# ELECTRONIC AMERICA

Stephen Meyer

**INFORMATION PLUS® REFERENCE SERIES**
Formerly Published by Information Plus, Wylie, Texas

GALE
CENGAGE Learning·

Farmington Hills, Mich • San Francisco • New York • Waterville, Maine
Meriden, Conn • Mason, Ohio • Chicago

**Electronic America**

Stephen Meyer

Kepos Media, Inc.: Steven Long and Janice
Jorgensen, Series Editors

Project Editor: Laura Avery

Rights Acquisition and Management: Ashley M.
  Maynard, Carissa Poweleit

Composition: Evi Abou-El-Seoud, Mary Beth
  Trimper

Manufacturing: Rita Wimberley

For product information and technology assistance, contact us at
**Gale Customer Support, 1-800-877-4253.**
For permission to use material from this text or product,
submit all requests online at **www.cengage.com/permissions.**
Further permissions questions can be e-mailed to
**permissionrequest@cengage.com**

Cover photograph: © 2121fisher/Shutterstock.com.

Gale
27500 Drake Rd.
Farmington Hills, MI 48331-3535

ISBN-13: 978-0-7876-5103-9 (set)
ISBN-13: 978-1-4103-6223-0

ISSN 1554-4397

This title is also available as an e-book.
ISBN-13: 978-1-4103-2539-6 (set)
Contact your Gale sales representative for ordering information.

Printed in the United States of America
1 2 3 4 5      21 20 19 18 17

# ELECTRONIC AMERICA

# TABLE OF CONTENTS

augmented reality, and the gamification of everyday life. The integration of electronics and information technologies into American vehicles and household appliances and utilities is also studied, as are developments in robotics.

# PREFACE

*Electronic America* is part of the *Information Plus Reference Series*. The purpose of each volume of the series is to present the latest facts on a topic of pressing concern in modern American life. These topics include the most controversial and studied social issues of the 21st century: abortion, capital punishment, care for the elderly, crime, energy, gambling, health care, immigration, national security, race and ethnicity, social welfare, youth, and many more. Although this series is written especially for high school and undergraduate students, it is an excellent resource for anyone in need of factual information on current affairs.

By presenting the facts, it is the intention of Gale, Cengage Learning, to provide its readers with everything they need to reach an informed opinion on current issues. To that end, there is a particular emphasis in this series on the presentation of scientific studies, surveys, and statistics. These data are generally presented in the form of tables, charts, and other graphics placed within the text of each book. Every graphic is directly referred to and carefully explained in the text. The source of each graphic is presented within the graphic itself. The data used in these graphics are drawn from the most reputable and reliable sources, such as from the various branches of the U.S. government and from private organizations and associations. Every effort has been made to secure the most recent information available. Readers should bear in mind that many major studies take years to conduct and that additional years often pass before the data from these studies are made available to the public. Therefore, in many cases the most recent information available in 2017 is dated from 2014 or 2015. Older statistics are sometimes presented as well, if they are landmark studies or of particular interest and no more-recent information exists.

Although statistics are a major focus of the *Information Plus Reference Series*, they are by no means its only content. Each book also presents the widely held positions and important ideas that shape how the book's subject is discussed in the United States. These positions are explained in detail and, where possible, in the words of their proponents. Some of the other material to be found in these books includes historical background, descriptions of major events related to the subject, relevant laws and court cases, and examples of how these issues play out in American life. Some books also feature primary documents or have pro and con debate sections that provide the words and opinions of prominent Americans on both sides of a controversial topic. All material is presented in an evenhanded and unbiased manner; readers will never be encouraged to accept one view of an issue over another.

## HOW TO USE THIS BOOK

During the late 20th and early 21st centuries the United States was transformed by the rapid development and adoption of new electronic devices, software programs, and other technologies. Computers, cell phones, cable television, e-mail, MP3s, DVDs, viruses, robots, spam, peer-to-peer networks, and massively multiplayer online role-playing games were in limited use in 1980, if they existed at all. By 2017 they had all become common, and many were ubiquitous. Their effect on the United States, and on the world, has been profound. New types of industries developed to produce and make use of these technologies. Existing businesses used them to become more efficient. New technologies also opened the door to new kinds of crime and criminals, and with them a need for changes in U.S. government and law enforcement. Last but not least, average Americans found that these technologies made it increasingly easy for them to communicate and find information, as well as to enjoy themselves, to be frustrated, or even to be victimized, in new and different ways.

*Electronic America* consists of nine chapters and three appendixes. Each chapter is devoted to a particular aspect of the changes in the United States brought about by high technology and its applications. For a summary of the information that is covered in each chapter, please see the synopses that are provided in the Table of Contents. Chapters generally begin with an overview of the basic facts and background information on the chapter's topic, then proceed to examine subtopics of particular interest. For example, Chapter 4: Technology and Crime opens with an overview of various categories of cybercrime, examining data compiled by the Federal Bureau of Investigation and the Federal Trade Commission. The chapter proceeds with an in-depth discussion of identity theft, analyzing methods used by criminals to steal sensitive personal information from consumers, assessing financial losses incurred by victims, and examining a number of high-profile court cases. The discussion also provides insights into the link between global hacking organizations and incidences of identity theft both in the United States and abroad, while surveying efforts by federal law enforcement officials to combat the crime. The chapter continues with a discussion of the role that the Internet has played in perpetuating fraud and other financial scams. A summary of computer viruses and other forms of malicious software (malware) follows, along with an assessment of tools that are used to protect networks and data from external attacks. After evaluating the impact of cybercrime on corporations and government agencies, the chapter considers the unique challenges involved with identifying and deterring copyright infringement in the digital age. It concludes with an examination of criminal activity that occurs on the Dark Web, an area of the Internet that remains undetectable on conventional web browsers, as well as the ways that law enforcement uses technology to fight cybercrime. Readers can find their way through a chapter by looking for the section and subsection headings, which are clearly set off from the text. They can also refer to the book's extensive Index, if they already know what they are looking for.

### Statistical Information

The tables and figures featured throughout *Electronic America* will be of particular use to readers in learning about this topic. These tables and figures represent an extensive collection of the most recent and valuable statistics on new technology and its impact on the United States. For example, graphics cover how many Americans use the Internet, how they use it, and how usage differs depending on demographic characteristics; the percentage of undergraduate students at degree-granting institutions who enrolled exclusively in distance learning programs; and the percentage of U.S. households that are victimized by identity theft. Gale, Cengage Learning, believes that making this information available to readers is the most important way to fulfill the goal of this book: to help readers understand the issues and controversies surrounding new technologies in the United States and reach their own conclusions.

Each table or figure has a unique identifier appearing above it, for ease of identification and reference. Titles for the tables and figures explain their purpose. At the end of each table or figure, the original source of the data is provided.

To help readers understand these often complicated statistics, all tables and figures are explained in the text. References in the text direct readers to the relevant statistics. Furthermore, the contents of all tables and figures are fully indexed. Please see the opening section of the Index at the back of this volume for a description of how to find tables and figures within it.

### Appendixes

Besides the main body text and images, *Electronic America* has three appendixes. The first is the Important Names and Addresses directory. Here, readers will find contact information for a number of government and private organizations that can provide further information on computers and high technology. The second appendix is the Resources section, which can also assist readers in conducting their own research. In this section, the author and editors of *Electronic America* describe some of the sources that were most useful during the compilation of this book. The final appendix is the Index. It has been greatly expanded from previous editions and should make it even easier to find specific topics in this book.

### COMMENTS AND SUGGESTIONS

The editors of the *Information Plus Reference Series* welcome your feedback on *Electronic America*. Please direct all correspondence to:

Editors
*Information Plus Reference Series*
27500 Drake Rd.
Farmington Hills, MI 48331-3535

# CHAPTER 1
# THE INTERNET AND THE ELECTRONIC AGE

*The Internet was a Cold War military project. It was designed for purposes of military communication in a United States devastated by a Soviet nuclear strike.... When I look at the Internet—that paragon of cyberspace today—I see something astounding and delightful. It's as if some grim fallout shelter had burst open and a full-scale Mardi Gras parade had come out.*

—Bruce Sterling, in "Literary Freeware—Not for Commercial Use" (with William Gibson), *Speeches to the National Academy of Sciences Convocation on Technology and Education*, Washington, D.C., May 10, 1993

Since the 1980s electronics and communications technologies have become integrated into nearly every aspect of American life, transforming the ways in which people shop, work, learn, and communicate with one another. The speed with which these new technologies have proliferated through U.S. homes and offices is nothing short of astounding. Cell phones, which were once novelties occupying the front seat of a car, can now be found in the pockets of many six-year-olds. Computers and the Internet, once accessible only to those who worked in government installations, large corporations, and academic institutions, are present in most American homes.

Jennifer Cheeseman Day, Alex Janus, and Jessica Davis report in *Computer and Internet Use in the United States: 2003* (October 2005, http://www.census.gov/prod/2005pubs/p23-208.pdf) that in 1984 only 8.2% of U.S. households had computers. By 2003 the number of homes with computers had increased to 61.8%. In *Technology Device Ownership: 2015* (October 29, 2015, http://www.pewinternet.org/files/2015/10/PI_2015-10-29_device-ownership_FINAL.pdf), Monica Anderson of the Pew Research Center reveals that in 2015 nearly three-quarters (73%) of all American adults owned a desktop or laptop computer. (See Table 1.1.) Meanwhile, the number of Americans who used the Internet also grew sharply during this period. Figure 1.1 shows the steady increase in Internet use among adults between 2000 and 2015. Slightly more than half (52%) of American adults used

the Internet in 2000; by 2015 that figure had risen to 84%. According to Internet Live Stats in "Internet Users by Country (2016)" (http://www.internetlivestats.com/internet-users-by-country), an estimated 286.9 million Americans had access to the Internet as of July 2016.

Since its inception, the Internet has reduced the time needed to complete dozens of mundane tasks, such as finding directions, writing personal correspondence, and conducting financial transactions. Because of these conveniences, Americans continue to use the Internet more each year. As Figure 1.2 indicates, Internet use among adults rose considerably across all age groups between 2000 and 2015. The percentage of Internet users 65 years of age and older more than quadrupled during this span, rising from only 14% in 2000 to 58% in 2015.

Although the development of technology has affected most people in a positive way, significant pitfalls have developed as well. Typically, underprivileged groups have been left at a bigger disadvantage because the most innovative technologies have been embraced faster by the well-educated and wealthy. The Internet and computer databases have also made fraud much easier. The number of cases of identity theft in the United States has skyrocketed. Each day thieves steal hundreds, if not thousands, of Social Security and credit card numbers by simply surfing the Internet or by sending out fraudulent electronic mail (e-mail) messages. The Federal Trade Commission (FTC) reports in "FTC Releases Annual Summary of Consumer Complaints" (March 1, 2016, https://www.ftc.gov/news-events/press-releases/2016/03/ftc-releases-annual-summary-consumer-complaints) that it received 490,220 identity theft complaints in 2015. This figure accounted for 16% of the nearly 3.1 million total consumer complaints the FTC received that year. (An extended discussion of technology and crime is presented in Chapter 4.)

**TABLE 1.1**

**Percentage of adults who own computers, by select characteristics, 2015**

| | |
|---|---|
| **U.S. adults** | 73 |
| **Sex** | |
| Men | 74 |
| Women | 71 |
| **Race/ethnicity** | |
| White | 79 |
| Black | 45 |
| Hispanic | 63 |
| **Age group** | |
| 18–29 | 78 |
| 30–49 | 81 |
| 50–64 | 70 |
| 65+ | 55 |
| **Household income** | |
| <$30K | 50 |
| $30K–$49,999 | 80 |
| $50K–$74,999 | 90 |
| $75K+ | 91 |
| **Educational attainment** | |
| Less than high school | 29 |
| High school | 63 |
| Some college | 81 |
| College+ | 90 |
| **Community type** | |
| Urban | 67 |
| Suburban | 78 |
| Rural | 67 |

SOURCE: Monica Anderson, "Computer Ownership Varies Greatly by Race and Ethnicity, Household Income and Educational Attainment," in *Technology Device Ownership: 2015*, Pew Research Center, October 29, 2015, http://www.pewinternet.org/files/2015/10/PI_2015-10-29_device-ownership_FINAL.pdf (accessed August 6, 2016)

**FIGURE 1.1**

**Percentage of adults online, 2000–15**

[% of all American adults who use the internet]

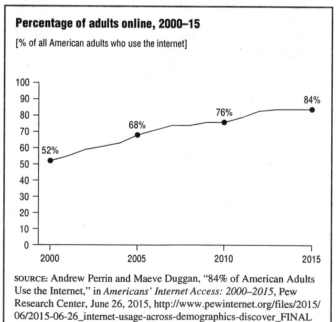

SOURCE: Andrew Perrin and Maeve Duggan, "84% of American Adults Use the Internet," in *Americans' Internet Access: 2000–2015*, Pew Research Center, June 26, 2015, http://www.pewinternet.org/files/2015/06/2015-06-26_internet-usage-across-demographics-discover_FINAL.pdf (accessed August 5, 2016)

**FIGURE 1.2**

**Percentage of adults online, by age, 2000–15**

[Among all American adults, the % who use the internet, by age]

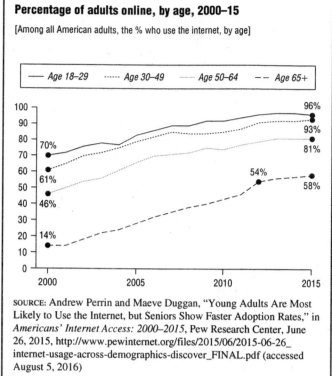

SOURCE: Andrew Perrin and Maeve Duggan, "Young Adults Are Most Likely to Use the Internet, but Seniors Show Faster Adoption Rates," in *Americans' Internet Access: 2000–2015*, Pew Research Center, June 26, 2015, http://www.pewinternet.org/files/2015/06/2015-06-26_internet-usage-across-demographics-discover_FINAL.pdf (accessed August 5, 2016)

Another problem that continues to confront owners of computers and mobile devices is the number of viruses, worms, botnets, and Trojan horses that make their way around the Internet. Viruses are programs or codes that "infect" computers by secretly infiltrating systems and interfering with proper functioning; worms are destructive codes that copy themselves over and over on a computer or network; robot networks, or botnets, are groups of computers that have been invaded by a malignant software that is controlled by a hacker or other outside source, effectively transforming the infected computers into "zombies" or "drones"; and Trojan horses are software programs or files that seem legitimate yet act maliciously on the computer or secretly provide access to information contained on the computer to outsiders. Collectively, these invasive programs are often referred to as malicious software, or malware. Not only do viruses, worms, and hackers cost time and energy from their victims but they also put valuable information at risk. David Emm et al. of the Kaspersky Lab, a leading antivirus software firm, report in *IT Threat Evolution in Q2 2016* (August 12, 2016, https://securelist.com/files/2016/08/Kaspersky_Q2_malware_report_ENG.pdf) that the firm "detected and repelled" 171.9 million online security threats during the second quarter of 2016.

In addition, mobile phones are also susceptible to virus attacks. In October 2004 the first mobile phone virus was detected in Southeast Asia. The virus, known as Cabir, infected mobile phone software and could be used to steal information from mobile phone address books. Since that time other viruses have been identified that target mobile devices, particularly smartphones and those with enhanced web and data capabilities. In some cases the viruses caused mobile phones to send mass text messages using a service that charged the sender a high fee for each message. Others erased stored data, disabled functions, or automatically routed phone calls through high-priced communications providers.

Despite such difficulties, technological innovation showed no sign of slowing down. In 2016 more and more Americans were carrying powerful portable computers such as an Android, iPhone, BlackBerry, or other handheld device. The consumer analytics firm Kantar Worldpanel reveals in "Smartphone OS Sales Market Share" (August 2016, http://www.kantarworldpanel .com/global/smartphone-os-market-share/) that Android was the nation's leading smartphone platform during the second quarter of 2016, accounting for nearly two-thirds (65.2%) of the U.S. market, followed by Apple's iOS platform (30.9%), Microsoft's Windows Phone (2.3%), and BlackBerry (0.2%). Meanwhile, trends toward wireless fidelity (Wi-Fi) connectivity, touch-screen functioning, voice-recognition software, and alternative power sources continued. One development expected to become commonplace is technology through which price tags at the grocery store will give off radio signals that automatically register the merchandise on a credit card when the buyer leaves the market. Meanwhile, robotic appliances are becoming available that automate some of the more tedious domestic chores, including lawn mowing, vacuuming, cleaning gutters, and folding laundry, while humanoid robots are now being used as cashiers, bartenders, and store greeters in both restaurant and retail settings.

## HISTORY OF THE INTERNET

At the center of the information technology and electronics revolution lies the Internet. Many believe the Internet had its origins on October 4, 1957, when the Soviet Union launched the *Sputnik 1* satellite into orbit with a military rocket. The news of *Sputnik 1*, a beeping steel sphere a little bigger in diameter than a basketball, sent the U.S. military into a frenzy. At the time, the United States and the Soviet Union were engaged in what became known as the Cold War (1947–1991), a period of sustained military buildup and ideological conflict. Americans were fearful that Soviet satellite technology could be used to spy on the United States or to launch missile attacks on U.S. targets. Technological superiority, the one advantage the United States thought it had over the Soviets, now seemed tenuous.

In response, the U.S. government formed the Advanced Research Projects Agency (ARPA; eventually, it was renamed the Defense Advanced Research Projects Agency and became responsible for the development of emerging

technologies within the U.S. military) within the U.S. Department of Defense in 1958. The central mission of this new agency was to develop state-of-the-art technology to stay well ahead of the Soviet Union. One of the first projects on ARPA's agenda was to create a system by which ARPA operational bases could communicate with one another and their contractors via computer. The agency wanted the system to be resilient enough to survive a nuclear attack.

Joseph Carl Robnett Licklider (1915–1990), a scientist at the Massachusetts Institute of Technology (MIT), was appointed to oversee the computer research program at ARPA in 1962. He conferred with some of the leading researchers in networking technology at the time, including Leonard Kleinrock (1934–), then an MIT graduate student, and Lawrence Roberts (1937–). Their solution, first published in 1967, was a nationwide network of ARPA computers known as ARPANET. In this network a user on any computer terminal in the network would be able to send a message to multiple users at other computer terminals. If any one computer was knocked out in a nuclear attack, the remaining stations could still communicate with each other.

For this network to function properly, the researchers established that the computers would first have to break down information into discrete packets. These packets were then to be sent along high-speed phone lines and reassembled upon reaching their destination at another computer. At the time, telephone conversations traveled across dedicated telephone wires in one long stream of data from one user to another like a single train traveling along a track. Although this was adequate for chatting with far-off relatives, it did not work well when one computer attempted to send data to several other computers on the network. By packetizing data, the information became more flexible. Much like cars on a highway, the packets could be routed easily to multiple computers. If one packet of information went bad during transmission, it did not disrupt the stream of data transmitting from one computer to another and could easily be resent. Packets could also carry information about themselves and where they were going, they could be compressed for speed, and they could be encrypted for security purposes.

After two years of engineering the parts needed for ARPANET, ARPA researchers set up the first four computer centers in the network. They were located at the University of California, Los Angeles (UCLA); the Stanford Research Institute; the University of California, Santa Barbara; and the University of Utah. Between these nodes, AT&T had laid down telephone lines that were capable of transmitting data at 50 kilobytes per second (Kbps). (Memory circuits are measured according to the base-two, or binary, number system. A kilobyte is equal to $2^{10}$ bytes, or 1,024 bytes.) The first test of the system commenced on October 29, 1969, when Charles S. Kline at UCLA tried logging into the Stanford system. On encountering the letter *g* in the word *login*, the system crashed. Recalling the event 40 years later in "Internet a Teenager at 40" (SMH.com, October 26, 2009), Kleinrock noted, "So, the first message was 'Lo' as in 'Lo and behold.'... We couldn't have a better, more succinct first message."

## A Loose Affiliation of Networks

Eventually, the researchers at UCLA worked out the problems, and two years later ARPANET was fully functional and had 15 nodes linked to it. Figure 1.3 shows ARPANET in September 1971. Throughout the early and mid-1970s the development of networking technologies progressed slowly. Raymond Tomlinson (1941–2016) invented the first e-mail program in 1971 to send typed messages across the network, and a year later the first computer-to-computer chat took place at UCLA. In 1973 Robert Metcalfe (1946–) of the Xerox Corporation developed the Ethernet to connect computers and printers in a large organization. Three years later at AT&T Bell Labs, Michael E. Lesk (1945–) put together the program Unix-to-Unix-copy protocol that allowed Unix computers, which were typically used by academics, to communicate with one another over the phone lines.

Technological developments such as these allowed people and organizations that were not connected into

**FIGURE 1.3**

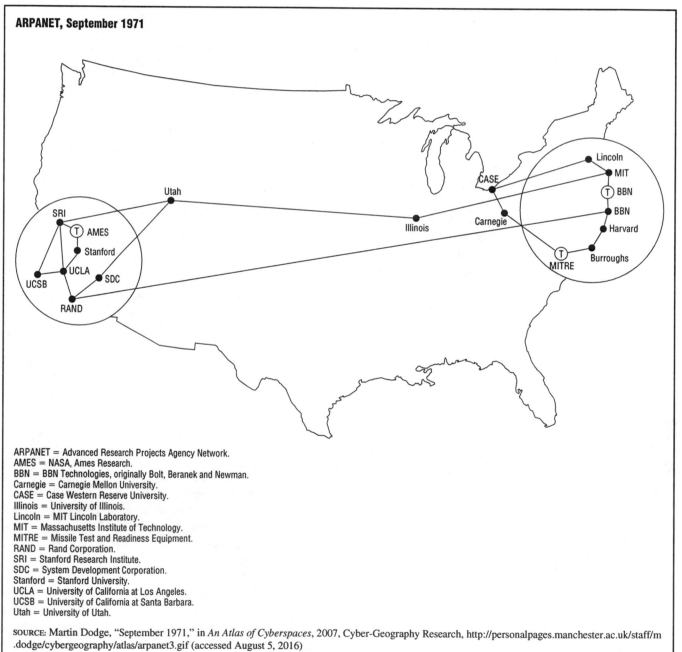

ARPANET, September 1971

ARPANET = Advanced Research Projects Agency Network.
AMES = NASA, Ames Research.
BBN = BBN Technologies, originally Bolt, Beranek and Newman.
Carnegie = Carnegie Mellon University.
CASE = Case Western Reserve University.
Illinois = University of Illinois.
Lincoln = MIT Lincoln Laboratory.
MIT = Massachusetts Institute of Technology.
MITRE = Missile Test and Readiness Equipment.
RAND = Rand Corporation.
SRI = Stanford Research Institute.
SDC = System Development Corporation.
Stanford = Stanford University.
UCLA = University of California at Los Angeles.
UCSB = University of California at Santa Barbara.
Utah = University of Utah.

SOURCE: Martin Dodge, "September 1971," in *An Atlas of Cyberspaces*, 2007, Cyber-Geography Research, http://personalpages.manchester.ac.uk/staff/m.dodge/cybergeography/atlas/arpanet3.gif (accessed August 5, 2016)

ARPANET to set up networks of their own by the early 1980s. One of the largest of these was the Computer Science Network, which was established by a number of universities with help from the National Science Foundation (NSF). These universities recognized the advantages in resource sharing and communication that ARPANET provided the Ivy League and West Coast schools and wanted to develop similar capabilities. Another network known as Usenet was initially established to connect researchers at Duke University and the University of North Carolina, and it eventually spread throughout the country. The Because It's Time Network (BITNET) was formed to connect computers in the City University of New York system. Most of these smaller networks used standard telephone lines to operate. They were set up primarily to transfer scientific data, share computing resources, post items on bulletin boards, and provide e-mail.

One major problem was that these different networks could not readily communicate with one another. Each network used different methods to identify the computers within the network. A computer in one network could not recognize the computers in different networks, and information packets sent out from one network could not navigate the other networks. The situation was analogous to a state in the United States having its own unique postal address system that no mail carriers outside of that state could understand.

During the 1970s the engineers Vinton G. Cerf (1943–) and Robert E. Kahn (1938–) devised the Transmission Control Program and the Internet Protocol (TCP/IP). This suite of programs created a universal address system that could be installed on any existing network. Once installed, the machines on the network could recognize and send information to a machine on any other network, provided they also had TCP/IP. In 1983 ARPANET was split into military and civilian sections, both of which adopted TCP/IP. Many consider the adoption of TCP/IP by ARPANET to be the event that gave birth to the Internet. To this day, each machine on the Internet has a unique IP address that identifies that machine on a network. Servers typically have permanent IP numbers assigned to them, whereas most personal computers (PCs) are given a different number by an Internet service provider (ISP) each time the user begins a new session.

In the year the Internet was born, home computing was still in its infancy. The Commodore 64 had just made its debut, sporting a 1 megahertz (or 1 million hertz, a unit used to measure computer processing speeds) microprocessor and 64 kilobytes of random access memory. Relatively few people owned home computers in 1983. Most of them used their machines for basic business applications, such as word processing and spreadsheets, and for playing games. Home users did not have direct access to the Internet. Low-speed modems were widely available by

the mid- to late 1980s, and people could dial directly into servers that were owned by CompuServe, Quantum Computer Services (later to be renamed America Online and then simply AOL), and Prodigy. These services allowed people to post messages, go into chat rooms, play games, or send and receive e-mail. Nevertheless, these services were not linked to the Internet, and e-mails could be sent only among people subscribing to the same service.

The only people who could surf the Internet freely were those who had access to powerful mainframe computers, most of which were owned by universities, the government, and large corporations. The Internet was an uninviting place during the early 1980s. Users connecting to the Internet had to know exactly what they were looking for to get it. To reach another computer or server on the Internet, users had to key in the IP address for that computer, which consisted of a string of up to 12 numbers, such as 69.32.146.63. To navigate a server, a computer operator had to type in computer code on a prompt line and sift through cryptic directories. There were no web browsers, colorful Internet pages, or search engines.

By 1984 the dedicated name server (DNS), developed by the University of Wisconsin, was introduced, making the Internet somewhat more user-friendly. A DNS is a computer server on the Internet with a database that pairs domain names with IP addresses, giving people the ability to type in a name instead of a multidigit number to reach an Internet destination. Modern Internet browsers contact one of many DNSs each time an address, such as http://www.google.com, is entered into the address bar. Most ISPs have a DNS that contains the names and IP address numbers of widely used sites. Once the browser makes the request from a DNS, the name server sends back the IP address number, which for Google is 209.85.225.105. The Internet browser then uses this IP address number to access the site (Google in this case).

Along with these name servers, a dedicated name system was also put into place so that no two names would be the same. Domain names with a minimum of two levels were established. The top level designated the country or economic sector a computer was in (e.g., .gov or .com), and a unique second-level domain name designated the organization itself (e.g., National Aeronautics and Space Administration [NASA] or Google). The Information Sciences Institute was put in charge of managing the root DNS in 1985 for all domains to make sure that no two were alike and to track who was registered for what name. Some of the first domain names to be registered were symbolics.com, mit.edu, think.com, and berkeley.edu.

## A Major Expansion during the Mid-1980s

In 1986 Internet use expanded exponentially when the NSF installed new supercomputers and a new backbone for the U.S. Internet service, giving rise to the NSFNet. By 2016

ISPs and cable companies typically had their own backbones, which were all tied into one another. When a home user connects to the Internet via phone, digital subscriber line, satellite link, or cable, the signal is directed to a bank of modems called a point of presence (POP) that is owned by the service provider. (See Figure 1.4.) Each POP from each service provider, be it AOL or Comcast or one of many others, feeds into a network access point (NAP). These NAPs are connected to one another via backbones that consist of bundles, or trunks, of fiber-optic cables that carry cross-country transmissions. The first NSF-funded backbone consisted of 56-Kbps wire to connect the access points. The wire was laid down by AT&T. The NSF also provided five supercomputers to route traffic between the NAPs and bundles. In 1988 the NSF upgraded the NSFNet when it installed supercomputers that could handle 1.5 gigabytes of traffic per second and fiber-optic line that could transfer information at 1.5 megabytes per second. (Computers process the long lines of complex computer code in small quantities known as bytes. Each byte consists of a string of eight ones and zeros that can be used to represent binary numbers from 0 to 255. In binary, which is a base-two number system, 1 is 00000001, 2 is 00000010, 3 is 00000011, and so on up to 255, which is represented as 11111111. A thousand bytes equal a kilobyte, a million bytes equal a megabyte, and a billion bytes equal a gigabyte.)

**FIGURE 1.4**

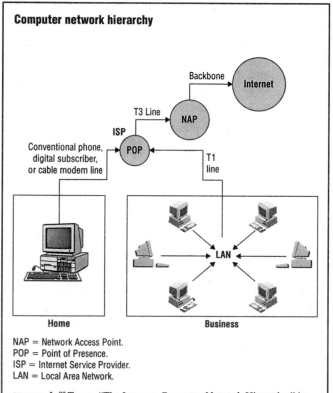

**Computer network hierarchy**

NAP = Network Access Point.
POP = Point of Presence.
ISP = Internet Service Provider.
LAN = Local Area Network.

SOURCE: Jeff Tyson, "The Internet: Computer Network Hierarchy," in *How Internet Infrastructure Works*, HowStuffWorks, Inc., 2004, http:// computer.howstuffworks.com/internet/basics/internet-infrastructure1 .htm (accessed August 5, 2016). Courtesy of HowStuffWorks.com.

The creation of the NSFNet ended the transmission bottlenecks that existed in the early Internet. The network also provided access for most major research institutions and universities. Academic departments and government agencies across the country jumped at the chance to set up servers and share information with their colleagues. Richard T. Griffiths notes in *History of the Internet, Internet for Historians* (October 11, 2002, http://www.let .leidenuniv.nl/history/ivh/chap2.htm) that from 1986 to 1987 the number of hosts (machines with a distinct IP address) on the Internet jumped from 5,000 to 28,000.

The NSF strictly prohibited the use of its site for commercial purposes. Although such a rule seemed limiting, it had the intended consequence of fostering the development of private Internet providers. In 1987 the UUNET became the first commercial Internet provider, offering service to Unix computers. Three years later, in 1990, The World (the first commercial provider of dial-up access) began operating, and computer scientists at McGill University in Montreal, Quebec, invented Archie, the first Internet search engine for finding computer files.

**An Internet for Everyone**

In 1991 Tim Berners-Lee (1955–) of the Conseil Européen pour la Recherche Nucléaire (CERN; European Organization for Nuclear Research) introduced the three technologies that would give rise to the World Wide Web. The first of Berners-Lee's technologies was the web browser, a program that allowed a user to jump from one server computer on the Internet to another. The second was the hypertext markup language (HTML), which was a programming language for creating web pages with links to other web pages and graphics. The third was the hypertext transfer protocol (HTTP), a command used by the browser to retrieve the HTML information contained on the server's website. In concert, these three innovations led to the World Wide Web as it became known during the early 21st century. On his server, Berners-Lee created the first website at CERN in 1990. Although this site is no longer active, an early screen shot of Berners-Lee's web browser may be accessed at http://info.cern.ch/NextBrowser .html. As the technology spread, many more web servers and sites quickly came into being. Internet Live Stats reports in "Total Number of Websites" (http://www.internetlivestats .com/total-number-of-websites) that by November 2016 the total number of websites had grown to more than 1.1 billion.

With Berners-Lee's invention, people were no longer required to use complex computer codes or sift through cryptic directories to retrieve information from other computers on the Internet. To reach a server with a website, a user simply types in the name of a server along with the HTTP command (e.g., http://www.google.com) into the address bar of his or her browser. The browser then contacts a DNS server to get the IP address of the server. Once the browser connects with the website, the browser then sends out the HTTP command. The HTTP tells the server to send the browser the HTML code for the specified website. On receiving the HTML code, the browser deciphers the code and simply displays the web page on the user's computer (e.g., Google's home page).

At the same time that these strides were being made in establishing the Internet, the U.S. government took a more active role in its development. In 1991 Senator Al Gore Jr. (1948–; D-TN) introduced the U.S. High Performance Computing Act into Congress. The act set aside more than $2 billion for further research into computing and to improve the infrastructure of the Internet. Although most of it was earmarked for large agencies such as the NSF and NASA, some of the funds were placed into the hands of independent software developers.

Marc Andreessen (1971?–) developed the Mosaic X web browser in 1993 using a federal grant received through this act. The browser was one of the first commercial browsers to employ the HTML program language and HTTP, and it became the first browser to be embraced by the general public. It was easy to set up, simple to use, and backed by a full customer support staff. It displayed images in an attractive way and contained many of the standard features used on present-day web browsers, such as the address prompt and Back and Forward buttons. Tens of thousands of copies of Mosaic X were sold.

Once Mosaic X became popular, more websites employing HTML and HTTP were posted. According to Robert H. Zakon, in *Hobbes' Internet Timeline 23* (January 1, 2016, http://www.zakon.org/robert/internet/timeline), in June 1994 there were 2,738 web servers, by June 1995 there were an estimated 23,500 servers, and by June 1996 there were an estimated 252,000 servers. Zakon indicates that the growth in hosts, or computers with a unique IP address, during the same period reflected an increase from 3 million in October 1994 to 13 million in June 1996.

The web was growing at such a rapid rate that the NSF created the Internet Network Information Center (InterNIC) as an agency to handle domain names. InterNIC contracted with Network Solutions to handle domain registration. By 1995 the companies that ran the older dial-up services for home users, such as CompuServe, AOL, and Prodigy, brought their clients to the Internet and offered Internet service for all. Internet network providers, such as MCI and Qwest, began laying fiber-optic cables and communications networks at a breakneck pace. Advertising appeared on the web for the first time (the first banner being for the alcoholic beverage Zima), e-shopping appeared on the Internet, and many companies such as Netscape went public. In the following years the Internet gained a firm foothold in American life. As of January 2016, the nonprofit Internet Systems Consortium (http://ftp.isc.org/www/survey/reports/

current) estimated the number of Internet hosts at nearly 1.05 billion.

## DIGITAL DIVIDE

Although the Internet swept into U.S. households at a faster rate than almost any other technology, many people were still not connected to the Internet well after the turn of the 21st century. In *Americans' Internet Access: 2000–2015* (June 26, 2015, http://www.pewinternet.org/files/2015/06/2015-06-26_internet-usage-across-demographics-discover_FINAL.pdf), Andrew Perrin and Maeve Duggan of the Pew Research Center examine the various demographics relating to Internet use. The biggest discrepancies were in age, income, and educational attainment. For example, 96% of respondents aged 18 to 29 years were Internet users in 2015; by comparison, only 58% of seniors aged 65 years and older went online. (See Figure 1.2.) Perrin and Duggan also reveal that those in typically disadvantaged demographics had the least exposure to the Internet. Seventy-four percent of adults living in households earning less than $30,000 per year went online in 2015, compared with 97% of adults living in households earning $75,000 or more per year. Whereas 95% of college graduates used the Internet in 2015, only two-thirds (66%) of adults who had never finished high school were Internet users that year.

According to Perrin and Duggan, there were also variations in Internet usage between different races and ethnicities in 2015. English-speaking Asian Americans (97%) were the most likely to be Internet users that year, followed by whites (85%), Hispanics (81%), and African Americans (78%). The type of community in which an individual lived was also a factor in determining Internet use during that time. In 2015 a comparable proportion of adults living in urban areas (85%) and adults living in suburban areas (85%) used the Internet, while fewer than four-fifths (78%) of rural Americans used the Internet that year. Roughly the same proportion of men (85%) and women (84%) were Internet users in 2015.

A more noticeable divide exists between those with faster, broadband connectivity and those with older equipment and slow connection speeds. For example, the overall number of Americans with access to broadband rose dramatically between 2000 and 2015. In 2000 only 1% of adults went online via broadband. (See Figure 1.5.) By 2013 this figure rose to 70%, before dipping to 67% in 2015. Still, research indicates significant demographic differences among broadband users. As Table 1.2 shows, 75% of adults aged 18 to 29 years accessed the Internet via broadband in 2015, compared with only 45% of adults aged 65 years and older.

Table 1.2 also shows that education plays an important role in determining whether an adult is more or less likely to go online via a high-speed connection. For

FIGURE 1.5

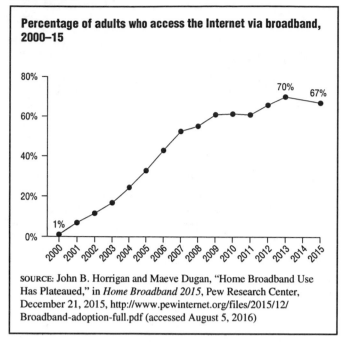

**Percentage of adults who access the Internet via broadband, 2000–15**

SOURCE: John B. Horrigan and Maeve Dugan, "Home Broadband Use Has Plateaued," in *Home Broadband 2015*, Pew Research Center, December 21, 2015, http://www.pewinternet.org/files/2015/12/Broadband-adoption-full.pdf (accessed August 5, 2016)

**TABLE 1.2**

**Broadband users by select characteristics, 2013 and 2015**

|  | 2013 | 2015 | % change |
|---|---|---|---|
| **All** | **70%** | **67%** | **−3** |
| Male | 70 | 66 | −4 |
| Female | 70 | 67 | −3 |
| Parents | 77 | 73 | −4 |
| Non-parents | 67 | 64 | −3 |
| White | 74 | 72 | −2 |
| African American | 62 | 54 | −8 |
| Hispanic | 56 | 50 | −6 |
| 18–29 | 81 | 75 | −6 |
| 30–49 | 77 | 74 | −3 |
| 50–64 | 68 | 65 | −3 |
| 65+ | 47 | 45 | −2 |
| Under $20K | 46 | 41 | −5 |
| $20K–$50K | 67 | 63 | −4 |
| $50K–$75K | 85 | 80 | −5 |
| $75K–$100K | 88 | 88 | 0 |
| Over $100K | 93 | 90 | −3 |
| High school grad or less | 50 | 47 | −3 |
| Some college/Assoc. deg. | 80 | 75 | −5 |
| College+ | 90 | 87 | −3 |
| Rural | 60 | 55 | −5 |
| Urban | 70 | 67 | −3 |
| Suburban | 74 | 70 | −4 |

SOURCE: John B. Horrigan and Maeve Dugan, "Broadband Adoption Decreases Slightly between 2013 and 2015," in *Home Broadband 2015*, Pew Research Center, December 21, 2015, http://www.pewinternet.org/files/2015/12/Broadband-adoption-full.pdf (accessed August 5, 2016)

example, adults with a college degree (87%) were significantly more likely than those with a high school diploma or who never finished high school (47%) to use a broadband Internet connection in 2015. Gaps in broadband use also existed between different races and ethnicities. That year, nearly three-quarters (72%) of whites accessed the Internet via broadband, compared with slightly more than half (54%) of African Americans and half (50%) of Hispanics. Geography also seemed to play a considerable role in determining whether or not Americans had access to high-speed Internet, as suburban (70%) and urban (67%) Americans were considerably more likely than rural Americans (55%) to go online using a broadband connection in 2015.

## THE FUTURE OF COMPUTING AND THE INTERNET

For many, the Internet has become an essential part of everyday life, and people increasingly want to be able to log on to the Internet from any location, in private or public spaces. It is therefore not surprising that more Americans are turning to wireless technologies. In *U.S. Smartphone Use in 2015* (April 1, 2015, http://www.pewinternet.org/files/2015/03/PI_Smartphones_0401151.pdf), Aaron Smith and Dana Page of the Pew Research Center indicate that nearly two-thirds (64%) of American adults owned smartphones in 2015. Eighty-five percent of adults aged 18 to 29 years owned smartphones that year, compared with 27% of adults over the age of 65. Hispanics (71%) and non-Hispanic African Americans (70%) were considerably more likely to own smartphones than non-Hispanic whites (61%) in 2015.

In 2015, 15% of all smartphone owners relied almost exclusively on their mobile devices to go online, while 10% had no broadband Internet access at home. (See Table 1.3.) That year, a quarter (25%) of adult smartphone owners aged 18 to 29 years had limited alternatives to accessing the Internet apart from using their devices. Among different racial and ethnic groups, Hispanics (13%) and non-Hispanic African Americans (12%) were three times more likely than non-Hispanic whites (4%) to describe themselves as "smartphone-dependent." Nearly a quarter (24%) of adult smartphone owners with a household income below $30,000 a year claimed to have few other ways to go online apart from using their mobile devices in 2015; by contrast, only 5% of adult smartphone owners earning $75,000 or more annually were almost entirely dependent on their smartphones to access the Internet.

Tablet computers also played a key role in the rise of wireless computing during these years. Anderson notes that 4% of American adults owned a tablet computer (such as an iPad) in 2010; by 2015 this figure had risen to 45%. Anderson notes that wealth and education were key factors in determining whether or not someone owned a tablet computer. Among adults earning $75,000 or more per year, 67% owned tablet computers, and 62% of college graduates were tablet owners. By comparison, only 19% of adults without a high school diploma and 28% of adults who made less than $30,000 per year owned a tablet computer in 2015.

**TABLE 1.3**

### Percentage of adults who rely on smartphones to go online, by select characteristics, 2015

[Percentage of American adults in each group who have a smartphone but lack broadband at home or have limited options for online access other than their cell phone]

% WHO HAVE A SMARTPHONE AND...

| | Do not have broadband at home | Have few access options other than cell phone | Total "Smartphone-Dependent"* |
|---|---|---|---|
| **All adults** | **10%** | **15%** | **7%** |
| Male | 10 | 12 | 5 |
| Female | 11 | 18 | 8 |
| 18–29 | 20 | 25 | 15 |
| 30–49 | 11 | 16 | 6 |
| 50–64 | 6 | 11 | 4 |
| 65+ | 4 | 7 | 2 |
| White, non-Hispanic | 7 | 12 | 4 |
| Black, non-Hispanic | 21 | 19 | 12 |
| Hispanic | 17 | 23 | 13 |
| HS grad or less | 15 | 19 | 9 |
| Some college | 10 | 16 | 7 |
| College+ | 4 | 7 | 2 |
| Less than $30,000/yr | 19 | 24 | 13 |
| $30,000–$74,999 | 8 | 14 | 5 |
| $75,000 or more | 3 | 5 | 1 |
| Urban | 12 | 17 | 8 |
| Suburban | 9 | 14 | 6 |
| Rural | 11 | 14 | 7 |

HS = High school graduate.
*"Smartphone dependent" users are those who own a smartphone but have no broadband at home, and have limited access options beyond their cell phone.

SOURCE: Aaron Smith and Dana Page, "Young Adults, Non-Whites, Lower Income Americans Are Especially Dependent on Smartphones for Online Access," in *U.S. Smartphone Use in 2015*, Pew Research Center, April 1, 2015, http://www.pewinternet.org/files/2015/03/PI_Smartphones_0401151.pdf (accessed August 5, 2016)

In "PC Is Dead. Cloud Computing, Mobile Devices Taking Over" (CSMonitor.com, June 8, 2011), Chad Brooks suggests that the popularity of tablet devices, combined with the proliferation of online data storage systems, or "cloud computing," might signal the end of the traditional desktop computer. "We don't need PCs anymore," Brooks quoted the technology expert John Quain as saying. "They are dead." Despite these predictions, U.S. PC sales experienced a slight increase in 2016. According to Gartner, Inc., in the press release "Gartner Says Worldwide PC Shipments Declined 5.2 Percent in Second Quarter of 2016" (July 11, 2016, http://www.gartner.com/newsroom/id/3373617), PC sales in the United States rose from 15 million during the second quarter of 2015 to 15.2 million during the second quarter of 2016, an increase of 1.4%. However, Gartner notes this increase came after five consecutive quarters of declining shipments for the U.S. PC industry.

The number of wireless networks has risen in response to increasing demand. According to WiGLE (https://wigle.net/stats#geostats), a wireless network mapping site, by November 2016 there were more than 294 million wireless networks worldwide. Nearly one-fifth (53.5 million, or 18.1%) of these were located in the United States. Germany had the second-highest number of wireless networks, with 8.9 million, followed by Great Britain (7.9 million), the Netherlands (6.1 million), and Canada (5.2 million).

### Increasing Mobile Connectivity

As wireless devices grow in popularity, several emerging technologies allow people to access high-speed Internet on their laptops wherever they go. Worldwide interoperability for microwave access (WiMAX) uses base-station transmitters much like those in a mobile phone network. Any laptop computer that is equipped with a WiMAX receiver should be able to instantly log on to one of these stations and receive high-speed Internet access up to 30 miles (48 km) away.

One of the most popular technologies on the market during the first decade of the 21st century was high-speed third-generation (3G) cell phone service. First introduced in the United States in 2003, 3G service allows cell phones to receive and send signals that contain much more information than standard cellular phone signals, enabling 3G cell phone users to access the Internet at speeds approaching those of a cable modem. This high connection speed also enables 3G cell phone users to download various applications (commonly known as "apps") such as games, videos, online tools, and websites. As wireless technology advanced, 3G phones were capable of offering data transmission speeds of between 400 and 4,000 Kbps.

By 2010 most major cellular operators in the United States were offering 3G service to their customers, and devices such as the BlackBerry, the Apple 3G iPhone, and Samsung Instinct were making multifunction smartphones relatively affordable. Proving consumer demand for such products, the Apple 3G iPhone, which combined 3G phone, Internet, personal data, and music capabilities in one device, sold more than a million units in three days following its release in July 2008. Following the success of the iPhone, a number of other 3G portable wireless devices were introduced, including the iPod Touch and the iPad from Apple Inc., the Droid from Motorola Inc., and the Zune from Microsoft Corporation.

During this period a new wireless technology, known as long-term evolution (LTE), or fourth-generation (4G) cell phone service, was beginning to emerge, with the promise of even faster connection speeds for consumers. Launched as an initiative by the International Telecommunications Union (ITU) in March 2008, the development of a new global 4G standard, offering connection speeds of between 100 megabytes and 1 gigabyte per second, became the top priority of telecommunications companies worldwide. With connection speeds that were expected to exceed those offered by 3G devices, 4G promised to enable cell phone users to stream much more advanced forms of data, such as live television broadcasts, interactive games, and other multimedia applications at a much faster rate. However, as companies became eager to sell 4G products to consumers, the ITU's efforts to establish universal 4G standards became a low priority for cell phone carriers and the organization abandoned the initiative. As a result, several of the first phones to be marketed as 4G were actually no faster than their 3G predecessors. In "3G vs. 4G: What's the Difference?" (PCMag.com, February 24, 2012), Sascha Segan notes that by 2012 so many 4G technologies had emerged that the term had become "almost meaningless." Still, as 4G-LTE networks continued to expand throughout the United States, the technology would eventually supersede 3G as the industry standard. In anticipation of this shift, Apple released its iPhone 5, the first iPhone to be compatible with 4G-LTE networks, in September 2012. By 2016 major telecommunications providers such as AT&T, Sprint, T-Mobile, and Verizon, had all built extensive 4G-LTE networks in the United States.

## Internet2

In the long term, however, the future of the Internet will likely be the Internet2. Internet2 is not a new Internet, but a collaboration of dozens of academic institutions and corporations working together to develop technologies that will be integrated into the Internet. According to the organization's website (May 2016, http://www.internet2 .edu/about-us), in 2016 the Internet2 community involved the cooperation of 317 U.S. universities and 81 corporations, in addition to 64 affiliates and 43 state and regional education networks. Globally, Internet2 also partnered with 65 research and education affiliates with sites in more than 100 countries worldwide. The group's guiding philosophy is based on a commitment to establishing a research climate that is conducive to the development and sharing of new technologies. "Innovation takes place when ideas are liberated to create practical, far-reaching solutions to the problems of society," the organization states. "Our community is laying the foundation for entirely new ideas: equipping the brightest people in the world with the most advanced technology in the world. If their previous track record is any indication, the future they create will be bold and brilliant."

One project the Internet2 consortium began testing in 2008 was version six of the Internet protocol (IPv6). By 2012 the number of computers, cell phones, and other devices using the Internet had grown exponentially. Each time one of these devices logs on to the Internet, it requires its own address. Until 2012 these devices all operated within version four of the Internet protocol (IPv4), which allowed for only a little more than 4 billion addresses. As the number of new IP addresses continued to rise, IPv4 would eventually prove insufficient to accommodate all users. IPv6 introduced a new Internet

address system that would allow for trillions upon trillions of new addresses. With such a network, Americans would be able to watch high-definition television via the Internet, teleconference with associates and family at any time, and easily access entire libraries of music and books online.

In June 2011 a number of companies and institutions, including Google, Facebook, and the U.S. Department of Commerce, participated in World IPv6 Day, an event that was designed to test the functionality of the new IP. The experiment proved a success, and IPv6 was officially launched on June 6, 2012. Iljitsch van Beijnum reports in "IPv6 on Its Way to Conquer the World after World IPv6 Launch" (ArsTechnica.com, August 1, 2012) that 19 million IPv6 addresses saw activity during the launch, with 71% of the total traffic occurring in the United States. According to Fahmida Y. Rashid, in "What to Expect for IPv6 Day" (PCMag.com, June 6, 2012), by the day of the launch 12% of existing Internet networks were compatible with the new protocol. By 2015, 28% of new Internet connections were expected to operate within the IPv6 system. Although the existing IPv4 network continued to operate alongside IPv6, by 2016 it seemed clear that the new protocol represented the networking platform of the future. In "IPv6 Adoption" (https://www .google.com/intl/en/ipv6/statistics.html), Google indicates that by November 2016 IPv6 accounted for 12.3% of all Internet traffic worldwide. According to the Internet content firm Akamai, in "IPv6 Adoption Visualization" (July 15, 2016, https://www.akamai.com/uk/en/our-thinking/ state-of-the-internet-report/state-of-the-internet-ipv6-adoption-visualization.jsp), adoption was particularly high in Belgium, where 47.8% of all web addresses used the IPv6 system in 2016, followed by the United States (29.2%), Greece (28.3%), Switzerland (27.2%), Germany (26.6%), and Portugal (18.3%).

## Future Incarnations of the Internet

As the Internet became integrated into society, many observers began raising questions about the ways an information-driven, interconnected world might transform human behavior. In *The Internet of Things Will Thrive by 2025* (May 14, 2014, http://www.pewinternet.org/files/2014/ 05/PIP_Internet-of-things_0514142.pdf), Janna Anderson and Lee Rainie surveyed more than 1,800 technology experts about how the Internet might evolve by 2025. By and large, the experts surveyed agreed that network technology would become increasingly interwoven into the physical world. This process would occur through the proliferation of digital tools designed to monitor and enhance everyday existence, creating what Anderson and Rainie describe as an "Internet of Things." Examples cited in the report include bodily devices that would measure the health, fitness, and dietary activities of individuals, as well as remote-control sensors that could regulate appliances in the home. Respondents also surmised that network technology would have the capacity to measure changes to the earth's environment, allowing scientists to keep track of pollution levels and shifts in weather patterns in real time. For some respondents, these future developments represented a source of enormous opportunity for society. For example, harnessing network technology to monitor the flow of goods in the marketplace will help increase efficiency while reducing waste. Other experts expressed a more cautionary perspective on the future of the Internet, notably in the ways that increased connectivity will erode, and ultimately destroy, any prospect for individual privacy.

At the same time, profound political ramifications are inherent in the expansion of network technologies. Indeed, questions concerning the free, open movement of information between individuals and societies are central to discussions of the Internet's future. In "Future Scenarios" (2016, http://www.internetsociety.org/internet/how-its-evolving/future-scenarios), the Internet Society, an advocacy group dedicated to ensuring that the World Wide Web remains accessible and open to all citizens, imagines several possible outcomes for the Internet. In one instance, the "Common Pool" scenario, the society envisions a future where barriers to online participation are eliminated, encouraging opportunity, innovation, and collaboration among all Internet users. By contrast, the "Moats and Drawbridges" scenario, in which the flow of information would be heavily controlled by government and corporate interests, would cripple innovation by forcing online participants to devote energy and resources to cultivating political connections to compete.

Meanwhile, by mid-decade government control of online information had become a serious threat to Internet freedom in a number of countries throughout the world. Freedom House, a human rights advocacy group headquartered in Washington, D.C., provides an assessment of Internet freedom in *Freedom on the Net 2015* (October 2015, https://freedomhouse.org/sites/default/files/FH_FOTN_2015Report.pdf). Of the 65 countries surveyed by Freedom House in the report, 14 implemented new laws authorizing increased online surveillance between 2014 and 2015. Furthermore, of the 3 billion people worldwide who had access to the Internet in 2015, more than three out of five (61%) lived in countries where online criticism of the government, military, or members of the royal family was subject to censorship. Nearly half (47%) of the world's Internet users lived in countries where individuals had been assaulted or murdered for posting particular content online during the previous year, while more than one-third (34%) lived in countries where the government had imposed general bans on Internet or mobile phone service at some point in 2014 and 2015.

To counter this threat to Internet freedom, a number of advocacy groups began taking steps to preserve the rights of individuals to post content online. According to Hannah Kuchler, in "How to Preserve the Web's Past for the Future" (FT.com, April 11, 2014), the Internet Archive, a digital library based in San Francisco, has the capacity to capture and preserve threatened material before governments have the chance to take it off the Internet. The archive is also dedicated to preserving documentation relating to ordinary life, organizing and maintaining information ranging from school curricula to traditional recipes. Meanwhile, events such as the Internet Freedom Festival (https://internetfreedomfestival.org/) act as global forums that allow individuals to coordinate their ongoing efforts to combat online censorship. In March 2016 more than 700 people representing 74 countries attended the Internet Freedom Festival in Valencia, Spain.

# CHAPTER 2
# DEVELOPMENTS IN TELECOMMUNICATIONS

Communication has undeniably been one of the central motivations behind the technical strides that have taken place since the beginning of the Cold War (1947–1991), a period of sustained military buildup and ideological conflict that pitted the United States and other capitalist powers against the Soviet Union and its communist allies. The Internet was first conceived as a way of connecting computers for the purpose of communication. By the 21st century, digital connectivity had become an indispensable aspect of everyday life in the United States, particularly among younger Americans. In 2015, 96% of adults between the ages of 18 and 29 years were Internet users. (See Figure 1.2 in Chapter 1.)

Electronic mail (e-mail) was the first application to gain acceptance and widespread use on the Internet. In "Email Statistics Report, 2016–2020" (March 2016, http://www.radicati.com/wp/wp-content/uploads/2016/03/Email-Statistics-Report-2016-2020-Executive-Summary.pdf), the Radicati Group, a technology marketing research firm, reports that in 2016 there were nearly 2.7 billion individual e-mail users worldwide.

E-mail is not the only communications system to flourish, however. Since the early 1980s a wireless phone system has sprung up across the United States. CTIA, a nonprofit communications advocacy group, reports on trends in wireless technology adoption in *Background on CTIA's Wireless Industry Survey* (2016, http://www.ctia.org/docs/default-source/default-document-library/ctia-survey-2015.pdf). According to CTIA, the number of wireless subscribers in the United States was nearly 5.3 million in 1990. At that time, wireless subscribers consisted solely of cell phone users. By 2015, as wireless devices came to include tablets, laptop computers, and smartphones, the number of wireless subscriber connections in the United States reached nearly 377.9 million. Furthermore, of the approximately 370 million wireless devices being used by Americans in 2015, 228 million (62%) were smartphones.

Meanwhile, the amount of revenue that was brought in by the wireless industry rose from $52.5 billion in 2000 to $191.9 billion in 2015.

As the 21st century progressed, more sophisticated modes of online communication continued to emerge. Instant messaging (IM) software allowed individuals to share text messages over the Internet almost instantly, while video chat platforms such as Skype, ooVoo, and Tango enabled users to have face-to-face conversations over their devices. Furthermore, with the rapid rise in popularity of social media, online communication became increasingly varied and complex. Through platforms such as Facebook, Twitter, and Instagram, Internet users began expressing themselves not only in writing but also by posting photographs, sharing links to websites, and "liking" certain social media pages using some or all of these forms of communication.

In some ways these new forms of communication have made life easier. Most Americans no longer have to look for a pay phone and search for change when they need to make a phone call away from home. Nor do most travelers have to worry about being stranded on a deserted roadway miles from a phone. Using e-mail and IM, online Americans can now easily stay in touch with anyone in any country around the world. In *The Web at 25 in the U.S.* (February 27, 2014, http://www.pewinternet.org/files/2014/02/PIP_25th-anniversary-of-the-Web_022714_pdf.pdf), Susannah Fox and Lee Rainie of the Pew Research Center note that, in general, Americans also feel that online communication helps strengthen their relationships with friends and family. At the same time, however, Americans now have to comb through spam daily, worry about unleashing e-mail viruses, and endure strangers' phone conversations and cell phone ring tones virtually everywhere they go.

## E-MAIL

E-mail was the first of these new communications technologies to emerge. Not more than two years after the initial ARPANET test in 1969, Raymond Tomlinson (1941–2016) of ARPANET created the first e-mail program. Tomlinson developed the idea from a program that had been used on mainframe computers with time-share operating systems. These computers, which were prevalent during the early 1960s, consisted of a number of remote terminals that were all connected to a central host computer, where all the office files and programs were stored. The remote terminals, which were typically spread throughout the office building, were little more than a screen and a keyboard, and the office workers shared the resources of the central computer. Programs were written for these systems wherein people could leave messages for one another within the core computer. Tomlinson simply adapted one of these static internal mail programs into a program that could send messages to other computers on ARPANET. The first mass e-mail Tomlinson sent out with his program was a message to all ARPANET employees telling them that "electronic mail" was now available. He instructed them to address one another using the following convention: "user's log-in name@host computer name." This same convention is still being used.

The first e-mail program was not user-friendly. The e-mails did not have subject lines or date lines, they had to be opened in the order that they were received, and they read as strings of continuous text. Despite these inconveniences, the e-mail application caught on in the ARPANET community quickly, and the computer scientists in the organization worked out most of the kinks. Within several years users could list messages by subject and date, delete selected messages, and forward messages to other users. E-mail soon became the most popular application for the busy researchers working at ARPANET. When communicating by e-mail, they did not have to worry about the formalities or the long delays inherent in letter writing. Unlike a phone conversation, no time was wasted on small talk, and a copy of the communication could be retained. People could also send e-mails to one another at any time of day or night. By the late 1970s e-mail discussion groups had formed within the ARPANET community. Two of the more popular discussion groups were a science-fiction group and a group that discussed the potential future social impacts of e-mail.

During the late 1970s and early 1980s other networks began to develop, such as Usenet and Because It's Time Network (BITNET), which consisted of mainframe computers that were connected to one another over telephone lines. The central purpose of these networks was to connect universities and government agencies that were not on ARPANET. Some of these networks, such as Usenet, were set up for the express purpose of sending e-mail and posting messages on newsgroups. Usenet consisted of computers of various sizes all over the country. A relatively small number of large, powerful computers formed the backbone of the network, and many smaller computers logged on to the network through the larger ones. For example, to send an e-mail from Indiana to South Carolina a person on a small computer in Indiana would first dial into and post an e-mail onto the nearest large computer. The person operating the large computer in Indiana would then pass the e-mail via modem along with other messages from the region to all the other large computers in the network, including those in South Carolina. When the recipient of the e-mail in South Carolina logged into the network through the nearest large computer, the e-mail would then automatically be downloaded to his or her smaller computer.

By the late 1980s e-mail was commercially available for home users to a limited extent. Companies such as Quantum Computer Services (now known as AOL) and Prodigy set up chat rooms and e-mail services that could be enjoyed by people with home computers. Quantum Link, for example, was a service compatible with the Commodore 64 computer. Home users dialed into local Quantum Link mainframes, which were located in most major cities around the country. The mainframes were interconnected via open phone lines, so that anyone using the service could e-mail or chat with anyone else logged onto the service across the country. A member, however, could not contact someone on another commercial service or on the much larger Internet.

## E-mail Becomes Widespread

The development of the National Science Foundation Internet and the standardization of Internet protocols during the mid-1980s brought most of the smaller academic networks such as BITNET together, allowing people throughout academia and government agencies to communicate with one another via e-mail. The invention of the World Wide Web, the Mosaic X web browser, and the widespread use of more powerful personal computers allowed home users access to Internet e-mail by the early 1990s. In 1994 AOL (known at the time as America Online) began offering people a limited service on the web with the ability to send and receive e-mail. Within a year, all the established dial-up services such as CompuServe and Prodigy moved their e-mail subscribers onto the larger Internet.

Since the mid-1990s e-mail has become the most used application on the Internet. In "Americans Going Online...Explosive Growth, Uncertain Destinations" (October 16, 1995, http://www.people-press.org/1995/10/16/americans-going-online-explosive-growth-uncertain-destinations), the Pew Research Center reports that 12 million adult Americans were regular users of e-mail in June 1995 (with "regular user" defined as someone who checked e-mail at least once per week). Since that time e-mail use has skyrocketed. Pew reports in "Usage over Time" (2014, http://www.pewinternet.org/files/2014/01/Usage-Over-Time-_May-2013.xlsx) that e-mail use reached an all-time high in May 2010, when 94% of online adults were e-mail users and 62% sent and received e-mails daily. E-mail use actually dipped slightly in 2011 and 2012, largely due to the increasing popularity of other platforms for online communication, notably IM and social networking sites such as Facebook. Still, with 89% of adults sending and receiving e-mails in 2012, e-mail remained the most prevalent form of online communication. Even as a large percentage of Americans became smartphone users, e-mail continued to serve as a primary means of communicating over the Internet. Aaron Smith and Dana Page of the Pew Research Center report in *U.S. Smartphone Use in 2015* (April 1, 2015, http://www.pewinternet.org/files/2015/03/PI_Smartphones_0401151.pdf) that among smartphone owners in 2015, 91% of those aged 18 to 29 years, 87% of those aged 30 to 49 years, and 87% of those aged 50 years and older used their devices to send or receive e-mail at least once during the previous week.

## Spam

By far one of the biggest problems facing e-mail in the early 21st century is spam, which is generally defined as unsolicited e-mail sent in bulk. Although different organizations gauge the number of e-mails sent worldwide differently, most agree that the vast majority of them are spam. In *Spam and Phishing in Q2 2016* (2016, https://kasperskycontenthub.com/securelist/files/2016/08/Spam-report_Q2-2016_final_ENG.pdf), Darya Gudkova et al. of the Kaspersky Lab, a leading antivirus software firm, indicate that 57.3% of all e-mail messages sent during the second quarter of 2016 were spam. The United States was responsible for 10.8% of all spam-generated e-mail during that quarter; Vietnam was the second-largest distributor, accounting for 10.1% of all spam e-mails, followed by India (10%), China (6.5%), and Mexico (4.6%).

The Spamhaus Project, an organization that tracks and works to eliminate spam, estimates in "The World's Worst Spammers" (https://www.spamhaus.org/statistics/spammers/) that as of November 2016 approximately 80% of the world's spam was being generated by a group of roughly 100 spam operations known as "spam gangs." Spamhaus reports in "Register of Known Spam Operations" (November 3, 2016, https://www.spamhaus.org/rokso/) that on average these gangs consisted of between one and five individual spammers; the total number of individual spammers involved in these operations was estimated to be between 300 and 400. In November 2016 one of the worst offenders was a long-running spam gang known as the Canadian Pharmacy. Believed to be based in Ukraine, the Canadian Pharmacy generated tens of millions of spam e-mail messages every day, primarily through botnets. According to Spamhaus, in "The World's Worst Spam Enabling Countries" (https://www.spamhaus.org/statistics/countries/), in November 2016

there were 3,062 high-volume spammers in the United States alone. Indeed, the United States was the country of origin for the largest number of spammers, followed by China with 2,704. Other countries with major spam operations in November 2016 included the Russian Federation (1,017), Ukraine (645), Japan (593), Hong Kong (579), Brazil (423), the United Kingdom (419), Turkey (385), and India (381).

ANTISPAM LEGISLATION. As early as 2003 many people worried that spam was reaching epidemic proportions and was on the verge of making e-mail an impractical means of communication. In response to the growing concerns, the U.S. government attempted to limit spam, when, on January 1, 2004, the Controlling the Assault of Non-solicited Pornography and Marketing Act of 2003 went into effect. Enforced by the Federal Trade Commission (FTC) and the states' attorneys general, this act lays out a number of provisions that commercial e-mail senders must follow. One provision states that commercial e-mail senders must clearly identify unsolicited e-mail as solicitations or advertisements for products and services. Commercial e-mail senders must also provide a way for the recipient of the mail to opt out of receiving any more e-mails from them, and all e-mails must contain a legitimate address and use honest subject lines. Although these provisions address the issue of spam in the United States, enforcement has been difficult. Creating a false identity on the Internet is easy, and once spammers know they are being tracked, they can easily relocate their operations to a different state or country. In "First Spam Felony Conviction Upheld: No Free Speech to Spam" (ArsTechnica.com, March 2, 2008), David Chartier reports that the U.S. spammer Jeremy Jaynes of Raleigh, North Carolina, was the first person convicted in U.S. federal court of sending spam. Jaynes was sentenced to serve nine years in prison for sending an estimated 10 million spam messages during July and August of 2003.

In the face of this seemingly unstoppable nuisance, Internet service providers (ISPs), along with web security firms, developed new technologies that were aimed at reducing the volume of spam being dumped in people's in-boxes. In *Spam Summit: The Next Generation of Threats and Solutions* (November 2007, http://www.ftc.gov/os/2007/12/071220spamsummitreport.pdf), the FTC's Division of Marketing Practices reports that approximately two-thirds of e-mail users used some form of spam-filtering software. In a study published in the report, researchers found that two web-based ISPs were able to block the majority of spam e-mails through the use of filtering software; one ISP succeeded in blocking 92% of all spam e-mails, and the other managed to filter 68% of spam.

Still, in 2016 the problem of spam remained a fact of life among Internet users. In June of that year the FTC filed charges against two Florida-based marketing firms—Tachht

Inc. and Teqqi LLC—for disseminating spam e-mail messages in an effort to sell weight-loss products. By using hacked e-mail accounts to deliver the spam, the perpetrators led recipients to believe they were receiving messages from people they knew, thereby making them more likely to click on fraudulent links. Although consumers typically object to spam, entrepreneurs recognize the potential profit in sending out unsolicited messages. Issuing spam costs next to nothing per message sent. Even if only 1% of people respond to a spam attack, be it for a legitimate digital cable filter or a fraudulent credit card scam, the spammer stands to make a lot of money or bring in a lot of credit card numbers. As long as a small percentage of the population responds to spam, it is potentially profitable. Bringing this number down to zero would likely be impossible. In the end, spam may just become another form of white noise that has to be endured in the modern world.

## INSTANT MESSAGING

IM is a tool that allows people to communicate via text messages in near real time over the Internet and is typically available on personal computers and many cell phones. According to Gizmo's Freeware, a freeware review site, in "Best Free Instant Messaging Client" (March 5, 2015, http://www.techsupportalert.com/best-free-instant-messaging-client.htm), the leading IM platforms in 2015 included Pidgin, Miranda IM, imo, Ebuddy, and Trillian.

IM provides people some unique advantages that other communication devices do not. Most IM applications are compact in size and easy to access, making IM easy to use while taking part in other activities. Eulynn Shiu and Amanda Lenhart of the Pew Research Center report in *How Americans Use Instant Messaging* (September 1, 2004, http://www.pewinternet.org/~/media//Files/Reports/2004/PIP_Instantmessage_Report.pdf.pdf) that in 2004, 32% of adult Americans said they were multitasking almost every time when they used IM. IM also has a clandestine aspect to it. A person can type a message without anyone knowing what he or she is doing. Nearly a quarter (24%) of all IM users said they used IM to converse with someone they were in close proximity to, typically because a class or meeting was in progress.

Like most forms of communication technology, IM evolved rapidly in the 21st century. According to the AOL–Associated Press survey "AP-AOL Instant Messaging Trends Survey Reveals Popularity of Mobile Instant Messaging" (BusinessWire.com, November 15, 2007), by 2007 roughly a quarter (24%) of IM users had begun sending and receiving instant messages from their cell phones. Over the next eight years the number of mobile IM users rose rapidly, driven largely by the increasing popularity of smartphone devices. Maeve Duggan of the Pew Research Center reports in *Mobile Messaging and Social Media 2015* (August 19, 2015, http://www.pewinternet.org/files/2015/08/Social-Media-Update-2015-FINAL2.pdf) that by 2015 more than one-third (36%) of smartphone owners used some form of messaging app on their mobile devices.

During this period IM began diversifying into new platforms. In April 2008 the popular social networking site Facebook introduced Facebook Chat, a communication tool that enabled users to initiate instant conversations with other people within their personal networks. In February 2010 Facebook reached an agreement with AOL to integrate their IM services, enabling users to communicate between the two IM platforms. Even as other messaging tools such as texting and Twitter were gaining popularity by decade's end, IM remained a vital form of rapid communication for many Internet users. As the Radicati Group reports in "Instant Messaging Market, 2016–2020" (February 2016, http://www.radicati.com/wp/wp-content/uploads/2016/01/Instant-Messaging-Market-2016-2020-Executive-Summary.pdf), the number of IM accounts worldwide exceeded 3.2 billion by 2016.

## SOCIAL NETWORKING

By 2016 social media had emerged as a popular way for people to maintain contact with friends and family members over the Internet. Indeed, social networking sites such as Facebook grew increasingly prevalent across all age demographics during this period. For example, in 2005 only 7% of all American adults used social media; by 2015 this figure had risen to 65%. (See Figure 2.1.) The increase in popularity of social networking sites was most pronounced among younger adults. Between 2005 and 2015 the proportion of adults aged 18 to 29 years who used social media rose from 12% to 90%. (See Figure 2.2.) As Figure 2.3 shows, women (68%) were somewhat more likely than men (62%) to be social media users in 2015.

Educational attainment and household income appear to be significant factors in determining whether or not adults use social media. As Figure 2.4 reveals, more than three-quarters (76%) of all college graduates were social media users in 2015. By contrast, a little over half (54%) of adults who had a high school diploma or who had never completed high school used social networking sites that year. Social media usage was also more prevalent among adults with higher household incomes. In 2015, 78% of adults with an annual household income of $75,000 or higher used social media, compared with only 56% of adults with an annual household income of $30,000 or less. (See Figure 2.5.) Among racial and ethnic groups, Hispanic (65%) and non-Hispanic white (65%) adults where considerably more likely than non-Hispanic African American (56%) adults to use social media in 2015. (See Figure 2.6.)

**FIGURE 2.1**

**Social networking use, 2005–15**

[Percentage of all American adults and internet-using adults who use at least one social networking site]

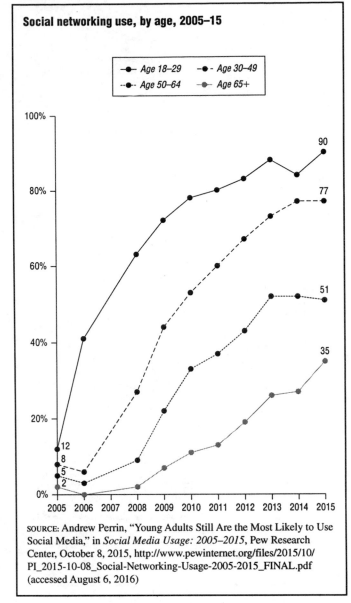

SOURCE: Andrew Perrin, "Social Networking Use Has Shot Up in Past Decade," in *Social Media Usage: 2005–2015*, Pew Research Center, October 8, 2015, http://www.pewinternet.org/files/2015/10/PI_2015-10-08_Social-Networking-Usage-2005-2015_FINAL.pdf (accessed August 6, 2016)

**FIGURE 2.2**

**Social networking use, by age, 2005–15**

SOURCE: Andrew Perrin, "Young Adults Still Are the Most Likely to Use Social Media," in *Social Media Usage: 2005–2015*, Pew Research Center, October 8, 2015, http://www.pewinternet.org/files/2015/10/PI_2015-10-08_Social-Networking-Usage-2005-2015_FINAL.pdf (accessed August 6, 2016)

Of the leading social networking sites, Facebook was by far the most popular among Internet users in 2016. Liis Hainla reports in "Top 15 Most Popular Social Networking Sites (and 10 Apps!)" (DreamGrow.com, November 2, 2016) that by September 2016 an estimated 1.7 billion people worldwide visited Facebook each month. By comparison, Instagram received 500 million monthly visitors. The vast majority of Twitter users lived abroad. By 2015 there were 254 million international Twitter users, compared with 65 million Twitter users in the United States. (See Figure 2.7.)

Use of social networking sites is also prevalent among teenagers. In *Teens, Social Media & Technology Overview 2015* (April 9, 2015, http://www.pewinternet.org/files/2015/04/PI_TeensandTech_Update2015_0409151.pdf), Amanda Lenhart and Dana Page of the Pew Research

Center indicate that 89% of all U.S. teens aged 13 to 17 years used social media in 2015. In addition, 71% of teens maintained accounts on two or more social networking sites that year. Overall, Facebook remained the most used social media platform among U.S. teens. Among teens who maintained only one social networking account, two-thirds (66%) used Facebook, compared with 13% who used Google+ and 13% who used Instagram. In addition, 41% of all teens claimed they visited Facebook more often than any other social media site in 2015, while 20% visited Instagram more than any other site, and 11% predominantly used Snapchat. Although Facebook was the site U.S. teens used more than any other social network in 2015, it was not the most popular social media platform. Kellen Beck notes in "Snapchat Is Now the Most Popular Social Network among Teens, According to New Study" (Mashable.com, April 14,

FIGURE 2.3

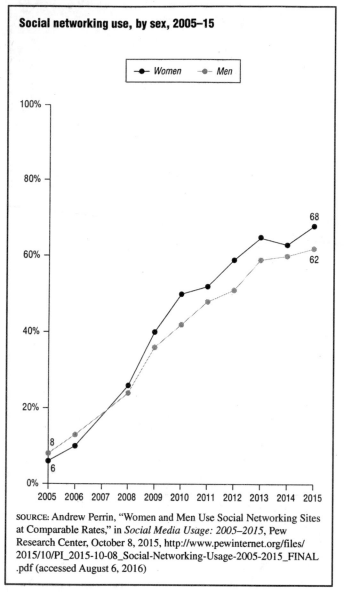

**Social networking use, by sex, 2005–15**

SOURCE: Andrew Perrin, "Women and Men Use Social Networking Sites at Comparable Rates," in *Social Media Usage: 2005–2015*, Pew Research Center, October 8, 2015, http://www.pewinternet.org/files/2015/10/PI_2015-10-08_Social-Networking-Usage-2005-2015_FINAL.pdf (accessed August 6, 2016)

FIGURE 2.4

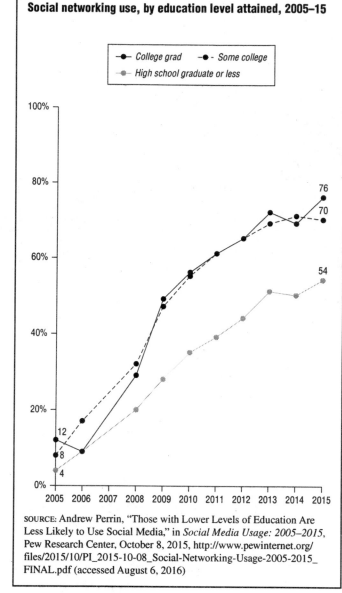

**Social networking use, by education level attained, 2005–15**

SOURCE: Andrew Perrin, "Those with Lower Levels of Education Are Less Likely to Use Social Media," in *Social Media Usage: 2005–2015*, Pew Research Center, October 8, 2015, http://www.pewinternet.org/files/2015/10/PI_2015-10-08_Social-Networking-Usage-2005-2015_FINAL.pdf (accessed August 6, 2016)

2016) that 28% of U.S. teens named Snapchat as the most important social network in 2016. Instagram was second in popularity, with 27% of teens naming it as the most important social media site.

At the same time, social networking and other online activities also play a role in promoting friendships among teens. In *Teens, Technology & Friendships* (August 6, 2015, http://www.pewinternet.org/files/2015/08/Teens-and-Friendships-FINAL2.pdf), Lenhart and Page report that more than half (57%) of all U.S. teens made friends online in 2014–15. Of these, 29% met five or more new friends online, while 22% made between two and five friends on the Internet. Nearly three-quarters (72%) of all U.S. teens used social media to communicate with their friends, while nearly a quarter (23%) did so every day. Overall, 56% of teenage girls communicated with friends via social media either every day (26%) or every few days (30%) in 2014–15; among teenage boys 19%

communicated with friends via social media every day, while 25% did so every few days.

## VOICE OVER INTERNET PROTOCOL

Another type of Internet communications technology is voice over Internet protocol (VoIP). VoIP is an application that allows the user to make phone calls over the Internet. The user attaches the phone to an adapter that sits between the phone and the computer. When a call is in progress, the adapter breaks down the voice stream into data packets and sends them over the Internet just like e-mail to the user's destination. (Regular phone conversations typically travel as streams of continuous data over a dedicated phone line that connects two people directly.) If the person on the other end of the call is also equipped with VoIP, then the entire conversation is treated by the Internet as nothing more than an instant

FIGURE 2.5

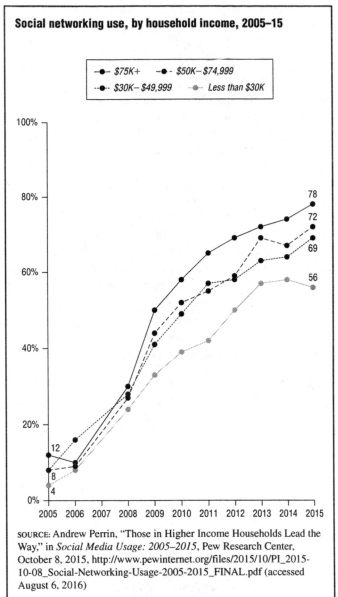

**Social networking use, by household income, 2005–15**

SOURCE: Andrew Perrin, "Those in Higher Income Households Lead the Way," in *Social Media Usage: 2005–2015*, Pew Research Center, October 8, 2015, http://www.pewinternet.org/files/2015/10/PI_2015-10-08_Social-Networking-Usage-2005-2015_FINAL.pdf (accessed August 6, 2016)

FIGURE 2.6

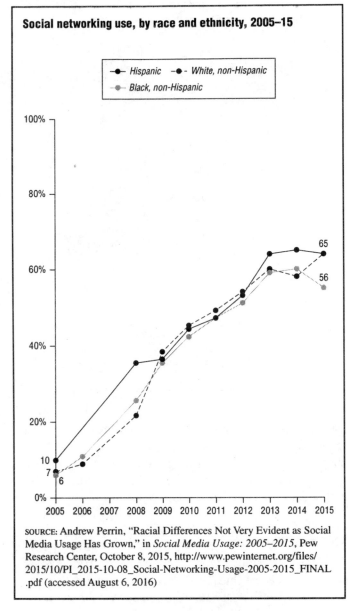

**Social networking use, by race and ethnicity, 2005–15**

SOURCE: Andrew Perrin, "Racial Differences Not Very Evident as Social Media Usage Has Grown," in *Social Media Usage: 2005–2015*, Pew Research Center, October 8, 2015, http://www.pewinternet.org/files/2015/10/PI_2015-10-08_Social-Networking-Usage-2005-2015_FINAL.pdf (accessed August 6, 2016)

message or e-mail. If the person using VoIP dials to a traditional phone, then the call must be converted into a continuous voice stream by a telecommunications company before the call reaches its destination. Leading VoIP providers in 2016 included Skype, Vonage, BroadVoice, Fonality, and Lingo.

VoIP began gaining widespread acceptance among consumers during the early part of the 21st century. According to the Pew Research Center and the New Millennium Research Council (June 2004, http://www.pewinternet.org/files/old-media//Files/Reports/2004/PIP_VOIP_DataMemo.pdf.pdf), by 2004, 34 million Americans (27% of Internet users) had heard of VoIP, and nearly 14 million (11%) had used VoIP at some point during their lifetime. The marketing research firm TeleGeography indicates in the press release "US VoIP Gains Mean RBOC Pain" (May 19, 2008, http://www.telegeography.com/press/

press-releases/2008/05/19/us-voip-gains-mean-rboc-pain/index.html) that "by the first quarter of 2008, 16.3 million consumer VoIP lines were in service, representing 13.8 percent of all U.S. households, and 27 percent of broadband households." This reflected growth of 758% since 2005, when 1.9 million households had subscribed to VoIP. In "Internet Phone Calling Is on the Rise" (August 1, 2013, http://www.pewinternet.org/2013/08/01/internet-phone-calling-is-on-the-rise), Pew reports that by December 2012 nearly one-third (30%) of Internet users had made a phone call online.

Meanwhile, the number of Americans using VoIP technology on their mobile devices also saw a substantial increase. Christina Sterling reports in "Numbers Don't Lie: Impressive Stats on the VoIP Industry" (VirtualPhone SystemReviews.com, October 17, 2013) that an estimated 228 million mobile phone owners were expected to use VoIP

FIGURE 2.7

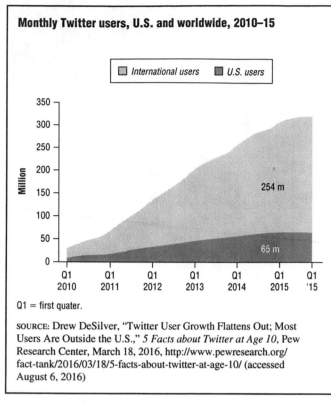

**Monthly Twitter users, U.S. and worldwide, 2010–15**

Q1 = first quater.

SOURCE: Drew DeSilver, "Twitter User Growth Flattens Out; Most Users Are Outside the U.S.," *5 Facts about Twitter at Age 10*, Pew Research Center, March 18, 2016, http://www.pewresearch.org/fact-tank/2016/03/18/5-facts-about-twitter-at-age-10/ (accessed August 6, 2016)

applications on their phones in 2013. VoIP technology also found massive growth potential in the business world by 2016, as providers such as RingCentral, Nextiva, and Vonage Business Solutions offered cost-effective alternatives to traditional business telephony systems.

## MOBILE PHONES

The cell phone is the only information technology adopted since the mid-1980s that has outpaced the Internet in terms of use. The development of the modern cell phone began during the mid-1940s, nearly 20 years before scientists even conceived of an Internet. In St. Louis, Missouri, the Bell System introduced the first commercial radio-telephone service that could connect to the national phone system. The radio-telephone, which was typically mounted under the front dashboard of a car or truck, received incoming telephone calls via radio waves that were transmitted from a large tower planted on a downtown building. A bell rang and a light went off on the radio-telephone to signify an incoming call. When the person using the radio-telephone answered, his or her side of the conversation was transmitted to one of several receiving stations around the city that were all open to the same frequencies. Both the incoming and outgoing signals were relayed through a switchboard and routed into the national phone system. From its inception in 1946, this system had a number of limitations. Calls had to be routed through a live switchboard operator, both parties involved in a conversation could not talk at once, and

only three conversations could take place citywide at any given time because of bandwidth restrictions.

### History and Development

D. H. Ring (1907–2000) at Bell Laboratories first posited the idea for the modern mobile cellular phone network in 1947 in an internal memorandum. The memo proposed a system that would overcome many of the flaws inherent in the Bell radio-telephone. The plan called for a network of low-powered cellular towers that could receive and transmit telephone calls via radio waves to and from mobile phones. Each tower would have a three-mile (4.8-km) broadcast radius. As the user of the mobile phone traveled across these cells, the call would be automatically routed from one tower to the next and the phone would switch frequencies. Because of a limited number of frequencies available in the spectrum, towers that were out of range of one another were to send and receive radio signals of the same frequency. That way two people who were three miles apart or more could carry on separate conversations using the same frequency without interfering with each other's reception.

To implement this vision on a large scale and make a profit, AT&T (the successor to Bell Laboratories) required more frequencies on the radio spectrum than the Federal Communications Commission (FCC) then allowed for two-way radio communications. The radio spectrum is essentially a long ribbon of frequencies that stretch from 3 kilohertz (kHz) to 300 gigahertz. Only one device in an area, be it a radio station or a television station, can use a particular part of this ribbon to broadcast or else interference will arise. The FCC regulates what type of devices can operate over various sections of the radio spectrum. Cell phones generally take up a large part of each spectrum because each cell phone requires two signals at two different frequencies (one signal for the incoming signal and one for the outgoing signal). With the limits the FCC imposed in 1947, only 23 cell phone conversations could take place in a metropolitan area equipped with Bell Laboratories' proposed cellular system. When AT&T approached the FCC and asked for additional room on the radio spectrum, the FCC granted AT&T only a fraction of the space requested.

Over the next 20 years mobile phone technology advanced slowly. In 1948 the Richmond Radiotelephone Company implemented the first automated radio-telephone service that did not require a live switchboard operator. In 1964 the Bell System rolled out the Improved Mobile Telephone Service to replace its aging radio-telephone network. This system allowed for both people to talk at once during a call. The bandwidth that each phone occupied on the radio spectrum was narrowed, so more people in a city could use it.

## Technological Developments after 1960

AT&T once again approached the FCC in 1958, this time asking for 75 megahertz (MHz) of spectrum located in the 800 MHz range of the radio spectrum. At the time, hardly anyone in the United States employed this part of the spectrum for broadcasting. The FCC did not review the proposal until 1968. It considered the request for two years and made a tentative decision to let AT&T use that part of the spectrum for two-way radio in 1970. Meanwhile, the Bell System, Motorola, and several other companies began engineering the technologies that were necessary for the cell phone network. In 1969 the Bell System installed the first working cell phone system aboard a train. The system consisted of a set of pay phones placed on the Metroliner trains that ran between New York City and Washington, D.C. Cell phone towers were set up along the track. As the train sped along, telephone conversations were routed from tower to tower just as described in the 1947 Bell Laboratories proposal. Four years after this first cell phone went into use, Martin Cooper (1928–) of Motorola Inc. developed the first personal, handheld cell phone. Motorola erected a single prototype cellular tower in New York City to test the phone. Cooper made his first call to his rival at Bell Laboratories, who was attempting to create a similar device.

In 1978 the FCC allowed AT&T to test an analog cellular telephone service. AT&T chose Chicago, Illinois, as one of the trial cities and set up 10 cellular towers, which covered 21,000 square miles (54,000 sq km) of the Chicago metropolitan area. Customers who wanted to use the service leased large, car-mounted telephones. The trial run was a success, and Ameritech, the regional Bell in metropolitan Chicago, launched the first commercial cellular service in the United States in 1983. (Other cell phone services had already begun operating in Europe, Asia, and the Middle East.) Two months after Ameritech began service, Cellular One offered service in the Washington-Baltimore area. Most people had car-mounted phones that occupied the middle of the front seat of a car. The alternatives were large portable phones that were so big they had to be carried around in a suitcase. At first, the cellular systems being put in place were not compatible with one another, and "roaming" outside of the calling area was not a possibility.

During the late 1980s the Telecommunications Industry Association established some basic standards for cell phone companies. The standards paved the way for a continuous, cross-country network that everyone could use regardless of which company was providing the service (oftentimes with extra charges for roaming outside one's home area). The first standard was for analog phones. Analog phones process signals in much the same way as car radios or traditional phones do. When a person speaks into the cell phone, the microphone turns the signal into a continuous stream of electrical impulses, which travels out from the phone's antennae and to the cellular tower. Both the outgoing signals and the incoming signals on modern analog phones were each allowed 30 kHz of space on the radio wave spectrum.

## Modern Cell Phone Networks

CTIA indicates in *Background on CTIA's Semi-annual Wireless Industry Survey* (2010, http://files.ctia.org/pdf/CTIA__Survey_Midyear_2010_Graphics.pdf) that by December 1990 the number of people using cell phones increased dramatically to 5.3 million subscribers. With the analog standard and the frequency limitations imposed by the FCC, fewer than 60 people in each network were able to use one cellular tower at once. If the number of cell phone subscriptions continued to increase at its then-current rate, then cell phone companies would soon require new technologies that allowed more cell phone conversations to take place in a given area. The cell phone companies' solution was to adopt digital technology.

A digital signal is a signal that is broken down into impulses representing ones and zeros. When a digital cell phone receives a digital signal, a chip inside the phone known as a digital signal processor (DSP) reads these ones and zeros and then constructs an analog signal that travels to the phone's speaker. Conversely, the DSP also processes the analog signal coming from the phone's microphone, converting it into ones and zeros, before sending the signal to a cell tower. By breaking down the signal into ones and zeros, more telephone calls can be handled by one-frequency cell phone towers. The process is analogous to breaking down and cutting up boxes to allow more to fit inside a recycling bin. The first digital system widely used by the cell phone companies was the time division multiple access (TDMA) method. Figure 2.8 and Figure 2.9 show the difference between the older, frequency division multiple access (FDMA) used for analog phones and TDMA. FDMA requires each phone to use a different frequency. TDMA allows three cell phone conversations to be contained in the same 30-kHz-wide band that holds only one analog conversation. By the early 1990s cellular companies were erecting digital cellular towers enabled with TDMA across the country.

Meanwhile, the TDMA systems were looking as if they might hit capacity. In response, the FCC auctioned off more frequency bands in the radio wave spectrum between the 1850 MHz and 1900 MHz range. Services set up on these bands were known as personal communications services (PCS). PCS networks were designed for handheld mobile phones instead of car phones and had smaller cells than the original cellular network. The PCS networks also employed a newer technology known as code division multiple access (CDMA). CDMA could pack up to 10 calls into one frequency band. (See Figure 2.10.) With so many bands available, cell phone companies introduced a multitude of

**FIGURE 2.8**

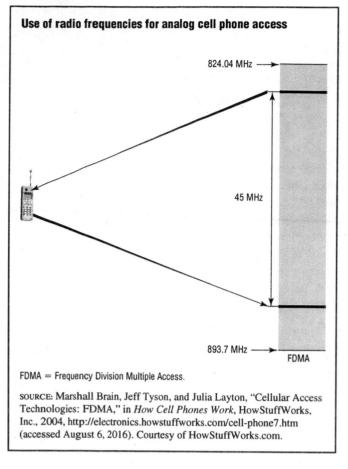

**Use of radio frequencies for analog cell phone access**

824.04 MHz →

45 MHz

893.7 MHz →

FDMA

FDMA = Frequency Division Multiple Access.

SOURCE: Marshall Brain, Jeff Tyson, and Julia Layton, "Cellular Access Technologies: FDMA," in *How Cell Phones Work*, HowStuffWorks, Inc., 2004, http://electronics.howstuffworks.com/cell-phone7.htm (accessed August 6, 2016). Courtesy of HowStuffWorks.com.

**FIGURE 2.9**

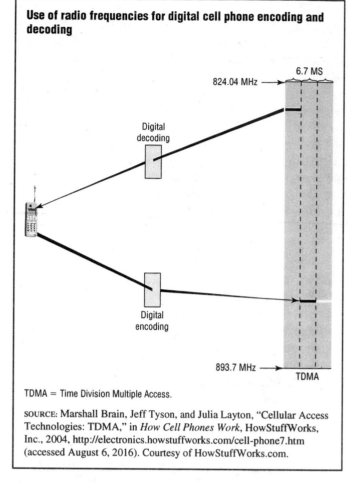

**Use of radio frequencies for digital cell phone encoding and decoding**

6.7 MS

824.04 MHz →

Digital decoding

Digital encoding

893.7 MHz →

TDMA

TDMA = Time Division Multiple Access.

SOURCE: Marshall Brain, Jeff Tyson, and Julia Layton, "Cellular Access Technologies: TDMA," in *How Cell Phones Work*, HowStuffWorks, Inc., 2004, http://electronics.howstuffworks.com/cell-phone7.htm (accessed August 6, 2016). Courtesy of HowStuffWorks.com.

standard features into their phones, such as the ability to send instant messages, surf the web, play games, send e-mail, and check the identity of callers.

High-speed fourth-generation (4G) cell phone service, the newest generation of wireless technology, allows for even more integration of Internet technologies into cell phones. Because it is an advanced form of CDMA, 4G allows more people to share a broader bandwidth of frequencies on the current cell phone networks. Cell phone providers installed software known as high-speed downlink packet access into cell phone base stations. This software increased the amount of data that could flow through cell phone networks and boosted Internet connection speeds to more than 1 megabyte per second. With such high-speed access, more people began using their cell phones to download and play video files, watch newscasts, and shop online. By 2016 all major telecommunications companies had introduced 4G long-term evolution mobile wireless products, many of them offering connection speeds of up to 1 gigabyte per second. Continued development of smaller electronics and display screens will bring about even higher-quality cameras, video games systems, and web cameras to cell phones.

For both adults and teens, by the second decade of the 21st century cell phones had become an integral part of their daily lives. By 2015, 92% of all adults owned a cell phone. (See Figure 2.11.) As Table 2.1 shows, younger adults were more likely than older adults to own cell phones. Among adults between the ages of 18 and 29 years, 98% owned cell phones in 2015; this figure was comparable for adults between the ages of 30 and 49 years, 96% of whom owned cell phones that year. By comparison, cell phone ownership fell to 90% among adults between the ages of 50 and 64 years, and just over three-quarters (78%) of seniors aged 65 years and older owned cell phones in 2015. Educational attainment and wealth were factors in determining whether or not U.S. adults owned cell phones. Whereas 95% of college-educated adults owned cell phones in 2015, 86% who had never finished high school owned cell phones that year. Among adults with an annual household income of $75,000 or higher, 98% owned cell phones in 2015; by contrast, 86% of adults with an annual household income of $30,000 or less had cell phones that year.

In *Parents, Teens and Digital Monitoring* (January 7, 2016, http://www.pewinternet.org/files/2016/01/PI_2016-01-07_Parents-Teens-Digital-Monitoring_FINAL.pdf), Monica Anderson, Aaron Smith, and Dana Page of the Pew Research Center report that 82% of teens aged 13 to 17 years owned

FIGURE 2.10

## Use of radio frequencies for code division multiple access

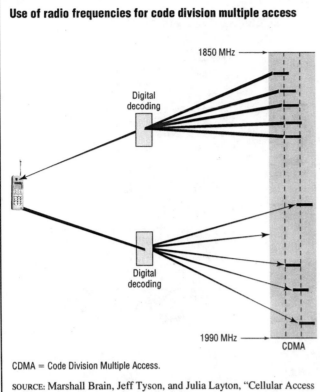

1850 MHz →

Digital decoding

Digital decoding

1990 MHz →

CDMA

CDMA = Code Division Multiple Access.

SOURCE: Marshall Brain, Jeff Tyson, and Julia Layton, "Cellular Access Technologies: CDMA," in *How Cell Phones Work*, HowStuffWorks, Inc., 2004, http://electronics.howstuffworks.com/cell-phone7.htm (accessed August 6, 2016). Courtesy of HowStuffWorks.com.

TABLE 2.1

## Percentage of adults who own cell phones, by age, gender, and other select characteristics, 2015

| | |
|---|---|
| **U.S. adults** | 92 |
| **Sex** | |
| Men | 92 |
| Women | 92 |
| **Race/ethnicity** | |
| White | 91 |
| Black | 94 |
| Hispanic | 92 |
| **Age group** | |
| 18–29 | 98 |
| 30–49 | 96 |
| 50–64 | 90 |
| 65+ | 78 |
| **Household income** | |
| <$30K | 86 |
| $30K–$49,999 | 94 |
| $50K–$74,999 | 91 |
| $75K+ | 98 |
| **Educational attainment** | |
| Less than high school | 86 |
| High school | 90 |
| Some college | 93 |
| College+ | 95 |
| **Community type** | |
| Urban | 94 |
| Suburban | 92 |
| Rural | 87 |

SOURCE: Monica Anderson, "Cellphone Ownership Is Common across All Major Demographic Groups," in *Technology Device Ownership: 2015*, Pew Research Center, October 29, 2015, http://www.pewinternet.org/files/2015/10/PI_2015-10-29_device-ownership_FINAL.pdf (accessed August 6, 2016)

FIGURE 2.11

## Percentage of adults who own electronic devices, by type of device, 2015

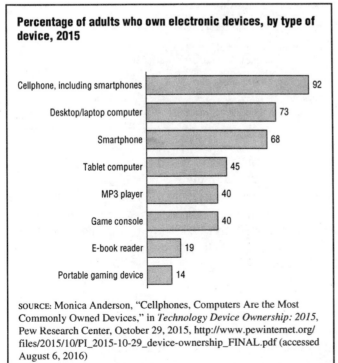

| Device | % |
|---|---|
| Cellphone, including smartphones | 92 |
| Desktop/laptop computer | 73 |
| Smartphone | 68 |
| Tablet computer | 45 |
| MP3 player | 40 |
| Game console | 40 |
| E-book reader | 19 |
| Portable gaming device | 14 |

SOURCE: Monica Anderson, "Cellphones, Computers Are the Most Commonly Owned Devices," in *Technology Device Ownership: 2015*, Pew Research Center, October 29, 2015, http://www.pewinternet.org/files/2015/10/PI_2015-10-29_device-ownership_FINAL.pdf (accessed August 6, 2016)

either a cell phone or a smartphone in 2015. According to Lenhart and Page, in *Teens, Technology & Friendships*, 80% of teenage girls engage in text messaging with their friends either every day (62%) or every few days (18%), while 71% of teenage boys send or receive text messages with friends either every day (48%) or every few days (23%). Nearly half (48%) of all teen cell phone owners use messaging applications such as WhatsApp, Kik Messenger, or Snapchat to communicate with friends. Teenage girls (46%) were considerably more likely than teenage boys (38%) to use messaging applications (apps) as a way to spend time with friends.

### Texting and Other Nonvoice Applications

Meanwhile, an increasing number of cell phone owners were using their mobile devices to access the Internet. As Table 2.2 shows, by 2015 just over two-thirds (68%) of all U.S. adults owned smartphones. As with traditional cell phones, smartphone ownership was more prevalent among younger adults. In 2015, 86% of adults between the ages of 18 and 29 years owned smartphones. The proportion of smartphone owners dropped slightly among adults between the ages of 30 and 49 years (83%), before dipping to 58% among adults aged 50 to 64 years. Smartphone ownership was lowest among seniors aged

**TABLE 2.2**

**Percentage of adults who own smartphones, by age, gender, and other select characteristics, 2015**

| | |
|---|---|
| **U.S. adults** | 68 |
| **Sex** | |
| Men | 70 |
| Women | 66 |
| **Race/ethnicity** | |
| White | 66 |
| Black | 68 |
| Hispanic | 64 |
| **Age group** | |
| 18–29 | 86 |
| 30–49 | 83 |
| 50–64 | 58 |
| 65+ | 30 |
| **Household income** | |
| <$30K | 52 |
| $30K–$49,999 | 69 |
| $50K–$74,999 | 76 |
| $75K+ | 87 |
| **Educational attainment** | |
| Less than high school | 41 |
| High school | 56 |
| Some college | 75 |
| College+ | 81 |
| **Community type** | |
| Urban | 72 |
| Suburban | 70 |
| Rural | 52 |

SOURCE: Monica Anderson, "Smartphone Owners More Likely to Be Younger, More Affluent and Highly Educated," in *Technology Device Ownership: 2015*, Pew Research Center, October 29, 2015, http://www .pewinternet.org/files/2015/10/PI_2015-10-29_device-ownership_FINAL.pdf (accessed August 6, 2016)

65 years and older; among adults in this age demographic, only 30% owned smartphones in 2015.

Younger adults were also considerably more likely to take advantage of the diverse technological features contained in smartphones. In 2014, 97% of smartphone owners between the ages of 18 and 29 years used their devices to access the Internet; 90% of smartphone owners between the ages of 30 and 49 years went online with their devices that year, while 80% of smartphone owners aged 50 years and older accessed the Internet with their devices. (See Figure 2.12.) Whereas three-quarters (75%) of smartphone owners aged 18 to 29 years used their devices to watch video content in 2014, fewer than half (46%) of smartphone owners between the ages of 30 and 49 years watched videos on their devices, and fewer than one-third (31%) of those over the age of 50 used their smartphones to view video content.

**Apps**

As ownership of smartphones and other portable computing devices increased, a wide range of mobile apps became available to consumers. An app is a software program that enables smartphone users to perform

**FIGURE 2.12**

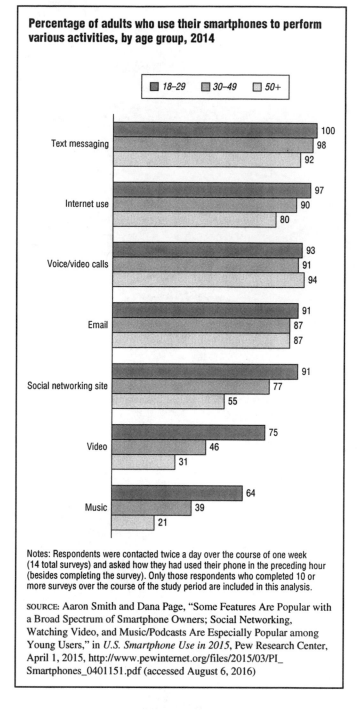

**Percentage of adults who use their smartphones to perform various activities, by age group, 2014**

Notes: Respondents were contacted twice a day over the course of one week (14 total surveys) and asked how they had used their phone in the preceding hour (besides completing the survey). Only those respondents who completed 10 or more surveys over the course of the study period are included in this analysis.

SOURCE: Aaron Smith and Dana Page, "Some Features Are Popular with a Broad Spectrum of Smartphone Owners; Social Networking, Watching Video, and Music/Podcasts Are Especially Popular among Young Users," in *U.S. Smartphone Use in 2015*, Pew Research Center, April 1, 2015, http://www.pewinternet.org/files/2015/03/PI_ Smartphones_0401151.pdf (accessed August 6, 2016)

certain functions on their mobile devices. Apps come in a variety of forms, from digital tools (such as appointment calendars or navigation systems) to music players to interactive online games. As smartphone use became increasingly widespread, many companies, including banks, retailers, and streaming content providers such as Netflix and HBO Go, created apps to enable their customers to conduct transactions or access their accounts from their mobile devices. At the same time, social networking sites such as Facebook created apps that allow users to update their status, upload photographs, and share their location from their phones. Artyom Dogtiev reports in "App Usage Statistics: 2015 Roundup"

(BusinessofApps.com, December 14, 2015) that in 2015 Americans spent an average of 2.8 hours per day interacting with digital media apps on their mobile devices. Overall, social media accounted for nearly one-third (29%) of all app usage that year. According to Dogtiev, app downloads in the United States topped 75 billion in 2015. Fifty billion of these apps were downloaded to devices using the Android operating system, while 25 billion apps were downloaded to phones using iOS.

The leading app distributors in 2016 included the Apple Store, the Windows Phone Store, and Google Play. Statista notes in "Most Popular Apple App Store Categories in September 2016, by Share of Available Apps" (http://www.statista.com/statistics/270291/popular-categories-in-the-app-store/) that games accounted for nearly a quarter (24.4%) of all apps downloaded from the Apple Store in September 2016; other popular app categories included business apps (10.1%), education apps (8.8%), and lifestyle apps (8.6%). Indeed, by 2015 smartphone owners were spending considerably more time using apps than web browsers. According to Greg Sterling, in "All Digital Growth Now Coming from Mobile Usage" (MarketingLand.com, April 3, 2016), by 2015 mobile app usage accounted for 65% of all time spent interacting with digital media in the United States.

## Issues and Concerns

DISTRACTED DRIVING. Although cell phones have brought a great deal of convenience to modern society, they have become a source of trouble as well. Cell phones contribute to automobile accidents because drivers cannot concentrate on the road appropriately while speaking or texting on a cell phone. As of November 2016, Congress continued to debate whether or not to institute a nationwide ban on handheld cell phone use in automobiles, but many states already had laws in place. Table 2.3 indicates which states had adopted cell phone driving laws as of August 2016; at that time 14 states and the District of Columbia had statewide bans on the use of handheld devices while driving. In addition, 46 states and the District of Columbia banned drivers from text messaging while behind the wheel; 38 states and the District of Columbia banned cell phones for drivers with learner permits or provisional licenses; and 20 states and the District of Columbia prohibited the use of cell phones by school bus drivers carrying passengers.

HEALTH RISKS. Health concerns associated with cell phone use have also been identified. In the landmark study "Nerve Cell Damage in Mammalian Brain after Exposure to Microwaves from GSM Mobile Phones" (*Environmental Health Perspectives*, vol. 111, no. 7, June 2003), Leif G. Salford et al. of Lund University found that cell phone radiation causes brain damage in rats. The researchers mounted a cell phone to the side of the rats' cage for two hours per day for 50 days to emulate the amount of exposure that is received by a habitual cell phone user. The rats' brains showed significant blood vessel leakage as well as areas of damaged neurons. Other studies followed but were inconclusive. Nevertheless, the University of Pittsburgh Cancer Institute warns in "The Case for Precaution in the Use of Cell Phones" (July 22, 2008, http://www.upci.upmc.edu/news/pdf/The-Case-for-Precaution-in-Cell-Phone-Use.pdf) that:

> Electromagnetic fields generated by cell phones should be considered a potential human health risk. Sufficient time has not elapsed in order for us to have conclusive data on the biological effects of cell phones and other cordless phones—a technology that is now universal.
>
> Studies in humans do not indicate that cell phones are safe, nor do they yet clearly show that they are dangerous. But, growing evidence indicates that we should reduce exposures, while research continues on this important question.

The institute emphasizes that children are particularly at risk because their brains are still developing and suggests that children should not use mobile phones except in emergencies. Nevertheless, other studies find no evidence of human health risks related to cell phone use. In "Reducing Exposure: Hands-free Kits and Other Accessories" (October 1, 2014, http://www.fda.gov/Radiation-EmittingProducts/RadiationEmittingProductsandProcedures/HomeBusinessandEntertainment/CellPhones/ucm116293.htm), the U.S. Food and Drug Administration (FDA) indicates that no specific health risks related to cell phone use have been identified. Nonetheless, the FDA also states that scientific research on the subject is still ongoing.

**TABLE 2.3**

## State cell phone and texting laws, August 2016

| State | Hand-held ban | All cell phone ban — School bus drivers | All cell phone ban — Novice drivers | Text messaging ban — All drivers | Text messaging ban — School bus drivers | Text messaging ban — Novice drivers | Crash data |
|---|---|---|---|---|---|---|---|
| Alabama | | | 16, or 17 w/intermediate license <6 months (primary) | Yes (primary) | Covered under all driver ban | | Yes |
| Alaska | | | | Yes (primary) | Covered under all driver ban | | Yes |
| Arizona | | Yes (primary) | | | | | Yes |
| Arkansas[a] | 18–20 years old (primary) | Yes (primary) | <18 (secondary) | Yes (primary) | Covered under all driver ban | | Yes |
| California | Yes (primary) | Yes (primary) | <18 (secondary) | Yes (primary) | Covered under all driver ban | | Yes |
| Colorado | | | <18 (primary) | Yes (primary) | Covered under all driver ban | | Yes |
| Connecticut | Yes (primary) | Yes (primary) | <18 (primary) | Yes (primary) | Covered under all driver ban | | |
| Delaware | Yes (primary) | Yes (primary) | Learner or intermediate license (primary) | Yes (primary) | Covered under all driver ban | | Yes |
| D.C. | Yes (primary) | Yes (primary) | Learner's permit (primary) | Yes (primary) | Covered under all driver ban | | Yes |
| Florida | | | | Yes (secondary) | Covered under all driver ban | | Yes |
| Georgia | | Yes (primary) | <18 (primary) | Yes (primary) | Covered under all driver ban | | Yes |
| Guam | Yes (primary) | | | Yes (primary) | Covered under all driver ban | | |
| Hawaii | Yes (primary) | | <18 (primary) | Yes (primary) | Covered under all driver ban | | Yes |
| Idaho | | | | Yes (primary) | Covered under all driver ban | | Yes |
| Illinois | Yes (primary) | Yes (primary) | <19 (primary) | Yes (primary) | Covered under all driver ban | | Yes |
| Indiana | | | <21 (primary) (eff. 7/2015) | Yes (primary) | Covered under all driver ban | | Yes |
| Iowa | | | Restricted or intermediate license (primary) | Yes (secondary) | Covered under all driver ban | | Yes |
| Kansas | | | Learner or intermediate license (primary) | Yes (primary) | Covered under all driver ban | | Yes |
| Kentucky | | Yes (primary) | <18 (primary) | Yes (primary) | Covered under all driver ban | | Yes |
| Louisiana | Learner or intermediate license (regardless of age) | Yes (primary) | 1st year of license (primary for <18) | Yes (primary) | Covered under all driver ban | | Yes |
| Maine | | | Learner or intermediate license (primary) | Yes (primary) | Covered under all driver ban | | Yes |
| Maryland | Yes (primary) | | <18 (primary) | Yes (primary) | Covered under all driver ban | | Yes |
| Massachusetts | | Yes (primary) | <18 (primary) | Yes (primary) | Covered under all driver ban | | Yes |
| Michigan | | Yes (primary) | Level 1 or 2 license (primary) | Yes (primary) | Covered under all driver ban | | Yes |
| Minnesota | | Yes (primary) | <18 w/Learner or provisional license (primary) | Yes (primary) | Covered under all driver ban | | Yes |
| Mississippi | | Yes (primary) | | Yes (primary) | Covered under all driver ban | | Yes |
| Missouri | | | | | | <21 (primary) | Yes |
| Montana | | | | | | | Yes |
| Nebraska | | | <18 w/Learner or intermediate license (secondary) | Yes (secondary) | Covered under all driver ban | | Yes |
| Nevada | Yes (primary) | | | Yes (primary) | Covered under all driver ban | | Yes |
| New Hampshire | Yes (primary) | | <18 (primary) | Yes (primary) | Covered under all driver ban | | |
| New Jersey | Yes (primary) | Yes (primary) | Permit or provisional license (primary) | Yes (primary) | Covered under all driver ban | | Yes |
| New Mexico | In state vehicles | | Learner or provisional license (primary) | Yes (primary) | Covered under all driver ban | | Yes |
| New York | Yes (primary) | | | Yes (primary) | Covered under all driver ban | | Yes |
| North Carolina | | Yes (primary) | <18 (primary) | Yes (primary) | Covered under all driver ban | | Yes |
| North Dakota | | | <18 (primary) | Yes (primary) | Covered under all driver ban | | Yes |
| Ohio | | | <18 (primary) | Yes (secondary) | Covered under all driver ban | | Yes |
| Oklahoma | Learner or intermediate license (primary) | | | Yes (primary) | Covered under all driver ban | | Yes |
| Oregon | Yes (primary) | | <18 (primary) | Yes (primary) | Covered under all driver ban | | Yes |
| Pennsylvania | | | | Yes (primary) | Covered under all driver ban | | Yes |
| Puerto Rico | Yes (primary) | | | Yes (primary) | Covered under all driver ban | | |
| Rhode Island | | Yes (primary) | <18 (primary) | Yes (primary) | Covered under all driver ban | | Yes |

**TABLE 2.3**

**State cell phone and texting laws, August 2016** [CONTINUED]

| State | Hand-held ban | All cell phone ban | | Text messaging ban | | | Crash data |
|---|---|---|---|---|---|---|---|
| | | School bus drivers | Novice drivers | All drivers | School bus drivers | Novice drivers | |
| South Carolina | | | | Yes (primary) | Covered under all driver ban | | Yes |
| South Dakota | | | Learner or intermediate license (secondary) | Yes (secondary) | Covered under all driver ban | | Yes |
| Tennessee | | Yes (primary) | Learner or intermediate license (primary) | Yes (primary) | Covered under all driver ban | | Yes |
| Texas[b] | | Yes, w/passenger <17 (primary) | <18 (primary) | | Yes, w/passenger <17 (primary) | <18 (primary) | Yes |
| Utah | | Yes (primary) | <18 (primary) | Yes (primary) | Covered under all driver ban | | Yes |
| Vermont | Yes (primary) | | <18 (primary) | Yes (primary) | Covered under all driver ban | | Yes |
| Virgin Islands | Yes (primary) | | | Yes (primary) | Covered under all driver ban | | Yes |
| Virginia | | Yes (primary) | <18 (secondary) | Yes (primary) | Covered under all driver ban | | Yes |
| Washington | Yes (primary) | | Learner or intermediate license (primary) | Yes (primary) | Covered under all driver ban | | Yes |
| West Virginia | Yes (primary) | | <18 w/Learner or intermediate license (primary) | Yes (primary) | Covered under all driver ban | | Yes |
| Wisconsin | | | Learner or intermediate license (primary) | Yes (primary) | Covered under all driver ban | | Yes |
| Wyoming | | | | Yes (primary) | Covered under all driver ban | | Yes |
| **Total states** | **14 + D.C. PR, Guam, Virgin Islands** All primary | **20 + D.C.** All primary | **38 + D.C.** primary (32 + D.C.) secondary (6) | **46 + D.C., PR, Guam, Virgin Islands** primary (41 + D.C., PR, Guam, Virgin Islands) secondary (5) | 1 primary | 2 primary | **48 + D.C., Virgin Islands** |

[a]Arkansas also bans the use of hand-held cell phones while driving in a school zone or in a highway construction zone. This law is secondarily enforced.
[b]Texas has banned the use of hand-held phones and texting in school zones.

SOURCE: "Distracted Driving Laws," in *State Laws and Funding*, Governors Highway Safety Association, August 2016, http://www.ghsa.org/html/stateinfo/laws/cellphone_laws.html (accessed August 6, 2016).

# CHAPTER 3
# INFORMATION TECHNOLOGY AND U.S. BUSINESS

The desire of U.S. corporations to make money fueled the proliferation of electronics and communications technologies during the 1980s and 1990s. High-technology (high-tech) companies such as Microsoft, Apple, and Intel strove to create affordable computers, Internet technologies, cell phones, and a variety of electronics-based products for use in the office, at home, and while on the go. A huge market segment, commonly referred to as the information technology (IT) industry, developed around the production of these new technologies and included the manufacture of computers and electronic products, software publishing, data processing services, advanced telecommunications, and computer systems design. The technology research firm Gartner, Inc., reports in "Gartner Says Worldwide IT Spending Is Forecast to Be Flat in 2016" (July 7, 2016, http://www.gartner.com/newsroom/id/3368517) that global spending on IT topped $3.4 trillion in 2015. However, IT spending was expected to remain roughly the same in 2016, as efforts by many corporations to reduce operating costs stalled overall growth in the industry.

As information technologies spread through U.S. offices and corporations, they also transformed other industries outside of the IT sector. In the financial industries, innovations such as interconnected bank networks and electronic bill pay greatly reduced the number of paper checks in circulation daily. The retail industry discovered a new way to sell merchandise. In "E-Stats 2014: Measuring the Electronic Economy" (June 7, 2016, https://www.census.gov/content/dam/Census/library/publications/2016/econ/e14-estats.pdf), the U.S. Census Bureau notes that in 2014, $298.6 billion in retail sales were conducted over the Internet. Furthermore, e-commerce manufacturing shipments in 2014 amounted to nearly $3.6 trillion. During the first quarter of 2015 e-commerce retail sales approached $80.6 billion; during the first quarter of 2016 online retail sales exceeded $92.8 billion, an increase of 15.2% over the same period the previous year. (See Table 3.1.) Overall, e-commerce accounted for an increasingly larger proportion of all retail sales between 2006 and 2016. In 2006 e-commerce represented just over 2.5% of overall retail sales; by the first quarter 2016 this figure rose to 7.8%. (See Figure 3.1.)

The economic impact of IT reverberated well beyond those industries that sold goods on the Internet, however. Every industry from trucking to real estate to health care to manufacturing incorporated new technologies that helped make doing business more efficient and affordable. Entire medical and law libraries were replaced by online databases that could be searched in minutes. Retail inventories, which used to be counted by hand, were linked directly to barcode scans taken at cash registers, a process that ultimately made ordering stock more efficient and reduced expensive storage costs. Bookkeeping and accounting, which was once an arduous task completed in thick, paper ledgers, was done in a fraction of the time and at a fraction of the cost using computer accounting software.

Nevertheless, IT did not have a positive effect on all businesses. For example, travel agencies saw an enormous drop in revenue because many people began making their own travel arrangements using online reservations sites. The growth in online bookings led to a 40% drop in the number of travel agency jobs in the United States between 1999 and 2013. In *National Occupational Employment and Wage Estimates* (May 2015, http://www.bls.gov/oes/current/oes_nat.htm), the U.S. Department of Labor's Bureau of Labor Statistics (BLS) indicates that 66,560 travel agents were employed in 2015, compared with 111,130 in 1999. The ease with which the typical consumer could make travel arrangements online was largely responsible for this decline.

The newspaper industry has also suffered a steady decline in the digital age, as online media sources offer

**TABLE 3.1**

Estimated quarterly U.S. retail sales, total and e-commerce, 2015–16

| Quarter | Retail sales (millions of dollars) | | E-commerce as a percent of total | Percent change from prior quarter | | Percent change from same quarter a year ago | |
| --- | --- | --- | --- | --- | --- | --- | --- |
| | Total | E-commerce | | Total | E-commerce | Total | E-commerce |
| **Adjusted[a]** | | | | | | | |
| 1st quarter 2016[b] | 1,183,863 | 92,801 | 7.8 | −0.2 | 3.7 | 2.2 | 15.2 |
| 4th quarter 2015 | 1,186,748 | 89,454 | 7.5 | 0.1 | 2.1 | 1.4 | 15.1 |
| 3rd quarter 2015 | 1,185,330 | 87,588 | 7.4 | 0.9 | 4.0 | 1.6 | 15.2 |
| 2nd quarter 2015 | 1,174,967 | 84,217 | 7.2 | 1.4 | 4.5 | 1.2 | 14.5 |
| 1st quarter 2015 | 1,158,391 | 80,569 | 7.0 | −1.0 | 3.7 | 2.1 | 14.6 |
| **Not adjusted** | | | | | | | |
| 1st quarter 2016[b] | 1,116,695 | 86,327 | 7.7 | −10.6 | −20.2 | 3.3 | 15.1 |
| 4th quarter 2015 | 1,249,081 | 108,175 | 8.7 | 5.1 | 33.5 | 1.7 | 14.8 |
| 3rd quarter 2015 | 1,188,363 | 81,020 | 6.8 | −0.1 | 2.8 | 1.6 | 15.4 |
| 2nd quarter 2015 | 1,189,836 | 78,784 | 6.6 | 10.1 | 5.1 | 1.1 | 14.7 |
| 1st quarter 2015 | 1,081,022 | 74,982 | 6.9 | −12.0 | −20.4 | 1.8 | 14.4 |

[a]Estimates are adjusted for seasonal variation, but not for price changes. Total sales estimates are also adjusted for trading day differences and moving holidays.
[b]Preliminary estimate.
Note: E-commerce sales are sales of goods and services where the buyer places an order, or the price and terms of the sale are negotiated over an Internet, mobile device (M-commerce), extranet, Electronic Data Interchange (EDI) network, electronic mail, or other comparable online system. Payment may or may not be made online.

SOURCE: Rebecca DeNale and Deanna Weidenhamer, "Table 1. Estimated Quarterly U.S. Retail Sales: Total and E-Commerce," in *Quarterly Retail E-Commerce Sales: 1st Quarter 2016*, U.S. Department of Commerce, U.S. Census Bureau, May 17, 2016, https://www.census.gov/retail/mrts/www/data/pdf/ec_current.pdf (accessed August 10, 2016)

**FIGURE 3.1**

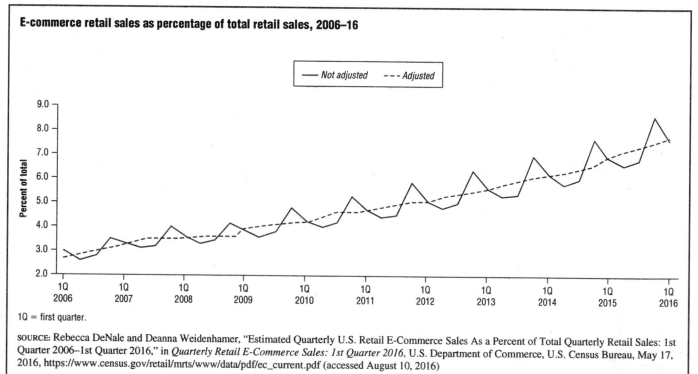

E-commerce retail sales as percentage of total retail sales, 2006–16

1Q = first quarter.

SOURCE: Rebecca DeNale and Deanna Weidenhamer, "Estimated Quarterly U.S. Retail E-Commerce Sales As a Percent of Total Quarterly Retail Sales: 1st Quarter 2006–1st Quarter 2016," in *Quarterly Retail E-Commerce Sales: 1st Quarter 2016*, U.S. Department of Commerce, U.S. Census Bureau, May 17, 2016, https://www.census.gov/retail/mrts/www/data/pdf/ec_current.pdf (accessed August 10, 2016)

convenient alternatives to traditional print publications. Michael Barthel of the Pew Research Center notes in "Newspapers: Fact Sheet" (June 15, 2016, http://www.journalism.org/2016/06/15/newspapers-fact-sheet/) that 126 daily newspapers went out of business nationwide between 2004 and 2014. Meanwhile, between the mid-1990s and 2015 the newspaper industry cut approximately 20,000 jobs, which was a decrease of 39%.

## IT INDUSTRY

Although IT has been around since the International Business Machines Corporation (IBM) began mass-producing computers during the early 1950s, it did not become a large part of the U.S. economy until the 1990s. A number of high-tech companies, such as Microsoft and Dell, had positioned themselves as the commercial leaders in Internet, personal computer, and cell phone technologies during the 1980s. When use of the World Wide Web became common in 1994 and the price of electronics began to drop, Americans flocked to these technologies. Revenues in the high-tech industry as a whole increased at a rate not seen in any industry since the postwar boom of the 1950s. Microsoft reported sales of $140 million in 1985. Ten years later its revenues had increased to $6 billion. Cisco Systems, the leading commercial maker of Internet routers and switches, grew at an even faster rate. Between 1990 and 2001 the company's revenues grew from $69 million to $22 billion. Dell, one of the top sellers of home computers in the U.S. market, saw sales increase from $300 million in 1989 to $25.3 billion in fiscal year (FY) 2000.

The growth of these companies along with the rest of the IT-producing industries had a tremendous impact on the economy. According to the U.S. Department of Commerce, in *Digital Economy 2003* (December 2003, http://www.esa.doc.gov/sites/default/files/dig_econ_2003.pdf), the IT industries made up roughly 8% to 9% of the U.S. domestic economy between 1996 and 2000. However, these industries were responsible for 1.4 percentage points of the nation's 4.6% annual average real gross domestic product (GDP) growth over these years. The GDP is one of the basic yardsticks used to measure the U.S. economy and is defined as the value, or sale price, of all goods that are produced in a country minus the cost of the materials that went into making those goods. In other words, the entire IT industry, which made up a little under one-tenth of the economy, accounted for more than one-third of the economic growth. Between 1993 and 2000 employment in the IT industries expanded rapidly as well. IT companies hired people at twice the rate of all private industries and added more than 1.8 million jobs to the workforce in sectors such as software and computer services, computer hardware, and communication services.

### End of the IT Boom

Toward the dawn of the 21st century many Americans thought the IT boom would continue indefinitely. They invested enormous sums of money in IT and IT-related stocks. From late 1998 to early 2000 the value of Microsoft stocks and Dell stocks doubled; Cisco Systems' stock value quadrupled. The National Association of Securities Dealers Automated Quotation System (NASDAQ), a stock index that tracks the value of many IT stocks, rose from 2,442 on August 10, 1999, to a peak value of 5,132 on Friday, March 10, 2000 (one of the largest increases of a major stock index in history). Many Americans invested not only in large, well-established corporations but also in small e-commerce companies such as Pets.com and eToys. Many of these dot-coms were brand-new businesses that had yet to produce any profits. People invested in them in the hope that these dot-coms would enjoy the sort of huge

rise in value that made early investors in Dell or Microsoft millionaires.

On Monday, March 13, 2000, the NASDAQ dropped roughly 300 points, from a high of 5,013 to a closing low of 4,706. The index dropped for a couple more days, rebounded to a point close to its all-time high, and then proceeded to fall intermittently for the next two-and-a-half years, finally hitting bottom on October 10, 2002, at 1,108. Other stock indexes, such as the Dow Jones Industrial Average and Standard and Poor's 500, followed this downward trend, ultimately returning to 1998 levels. The stock bubble burst because investors began to fear that many IT and IT-related companies were not living up to expectations and pulled their money out of the market.

The entire nation slipped into a recession. By 2001 numerous dot-coms were out of business, and many established IT companies were beginning to post losses. Between 2001 and 2002 Cisco Systems' sales dropped more than $3.4 billion, and Dell's annual earnings dipped by roughly $700 million. The Department of Commerce explains in *Digital Economy 2003* that the main reason for the slowdown in the IT industries was that the private business sector stopped buying equipment. Throughout the 1990s just about every type of business (from law firms to paper producers to grocery stores to auto shops) was either buying or updating its computers, printers, and networks. Businesses that did not make such investments quickly became outdated and inefficient and did not survive. By the dawn of the 21st century many companies outside of the IT industries had already made an initial investment in IT equipment and required only upgrades as hardware needed replacement or as software was updated. In addition, the components that make up the infrastructure for the Internet (fiber-optic cables, routers, and switches) had largely been laid down by the late 1990s, so the need for these components greatly diminished as well.

The industries that produced hardware components and communications equipment were the hardest hit. The overall GDP for these industries dropped 22% in 2000 and 18% in 2001. The Department of Commerce reports that among the most negatively affected industries, semiconductor manufacturing fell from $67.9 billion in 2000 to $44.1 billion in 2001, a 35% decrease. The industries that did reasonably well during this recessionary period were the software and services industries and the communications services industries. Prepackaged software, computer processing, information retrieval services, computer services management, computer maintenance and repair, and other computer-related services all showed modest gains. Although U.S. businesses as a whole had bought much of their hardware, many still had the need for new software, Internet service, and computer maintenance.

## Lost Jobs

To cut their losses in this down market, IT companies began laying off many of the workers they had hired during the 1990s. In *Digital Economy 2003*, the Department of Commerce reports that roughly 600,000 jobs were shed in the IT industries between 2000 and 2002. This job loss accounted for more than a quarter of all the jobs that were lost during the recession. The rate of job loss in the IT industries was six times that of all private industry. Not surprisingly, the industry that lost the most jobs was computer hardware, from a high of nearly 1.7 million jobs in 2000 to 1.4 million in 2002.

Although many of the jobs that were lost simply ceased to exist, two additional trends combined to decrease the number of traditional employment positions. The term *outsourcing* refers to work that is contracted to nonemployees such as temporary workers; *offshoring* refers to situations in which the positions are assumed by workers located in another country where wages are less. With the advent of e-mail, the Internet, and low-cost international phone calls, offices separated by continents could be linked through cyberspace. Geography was no longer a predominant concern for many companies. In India, for example, there were large numbers of highly educated people who spoke English, were knowledgeable about computer science, and were more than happy to work for a fraction of the typical U.S. hourly wage. Companies such as Dell moved high-paying technical assistance jobs, low- to midlevel computer programming jobs, and even technical documentation jobs to other countries.

## IT Becomes a Mature Industry

According to the Department of Commerce, in *Digital Economy 2003*, by 2003 the IT industries showed signs of recovery. The GDP in the IT-producing industries grew 4.8% to $871.9 billion in 2003 as business spending on IT equipment began to accelerate. During the first nine months of 2003 IT spending by the private sector as a whole rose an estimated 2.3% on average. Consumer and household spending on IT equipment, which did not abate as sharply during the recession, grew faster through 2002 and into 2003. In addition, the IT industries did not cut back on research and development during the recession. Consequently, many new products were being developed by the end of the recession. Nevertheless, employment numbers in the IT industries had not recovered significantly by 2003. The Department of Commerce considered these developments taken together to indicate that the IT industries had settled into maturity and predicted that future growth would likely be more modest and less volatile than it was during the 1980s and 1990s.

By 2015 the information and telecommunications industries reached a gross output of $1.6 trillion. (See Table 3.2; gross output equals the value of the industry's total sales and other operating income.) This figure represented growth of 4% over the $1.5 trillion in gross output experienced in 2014. Indeed, in spite of the general economic uncertainty of these years, many high-tech companies such as Google and Apple saw their revenues exceed expectations during this period.

Apple reported sales of $231.3 billion in 2015, an increase of 35% compared with the $170.9 billion in revenues the company generated in 2013. Google, which posted sales of $59.7 billion in FY 2013, saw revenues rise to $73.6 billion in 2015, an increase of 23%. Microsoft, which posted revenues of $77.7 billion in 2013, saw sales grow to $93 billion in 2015, an increase of 20%.

Trends in IT employment during this span also showed signs of the industry's economic rebound. In "Mass Layoff Statistics" (May 13, 2013, http://www.bls.gov/mls/miltprod.htm), the most recent report on this topic as of November 2016, the BLS charts a steep rise in IT layoffs between 2007 and 2009. (An extended mass layoff, as defined by the BLS, is one that affects at least 50 individuals from a single employer for a period of at least 31 days; the number of events and of workers affected in mass layoff statistics do not reflect totals for the industry, but are indicative of overall trends.) Extended mass layoffs in the IT sector swelled from 5,363 in 2007 to 8,259 in 2008, an increase of 54%. The industry's employment prospects declined even more sharply in 2009, when 11,824 extended mass layoffs were reported, an increase of 3,565 compared with the previous year. This trend was particularly notable in the computer hardware business, where extended mass layoff events rose from 91 in 2007 to 345 in 2009, an increase of 279%.

By decade's end, extended mass layoff events in the IT sector began to decline. After falling to 7,247 in 2010, extended mass layoffs for the IT sector dropped to 6,596 in 2011, before falling to 6,500 in 2012. Figures for the first part of 2013 revealed even stronger signs of recovery. Extended mass IT layoffs for the first quarter of 2013 fell to 914, which was nearly a 30% drop from the 1,294 extended mass layoffs the industry recorded for the first quarter of 2012.

## EFFECT OF IT ON U.S. BUSINESSES

The rise of the IT industries, although dramatic, did not affect the U.S. economy nearly as much as the products that these industries produced. Nearly every task in a modern office, regardless of the business, employs some piece of technology that either was not present before the proliferation of IT or was present in only a limited way. These technologies have had a profound effect on both the productivity of businesses and individual employees.

Figure 3.2 charts shifts in productivity in the private, nonfarm business sector between 1947 and 2015.

**TABLE 3.2**

## Gross output by industry, 2013–15

[Millions of dollars]

| Line | | 2013 | 2014 | 2015 |
|---|---|---|---|---|
| 1 | All industries | 29,571,553 | 30,971,025 | 31,386,507 |
| 2 | Private industries | 26,187,054 | 27,532,868 | 27,907,037 |
| 3 | Agriculture, forestry, fishing, and hunting | 482,232 | 488,824 | 454,155 |
| 4 | Farms | 433,554 | 435,775 | 401,883(u) |
| 5 | Forestry, fishing, and related activities | 48,678 | 53,048 | 52,272(u) |
| 6 | Mining | 619,908 | 666,540 | 425,864 |
| 7 | Oil and gas extraction | 393,844 | 430,484 | 244,810(u) |
| 8 | Mining, except oil and gas | 126,425 | 130,222 | 113,771(u) |
| 9 | Support activities for mining | 99,639 | 105,833 | 67,283(u) |
| 10 | Utilities | 392,452 | 417,777 | 390,852 |
| 11 | Construction | 1,128,331 | 1,204,025 | 1,319,599 |
| 12 | Manufacturing | 5,942,483 | 6,178,070 | 5,940,301 |
| 13 | Durable goods | 2,783,587 | 2,974,366 | 3,027,437 |
| 14 | Wood products | 89,604 | 97,834 | 98,724(u) |
| 15 | Nonmetallic mineral products | 105,238 | 116,432 | 117,439(u) |
| 16 | Primary metals | 263,363 | 281,905 | 250,619(u) |
| 17 | Fabricated metal products | 360,714 | 379,053 | 378,248(u) |
| 18 | Machinery | 390,378 | 405,049 | 396,783(u) |
| 19 | Computer and electronic products | 369,003 | 387,090 | 402,856(u) |
| 20 | Electrical equipment, appliances, and components | 122,194 | 125,597 | 123,382(u) |
| 21 | Motor vehicles, bodies and trailers, and parts | 546,950 | 596,080 | 662,472(u) |
| 22 | Other transportation equipment | 305,666 | 346,172 | 345,255(u) |
| 23 | Furniture and related products | 68,777 | 71,813 | 76,717(u) |
| 24 | Miscellaneous manufacturing | 161,698 | 167,341 | 174,944(u) |
| 25 | Nondurable goods | 3,158,896 | 3,203,704 | 2,912,864 |
| 26 | Food and beverage and tobacco products | 927,375 | 970,305 | 963,969(u) |
| 27 | Textile mills and textile product mills | 56,593 | 55,121 | 54,672(u) |
| 28 | Apparel and leather and allied products | 37,586 | 39,213 | 39,610(u) |
| 29 | Paper products | 184,610 | 193,924 | 192,922(u) |
| 30 | Printing and related support activities | 84,042 | 85,559 | 89,119(u) |
| 31 | Petroleum and coal products | 833,228 | 818,282 | 542,126(u) |
| 32 | Chemical products | 810,905 | 810,147 | 803,123(u) |
| 33 | Plastics and rubber products | 224,557 | 231,154 | 227,324(u) |
| 34 | Wholesale trade | 1,495,021 | 1,576,810 | 1,574,044 |
| 35 | Retail trade | 1,512,360 | 1,550,260 | 1,610,345 |
| 36 | Motor vehicle and parts dealers | 248,142 | 252,199 | 276,572(u) |
| 37 | Food and beverage stores | 215,483 | 222,658 | 229,171(u) |
| 38 | General merchandise stores | 217,898 | 221,933 | 227,779(u) |
| 39 | Other retail | 830,837 | 853,470 | 876,823(u) |
| 40 | Transportation and warehousing | 1,006,563 | 1,068,982 | 1,071,332 |
| 41 | Air transportation | 181,418 | 188,759 | 189,273(u) |
| 42 | Rail transportation | 81,732 | 88,582 | 82,406(u) |
| 43 | Water transportation | 60,549 | 62,989 | 62,771(u) |
| 44 | Truck transportation | 310,358 | 332,411 | 329,273(u) |
| 45 | Transit and ground passenger transportation | 54,083 | 56,697 | 58,658(u) |
| 46 | Pipeline transportation | 29,216 | 33,393 | 31,686(u) |
| 47 | Other transportation and support activities | 201,745 | 215,979 | 222,409(u) |
| 48 | Warehousing and storage | 87,462 | 90,173 | 94,856(u) |
| 49 | Information | 1,426,062 | 1,510,770 | 1,571,223 |
| 50 | Publishing industries, except internet (includes software) | 313,415 | 330,515 | 335,488(u) |
| 51 | Motion picture and sound recording industries | 148,847 | 153,206 | 160,705(u) |
| 52 | Broadcasting and telecommunications | 775,036 | 819,545 | 847,851(u) |
| 53 | Data processing, internet publishing, and other information services | 188,764 | 207,505 | 227,179(u) |
| 54 | Finance, insurance, real estate, rental, and leasing | 5,020,443 | 5,298,861 | 5,538,984 |
| 55 | Finance and insurance | 2,080,117 | 2,181,681 | 2,274,836 |
| 56 | Federal Reserve banks, credit intermediation, and related activities | 676,343 | 704,717 | 748,399(u) |
| 57 | Securities, commodity contracts, and investments | 449,116 | 479,064 | 475,831(u) |
| 58 | Insurance carriers and related activities | 817,356 | 846,564 | 894,549(u) |
| 59 | Funds, trusts, and other financial vehicles | 137,301 | 151,338 | 156,056(u) |

Between 1979 and 1990 the productivity of workers in the United States increased at a rate of 1.5% per year. Between 1990 and 2000, the period in which the Internet became widespread, the productivity of workers rose significantly, to 2.2% growth per year. This upward trend continued for the next seven years, as annual productivity rates grew an average of 2.6% between 2000 and 2007, before dropping to 1.3% between 2007 and 2015.

TABLE 3.2

## Gross output by industry, 2013–15 [CONTINUED]

[Millions of dollars]

| Line | | 2013 | 2014 | 2015 |
|---|---|---|---|---|
| 60 | **Real estate and rental and leasing** | **2,940,326** | **3,117,180** | **3,264,148** |
| 61 | Real estate | 2,622,250 | 2,777,992 | 2,915,714(u) |
| 62 | Housing | 1,748,409 | 1,822,097 | 1,897,170(u) |
| 63 | Other real estate | 873,841 | 955,895 | 1,018,544(u) |
| 64 | Rental and leasing services and lessors of intangible assets | 318,076 | 339,188 | 348,434(u) |
| 65 | **Professional and business services** | **3,139,289** | **3,336,611** | **3,499,410** |
| 66 | **Professional, scientific, and technical services** | **1,804,155** | **1,898,837** | **1,979,325** |
| 67 | Legal services | 302,124 | 307,754 | 318,726(u) |
| 68 | Computer systems design and related services | 338,689 | 353,418 | 366,321(u) |
| 69 | Miscellaneous professional, scientific, and technical services | 1,163,343 | 1,237,665 | 1,294,278(u) |
| 70 | **Management of companies and enterprises** | **558,999** | **598,387** | **629,363** |
| 71 | **Administrative and waste management services** | **776,135** | **839,388** | **890,722** |
| 72 | Administrative and support services | 688,605 | 747,595 | 803,559(u) |
| 73 | Waste management and remediation services | 87,529 | 91,793 | 87,163(u) |
| 74 | **Educational services, health care, and social assistance** | **2,301,268** | **2,407,020** | **2,566,588** |
| 75 | **Educational services** | **307,787** | **319,912** | **332,166** |
| 76 | **Health care and social assistance** | **1,993,480** | **2,087,108** | **2,234,421** |
| 77 | Ambulatory health care services | 891,876 | 931,939 | 996,008(u) |
| 78 | Hospitals and nursing and residential care facilities | 935,927 | 983,852 | 1,057,245(u) |
| 79 | Hospitals | 721,842 | 759,635 | 824,188(u) |
| 80 | Nursing and residential care facilities | 214,084 | 224,218 | 233,057(u) |
| 81 | Social assistance | 165,677 | 171,317 | 181,169(u) |
| 82 | **Arts, entertainment, recreation, accommodation, and food services** | **1,118,572** | **1,186,791** | **1,271,919** |
| 83 | **Arts, entertainment, and recreation** | **279,877** | **294,114** | **310,882** |
| 84 | Performing arts, spectator sports, museums, and related activities | 148,304 | 155,960 | 168,290(u) |
| 85 | Amusements, gambling, and recreation industries | 131,573 | 138,154 | 142,593(u) |
| 86 | **Accommodation and food services** | **838,695** | **892,677** | **961,037** |
| 87 | Accommodation | 212,037 | 227,160 | 242,344(u) |
| 88 | Food services and drinking places | 626,659 | 665,517 | 718,693(u) |
| 89 | **Other services, except government** | **602,071** | **641,527** | **672,421** |
| 90 | **Government** | **3,384,499** | **3,438,157** | **3,479,470** |
| 91 | **Federal** | **1,098,399** | **1,094,188** | **1,102,744** |
| 92 | General government | 1,007,569 | 1,001,935 | 1,006,977(u) |
| 93 | National defense | 639,655 | 624,409 | 620,680(u) |
| 94 | Nondefense | 367,914 | 377,525 | 386,297(u) |
| 95 | Government enterprises | 90,830 | 92,254 | 95,767(u) |
| 96 | **State and local** | **2,286,100** | **2,343,969** | **2,376,726** |
| 97 | General government | 2,015,823 | 2,066,313 | 2,089,018(u) |
| 98 | Government enterprises | 270,277 | 277,656 | 287,708(u) |
| 99 | **Addenda:** | | | |
| 100 | Private goods-producing industries[a] | 8,172,954 | 8,537,458 | 8,139,919 |
| 101 | Private services-producing industries[b] | 18,014,101 | 18,995,410 | 19,767,118 |
| 102 | Information-communications-technology-producing industries[c] | 1,691,800 | 1,791,000 | — |

(u): Underlying detail. All statistics for 2015 are prepared by taking the average of the corresponding quarterly series. For annual series marked as underlying detail, the quarterly statistics on which these estimates rely are of lower quality and pass through a less rigorous review process than the higher level aggregates in which they are included.
[a]Consists of agriculture, forestry, fishing, and hunting; mining; construction; and manufacturing.
[b]Consists of utilities; wholesale trade; retail trade; transportation and warehousing; information; finance, insurance, real estate, rental, and leasing; professional and business services; educational services, health care, and social assistance; arts, entertainment, recreation, accommodation, and food services; and other services, except government.
[c]Consists of computer and electronic product manufacturing (excluding navigational, measuring, electromedical, and control instruments manufacturing); software publishers; broadcasting and telecommunications; data processing, hosting and related services; internet publishing and broadcasting and web search portals; and computer systems design and related services.

SOURCE: Adapted from "Gross Output by Industry," in *Gross-Domestic-Product-(GDP)-by-Industry Data*, U.S. Department of Commerce, Bureau of Economic Analysis, April 21, 2016, http://www.bea.gov/industry/xls/GDPbyInd_GO_1947-2015.xlsx (accessed August 10, 2016)

In *Digital Economy 2003*, the Department of Commerce investigates some of the causes behind the sudden rise in worker productivity during the 1990s. To determine if this sudden acceleration in worker productivity was indeed because of the introduction of IT into the workplace, the department separates all private industry into those that were IT intensive, such as finance and retail, and those that were less IT intensive, such as construction. The department reports that IT-intensive industries, which already had a relatively high worker productivity growth per year, increased in productivity much faster than less IT-intensive industries in 1995.

FIGURE 3.2

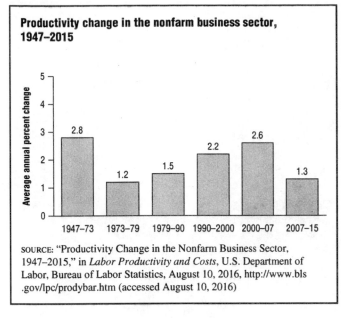

**Productivity change in the nonfarm business sector, 1947–2015**

SOURCE: "Productivity Change in the Nonfarm Business Sector, 1947–2015," in *Labor Productivity and Costs*, U.S. Department of Labor, Bureau of Labor Statistics, August 10, 2016, http://www.bls.gov/lpc/prodybar.htm (accessed August 10, 2016)

FIGURE 3.3

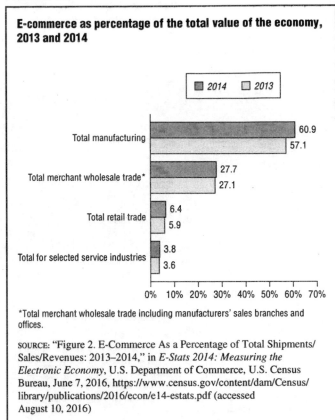

**E-commerce as percentage of the total value of the economy, 2013 and 2014**

*Total merchant wholesale trade including manufacturers' sales branches and offices.

SOURCE: "Figure 2. E-Commerce As a Percentage of Total Shipments/Sales/Revenues: 2013–2014," in *E-Stats 2014: Measuring the Electronic Economy*, U.S. Department of Commerce, U.S. Census Bureau, June 7, 2016, https://www.census.gov/content/dam/Census/library/publications/2016/econ/e14-estats.pdf (accessed August 10, 2016)

During the recessionary period in 2000 and 2001, the IT-intensive industries' worker productivity did not wane. Conversely, yearly growth in worker productivity in non-IT-intensive industries did not occur before 1995; it then rose 1% per year until 2000 before turning negative. Such results suggest that the introduction of IT into the workplace not only improved worker productivity for the long term but also increased the rate at which it improves.

### How IT Has Increased Productivity

The ways in which IT has increased productivity and made businesses more profitable are nearly endless. Word processors and desktop publishing software dramatically reduced the time necessary to complete many mundane office tasks, particularly in the communications industry. The reduction of paper filing systems in the workplace reduced corporate storage needs and made document retrieval more efficient. Computer systems in factories allowed manufacturers precise control over production lines, increasing efficiency and thus saving millions of dollars. Interoffice and Internet networks gave corporations daily access to sales numbers and profit margins, enabling them to make faster decisions to increase profitability. For example, if a line of clothing was not selling, a company could see the sales figures immediately and pull the line from the stores, rather than allow it to take up valuable retail space.

### E-COMMERCE

E-commerce, which is simply the sale of goods and services over the Internet, has grown steadily every year since the debut of the World Wide Web in 1991. Figure 3.3 provides a breakdown of e-commerce as a percentage of the value of sales in each industry that did business online in 2014, while Figure 3.4 shows total revenues generated by e-commerce for each industry. By far, most e-commerce that year occurred in manufacturing, where shipments ordered online accounted for 60.9% ($3.6 trillion) of the total value of all manufacturing shipments. Merchant wholesalers conducted e-commerce sales representing 27.7% ($2.2 trillion) of business in 2014, and e-commerce accounted for 6.4% ($298.6 billion) of all retail sales. Selected services revenues were sales made by a number of sectors in the services industry and include businesses such as travel brokers and online publications. Approximately 3.8% ($510 billion) of the total revenues generated by the selected services industry came from e-commerce in 2014.

Manufacturers are companies that take raw materials and parts and manufacture products that are used by other businesses or individuals. For instance, a soft drink company typically buys its cans from a manufacturer that makes the cans from raw aluminum. Dell buys computer components from dozens of manufacturers around the world to assemble its computers. The reason so many manufacturers use the Internet to conduct business transactions is that the Internet cuts costs and streamlines the processes that are involved in buying and selling manufactured goods. E-commerce allows the buyer to compare competitors' prices, reduces the costs of writing up and sending paper purchase orders and

**FIGURE 3.4**

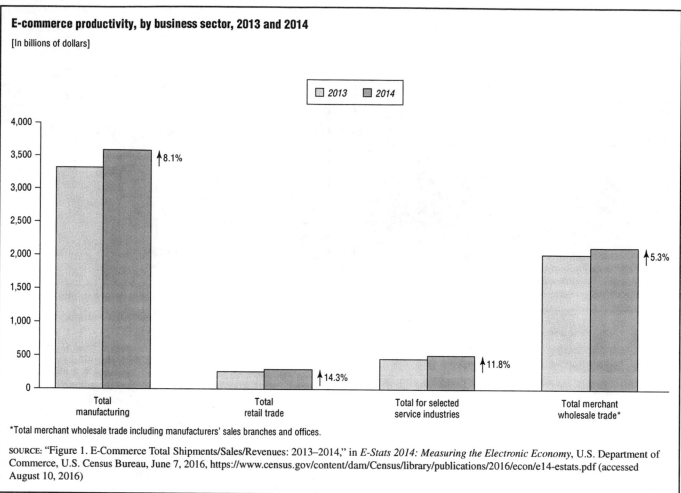

E-commerce productivity, by business sector, 2013 and 2014

[In billions of dollars]

*Total merchant wholesale trade including manufacturers' sales branches and offices.

SOURCE: "Figure 1. E-Commerce Total Shipments/Sales/Revenues: 2013–2014," in *E-Stats 2014: Measuring the Electronic Economy*, U.S. Department of Commerce, U.S. Census Bureau, June 7, 2016, https://www.census.gov/content/dam/Census/library/publications/2016/econ/e14-estats.pdf (accessed August 10, 2016)

invoices, maintains an electronic copy of each sale, and decreases the time it takes for the goods to reach the buyer.

As Table 3.3 shows, the proportion of manufactured goods shipped through e-commerce has risen considerably since the end of the 20th century. In 1999 e-commerce accounted for nearly $729.6 billion (18%) of the $4 trillion in total manufacturing shipments; by 2014 e-commerce accounted for $3.6 trillion (61%) of the $5.9 trillion in total manufacturing shipments. Meanwhile, growth in the value of manufactured goods shipped through e-commerce has continued at a much faster pace than the overall growth of the sector as a whole. Between 2013 and 2014 the value of manufactured goods shipped through e-commerce rose 8.1%, nearly seven times the 1.2% for total manufacturing shipments. (See Table 3.4.) Apparel manufacturing enjoyed the largest percentage boost in e-commerce sales, rising from $4.6 billion in 2013 to $5.9 billion in 2014, an increase of 28.2%. Only the petroleum and coal products and beverage and tobacco product manufacturing sectors saw a decline in e-commerce shipments during this span, falling 4.9% and 0.1%, respectively, between 2013 and 2014.

Merchant wholesale trade sales made up the second-largest block of e-commerce transactions in 2014. Wholesalers act as a mediator between manufacturers and retailers. Wholesalers typically buy large quantities of goods from a number of manufacturers and then resell these goods in bulk to retail outlets. The wholesalers save the retailers the trouble of contacting each manufacturer separately. Table 3.5 presents U.S. merchant wholesale trades in 2013 and 2014. Year-over-year wholesale e-commerce increased 5.3% between 2013 and 2014, which was considerably higher than the 3% growth generated by wholesale trades overall. Wholesale e-commerce growth outstripped overall merchant wholesale trades in several key businesses. For example, between 2013 and 2014 e-commerce sales of farm product raw materials rose 11.9%, compared with an overall decline of 5.5% in overall sales for that sector as a whole.

**E-Commerce and Retail**

Retail sales consist of any product that is sold to an individual customer or company for use. Since the late 1990s nearly every major retailer from AutoZone to Neiman Marcus to Wal-Mart has created a website. Many

# TABLE 3.3

## Total and e-commerce value of manufacturing shipments, 1999–2014

[Estimates are based on data from the Annual Survey of Manufactures and the Economic Census. Value of Shipments estimates are shown in millions of dollars, consequently industry group estimates may not be additive.]

### Value of shipments

| NAICS code | Description | 1999 Total | 1999 E-commerce | 2000 Total | 2000 E-commerce | 2001 Total | 2001 E-commerce | 2002 Total | 2002 E-commerce | 2003 Total | 2003 E-commerce |
|---|---|---|---|---|---|---|---|---|---|---|---|
| | Total manufacturing | 4,031,882 | 729,563 | 4,208,582 | 755,807 | 3,970,500 | 724,228 | 3,920,632 | 751,985 | 4,015,081 | 842,666 |
| 311 | Food products manufacturing | 426,000 | 45,757 | 435,230 | 54,837 | 451,386 | 53,556 | 460,020 | 51,094 | 483,226 | 59,576 |
| 312 | Beverage and tobacco manufacturing | 106,920 | 35,138 | 111,692 | 42,862 | 118,786 | 45,665 | 105,691 | 45,419 | 108,806 | 46,998 |
| 313 | Textile mills | 54,306 | 6,016 | 52,112 | 5,214 | 45,681 | 4,435 | 45,549 | 3,977 | 42,588 | 3,639 |
| 314 | Textile product mills | 32,689 | 7,284 | 33,654 | 5,800 | 31,971 | 7,409 | 31,807 | 7,491 | 31,261 | 7,244 |
| 315 | Apparel manufacturing | 62,305 | 16,485 | 60,339 | 12,063 | 54,598 | 10,652 | 44,515 | 9,726 | 38,668 | 9,137 |
| 316 | Leather and allied product manufacturing | 9,653 | 2,336 | 9,647 | 2,122 | 8,834 | 1,438 | 6,299 | 783 | 5,784 | 653 |
| 321 | Wood product manufacturing | 97,311 | 4,275 | 93,669 | 5,957 | 87,250 | 4,919 | 88,985 | 4,567 | 92,119 | 5,753 |
| 322 | Paper manufacturing | 156,915 | 15,312 | 165,297 | 20,617 | 155,846 | 20,208 | 153,655 | 18,385 | 151,094 | 18,683 |
| 323 | Printing and related support activites | 101,536 | 7,319 | 104,396 | 5,966 | 100,792 | 5,885 | 95,388 | 4,725 | 92,663 | 4,452 |
| 324 | Petroleum and coal products manufacturing | 162,620 | 19,881 | 235,134 | 16,647 | 219,075 | 16,312 | 215,190 | 25,523 | 247,316 | 51,586 |
| 325 | Chemicals manufacturing | 420,320 | 58,827 | 449,159 | 52,974 | 438,410 | 54,041 | 460,451 | 68,674 | 486,563 | 85,186 |
| 326 | Plastics and rubber products manufacturing | 171,885 | 27,795 | 178,236 | 28,400 | 170,717 | 27,324 | 173,901 | 23,953 | 178,328 | 26,954 |
| 327 | Nonmetallic mineral products manufacturing | 96,153 | 7,282 | 97,329 | 8,174 | 94,861 | 7,887 | 95,265 | 7,144 | 96,923 | 8,631 |
| 331 | Primary metals manufacturing | 156,647 | 15,470 | 156,598 | 15,403 | 138,245 | 14,274 | 139,449 | 12,828 | 138,142 | 12,578 |
| 332 | Fabricated metal products manufacturing | 257,072 | 29,509 | 268,212 | 25,798 | 253,113 | 24,168 | 246,734 | 21,427 | 245,550 | 23,735 |
| 333 | Machinery manufacturing | 276,901 | 48,452 | 291,548 | 40,441 | 266,553 | 35,670 | 253,135 | 30,390 | 257,375 | 34,797 |
| 334 | Computer and electronic products manufacturing | 467,059 | 65,336 | 510,639 | 77,933 | 429,471 | 73,221 | 358,258 | 73,406 | 352,636 | 67,476 |
| 335 | Electrical equipment, appliances, and components | 118,313 | 27,067 | 125,443 | 30,003 | 114,067 | 27,845 | 104,472 | 23,043 | 100,140 | 23,722 |
| 336 | Transportation equipment manufacturing | 676,328 | 268,667 | 639,861 | 281,396 | 602,496 | 264,326 | 637,675 | 297,280 | 661,142 | 327,401 |
| 337 | Furniture and related products manufacturing | 72,659 | 7,623 | 75,107 | 8,400 | 72,147 | 9,348 | 77,242 | 8,082 | 75,423 | 9,983 |
| 339 | Miscellaneous manufacturing | 108,290 | 13,732 | 115,280 | 14,800 | 116,201 | 15,644 | 126,951 | 14,068 | 129,334 | 14,482 |

### Value of shipments

| NAICS code | Description | 2004 Total | 2004 E-commerce | 2005 Total | 2005 E-commerce | 2006 Total | 2006 E-commerce | 2007 Total | 2007 E-commerce | 2008 Total | 2008 E-commerce |
|---|---|---|---|---|---|---|---|---|---|---|---|
| | Total manufacturing | 4,308,971 | 996,174 | 4,742,076 | 1,343,852 | 5,015,553 | 1,566,799 | 5,338,307 | 1,879,424 | 5,468,093 | 2,170,818 |
| 311 | Food products manufacturing | 512,340 | 64,121 | 532,402 | 99,090 | 536,939 | 153,996 | 589,859 | 203,693 | 649,906 | 247,132 |
| 312 | Beverage and tobacco manufacturing | 113,737 | 52,783 | 124,086 | 60,651 | 124,033 | 68,046 | 128,286 | 72,038 | 125,099 | 67,894 |
| 313 | Textile mills | 40,898 | 4,416 | 42,328 | 7,512 | 38,829 | 12,377 | 36,185 | 14,494 | 32,052 | 13,186 |
| 314 | Textile product mills | 33,636 | 8,472 | 35,022 | 7,189 | 33,264 | 11,588 | 28,881 | 13,470 | 26,836 | 11,723 |
| 315 | Apparel manufacturing | 32,873 | 8,694 | 31,401 | 8,908 | 30,325 | 9,182 | 24,096 | 7,072 | 19,140 | 5,938 |
| 316 | Leather and allied product manufacturing | 5,812 | 611 | 6,181 | 826 | 5,941 | 926 | 5,615 | 1,281 | 5,212 | 1,095 |
| 321 | Wood product manufacturing | 104,135 | 7,974 | 112,095 | 12,248 | 112,403 | 14,960 | 102,029 | 19,468 | 87,765 | 19,375 |
| 322 | Paper manufacturing | 155,381 | 19,631 | 161,928 | 30,579 | 169,033 | 40,842 | 176,108 | 62,644 | 179,249 | 67,810 |
| 323 | Printing and related support activites | 93,595 | 8,259 | 96,922 | 15,592 | 99,800 | 19,181 | 103,432 | 25,649 | 98,634 | 29,993 |
| 324 | Petroleum and coal products manufacturing | 330,439 | 77,527 | 475,787 | 130,869 | 546,811 | 160,177 | 615,548 | 195,309 | 769,699 | 339,211 |
| 325 | Chemicals manufacturing | 540,883 | 102,967 | 610,873 | 173,747 | 657,082 | 203,168 | 724,081 | 252,390 | 738,669 | 296,059 |
| 326 | Plastics and rubber products manufacturing | 184,711 | 33,220 | 200,304 | 43,123 | 211,299 | 48,686 | 210,377 | 62,188 | 203,669 | 72,858 |
| 327 | Nonmetallic mineral products manufacturing | 102,880 | 10,850 | 114,849 | 16,469 | 126,263 | 20,726 | 128,066 | 23,173 | 115,456 | 26,621 |
| 331 | Primary metals manufacturing | 181,602 | 33,410 | 203,263 | 47,608 | 234,384 | 59,376 | 257,277 | 80,850 | 282,623 | 109,316 |
| 332 | Fabricated metal products manufacturing | 261,101 | 33,992 | 289,432 | 50,661 | 317,214 | 64,109 | 345,393 | 84,030 | 358,257 | 98,342 |
| 333 | Machinery manufacturing | 272,123 | 52,292 | 302,650 | 72,390 | 326,583 | 93,763 | 351,531 | 111,074 | 355,600 | 129,569 |
| 334 | Computer and electronic products manufacturing | 365,545 | 76,197 | 372,882 | 113,704 | 390,813 | 120,947 | 403,001 | 142,777 | 383,914 | 148,576 |
| 335 | Electrical equipment, appliances, and components | 105,084 | 25,177 | 111,977 | 30,602 | 119,402 | 34,211 | 129,737 | 40,737 | 130,334 | 44,442 |
| 336 | Transportation equipment manufacturing | 662,001 | 346,473 | 690,743 | 381,600 | 699,034 | 383,560 | 744,893 | 411,782 | 672,784 | 378,464 |
| 337 | Furniture and related products manufacturing | 78,279 | 11,264 | 84,181 | 16,233 | 85,618 | 18,187 | 85,534 | 22,483 | 79,829 | 24,722 |
| 339 | Miscellaneous manufacturing | 131,916 | 17,844 | 142,770 | 24,251 | 150,481 | 28,790 | 148,377 | 32,821 | 153,367 | 38,491 |

**TABLE 3.3**

## Total and e-commerce value of manufacturing shipments, 1999–2014 [CONTINUED]

[Estimates are based on data from the Annual Survey of Manufactures and the Economic Census. Value of Shipments estimates are shown in millions of dollars, consequently industry group estimates may not be additive.]

| NAICS code | Description | 2009 Total | 2009 E-commerce | 2010 Total | 2010 E-commerce | 2011 Total | 2011 E-commerce | 2012 Total | 2012 E-commerce | 2013 revised Total | 2013 revised E-commerce | 2014 Total | 2014 E-commerce |
|---|---|---|---|---|---|---|---|---|---|---|---|---|---|
| | **Total manufacturing** | **4,419,501** | **1,891,533** | **4,905,446** | **2,350,457** | **5,481,368** | **2,703,962** | **5,736,714** | **3,004,749** | **5,809,745** | **3,315,694** | **5,880,890** | **3,584,019** |
| 311 | Food products manufacturing | 627,185 | 262,608 | 649,339 | 300,280 | 708,683 | 340,436 | 738,515 | 385,649 | 762,848 | 417,687 | 790,509 | 463,169 |
| 312 | Beverage and tobacco manufacturing | 127,943 | 77,180 | 130,551 | 82,329 | 134,765 | 85,357 | 142,494 | 97,299 | 147,005 | 102,221 | 145,492 | 102,079 |
| 313 | Textile mills | 26,324 | 12,589 | 29,331 | 15,505 | 30,890 | 14,974 | 30,328 | 13,899 | 31,539 | 16,861 | 31,714 | 18,770 |
| 314 | Textile product mills | 21,366 | 10,019 | 20,969 | 9,804 | 22,368 | 10,805 | 22,048 | 11,485 | 22,889 | 12,710 | 24,308 | 14,073 |
| 315 | Apparel manufacturing | 13,909 | 5,179 | 13,366 | 5,159 | 12,784 | 5,135 | 12,739 | 4,977 | 12,053 | 4,618 | 11,776 | 5,919 |
| 316 | Leather and allied product manufacturing | 4,327 | 1,102 | 4,953 | 1,128 | 5,665 | 1,405 | 5,203 | 1,542 | 5,104 | 1,693 | 5,009 | 1,786 |
| 321 | Wood product manufacturing | 65,000 | 16,538 | 69,566 | 19,712 | 70,091 | 21,805 | 77,913 | 25,997 | 88,618 | 35,084 | 95,176 | 40,743 |
| 322 | Paper manufacturing | 161,636 | 69,312 | 170,043 | 78,953 | 175,552 | 86,897 | 181,261 | 98,839 | 185,895 | 116,715 | 186,836 | 126,720 |
| 323 | Printing and related support activites | 82,919 | 26,274 | 82,410 | 29,105 | 82,380 | 32,659 | 81,979 | 32,441 | 82,425 | 37,014 | 83,319 | 38,725 |
| 324 | Petroleum and coal products manufacturing | 495,777 | 219,546 | 627,092 | 328,817 | 838,083 | 441,837 | 850,621 | 446,068 | 852,802 | 487,594 | 786,513 | 463,601 |
| 325 | Chemicals manufacturing | 624,367 | 263,587 | 697,812 | 313,317 | 773,080 | 365,155 | 794,709 | 399,590 | 785,616 | 426,671 | 788,685 | 451,944 |
| 326 | Plastics and rubber products manufacturing | 171,115 | 69,935 | 188,785 | 82,925 | 203,757 | 94,519 | 218,603 | 107,807 | 225,763 | 122,231 | 235,197 | 133,981 |
| 327 | Nonmetallic mineral products manufacturing | 89,662 | 24,250 | 90,104 | 28,053 | 92,585 | 30,988 | 98,464 | 38,167 | 106,182 | 45,860 | 113,667 | 50,575 |
| 331 | Primary metals manufacturing | 168,927 | 68,168 | 232,791 | 112,076 | 278,729 | 140,088 | 267,524 | 145,999 | 263,208 | 152,193 | 263,559 | 170,847 |
| 332 | Fabricated metal products manufacturing | 280,939 | 89,201 | 293,889 | 107,911 | 323,664 | 125,931 | 339,775 | 138,360 | 347,105 | 161,245 | 358,962 | 176,934 |
| 333 | Machinery manufacturing | 288,006 | 118,721 | 317,697 | 150,834 | 365,010 | 177,872 | 407,423 | 217,991 | 393,531 | 215,920 | 400,444 | 246,896 |
| 334 | Computer and electronic products manufacturing | 320,724 | 134,103 | 331,330 | 155,903 | 338,047 | 169,484 | 339,358 | 172,745 | 308,530 | 153,710 | 304,703 | 168,766 |
| 335 | Electrical equipment, appliances, and components | 105,417 | 42,354 | 110,036 | 49,866 | 118,500 | 55,544 | 123,534 | 64,166 | 123,513 | 68,096 | 125,495 | 73,552 |
| 336 | Transportation equipment manufacturing | 539,921 | 318,687 | 636,825 | 406,408 | 691,937 | 422,036 | 787,705 | 512,940 | 841,010 | 640,709 | 903,328 | 728,362 |
| 337 | Furniture and related products manufacturing | 60,287 | 20,685 | 59,048 | 23,398 | 62,285 | 27,006 | 66,706 | 29,962 | 68,219 | 31,031 | 69,570 | 35,233 |
| 339 | Miscellaneous manufacturing | 143,749 | 41,495 | 149,509 | 48,974 | 152,514 | 54,028 | 149,813 | 58,826 | 155,889 | 65,833 | 156,628 | 71,344 |

NAICS = North American Industry Classification System.
Note: Estimates are not adjusted for price changes. Estimates include data only for businesses with paid employees and are subject to revision.

SOURCE: "Table 1. U.S. Manufacturing Shipments—Total and E-Commerce Value: 2014–1999," in *2014 E-Commerce Multi-Sector Data Tables*, U.S. Department of Commerce, U.S. Census Bureau, June 7, 2016, http://www2.census.gov/programs-surveys/e-stats/tables/2014/historic/table_1.xlsx (accessed August 12, 2016)

**TABLE 3.4**

## Total and e-commerce value of manufacturing shipments, 2013 and 2014

[Data are based on the 2014 Annual Survey of Manufactures and the 2013 Annual Survey of Manufactures. Value of Shipments are shown in millions of dollars, consequently subsector estimates may not be additive. Estimated measures of sampling variability for these estimates are provided in the Measures of Sampling Variability—U.S. Manufacturing Shipments—Total and E-commerce Value: 2014 and 2013]

| NAICS code | Description | Value of shipments | | | | Year-over-year percent change | | E-commerce as percent of total shipments | | Percent distribution of e-commerce Shipments |
| --- | --- | --- | --- | --- | --- | --- | --- | --- | --- | --- |
| | | 2014 | | 2013 | | | | | | |
| | | Total | E-commerce | Revised total | Revised e-commerce | Total shipments | E-commerce shipments | 2014 | 2013 | 2014 |
| | **Total manufacturing** | **5,880,890** | **3,584,019** | **5,809,745** | **3,315,694** | **1.2** | **8.1** | **60.9** | **57.1** | **100.0** |
| 311 | Food manufacturing | 790,509 | 463,169 | 762,848 | 417,687 | 3.6 | 10.9 | 58.6 | 54.8 | 12.9 |
| 312 | Beverage and tobacco product manufacturing | 145,492 | 102,079 | 147,005 | 102,221 | -1.0 | -0.1 | 70.2 | 69.5 | 2.8 |
| 313 | Textile mills | 31,714 | 18,770 | 31,539 | 16,861 | 0.6 | 11.3 | 59.2 | 53.5 | 0.5 |
| 314 | Textile product mills | 24,308 | 14,073 | 22,889 | 12,710 | 6.2 | 10.7 | 57.9 | 55.5 | 0.4 |
| 315 | Apparel manufacturing | 11,776 | 5,919 | 12,053 | 4,618 | -2.3 | 28.2 | 50.3 | 38.3 | 0.2 |
| 316 | Leather and allied product manufacturing | 5,009 | 1,786 | 5,104 | 1,693 | -1.9 | 5.5 | 35.7 | 33.2 | 0.0 |
| 321 | Wood product manufacturing | 95,176 | 40,743 | 88,618 | 35,084 | 7.4 | 16.1 | 42.8 | 39.6 | 1.1 |
| 322 | Paper manufacturing | 186,836 | 126,720 | 185,895 | 116,715 | 0.5 | 8.6 | 67.8 | 62.8 | 3.5 |
| 323 | Printing and related support activities | 83,319 | 38,725 | 82,425 | 37,014 | 1.1 | 4.6 | 46.5 | 44.9 | 1.1 |
| 324 | Petroleum and coal products manufacturing | 786,513 | 463,601 | 852,802 | 487,594 | -7.8 | -4.9 | 58.9 | 57.2 | 12.9 |
| 325 | Chemical manufacturing | 788,685 | 451,944 | 785,616 | 426,671 | 0.4 | 5.9 | 57.3 | 54.3 | 12.6 |
| 326 | Plastics and rubber products manufacturing | 235,197 | 133,981 | 225,763 | 122,231 | 4.2 | 9.6 | 57.0 | 54.1 | 3.7 |
| 327 | Nonmetallic mineral product manufacturing | 113,667 | 50,575 | 106,182 | 45,860 | 7.0 | 10.3 | 44.5 | 43.2 | 1.4 |
| 331 | Primary metal manufacturing | 263,559 | 170,847 | 263,208 | 152,193 | 0.1 | 12.3 | 64.8 | 57.8 | 4.8 |
| 332 | Fabricated metal product manufacturing | 358,962 | 176,934 | 347,105 | 161,245 | 3.4 | 9.7 | 49.3 | 46.5 | 4.9 |
| 333 | Machinery manufacturing | 400,444 | 246,896 | 393,531 | 215,920 | 1.8 | 14.3 | 61.7 | 54.9 | 6.9 |
| 334 | Computer and electronic product manufacturing | 304,703 | 168,766 | 308,530 | 153,710 | -1.2 | 9.8 | 55.4 | 49.8 | 4.7 |
| 335 | Electrical equipment, appliance, and components | 125,495 | 73,552 | 123,513 | 68,096 | 1.6 | 8.0 | 58.6 | 55.1 | 2.1 |
| 336 | Transportation equipment manufacturing | 903,328 | 728,362 | 841,010 | 640,709 | 7.4 | 13.7 | 80.6 | 76.2 | 20.3 |
| 337 | Furniture and related product manufacturing | 69,570 | 35,233 | 68,219 | 31,031 | 2.0 | 13.5 | 50.6 | 45.5 | 1.0 |
| 339 | Miscellaneous manufacturing | 156,628 | 71,344 | 155,889 | 65,833 | 0.5 | 8.4 | 45.5 | 42.2 | 2.0 |

NAICS = North American Industry Classification System.
Note: Estimates are not adjusted for price changes. Establishments representing approximately 7 percent of the 2014 and 2013 value of shipments did not have an opportunity to report e-commerce receipts. Estimates include data only for businesses with paid employees and are subject to revision.

SOURCE: "Table 1. U.S. Manufacturing Shipments—Total and E-Commerce Value: 2014 and 2013," in *2014 E-Commerce Multi-Sector Data Tables*, U.S. Department of Commerce, U.S. Census Bureau, June 7, 2016, http://www2.census.gov/programs-surveys/e-stats/tables/2014/table_1.xlsx (accessed August 10, 2016)

# TABLE 3.5

## Total and e-commerce wholesale trade sales, 2013 and 2014

[Estimates are based on data from the 2014 Annual Wholesale Trade Survey. Sales estimates are shown in millions of dollars, consequently industry group estimates may not be additive. Estimated measures of sampling variability for these estimates are provided in Measures of Sampling Variability for U.S. Merchant Wholesale Trade Sales, Including Manufacturers' Sales Branches and Offices—Total and E-commerce: 2014 and 2013]

| NAICS code | Description | Value of sales | | | | Year-over-year percentage change | | E-commerce as percent of total sales | | Percent distribution of e-commerce sales |
| | | 2014 | | 2013 | | | | | | |
| | | Total | E-commerce | Revised total | Revised e-commerce | Total sales | E-commerce sales | 2014 | 2013 | 2014 |
|---|---|---|---|---|---|---|---|---|---|---|
| 42 | **Total merchant wholesale trade including manufacturers' sales branches and offices** | **7,692,210** | **2,127,755** | **7,468,122** | **2,020,819** | **3.0** | **5.3** | **27.7** | **27.1** | **100.0** |
| **423** | **Durable goods** | **3,389,878** | **913,643** | **3,255,292** | **874,317** | **4.1** | **4.5** | **27.0** | **26.9** | **42.9** |
| 4231 | Motor vehicle and motor vehicle parts and supplies | 784,490 | 405,803 | 753,209 | 389,846 | 4.2 | 4.1 | 51.7 | 51.8 | 19.1 |
| 4232 | Furniture and home furnishings | 97,885 | 15,475 | 92,285 | 15,201 | 6.1 | 1.8 | 15.8 | 16.5 | 0.7 |
| 4233 | Lumber and other construction materials | 160,230 | 19,324 | 149,967 | 17,659 | 6.8 | 9.4 | 12.1 | 11.8 | 0.9 |
| 4234 | Professional and commercial equipment and supplies | 522,950 | 132,538 | 508,119 | 128,117 | 2.9 | 3.5 | 25.3 | 25.2 | 6.2 |
| 42343 | Computer and computer peripheral equipment and software | 243,284 | 61,725 | 237,119 | 61,908 | 2.6 | -0.3 | 25.4 | 26.1 | 2.9 |
| 4235 | Metals and minerals, ex. petroleum | 244,603 | 30,664 | 231,812 | 29,409 | 5.5 | 4.3 | 12.5 | 12.7 | 1.4 |
| 4236 | Electrical goods | 605,194 | 152,971 | 578,105 | 144,144 | 4.7 | 6.1 | 25.3 | 24.9 | 7.2 |
| 4237 | Hardware, and plumbing and heating equipment and supplies | 155,207 | 25,904 | 146,629 | 22,996 | 5.9 | 12.6 | 16.7 | 15.7 | 1.2 |
| 4238 | Machinery, equipment and supplies | 565,431 | 98,620 | 539,066 | 95,150 | 4.9 | 3.6 | 17.4 | 17.7 | 4.6 |
| 4239 | Miscellaneous durable goods | 253,888 | 32,344 | 256,100 | 31,795 | -0.9 | 1.7 | 12.7 | 12.4 | 1.5 |
| **424** | **Nondurable goods** | **4,302,332** | **1,214,112** | **4,212,830** | **1,146,502** | **2.1** | **5.9** | **28.2** | **27.2** | **57.1** |
| 4241 | Paper and paper products | 143,788 | 52,216 | 141,053 | 50,542 | 1.9 | 3.3 | 36.3 | 35.8 | 2.5 |
| 4242 | Drugs and druggists' sundries | 771,139 | 544,789 | 710,319 | 495,523 | 8.6 | 9.9 | 70.6 | 69.8 | 25.6 |
| 4243 | Apparel, piece goods, and notions | 166,422 | 43,380 | 160,441 | 41,075 | 3.7 | 5.6 | 26.1 | 25.6 | 2.0 |
| 4244 | Groceries and related products | 876,580 | 237,781 | 835,786 | 221,717 | 4.9 | 7.2 | 27.1 | 26.5 | 11.2 |
| 4245 | Farm product raw materials | 254,820 | 12,215 | 269,739 | 10,912 | -5.5 | 11.9 | 4.8 | 4.0 | 0.6 |
| 4246 | Chemicals and allied products | 225,902 | 41,449 | 219,059 | 39,115 | 3.1 | 6.0 | 18.3 | 17.9 | 1.9 |
| 4247 | Petroleum and petroleum products | 1,383,304 | 196,267 | 1,392,740 | 204,245 | -0.7 | -3.9 | 14.2 | 14.7 | 9.2 |
| 4248 | Beer, wine, and distilled alcoholic beverages | 147,174 | 13,156 | 145,111 | 12,462 | 1.4 | 5.6 | 8.9 | 8.6 | 0.6 |
| 4249 | Miscellaneous nondurable goods | 333,203 | 72,859 | 338,582 | 70,911 | -1.6 | 2.7 | 21.9 | 20.9 | 3.4 |

NAICS = North American Industry Classification System (US Census Bureau).

Note: Estimates have not been adjusted for price changes. Measures of Sampling Variability—U.S. Merchant Wholesale Trade Sales, Including Manufacturers' Sales Branches and Offices—Total and E-commerce: 2014 and 2013 provides estimated measures of sampling variability. Estimates include data only for businesses with paid employees and are subject to revision.

SOURCE: "Table 2.0. U.S. Merchant Wholesale Trade Sales, Including Manufacturers' Sales Branches and Offices—Total and E-Commerce: 2014 and 2013," in 2014 E-Commerce Multi-Sector Data Tables, U.S. Department of Commerce, U.S. Census Bureau, June 7, 2016, http://www2.census.gov/programs-surveys/e-stats/e-stats/tables/2014/table_2.0.xls (accessed August 10, 2016)

offer a greater variety of merchandise online than what is available in the store. The growth of such websites has allowed Americans to order just about anything and have it delivered to their home within days.

The amount of money made from e-commerce in retail increased rapidly from the late 1990s. The Census Bureau reveals in *E-Commerce Statistics (E-STATS)* (2016, http://www.census.gov/programs-surveys/e-stats/data/tables.html) that e-commerce accounted for only 0.2% ($5 billion) of all retail sales in 1998. This percentage more than doubled to 0.5% ($15.4 billion) in 1999 and nearly doubled again to 0.9% ($28.2 billion) in 2000. In 2002 e-commerce represented 1.4% ($44.3 billion) of retail sales. E-commerce revenues increased 574% by 2014, when online transactions accounted for 6.4% ($298.6 billion) of all retail sales. As Table 3.6 shows, two-thirds (66%, or $254.7 billion) of all sales revenues for electronic shopping and mail-order houses came from e-commerce transactions in 2014. By comparison, e-commerce accounted for just 0.2% of sales of food and beverage stores, which generated $1.1 billion in revenues from online transactions.

Table 3.7 presents sales information on the electronic shopping and mail-order house segment of retail. Many of the businesses in this category, such as Dell, sell their products primarily online and through catalogs. Others are divisions of larger department stores, such as Nordstrom, and were created to sell the stores' products online. Online sales accounted for $254.7 billion in revenues for electronic shopping and mail-order businesses in 2014, an increase of 15.2% over 2013. Regarding individual types of products, 90.6% of the revenues from the sale of books and magazines came from online sales in 2014. This represented the highest reported percentage of online sales for any type of product in this retail segment, followed by furniture and home furnishings (88.2%). In terms of sheer sales volume, more clothing and accessories ($46.8 billion) were sold online than any other type of product.

## Online Auctions

When e-commerce developed during the mid-1990s, many small business owners created modest commercial websites, hoping to sell their wares. However, Internet fraud and the propagation of questionable websites made people reluctant to give personal information to unknown vendors on the web. Smaller vendors and buyers needed a common marketplace with rules and regulations to trade goods.

In 1998 Pierre Omidyar (c. 1967–), Jeff Skoll (1965–), and Meg Whitman (1956–) went public with eBay. The company, which was at first an auction site for collectibles such as Beanie Babies, quickly attracted the attention of small business owners. For a modest insertion fee, people could list their products on eBay's website. Buyers then bid on the objects, and when a sale was final, the seller paid eBay a commission of 1.3% to 5% of the item's sale price. The website included payment options that did not require the purchaser to provide credit card information, and it even offered protections against fraud.

The eBay website and its imitators created a whole new economic outlet for small business owners and people who simply wanted to pawn off their used goods. No longer was someone who wanted to sell embroidered pillows relegated to local flea markets. Individual vendors from crafters to high-end car salespeople could reach out to a nationwide audience. Even people with used stuff suddenly had more options than simply giving it to charity or holding a garage sale. As of November 2016, eBay (2016, https://www.ebayinc.com/our-company/who-we-are/) had 165 million active users worldwide, with more than 1 billion items listed for sale.

## Virtual Goods and Currencies

One of the more unusual industries to develop, due in part to eBay, was the sale of virtual goods. Games such as *World of Warcraft* and *EverQuest* place players in virtual worlds with thousands of other people where they can buy virtual property, kill monsters, and collect gold and other valuable virtual artifacts. Some of these online games even provide the player with the option to marry and build houses in a virtual world. Progressing far in these games and obtaining a high level, however, requires hundreds of hours of playtime. As a result, an entire cottage industry developed around the sale of virtual gold and characters on auction sites such as eBay. Typically, a player would buy the game, build up a character and gold, and then sell his or her password to the game to a buyer on eBay, sometimes fetching hundreds of dollars. Such sales represented the first industry that was centered on completely virtual goods. Soon, other sites began trading in virtual currencies, as the online community bought and sold everything from virtual gaming weapons to virtual flowers. Rip Empson reports in "Study: U.S. Consumer Spending on Virtual Goods Grew to $2.3 Billion in 2011" (TechCrunch.com, February 29, 2012) that U.S. sales of virtual goods topped $2.3 billion in 2011 and was expected to reach $2.9 billion in 2012. According to Matt Bodimeade, in "27 Million Virtual Goods Market Users Purchase through Facebook Payments" (CompaniesandMarkets.com, March 11, 2013), the worldwide market for virtual goods was $14.8 billion in 2012.

These years also saw a rise in the use of virtual currencies, a form of electronic money accepted as payment in certain online communities. To acquire a virtual currency, individuals visit an online exchange, where they can trade legal tender for some digital equivalent at a specified exchange rate. Virtual currencies appeal to Internet users who want to conduct business anonymously, or to vendors who want to avoid paying fees to banks. As of

**TABLE 3.6**

**Total and e-commerce retail sales, 2013 and 2014**

[Estimates are based on data from the 2014 Annual Retail Trade Survey. Sales estimates are shown in millions of dollars, consequently industry group estimates may not be additive.]

| NAICS code | Description | Value of sales | | | | Year-over-year percentage change | | E-commerce as percent of total sales | | Percent distribution of e-commerce sales |
| --- | --- | --- | --- | --- | --- | --- | --- | --- | --- | --- |
| | | **2014** | | **2013** | | | | | | |
| | | Total sales | E-commerce | Revised total sales | Revised e-commerce | Total sales | E-commerce | 2014 | 2013 | 2014 |
| | **Total retail trade** | **4,636,345** | **298,595** | **4,459,003** | **261,206** | **4.0** | **14.3** | **6.4** | **5.9** | **100.0** |
| 441 | Motor vehicles and parts dealers | 1,021,184 | 28,278 | 959,188 | 26,456 | 6.5 | 6.9 | 2.8 | 2.8 | 9.5 |
| 442 | Furniture and home furnishings stores | 99,687 | 651 | 95,331 | 544 | 4.6 | 19.7 | 0.7 | 0.6 | 0.2 |
| 443 | Electronics and appliance stores | 104,012 | 1,308 | 103,264 | 1,238 | 0.7 | 5.7 | 1.3 | 1.2 | 0.4 |
| 444 | Building materials and garden equipment and supplies stores | 317,715 | a | 301,792 | 1,233 | 5.3 | a | a | 0.4 | a |
| 445 | Food and beverage stores | 669,902 | 1,079 | 641,138 | 933 | 4.5 | 15.6 | 0.2 | 0.1 | 0.4 |
| 446 | Health and personal care stores | 299,891 | 659 | 282,176 | 688 | 6.3 | −4.2 | 0.2 | 0.2 | 0.2 |
| 447 | Gasoline stations | 534,670 | a | 547,489 | a | −2.3 | a | a | a | a |
| 448 | Clothing and clothing accessories stores | 250,775 | 4,199 | 246,313 | 3,583 | 1.8 | 17.2 | 1.7 | 1.5 | 1.4 |
| 451 | Sporting goods, hobby, book, and music stores | 85,375 | 2,471 | 84,550 | 2,141 | 1.0 | 15.4 | 2.9 b | 2.5 b | 0.8 b |
| 452 | General merchandise stores | 666,873 | 102 | 651,868 | 88 | 2.3 | 15.9 | | | |
| 453 | Miscellaneous store retailers | 116,065 | 2,713 | 112,454 | 2,412 | 3.2 | 12.5 | 2.3 | 2.1 | 0.9 |
| 454 | Nonstore retailers | 470,196 | 255,578 | 433,440 | 221,884 | 8.5 | 15.2 | 54.4 | 51.2 | 85.6 |
| 4541 | Electronic shopping and mail-order houses | 386,135 | 254,712 | 350,836 | 221,040 | 10.1 | 15.2 | 66.0 | 63.0 | 85.3 |

[a]Estimate does not meet publication standards because of high sampling variability (coefficient of variation is greater than 30%) or poor response quality (total quantity response rate is less than 50%), or other concerns about the estimate's quality. Unpublished estimates derived from this table by subtraction are subject to these same limitations and should not be attributed to the U.S. Census Bureau.

[b]Estimate is less than $500,000 or 0.05%.

NAICS = North American Industry Classification System (U.S. Census Bureau).

Note: Retail and food services total and other subsector totals may include data for kinds of business not shown. Estimates have not been adjusted for price changes. Estimates include data for businesses with or without paid employees and are subject to revision.

SOURCE: "Table 4. U.S. Retail Trade Sales—Total and E-Commerce: 2014 and 2013," in *2014 E-Commerce Multi-Sector Data Tables*, U.S. Department of Commerce, U.S. Census Bureau, June 7, 2016, http://www2.census.gov/programs-surveys/e-stats/tables/2014/table_4.xls (accessed August 10, 2016)

# TABLE 3.7

## Total and e-commerce sales of electronic shopping and mail-order houses by merchandise line, 2013 and 2014

[Estimates are based on data from the 2014 Annual Retail Trade Survey. Sales estimates are shown in millions of dollars, consequently merchandise line estimates may not be additive.]

| Merchandise lines | Value of sales 2014 | | Value of sales 2013 | | Year-over-year percent change | | E-commerce as percent of total sales | Percent distribution | |
| --- | --- | --- | --- | --- | --- | --- | --- | --- | --- |
| | Total sales | E-commerce | Revised total sales | Revised e-commerce | Total sales | E-commerce sales | 2014 | Total sales 2014 | E-commerce sales 2014 |
| **Total electronic shopping and mail-order houses (NAICS 4541)** | **386,135** | **254,712** | **350,836** | **221,040** | **10.1** | **15.2** | **66.0** | **100.0** | **100.0** |
| Books and magazines | 12,004 | 10,870 | 11,514 | 10,298 | 4.3 | 5.6 | 90.6 | 3.1 | 4.3 |
| Clothing and clothing accessories (includes footwear) | 53,892 | 46,833 | 46,855 | 40,262 | 15.0 | 16.3 | 86.9 | 14.0 | 18.4 |
| Computer hardware | 28,896 | 16,029 | 26,503 | 14,780 | 9.0 | 8.5 | 55.5 | 7.5 | 6.3 |
| Computer software | 9,601 | 6,422 | 8,378 | 5,452 | 14.6 | 17.8 | 66.9 | 2.5 | 2.5 |
| Drugs, health aids, and beauty aids | 94,026 | 18,870 | 91,447 | 17,451 | 2.8 | 8.1 | 20.1 | 24.4 | 7.4 |
| Electronics and appliances | 27,378 | 23,370 | 27,041 | 23,189 | 1.2 | 0.8 | 85.4 | 7.1 | 9.2 |
| Food, beer, and wine | 8,331 | 6,307 | 7,479 | 5,231 | 11.4 | 20.6 | 75.7 | 2.2 | 2.5 |
| Furniture and home furnishings | 27,508 | 24,257 | 23,571 | 20,394 | 16.7 | 18.9 | 88.2 | 7.1 | 9.5 |
| Music and videos | c | c | 11,319 | 10,362 | c | c | c | c | c |
| Office equipment and supplies | c | c | 8,061 | c | c | c | c | c | c |
| Sporting goods | 11,018 | 9,425 | 9,928 | 7,928 | 11.0 | 18.9 | 85.5 | 2.9 | 3.7 |
| Toys, hobby goods, and games | 10,527 | 8,872 | 9,152 | c | 15.0 | c | 84.3 | 2.7 | 3.5 |
| Other merchandise[a] | 54,988 | 40,882 | 47,874 | 33,964 | 14.9 | 20.4 | 74.3 | 14.2 | 16.1 |
| Nonmerchandise receipts[b] | 25,746 | 22,593 | 21,714 | 17,839 | 18.6 | 26.6 | 87.8 | 6.7 | 8.9 |

[a]Includes other merchandise such as collectibles, souvenirs, auto parts and accessories, hardware, lawn and garden equipment and supplies, and jewelry.
[b]Includes nonmerchandise receipts such as auction commissions, customer training, customer support, advertising, and shipping and handling.
[c]Estimate does not meet publication standards because of high sampling variability or poor response quality (total quantity response rate is less than 50%).

NAICS = North American Industry Classification System (US Census Bureau).

Note: Estimates have not been adjusted for price changes. Estimates include data for businesses with or without paid employees, are grouped according to merchandise categories used in the Annual Retail Trade Survey, and are subject to revision.

SOURCE: "Table 5. U.S. Electronic Shopping and Mail-Order Houses (NAICS 4541)—Total and E-Commerce Sales by Merchandise Line: 2014 and 2013," in *2014 E-Commerce Multi-Sector Data Tables*, U.S. Department of Commerce, U.S. Census Bureau, June 7, 2016, http://www2.census.gov/programs-surveys/e-stats/tables/2014/table_5.xls (accessed August 10, 2016)

2016, the most prominent virtual currency was Bitcoin. First introduced by its anonymous creator in 2009, Bitcoin quickly became the most prevalent form of exchange among online virtual currency users. After reaching a peak value of $1,151 per Bitcoin in December 2013, the digital currency's worth plunged precipitously in early 2014 amid ongoing uncertainties concerning its future legal status. By October 2016 the price of a single Bitcoin was hovering between $610 and $742. Although virtual currencies remained largely unregulated in 2016, the U.S. government was exploring ways to assert control over their use. In March 2014 the Internal Revenue Service ruled that Bitcoins were technically considered property, rather than currency, making them subject to capital gains tax. At the same time, Bitcoin and other electronic forms of money were increasingly being used to obtain controlled substances, weapons, and other illicit goods over the Internet, a source of growing concern among law enforcement officials worldwide. (For more on the relationship between virtual currency and online trafficking, see Chapter 4.)

## E-Commerce in the Services Industries

The services industries in the United States are enormous and encompass everything from brokerage houses to real estate companies to travel agents to health care. Generally, any business that sells its services or some type of expertise belongs in this category. Of all the industries presented in Figure 3.3, e-commerce revenue made up the smallest percentage of total revenue for the services industries in 2014. In those areas of the services industry where e-commerce has broken through, however, it has created much change.

TRAVEL INDUSTRY. Probably no other type of business in the services sector was affected more by the Internet than travel reservation services. Before the Internet, travelers either combed through travel books and called airlines, hotels, restaurants, and other venues one by one, or hired a travel agent to do it for them. When the Internet became widely available, businesses such as Expedia, Priceline, and Travelocity set up websites where anyone could search for rates and make travel reservations with most airlines and hotels. Existing businesses, such as the airlines, developed websites of their own. These Internet innovations made it much easier for travelers to comparison shop and make travel plans on their own. E-commerce made up $14.2 billion (36.7%) of the $38.7 billion in total revenues for travel arrangement and reservation services in 2014. (See Table 3.8.) In *Profile of U.S. Resident Travelers Visiting Overseas Destinations: 2014 Outbound* (July 2015, http://travel.trade.gov/outreachpages/download_data_table/2014_Outbound_Profile.pdf), the International Trade Administration of the Department of Commerce notes that 31% of Americans traveling overseas for leisure purposes used the Internet to book their trips in 2014, compared with 21% who used travel agents.

FINANCIAL SERVICES. Another services industry that experienced a great deal of change because of IT was the financial brokerage business. Beginning in the early 1980s many of those who worked in the industry employed powerful computers and networking capabilities to track financial markets in real time and make financial transactions electronically. When the Internet became mainstream, large financial services organizations, such as Fidelity Investments and Charles Schwab, offered brokerage accounts to customers, allowing them to trade stocks online. Customers also had access to many of the research services that were available only to stockbrokers before the introduction of the World Wide Web. As Table 3.8 shows, of the $255.8 billion generated in securities and commodities trading in 2014, $17.2 billion (6.7%) came from online transactions.

Dave Pettit and Rich Jaroslovsky indicate in *Wall Street Journal Online's Guide to Online Investing: How to Make the Most of the Internet in a Bull or Bear Market* (2002) that in 1996, 1.5 million brokerage accounts existed online; by 2001 this number had increased to 20 million. Even after the collapse of the global financial markets in 2008, competition among the top online brokerage firms remained fierce. In "As Economy Heals, Online Brokerages Go after Investors" (USAToday.com, January 19, 2010), Matt Krantz describes how several of the large online brokerage firms began slashing their commissions and fees as a way of attracting new investors. According to Krantz, much of the competition for clients was actually between Internet brokerages and traditional full-service firms, because consumers were turning to online investing as a way of reducing their costs.

This trend toward discounted online trading eventually caught the attention of the larger investment houses. In July 2010 Merrill Lynch entered the virtual brokerage business with the creation of Merrill Edge, a new online investment account service. Theresa W. Carey reports in "Best Online Brokers: Fidelity Wins in Barron's 2016 Survey" (Barrons.com, March 19, 2016) that by 2016 many brokerage firms had introduced a wide range of technological tools to attract investors, including trading applications (apps) that can be used with both smartphones and smartwatches.

REAL ESTATE SERVICES. The real estate brokerage sector was another services industry that underwent many changes because of the Internet. Before the Internet became widely available, people could find real estate listings only in the newspaper or at a real estate agency. Many websites, such as Realtor.com, began listing thousands of houses for sale in every region of the country. These sites made it possible for people in Connecticut, for example, to gain an understanding of real estate properties and prices in Arizona, Idaho, or even in their own neighborhood. The National Association of Realtors reports in "Realtor.com

**TABLE 3.8**

## Total and e-commerce revenue, selected services, 2013 and 2014

[Except where indicated, estimates are based on data from the 2014 Service Annual Survey. Revenue estimates are shown in millions of dollars, consequently industry group estimates may not be additive. Estimated measures of sampling variability for these estimates are provided in Measures of Sampling Variability for U.S. Selected Services Revenue—Total and E-commerce: 2014 and 2013. Estimates have been adjusted using results of the 2012 Economic Census where applicable]

| NAICS code | Description | Value of revenue 2014 Total | Value of revenue 2014 E-commerce | Value of revenue 2013 Total | Value of revenue 2013 E-commerce | Year-over-year percent change Total revenue | Year-over-year percent change E-commerce revenue | E-commerce as a percent of total revenue 2014 | E-commerce as a percent of total revenue 2013 | Percent distribution of e-commerce revenue 2014 |
|---|---|---|---|---|---|---|---|---|---|---|
| | Total for selected service industries[a] | 13,417,986 | 509,999 | 12,684,359 | 456,281 | 5.8% | 11.8% | 3.8% | 3.6% | 100.0% |
| 22 | Utilities[b] | 605,470 | 304 | 561,580 | 281 | 7.8% | 8.2% | 0.1% | 0.1% | 0.1% |
| 4849y | Transportation and warehousing[c] | 859,346 | 100,489 | 805,221 | 94,358 | 6.7% | 6.5% | 11.7% | 11.7% | 19.7% |
| 481 | Air transportation | 199,991 | 57,184 | 189,149 | 56,177 | 5.7% | 1.8% | 28.6% | 29.7% | 11.2% |
| 483 | Water transportation | 45,106 | 6,104 | 42,807 | 5,475 | 5.4% | 11.5% | 13.5% | 12.8% | 1.2% |
| 484 | Truck transportation | 262,973 | 19,778 | 245,445 | 17,603 | 7.1% | 12.4% | 7.5% | 7.2% | 3.9% |
| 485 | Transit and ground passenger transportation | 32,971 | 902 | 31,306 | 761 | 5.3% | 18.5% | 2.7% | 2.4% | 0.2% |
| 486 | Pipeline transportation | 42,071 | 3,268 | 38,813 | | 8.4% | | 7.8% | | 0.6% |
| 487 | Scenic and sightseeing transportation | 3,355 | 387 | 3,271 | 365 | 2.6% | 6.0% | 11.5% | 11.2% | 0.1% |
| 488 | Support activities for transportation | 167,587 | | 153,325 | 10,132 | 9.3% | | | 6.6% | |
| 51 | Information | 1,352,716 | 138,924 | 1,283,897 | 124,071 | 5.4% | 12.0% | 10.3% | 9.7% | 27.2% |
| 511 | Publishing industries (except Internet) | 293,659 | 76,032 | 280,825 | 68,087 | 4.6% | 11.7% | 25.9% | 24.2% | 14.9% |
| 512 | Motion picture and sound recording industries | 96,486 | 4,839 | 95,091 | 4,505 | 1.5% | 7.4% | 5.0% | 4.7% | 0.9% |
| 515 | Broadcasting (except Internet) | 140,205 | 1,476 | 130,838 | 1,251 | 7.2% | 18.0% | 1.1% | 1.0% | 0.3% |
| 517 | Telecommunications | 588,109 | 9,313 | 558,926 | 8,330 | 5.2% | 11.8% | 1.6% | 1.5% | 1.8% |
| 518 | Data processing, hosting, and related services | 118,145 | 14,053 | 114,878 | 13,361 | 2.8% | 5.2% | 11.9% | 11.6% | 2.8% |
| 519 | Other information services | 116,112 | 33,211 | 103,339 | 28,537 | 12.4% | 16.4% | 28.6% | 27.6% | 6.5% |
| 52 | Finance and insurance[d] | 3,934,801 | 109,302 | 3,738,149 | 94,875 | 5.3% | 15.2% | 2.8% | 2.5% | 21.4% |
| 5223 | Activities related to credit intermediation | 88,171 | 14,298 | 86,052 | 13,675 | 2.5% | 4.6% | 16.2% | 15.9% | 2.8% |
| 5231 | Securities and commodity contracts intermediation and brokerage | 255,812 | 17,170 | 243,520 | 17,029 | 5.0% | 0.8% | 6.7% | 7.0% | 3.4% |
| 53 | Real estate and rental and leasing[e] | 564,440 | 28,728 | 524,135 | 26,882 | 7.7% | 6.9% | 5.1% | 5.1% | 5.6% |
| 532 | Rental and leasing services | 145,771 | 23,365 | 135,780 | 22,048 | 7.4% | 6.0% | 16.0% | 16.2% | 4.6% |
| 54 | Professional, scientific, and technical services[f] | 1,582,313 | 27,420 | 1,508,353 | 25,236 | 4.9% | 8.7% | 1.7% | 1.7% | 5.4% |
| 5415 | Computer systems design and related services | 343,367 | 8,393 | 330,428 | 7,299 | 3.9% | 15.0% | 2.4% | 2.2% | 1.6% |
| 56 | Administrative and support and waste management and remediation services | 766,484 | 26,428 | 700,871 | 21,688 | 9.4% | 21.9% | 3.4% | 3.1% | 5.2% |
| 5615 | Travel arrangement and reservation services | 38,725 | 14,225 | 36,177 | 12,026 | 7.0% | 18.3% | 36.7% | 33.2% | 2.8% |
| 61 | Educational services[g] | 58,396 | 5,498 | 55,000 | 4,685 | 6.2% | 17.4% | 9.4% | 8.5% | 1.1% |
| 62 | Health care and social assistance | 2,190,999 | 1,120 | 2,093,015 | 1,019 | 4.7% | 9.9% | 0.1% | 0.1% | 0.2% |
| 71 | Arts, entertainment, and recreation | 223,162 | 8,608 | 211,222 | 7,239 | 5.7% | 18.9% | 3.9% | 3.4% | 1.7% |
| 72 | Accommodation and food services[h] | 796,991 | | 751,407 | | 6.1% | | | | |
| 81 | Other services (except public administration)[i] | 482,868 | 11,688 | 451,509 | 11,126 | 6.9% | 5.1% | 2.4% | 2.5% | 2.3% |
| 811 | Repair and maintenance | 155,869 | 1,071 | 147,993 | 1,071 | 5.3% | | | 0.7% | |
| 812 | Personal and laundry services | 96,800 | 2,635 | 91,205 | 2,384 | 6.1% | 10.5% | 2.7% | 2.6% | 0.5% |
| 813 | Religious, grantmaking, civic, professional, and similar organizations[j] | 230,199 | 7,992 | 212,311 | 7,671 | 8.4% | 4.2% | 3.5% | 3.6% | 1.6% |

## TABLE 3.8

### Total and e-commerce revenue, selected services, 2013 and 2014 [CONTINUED]

[Except where indicated, estimates are based on data from the 2014 Service Annual Survey. Revenue estimates are shown in millions of dollars, consequently industry group estimates may not be additive. Estimated measures of sampling variability for these estimates are provided in Measures of Sampling Variability for U.S. Selected Services Revenue—Total and E-commerce: 2014 and 2013. Estimates have been adjusted using results of the 2012 Economic Census where applicable]

[a] Includes NAICS 22 (Utilities), NAICS 4849y (Transportation and Warehousing), NAICS 51 (Information), NAICS 52 (Finance and Insurance), NAICS 53 (Real Estate and Rental and Leasing), NAICS 54 (Selected Professional, Scientific, and Technical Services), NAICS 56 (Administrative and Support and Waste Management and Remediation Services), NAICS 61 (Educational Services), NAICS 62 (Health Care and Social Assistance), NAICS 71 (Arts, Entertainment, and Recreation), NAICS 72 (Accommodation and Food Services), and NAICS 81 (Other Services (except Public Administration)).

[b] Excludes government owned utilities.

[c] Excludes NAICS 482 (Rail Transportation) and NAICS 491 (Postal Service).

[d] Excludes NAICS 525 (Funds, Trusts, and Other Financial Vehicles).

[e] NAICS published according to the 2007 NAICS definition, as is the 2007 Economic Census. The 2007 NAICS definition includes equity Real Estate Investment Trusts (REITs).

[f] Excludes NAICS 54112 (Offices of Notaries).

[g] Excludes NAICS 6111 (Elementary and Secondary Schools), NAICS 6112 (Junior Colleges), and NAICS 6113 (Colleges, Universities, and Professional Schools).

[h] Estimates are based on data from the 2014 Annual Retail Trade Survey. Estimates have been adjusted using results of the 2012 Economic Census.

[i] Excludes NAICS 81311 (Religious Organizations), NAICS 81393 (Labor Unions and Similar Labor Organizations), NAICS 81394 (Political Organizations), and NAICS814 (Private Households).

[j] Excludes NAICS 81311 (Religious Organizations), NAICS 81393 (Labor Unions and Similar Labor Organizations), and NAICS 81394 (Political Organizations).

[k] Estimate does not meet publication standards because of high sampling variability (coefficient of variation is greater than 30%) or poor response quality (total quantity response rate is less than 50%), or other concerns about the estimate's quality. Unpublished estimates derived from this table by subtraction are subject to these same limitations and should not be attributed to the U.S. Census Bureau.

[l] Estimate in table is withheld to avoid disclosing data of individual companies; data are included in higher level totals.

[m] Absolute value is less than 0.05.

NAICS = North American Industry Classification System (U.S. Census Bureau).

Note: Estimates are not adjusted for price changes. Estimates are subject to revision and include data only for businesses with paid employees except for Accommodation and Food Services, which also includes businesses without paid employees.

SOURCE: "Table 3. U.S. Selected Services Revenue—Total and E-Commerce: 2014 and 2013," in 2014 E-Commerce Multi-Sector Data Tables, U.S. Department of Commerce, U.S. Census Bureau, June 7, 2016, http://www2.census.gov/programs-surveys/e-stats/tables/2014/table_3.xls (accessed August 10, 2016)

Traffic" (June 2016, http://www.realtor.org/sites/default/files/reports/2016/2016-08-nar-website-traffic-stats-08-05-2016.pdf) that Internet traffic on its site reached 42 million unique visitors in June 2016, up from 34.1 million unique visitors in June 2015.

The Internet has also become a valuable tool for real estate brokers and agents. According to J. Barlow Herget, in "Internet Now an Indispensable Tool for Veteran Realtors Who Were Once Skeptical" (NewsObserver.com, July 14, 2012), e-mail and mobile phones enable realtors to maintain contact with a wider range of prospective homeowners, including those who live out of state or even overseas. Meanwhile, the Internet empowers consumers to identify desirable properties on their own, allowing real estate agents to streamline the home viewing process. Herget quotes Phyllis Brookshire of Allen Tate Realtors in Charlotte, North Carolina, as saying, "The Internet is an agent's best partner if they learn how to use it. You absolutely have to have it."

## M-Commerce

As more Americans own handheld devices, retailers are beginning to explore ways to reach consumers through mobile wireless technology. This emerging trend, known as mobile commerce (m-commerce), has become a vital mode of communication between sellers and consumers in the 21st century. Katie Evans reports in "The 2017 Mobile 500: The Next Generation of Mobile Commerce" (Interne Retailer.com, August 12, 2016) that in 2015 m-commerce accounted for an estimated $143.7 billion in sales in the United States, compared with $89.5 billion in 2014. Furthermore, m-commerce sales were projected to top $220.4 billion in 2016, an annual increase of 53.4%. The versatility and ease of mobile shopping also enabled consumers to perform a variety of tasks on their phone before making a purchase. In "Shop 'Til They Drop ... or at Least Until Their Thumbs Hurt: Getting to Know the Mobile Shopper" (May 10, 2016, http://www.nielsen.com/us/en/insights/news/2016/shop-til-they-drop-or-at-least-until-their-thumbs-hurt-getting-to-know-mobile-shoppers.html), the Nielsen Company reports that during the fourth quarter of 2015, 72% of smartphone shoppers used their mobile devices to research product information, while 70% used their phones to check the price of a product. In addition, 60% of mobile shoppers used a store locator app to get directions to a retail outlet. Overall, more than one-third (36%) of mobile shoppers completed a transaction on their smartphone during the fourth quarter of 2015.

## IT AND CURRENCY

IT has not only changed how people pay for merchandise but also how people make and receive payments in general. Credit cards, debit cards, electronic bank transfers, and online banking have eliminated much of the need to carry cash and personal checks. Neil B. Murphy of Virginia Commonwealth University reports in "The Future of Banking in America: The Effect on U.S. Banking of Payment System Changes" (*FDIC Banking Review*, vol. 16, no. 2, 2004) that 88% of households in the United States used some form of electronic payment in 2001. NACHA—The Electronic Payments Association (formerly the National Automated Clearing House Association) notes in "ACH Volume Grows by 5.6 Percent Adding 1.3 Billion Payments in 2015" (April 14, 2016, https://www.nacha.org/news/ach-volume-grows-56-percent-adding-13-billion-payments-2015-0) that automated clearing houses (ACHs) processed more than 24 billion electronic payment transactions in 2015, with an overall value of $41.6 trillion.

The advantages of a cashless system are undeniable. With credit and debit cards people always have buying power at their disposal, they can make purchases instantly, and they can access and transfer money online. Banks and businesses are no longer required to spend money moving paper bills and checks all over the country. Furthermore, store owners do not have to worry about the security risks that are inherent with keeping large amounts of cash on hand. At the same time, electronic financial transactions have a positive impact on the environment. According to The Paperless Project, in "Managing Financial Documents in a Paperless World" (2016, http://www.thepaperlessproject.com/managing-financial-documents-in-a-paperless-world/), the average household could save up to 6.6 pounds (3 kg) of paper and reduce carbon emissions by 171 pounds (78 kg) annually by conducting all their financial activities online.

## Credit and Debit Cards

In the 21st century credit and debit cards have become the predominant mode of payment for the majority of American consumers. By enabling individuals to make an array of purchases with a single piece of plastic, credit and debit cards bring unprecedented convenience to a range of financial transactions, from shopping at retail outlets to paying bills online. Furthermore, credit and debit card accounts allow individuals to track their spending over the Internet, providing them with a range of new tools designed to help them manage their spending more easily and efficiently. In the United States, the credit card industry is dominated by Visa, American Express, Master-Card, and Discover. Tamara E. Holmes notes in "Credit Card Market Share Statistics" (CreditCards.com, 2016) that these four companies accounted for 57% of all the cards issued in the United States in 2016.

However, the ubiquity of credit and debit cards has also created unique risks for 21st-century consumers. For one, credit and debit cards provide potential thieves with relatively easy access to peoples' sensitive personal and financial information, leading to dramatic increases in the number of unauthorized purchases and identity theft cases. (See Chapter 4.) Also, credit card companies and banks charge transaction fees for credit and debit card purchases, which imposes additional expenses on merchants and retailers. In "Hidden from View, Credit Card 'Swipe Fees' May Still Raise Prices" (LATimes.com, July 17, 2012), David Lazarus reports that these additional costs are sometimes passed on to consumers, usually in the form of higher prices. "A lot of merchants will consider it a cost of doing business and will raise all their prices," the consumer advocate Linda Sherry told Lazarus. "Consumers won't know if this is for the processing fees or not." Furthermore, the ease of using credit and debit cards makes it challenging for some consumers to manage their money effectively. Jamie Gonzalez and Tamara E. Holmes indicate in "Credit Card Debt Statistics" (CreditCards.com, 2016) that revolving debt (debt that changes from month to month, based on consumer purchases and payments) in the United States reached $953.3 billion in May 2016.

CREDIT CARDS. The most firmly established of these electronic payment methods is the credit card. Diners Club issued the first general-purpose credit card in 1950. This credit card allowed restaurant patrons in Manhattan to charge a meal at any restaurant that participated in the program. Although credit card use has increased almost every year since then, credit card transactions took place entirely on paper at first, which kept some people away. During the 1980s a computerized, networked credit card system was put into place using modems and other networking technologies. The result was that credit card use skyrocketed. Murphy estimates that in 2004 there were more than 1.2 billion credit cards in the United States. A little under half (551.9 million) of these cards were issued directly by retailers under a private label (e.g., Banana Republic or JC Penney). The rest were issued by banks or as travel and entertainment cards. Murphy reports that between 1997 and 2001 the number of credit card transactions grew from 12.9 billion to 17 billion. In *The 2013 Federal Reserve Payments Study: Recent and Long-Term Payment Trends in the United States: 2003–2012* (December 19, 2013, http://www.frbservices.org/files/communications/pdf/research/2013_payments_study_summary.pdf), the most recent report on this topic as of November 2016, the Federal Reserve System determines that 26.2 billion general-purpose credit card transactions, with a total value of $2.2 trillion, were processed in the United States in 2012. That year, the average general-purpose credit card transaction was $93.

DEBIT CARDS. Since their introduction to the U.S. market during the 1980s, debit cards have also become a popular method of payment for many Americans. Debit cards remove existing money from a money market or bank account when used, unlike credit cards, which are effectively making loans to their users. A debit card user does not owe money after the transaction, but must have sufficient funds in his or her account to cover the transaction.

Debit cards grew out of the automated teller machine (ATM) system that became widespread during the early 1980s. The first U.S. ATM was a Chemical Bank cash dispenser that went into operation in Long Island, New York, in 1969. Some ATM networks, which were originally constructed to allow bank cards access to ATMs at multiple banks, expanded their networks to grocery stores and select mainstream retail stores such as Wal-Mart. Customers could then use their ATM cards to buy groceries or merchandise at the register without first having to withdraw cash from a machine. When this debit card system appeared as if it might become widely used, Visa and MasterCard responded by opening their extensive networks to banks and debit card users. Since 1995 the use of debit cards has grown at a rapid pace. According to Murphy, between 1995 and 2001 the percentage of American households using a debit card grew from 17.6% to 47%. In 1995 there were 1.4 billion debit card transactions, and by 2000 the number of transactions had increased to 8.3 billion. The Federal Reserve notes in *2013 Federal Reserve Payments Study* that the total number of debit card transactions rose from 37.5 billion in 2009 to 47 billion in 2012, an increase of 7.7%. The total value of all debit card transactions exceeded $1.8 trillion in 2012, and debit cards accounted for more than one-third (38%) of all noncash payment transactions.

## Electronic Transfer of Money

Another type of paperless monetary transaction that has grown in popularity is the electronic transfer of money, formally known as the ACH system. Electronic transfer is an electronic form of the checking system. When making an ACH transaction, the person or business with the checking account provides the account and routing number to another party along with the authorization to wire money directly into or out of the account. For the most part, large corporations employ this method of payment and receipt more extensively than individual households. Murphy notes that 97% of large corporations used the ACH system extensively in 2002, largely for business-to-business (B2B) transactions involving substantial amounts of money.

Individuals who use the ACH system typically do so to receive regular salary or Social Security payments and to make regular monthly payments. According to the Social Security Administration (https://www.ssa.gov/deposit/GIS/data/Reports/T2StateSum.htm), as of November 2016, 98.8% of Social Security recipients received their payments through direct deposit.

Many Americans also file their tax returns and receive refunds through an electronic payment method. The Internal Revenue Service (November 4, 2016, https://www.irs.gov/uac/newsroom/filing-season-statistics-for-week-ending-oct-21-2016) indicates that through October 2016, 131.6 million (85.1%) out of 151.2 million 2015 tax returns had been filed electronically. Meanwhile, the government paid $259.9 billion out of a total of $305.3 billion in tax refunds through direct deposit.

As electronic transfers have become more common, the number of paper checks written by Americans has steadily declined. According to the Federal Reserve, in *2013 Federal Reserve Payments Study*, Americans wrote 18.3 billion checks in 2012, a 9.2% decrease from the 24.5 billion checks written in 2009. During this same period, the debit card surpassed the personal check as the most prevalent form of noncash payment in the United States. In 2012 the largest percentage of checks were those written by consumers to businesses (46%), followed by B2B check payments (28%) and business-to-consumer checks (15%).

Because the cost of creating, mailing, and handling so many paper checks is enormous, the U.S. government has made efforts to reduce the number of paper checks in the system. Early in 2003 the Federal Reserve reduced what it charges banks for processing electronic transfers and raised the prices it charges banks for processing paper checks. Then in October 2003 Congress passed and President George W. Bush (1946–) signed the Check Truncation Act, which went into effect in October 2004. Under this act, banks are no longer required to hold onto the original paper checks they receive. Instead, when a payee deposits a check in a bank, the bank makes a digital copy of the check and shreds the original. The bank then simply wires the payer's bank for the money, avoiding the postage and processing involved in sending the actual check to the payer's bank. If the payer needs a copy of the check, the stored digital image can be printed. At the same time, more and more bank customers were using digital technology to deposit checks into their accounts remotely. In "How to Deposit Checks with Your Smartphone" (USNews.com, October 9, 2012), Susan Johnston notes that by 2012 a number of banks had created mobile apps that enabled customers to take photographs of an endorsed check and then upload it to their accounts using their phones.

## WILL AMERICANS ABANDON THE BANK?

Dennis Jacobe reports in "Banking Customers Still Love Bricks and Mortar" (June 10, 2003, http://www.gallup.com/poll/8593/Banking-Customers-Still-Love-Bricks-Mortar.aspx) that in 2003 Americans wanted both the option of banking electronically and of visiting their local bank branch. Because of the high costs of hiring tellers and leasing branch space, banks have encouraged the use of electronic banking among customers as a whole. The banks' efforts appear to be working. In March 2000 only 7% of Americans reported any experience with online banking, and by 2003, 29% of Americans said they banked online from home at least once a month. In *Usage over Time* (2014, http://www.pewinternet.org/files/2014/01/Usage-Over-Time-_May-2013.xlsx), the Pew Research Center reports that in March 2000, 17% of Internet users reported that they had banked online at some time. In January 2005 this percentage had increased to 44%. By May 2013 more than three-fifths (61%) of Internet users had used an online banking service at some point. In *U.S. Smartphone Use in 2015* (April 1, 2015, http://www.pewinternet.org/files/2015/03/PI_Smartphones_0401151.pdf), Aaron Smith and Dana Page of the Pew Research Center note that 57% of smartphone owners conducted online banking via their devices in 2014. Mobile banking is particularly prevalent among young adults. Smith and Page note, in 2014 nearly three-quarters (72%) of adults aged 18 to 29 years used their smartphone to conduct banking transactions. By contrast, only one-third (34%) of adults aged 50 years and older engaged in mobile banking with their smartphones.

## ANTITRUST LITIGATION

Throughout U.S. history, technological innovation has tended to give rise to the formation of monopolies. Those companies that create a widespread demand and a standard for new technologies often become the only producer of that technology, shutting down further competition in that industry. Since the passage of the Sherman Antitrust Act in 1890, companies in the private sector have been forbidden from blocking competitors from entering the market. If a company grows large enough and powerful enough to keep competitors out of the market and becomes a monopoly, then the U.S. Department of Justice (DOJ) typically intervenes and either reaches a settlement with the company or files an antitrust suit and takes the company to court. The U.S. government takes the stance that monopolies reduce competition, which impedes economic progress and innovation. Although this law may appear easy to understand, the courts and the DOJ have to weigh a number of factors before breaking up a monopoly, including the negative effects the ruling may have on consumers.

In 1998 the DOJ and the attorneys general of 20 states filed an antitrust suit against the Microsoft Corporation. Along with other charges, the government claimed that Microsoft violated antitrust law when it integrated its Internet Explorer web browser software with Windows. At the time, Windows was the only operating system widely available for the personal computer (PC). When Microsoft integrated Internet Explorer and Windows, other web browsers such as Netscape could not compete. The DOJ maintained that this act created unfair competition for those other companies that made browsers for PC systems. Microsoft officials claimed that Internet Explorer was now part of Windows and that separating the two would destroy the most current versions of the operating system and years of development on their part.

In November 1999 Judge Thomas Penfield Jackson (1937–2013) of the U.S. district court presented a preliminary ruling, which asserted that Microsoft did have a monopoly with its PC operating system and that the monopoly prevented fair competition among companies that made software for PCs. Five months later, in April 2000, Judge Jackson gave his final ruling, ordering that Microsoft should be split into two separate units: one that would produce the operating system and one that would produce other software components such as Internet Explorer.

Microsoft immediately appealed, and the case went to the federal appeals court under Judge Colleen Kollar-Kotelly (1943–). In the midst of the judicial review, the White House administration changed, and the DOJ, now led by John D. Ashcroft (1942–), came to an agreement with Microsoft that did not involve the breakup of the company. However, several of the states continued to battle the software giant in court. In November 2002 Judge Kollar-Kotelly ruled that the company should not be broken up and should follow the agreement laid down by the DOJ and accepted by the attorneys general of Illinois, Kentucky, Louisiana, Maryland, Michigan, New York, North Carolina, Ohio, and Wisconsin. Additional remedies proposed by California, Connecticut, the District of Columbia, Florida, Iowa, Kansas, Massachusetts, Minnesota, Utah, and West Virginia were dismissed. The agreement required Microsoft to take a number of steps that would allow competitors to once again compete in the market. Among these provisions, Microsoft was required to give computer makers the option of removing Internet Explorer and other Microsoft programs that run on top of the Windows operating system. Microsoft was also forced to reveal details about the Windows operating system that would allow makers of other software to better integrate software with Windows. The terms of the final judgment in the case required Microsoft to share technical documentation, provide feedback to software developers, promote data portability, and support interoperability among systems.

While the DOJ awaited a resolution of the Microsoft antitrust case, other high-profile tech companies came under scrutiny for allegedly monopolistic business practices. In "IBM Hits Back at 'Mainframe Monopoly' Accusations" (Information-Age.com, March 15, 2010), Daniel Shane reports that in 2010 the Indian Council for Research on International Economic Relations filed a report claiming that IBM had attempted to assert monopoly control over India's computer mainframe business sector. Two years later, Google found itself the target of a European Union investigation, amid charges that the company had violated European antitrust law. Indeed, Susan P. Crawford notes in "Is Google a Monopoly? Wrong Question" (Bloomberg-view.com, July 8, 2012) that in 2012 Google accounted for 80% of all search engine traffic on the European continent. Furthermore, according to Tom Warren, in "Ballmer Calls Google a 'Monopoly' That Authorities Should Control" (Verge.com, September 20, 2013), Google controlled more than two-thirds (67%) of all U.S. search engine traffic in 2013; by contrast, its nearest competitor, Bing, controlled only 17.9%. Meanwhile, Google became the target of another antitrust challenge in April 2016, when the European Union accused the company of using its Android operating system to stifle smartphone competition in Europe. As the Microsoft, IBM, and Google cases illustrate, the era of economic globalization not only offered new opportunities for American tech companies to extend their reach into overseas markets but also introduced a range of potential new legal obstacles to overseas expansion.

# CHAPTER 4
# TECHNOLOGY AND CRIME

New technologies almost always introduce new problems into a society. The information technology that became widespread during the 1980s and 1990s is no exception. The advent of online shopping and the increased use of electronic currency have given rise to an identity theft epidemic. The digitization of music, movies, television, and the printed word has led to widespread intellectual property theft and losses of millions of dollars for the entertainment industry.

High-technology (high-tech) crime—also known as cybercrime, web crime, computer crime, netcrime, and electronic crime (e-crime)—has grown ever more common in the 21st century. The Federal Bureau of Investigation's (FBI) Internet Crime Complaint Center (IC3) reports in *2015 Internet Crime Report* (May 2016, https://pdf.ic3 .gov/2015_IC3Report.pdf) that 288,012 cybercrime incidents were reported to the IC3 in 2015. (See Figure 4.1.) Although this figure represented an 8.3% decline from 2011, when the center received 314,246 complaints, it was still 9.6% higher than the 262,813 complaints received in 2013. Cases involving either nonpayment for or nondelivery of goods or services (67,375) accounted for the largest number of victims in 2015. (See Table 4.1.) In addition, the Federal Trade Commission (FTC) notes in "FTC Releases Annual Summary of Consumer Complaints" (March 1, 2016, https://www.ftc.gov/news-events/press-releases/2016/03/ftc-releases-annual-summary-consumer-complaints) that its Consumer Sentinel Network received nearly 3.1 million consumer complaints in 2015. (See Table 4.2.) Unlawful debt collection accounted for 897,655 complaints that year, more than any other category. As the FTC notes, it marked the first time in 15 years that identity theft did not represent the top category of complaints to the Consumer Sentinel Network. Still, identity theft accounted for the second-highest total in 2015, with 490,220 complaints. Among victims reporting their age to the Consumer Sentinel Network in 2015, more than

two out of five (41%) were between the ages 50 and 69 years. (See Table 4.3.) As Table 4.4 indicates, the network also received 96,578 complaints from members of the military in 2015, with individuals enlisted in the U.S. Army accounting for nearly half (48%) of all victims.

## IDENTITY THEFT

The FTC has the responsibility of tracking identity theft and consumer fraud in the United States. Each year the FTC gathers consumer complaints of fraud and identity theft and logs them into its Consumer Sentinel database. Simply put, identity theft is the theft of an individual's personal information such as a telephone number, address, credit card number, or Social Security number. Thieves use this information to buy things, set up false credit card and cell phone accounts, or perpetrate other crimes. With a victim's Social Security number, address, and phone number, a thief can apply for credit cards in the victim's name and proceed to run up the limits on these cards. Such a crime leaves the victim's credit history in shambles, making it difficult to apply for loans or additional cards in the future. In 2015 identity theft accounted for 16% of all fraud complaints. (See Table 4.5.) Overall, identity theft cost victims a total of nearly $57.3 million that year. (See Table 4.6.)

In some instances, identity theft is perpetrated on a massive scale by sophisticated criminal networks. One of the most extensive identity theft cases was broken in 2008, when federal prosecutors brought indictments against 11 individuals accused of operating an international identity theft ring. According to the press release "Retail Hacking Ring Charged for Stealing and Distributing Credit and Debit Card Numbers from Major U.S. Retailers" (August 5, 2008, http://www.usdoj.gov/opa/pr/2008/August/08-ag-689.html), between 2006 and 2008 the 11 defendants in the case stole an estimated 40 million credit and debit card numbers from patrons of retail chains throughout the United States. According to U.S. Department of Justice

FIGURE 4.1

**Complaints received by the Internet Crime Complaint Center, 2010–15**

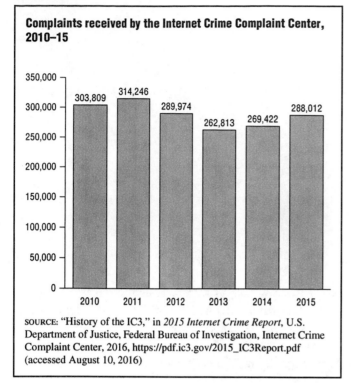

SOURCE: "History of the IC3," in *2015 Internet Crime Report*, U.S. Department of Justice, Federal Bureau of Investigation, Internet Crime Complaint Center, 2016, https://pdf.ic3.gov/2015_IC3Report.pdf (accessed August 10, 2016)

TABLE 4.1

**Complaints received by the Internet Crime Complaint Center, by crime type and victim count, 2015**

[By victim count]

| Crime type | Victim count |
|---|---|
| Non-payment/non-delivery | 67,375 |
| 419/overpayment | 30,855 |
| Identity theft | 21,949 |
| Auction | 21,510 |
| Other | 19,963 |
| Personal data breach | 19,632 |
| Employment | 18,758 |
| Extortion | 17,804 |
| Credit card fraud | 17,172 |
| Phishing/vishing/smishing/pharming | 16,594 |
| Advanced fee | 16,445 |
| Harassment/threats of violence | 14,812 |
| Confidence fraud/romance | 12,509 |
| No lead value | 12,187 |
| Government impersonation | 11,832 |
| Real estate/rental | 11,562 |
| Business email compromise | 7,837 |
| Misrepresentation | 5,458 |
| Lottery/sweepstakes | 5,324 |
| Malware/scareware | 3,294 |
| Corporate data breach | 2,499 |
| Ransomware | 2,453 |
| IPR/copyright and counterfeit | 1,931 |
| Investment | 1,806 |
| Crimes against children | 1,348 |
| Civil matter | 1,148 |
| Re-shipping | 1,073 |
| Denial of service | 1,020 |
| Virus | 971 |
| Health care related | 465 |
| Charity | 411 |
| Terrorism | 361 |
| Hacktivist | 211 |
| Gambling | 131 |
| Criminal forums | 62 |
| **Descriptors*** | |
| Social media | 19,967 |
| Virtual currency | 1,920 |

*These descriptors are used by the Internet Crime Complaint Center for tracking purposes only and are only available after another crime type has been selected.

SOURCE: Adapted from "2015 Crime Types," in *2015 Internet Crime Report*, U.S. Department of Justice, Federal Bureau of Investigation, Internet Crime Complaint Center, 2016, https://pdf.ic3.gov/2015_IC3Report.pdf (accessed August 12, 2016)

(DOJ) allegations, the accused defendants hacked into the wireless computer networks of TJX Companies, BJ's Wholesale Club, OfficeMax, Boston Market, Barnes & Noble, Sports Authority, Forever 21, and DSW to install "sniffer" programs that capture customers' account information. Once in possession of the credit and debit card numbers, the conspirators used them to encode the magnetic strips of blank cards, or else sold them to other criminals. In "Leader of Hacking Ring Sentenced for Massive Identity Thefts from Payment Processor and U.S. Retail Networks" (March 26, 2010, http://www.justice.gov/opa/pr/2010/March/10-crm-329.html), the DOJ reports the ringleader of the scam, Albert Gonzalez, was eventually convicted on multiple charges, including aggravated identity theft, and sentenced to 20 years in prison.

Another high-profile case, dubbed Operation Swiper, was exposed in October 2011. Julia Greenberg notes in "111 Indicted in One of Largest Identity-Theft Cases in the U.S." (IBTimes.com, October 7, 2011) that the ringleaders of the scam recruited bank tellers, restaurant employees, and retail associates throughout the New York City borough of Queens to steal credit card information from customers. One of the four principal organizers of the operation, Amar Singh, was eventually sentenced to 64 to 128 months in prison for his role in the scam, according to Allie Compton, in "Largest ID Theft Case in U.S. History: Amar Singh and Wife, Neha Punjani-Singh, Plead Guilty to Massive Fraud" (HuffingtonPost.com, August 7, 2012).

In June 2016 the FBI arrested four people in connection with an international conspiracy to use stolen identities as a means of accumulating millions of dollars through fraudulent credit card charges. In "International Identity-Theft Ring Victimized Hundreds, Including Hollywood Actress, Authorities Say" (WashingtonPost.com, June 17, 2016), Rachel Weiner explains that the perpetrators employed a variety of schemes to steal people's identities, including sham travel websites. In one instance, the conspirators obtained Social Security numbers and other personal information after posting online job listings for a phony company called the Deutche Group. According to Weiner, the leader of the group's operations in the United States, Amit Chaudhry, worked with relatives and other associates in India to create fake passports, credit cards, and companies using the stolen identities. Among the people victimized was the Canadian-born actress Laura Vandervoort (1984–), whose image appeared on a fake passport discovered by the FBI and ultimately helped it establish a timeline for the scam. As of November 2016, the full extent of the conspiracy, known as the Deutche Group case, was still being investigated.

Each year, the Internal Revenue Service (IRS) reports on criminal cases involving the use of identity theft to perpetrate tax fraud. A breakdown of several cases from 2016 is provided in "Examples of Identity Theft Investigations—Fiscal Year 2016" (October 17, 2016, https://www.irs.gov/uac/examples-of-identity-theft-investigations-fiscal-year-2016). According to the IRS, the use of false identities to claim fraudulent tax refunds costs the federal government tens of millions of dollars each year. In June 2016 a Florida judge sentenced nine people to prison for their involvement in a conspiracy that claimed more than $11 million in fraudulent tax refunds. In another notable case Carl Joseph Cappel was sentenced in 2016 to six years and three months in prison after using stolen identities to claim nearly $1.3 million in tax refunds over a four-year period.

Since the 1980s credit card companies and other financial institutions have made obtaining a credit card or setting up a financial account much easier. Because of the convenience of debit and credit cards, nearly every brick-and-mortar store, website, and catalog now accepts them, often with no proof of identification. Consequently, identity theft is not difficult, and it continues to grow. In *Consumer Sentinel Network Data Book for January–December 2015* (February 2016, https://www.ftc.gov/system/files/documents/reports/consumer-sentinel-net work-data-book-january-december-2015/160229csn-2015 databook.pdf), the FTC reports that in 2015 it received roughly 3.1 million complaints. (See Figure 4.2.) Of these, 16% were related to identity theft.

Table 4.7 displays reported incidents of identity theft by state. California had the highest number of complaints in the country in 2015, with 55,305. Missouri topped the list with the highest rate of reported cases of identity theft per capita, registering 364.3 complaints per 100,000 population. The FTC notes that if the District of Columbia were included among the states listed in Table 4.7, then it would be second with a rate of

**TABLE 4.2**

Complaints received by the Consumer Sentinel Network, by complaint type, 2001–15

| Calendar year | Consumer Sentinel Network complain count | | | Total complaints |
|---|---|---|---|---|
| | Fraud | Identity theft | Other | |
| 2001 | 137,306 | 86,250 | 101,963 | 325,519 |
| 2002 | 242,783 | 161,977 | 146,862 | 551,622 |
| 2003 | 331,366 | 215,240 | 167,051 | 713,657 |
| 2004 | 410,298 | 246,909 | 203,176 | 860,383 |
| 2005 | 437,585 | 255,687 | 216,042 | 909,314 |
| 2006 | 423,672 | 246,214 | 236,243 | 906,129 |
| 2007 | 505,563 | 259,314 | 305,570 | 1,070,447 |
| 2008 | 620,832 | 314,587 | 325,705 | 1,261,124 |
| 2009 | 708,781 | 278,360 | 441,836 | 1,428,977 |
| 2010 | 820,072 | 251,074 | 399,160 | 1,470,306 |
| 2011 | 1,041,517 | 279,191 | 577,835 | 1,898,543 |
| 2012 | 1,112,627 | 369,145 | 631,843 | 2,113,615 |
| 2013 | 1,212,719 | 290,102 | 672,534 | 2,175,355 |
| 2014 | 1,578,565 | 332,647 | 718,775 | 2,629,987 |
| 2015 | 1,246,849 | 490,220 | 1,346,310 | 3,083,379 |

Note: Complaint counts from calendar year 2001 to calendar year 2010 represent historical figures as per the Consumer Sentinel Network's five-year data retention policy. These complaint figures exclude National Do Not Call Registry complaints.

SOURCE: "Consumer Sentinel Network Complaint Type Count, Calendar Years 2001 through 2015," in *Consumer Sentinel Network Data Book for January–December 2015*, Federal Trade Commission, February 2016, https://www.ftc.gov/system/files/documents/reports/consumer-sentinel-network-data-book-january-december-2015/160229csn-2015databook.pdf (accessed August 12, 2016)

**TABLE 4.3**

Complaints received by the Consumer Sentinel Network, by age of victim, 2013–15

| Consumer age | Calendar year 2013 | | Calendar year 2014 | | Calendar year 2015 | |
|---|---|---|---|---|---|---|
| | Complaints | Percentages | Complaints | Percentages | Complaints | Percentages |
| 19 and under | 11,093 | 2% | 12,656 | 2% | 6,339 | 1% |
| 20–29 | 67,608 | 15% | 83,398 | 14% | 50,926 | 11% |
| 30–39 | 77,124 | 17% | 102,108 | 17% | 68,393 | 15% |
| 40–49 | 86,648 | 19% | 111,126 | 18% | 75,350 | 16% |
| 50–59 | 94,509 | 20% | 127,742 | 21% | 95,377 | 20% |
| 60–69 | 74,580 | 16% | 110,973 | 18% | 96,860 | 21% |
| 70 and over | 49,952 | 11% | 59,862 | 10% | 75,144 | 16% |
| **Total reporting age** | **461,514** | | **607,865** | | **468,389** | |

Note: Percentages are based on the total number of consumers reporting their age for Consumer Sentinel Network (CSN) fraud complaints each calendar year: calendar year 2013 = 461,514; calendar year 2014 = 607,865; and calendar year 2015 = 468,389. Of the total, 38% of consumers reported this information during calendar year 2015, 39% in calendar year 2014 and 38% for calendar year 2013.

SOURCE: "Consumer Sentinel Network Fraud Complaints by Consumer Age, Calendar Years 2013 through 2015," in *Consumer Sentinel Network Data Book for January–December 2015*, Federal Trade Commission, February 2016, https://www.ftc.gov/system/files/documents/reports/consumer-sentinel-network-data-book-january-december-2015/160229csn-2015databook.pdf (accessed August 12, 2016)

TABLE 4.4

**Complaints received by the Consumer Sentinel Network from victims in the military, by military branch, 2015**

| Military branch | Complaints | Percentages |
|---|---|---|
| U.S. Army | 45,976 | 48% |
| U.S. Navy | 20,559 | 21% |
| U.S. Air Force | 19,006 | 20% |
| U.S. Marines | 9,238 | 10% |
| U.S. Coast Guard | 1,799 | 2% |
| **Total** | **96,578** | |

Note: Percentages are based on the total number of Consumer Sentinel Network (CSN) complaints from military consumers reporting their branch of service (96,578) between January 1 and December 31, 2015. Of the 109,934 military consumers, 88% reported this information during calendar year 2015.

SOURCE: "Consumer Sentinel Network Military Complaints by Consumer Military Branch, January 1–December 31, 2015," in *Consumer Sentinel Network Data Book for January–December 2015*, Federal Trade Commission, February 2016, https://www.ftc.gov/system/files/documents/reports/consumer-sentinel-network-data-book-january-december-2015/160229csn-2015databook.pdf (accessed August 12, 2016)

TABLE 4.5

**Top consumer fraud complaints reported to the Consumer Sentinel Network, 2015**

| Rank | Category | No. of complaints | Percentages* |
|---|---|---|---|
| 1 | Debt collection | 897,655 | 29% |
| 2 | Identity theft | 490,220 | 16% |
| 3 | Impostor scams | 353,770 | 11% |
| 4 | Telephone and mobile services | 275,754 | 9% |
| 5 | Prizes, sweepstakes and lotteries | 140,136 | 5% |
| 6 | Banks and lenders | 131,875 | 4% |
| 7 | Shop-at-home and catalog sales | 96,363 | 3% |
| 8 | Auto-related complaints | 93,917 | 3% |
| 9 | Television and electronic media | 47,728 | 2% |
| 10 | Credit bureaus, information furnishers and report users | 43,939 | 1% |
| 11 | Internet services | 40,106 | 1% |
| 12 | Credit cards | 37,750 | 1% |
| 13 | Health care | 34,669 | 1% |
| 14 | Investment-related complaints | 26,453 | 1% |
| 15 | Foreign money offers and counterfeit check scams | 25,324 | 1% |
| 16 | Advance payments for credit services | 24,433 | 1% |
| 17 | Travel, vacations and timeshare plans | 24,171 | 1% |
| 18 | Business and job opportunities | 17,314 | 1% |
| 19 | Office supplies and services | 10,287 | <1% |
| 20 | Mortgage foreclosure relief and debt management | 10,210 | <1% |
| | | | <1% |
| 21 | Magazines and books | 8,866 | |
| 22 | Home repair, improvement and products | 8,364 | <1% |
| 23 | Computer equipment and software | 8,119 | <1% |
| 24 | Education | 6,973 | <1% |
| 25 | Grants | 4,077 | <1% |
| 26 | Tax preparers | 2,991 | <1% |
| 27 | Charitable solicitations | 2,747 | <1% |
| 28 | Internet auction | 2,430 | <1% |
| 29 | Buyers' clubs | 1,168 | <1% |
| 30 | Funeral services | 1,123 | <1% |

*Percentages are based on the total number of Consumer Sentinel Network (CSN) complaints (3,083,379) received by the Federal Trade Commission (FTC) between January 1 and December 31, 2015. Four percent (126,482) of the CSN complaints received by the FTC were coded "Other."

SOURCE: "Consumer Sentinel Network Complaint Categories, January 1–December 31, 2015," in *Consumer Sentinel Network Data Book for January–December 2015*, Federal Trade Commission, February 2016, https://www.ftc.gov/system/files/documents/reports/consumer-sentinel-network-data-book-january-december-2015/160229csn-2015databook.pdf (accessed August 10, 2016)

228 identity theft victimization reports per 100,000 population. Connecticut (225 per 100,000 population) and Florida (217.4) also experienced rates higher than 200 complaints per 100,000 population. Hawaii (62.6) and South Dakota (63.1) had the lowest number of reported victims of identity theft per 100,000 population in 2015.

The FBI monitors U.S. and global cybercrime incidents through its IC3, which publishes its findings annually. In *2015 Internet Crime Report*, the IC3 indicates that it received 288,012 cybercrime complaints in 2015; approximately 80.2% of these complaints originated in the United States. (See Figure 4.3.) As Figure 4.4 shows, the highest percentage of complaints came from California, which accounted for 14.5% of all complaints originating in the United States in 2015. That year, California generated 34,842 cybercrime complaints, while the second-leading state, Florida, generated 20,306 complaints. (See Table 4.8.) California was also the leading state in terms of financial losses linked to cybercrime that year, with a total of nearly $195.5 million reported lost; this figure represented more than one-fifth (21.8%) of all financial losses reported to the IC3 in 2015. (See Table 4.9.)

According to the FTC, in *Consumer Sentinel Network Data Book for January–December 2015*, more than half of those reporting identity theft in the calendar years (CYs) 2013 to 2015 were aged 40 years and older. (See Table 4.10; note that total numbers do not coincide with those in Table 4.5 because not all victims reported their age.) In CY 2015 nearly a quarter (24%) of complaints came from those between the ages of 50 and 59 years, while one-fifth (20%) were received from those aged 40 to 49 years. Between CYs 2013 and 2015 the number of identity theft complaints received from those 19 years old and younger increased by 37%, from 15,226 to

20,905. On the whole, men registered more complaints than women with the IC3 in 2015; the one exception was among adults between the ages of 40 and 49, where women (29,559) registered more complaints than men (28,694) that year. (See Table 4.11.)

The FTC also provides information on how identity theft victims' information was misused. Overall, nearly half (49.2%) of victims reported that someone had used their identity to obtain government benefits or documents, including tax- or wage-related fraud (45.3%), benefits fraud (2.5%), and driver's license fraud (0.3%) in CY 2015. (See Table 4.12.) Another 15.8% of victims suffered credit card fraud in CY 2015, with 11.6% reporting that new accounts were set up in their name and 4.2% reporting bogus charges made to their existing accounts. These figures represented a decrease from CY 2014, when 17.4% of victims

**TABLE 4.6**

**Complaints received by the Internet Crime Complaint Center, by crime type and total financial loss, 2015**

[By victim loss]

| Crime type | Loss amount |
| --- | --- |
| Business email compromise | $246,226,016 |
| Confidence fraud/romance | $203,390,531 |
| Non-payment/non-delivery | $121,329,122 |
| Investment | $119,177,899 |
| Identity theft | $57,294,589 |
| Other | $56,153,977 |
| Advanced fee | $50,721,226 |
| 419/overpayment | $49,217,119 |
| Personal data breach | $43,477,526 |
| Credit card fraud | $41,503,502 |
| Real estate/rental | $41,417,647 |
| Corporate data breach | $38,800,430 |
| Employment | $33,890,824 |
| Lottery/sweepstakes | $19,365,223 |
| Auction | $18,906,416 |
| Misrepresentation | $17,974,014 |
| Extortion | $14,799,705 |
| Harassment/threats of violence | $13,126,123 |
| Government impersonation | $12,090,159 |
| Civil matter | $9,946,345 |
| Phishing/vishing/smishing/pharming | $8,174,316 |
| IPR/copyright and counterfeit | $7,230,803 |
| Re-shipping | $3,831,957 |
| Malware/scareware | $2,912,628 |
| Denial of service | $2,770,978 |
| Ransomware | $1,620,814 |
| Charity | $1,328,153 |
| Virus | $1,230,812 |
| Gambling | $955,360 |
| Health care related | $906,343 |
| Hacktivist | $171,601 |
| Crimes against children | $97,584 |
| Terrorism | $65,789 |
| Criminal forums | $55,996 |
| No lead value | $0 |
| **Descriptors*** | |
| Social media | $98,652,510 |
| Virtual currency | $8,951,910 |

*These descriptors are used by the Internet Crime Complaint Center for tracking purposes only and are only available after another crime type has been selected.

SOURCE: Adapted from "2015 Crime Types," in *2015 Internet Crime Report*, U.S. Department of Justice, Federal Bureau of Investigation, Internet Crime Complaint Center, 2016, https://pdf.ic3.gov/2015_IC3Report.pdf (accessed August 12, 2016)

**FIGURE 4.2**

**Percentage of identity theft and other fraud complaints received by the Consumer Sentinel Network, 2013–15**

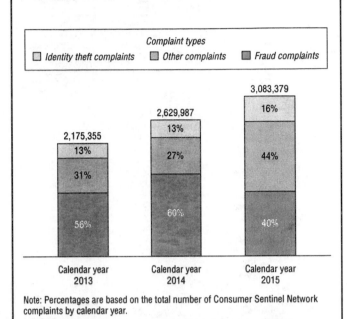

Note: Percentages are based on the total number of Consumer Sentinel Network complaints by calendar year.

SOURCE: "Consumer Sentinel Network Complaint Type Percentages, Calendar Years 2013 through 2015," in *Consumer Sentinel Network Data Book for January–December 2015*, Federal Trade Commission, February 2016, https://www.ftc.gov/system/files/documents/reports/consumer-sentinel-network-data-book-january-december-2015/160229csn-2015databook.pdf (accessed August 10, 2016)

experienced credit card fraud. Phone and utilities fraud was reported by 9.9% of victims in CY 2015, with 3.7% indicating that imposters set up wireless accounts in their name and another 0.5% claiming that bogus telephone accounts had been established under their personal information. Bank fraud, which was reported by 8.2% of identity theft victims in CY 2014, fell to 5.9% in CY 2015. Bank fraud complaints included unauthorized electronic fund transfers (2.3%), fraudulent new accounts (2%), and misuse of existing accounts (1.1%). Loan fraud was reported by 3.5% of identity theft victims in CY 2015. Those reporting identity theft crimes to the FTC in CY 2015 experienced many other types of fraud, including everything from phony child-support claims to property rental fraud. In addition, 14% of identity theft complaints in CY 2015 included more than one type of fraud.

## Identity Theft and the Internet

Identity thieves can operate alone or as part of a large crime organization. They can be someone the victim knows or a complete stranger. They gather personal information in various ways, stealing wallets and checkbooks or going through trash bins outside of homes and businesses to dig out credit card statements, old checkbooks, and receipts. Some pilfer financial statements and other private information from open mailboxes. Since the mid-1990s, many thieves have turned to the Internet to steal information.

There are a number of ways in which thieves employ the Internet to retrieve personal information. Tech-savvy crooks will often take the direct method and hack into business and bank servers and make off with hundreds of credit card numbers. Most identity thieves, however, do not deal in such sophisticated methods. According to Duncan Graham-Rowe, in "Internet Fuels Boom in ID Theft" (NewScientist.com, March 13, 2004), one of the easiest ways to steal identities is simply to use a search engine such as Google. Many people naively post all manner of personal information on home and even office websites, including their Social Security number, date of birth, mother's maiden name, current address, and phone number. Simply typing "driver's license" or "passport"

TABLE 4.7

**Fraud, identity theft, and other complaints received by the Consumer Sentinel Network, by state, 2015**

| | Fraud and other complaints | | | | Identity theft complaints | | |
|---|---|---|---|---|---|---|---|
| Rank | Consumer state | Complaints per 100,000 population* | Complaints | Rank | Victim state | Complaints per 100,000 population* | Complaints |
| 1 | Florida | 1,510.2 | 306,133 | 1 | Missouri | 364.3 | 22,164 |
| 2 | Georgia | 1,208.3 | 123,429 | 2 | Connecticut | 225.0 | 8,078 |
| 3 | Michigan | 1,143.6 | 113,474 | 3 | Florida | 217.4 | 44,063 |
| 4 | Texas | 941.3 | 258,579 | 4 | Maryland | 183.2 | 11,006 |
| 5 | Nevada | 836.9 | 24,194 | 5 | Illinois | 158.7 | 20,414 |
| 6 | Delaware | 807.8 | 7,641 | 6 | Michigan | 158.1 | 15,684 |
| 7 | Rhode Island | 764.7 | 8,078 | 7 | Georgia | 149.1 | 15,230 |
| 8 | California | 750.2 | 293,662 | 8 | Texas | 144.3 | 39,630 |
| 9 | Maryland | 749.0 | 44,985 | 9 | New Hampshire | 142.0 | 1,890 |
| 10 | Alabama | 738.1 | 35,865 | 10 | California | 141.3 | 55,305 |
| 11 | Tennessee | 670.3 | 44,241 | 11 | Rhode Island | 141.2 | 1,491 |
| 12 | Louisiana | 663.7 | 30,999 | 12 | Ohio | 134.4 | 15,611 |
| 13 | Virginia | 645.3 | 54,093 | 12 | Wisconsin | 134.4 | 7,756 |
| 14 | New Jersey | 626.5 | 56,121 | 14 | Arizona | 133.8 | 9,136 |
| 15 | Pennsylvania | 626.3 | 80,180 | 15 | Washington | 126.1 | 9,043 |
| 16 | Arizona | 623.5 | 42,575 | 15 | Oregon | 126.1 | 5,081 |
| 17 | Missouri | 609.3 | 37,068 | 17 | New Jersey | 125.8 | 11,266 |
| 18 | Ohio | 606.8 | 70,470 | 18 | Massachusetts | 125.5 | 8,530 |
| 19 | New Mexico | 594.1 | 12,387 | 19 | Nevada | 125.0 | 3,613 |
| 20 | Colorado | 592.6 | 32,333 | 20 | Delaware | 124.9 | 1,181 |
| 21 | New Hampshire | 572.0 | 7,611 | 21 | Colorado | 123.2 | 6,724 |
| 22 | Massachusetts | 557.6 | 37,884 | 21 | Virginia | 123.2 | 10,329 |
| 23 | Connecticut | 554.1 | 19,898 | 23 | New York | 122.0 | 24,157 |
| 24 | South Carolina | 553.3 | 27,091 | 24 | Oklahoma | 120.0 | 4,695 |
| 25 | North Carolina | 550.3 | 55,266 | 25 | Pennsylvania | 116.2 | 14,877 |
| 26 | New York | 524.9 | 103,918 | 26 | Maine | 113.9 | 1,514 |
| 27 | Illinois | 517.2 | 66,510 | 27 | Kansas | 112.7 | 3,282 |
| 28 | Mississippi | 516.3 | 15,450 | 28 | Tennessee | 107.9 | 7,121 |
| 29 | Indiana | 511.1 | 33,836 | 29 | North Carolina | 106.0 | 10,646 |
| 30 | Oregon | 506.0 | 20,387 | 30 | Alabama | 102.3 | 4,973 |
| 31 | Washington | 505.7 | 36,264 | 30 | South Carolina | 102.3 | 5,010 |
| 32 | Oklahoma | 493.6 | 19,307 | 32 | Idaho | 101.3 | 1,676 |
| 33 | Arkansas | 478.4 | 14,248 | 33 | New Mexico | 101.1 | 2,109 |
| 34 | Kentucky | 467.2 | 20,674 | 34 | Nebraska | 100.5 | 1,905 |
| 35 | Maine | 447.1 | 5,943 | 35 | Mississippi | 98.8 | 2,955 |
| 36 | West Virginia | 446.8 | 8,240 | 36 | Minnesota | 97.8 | 5,368 |
| 37 | Montana | 442.6 | 4,572 | 37 | Arkansas | 97.7 | 2,911 |
| 37 | Wisconsin | 442.6 | 25,544 | 38 | Wyoming | 96.6 | 566 |
| 39 | Minnesota | 438.2 | 24,055 | 39 | Louisiana | 94.4 | 4,410 |
| 40 | Kansas | 426.9 | 12,430 | 40 | Alaska | 94.3 | 696 |
| 41 | Idaho | 423.1 | 7,002 | 41 | Indiana | 93.9 | 6,217 |
| 42 | Wyoming | 415.5 | 2,435 | 42 | Iowa | 89.7 | 2,803 |
| 43 | Vermont | 406.7 | 2,546 | 43 | Montana | 87.2 | 901 |
| 44 | Nebraska | 403.3 | 7,648 | 44 | Utah | 85.7 | 2,567 |
| 45 | Utah | 396.2 | 11,870 | 45 | Vermont | 83.9 | 525 |
| 46 | Alaska | 395.0 | 2,917 | 46 | Kentucky | 80.9 | 3,581 |
| 47 | Hawaii | 371.3 | 5,315 | 47 | West Virginia | 79.9 | 1,474 |
| 48 | South Dakota | 356.0 | 3,056 | 48 | North Dakota | 76.0 | 575 |
| 49 | Iowa | 349.2 | 10,909 | 49 | South Dakota | 63.1 | 542 |
| 50 | North Dakota | 278.8 | 2,110 | 50 | Hawaii | 62.6 | 896 |

*Per 100,000 unit of population estimates are based on the 2015 U.S. Census population estimates. Numbers for the District of Columbia are: Fraud and Others = 8,928 complaints and 1,328.1 complaints per 100,000 population; Identity Theft = 1,533 victims and 228.0 victims per 100,000 population.

Note: In calculating the state and metropolitan areas rankings, we excluded 20 state-specific data contributors' complaints (the Hawaii Office of Consumer Protection, the Montana, North Carolina and Oregon Departments of Justice, the South Carolina Department of Consumer Affairs, the Tennessee Division of Consumer Affairs, and the Offices of the Attorneys General for Alaska, California, Colorado, Idaho, Indiana, Iowa, Louisiana, Maine, Massachusetts, Michigan, Mississippi, Nevada, Ohio, and Washington).

SOURCE: "Consumer Sentinel Network State Complaint Rates, January 1–December 31, 2015," in *Consumer Sentinel Network Data Book for January–December 2015*, Federal Trade Commission, February 2016, https://www.ftc.gov/system/files/documents/reports/consumer-sentinel-network-data-book-january-december-2015/160229csn-2015databook.pdf (accessed August 10, 2016)

into a search engine yields hundreds of photos of driver's licenses and passports from around the country and the world.

Businesses or institutions that keep lists of Social Security and credit card numbers sometimes inadvertently place the information in an insecure location. In "Foreign Hacker Steals 3.6 Million Social Security Numbers from State Department of Revenue" (GreenvilleOnline.com, October 26, 2012), Tim Smith reports that between August and October 2012 a hacker exploited a vulnerability in the South Carolina Revenue Department's database, stealing millions of Social Security and credit card numbers of state residents.

## FIGURE 4.3

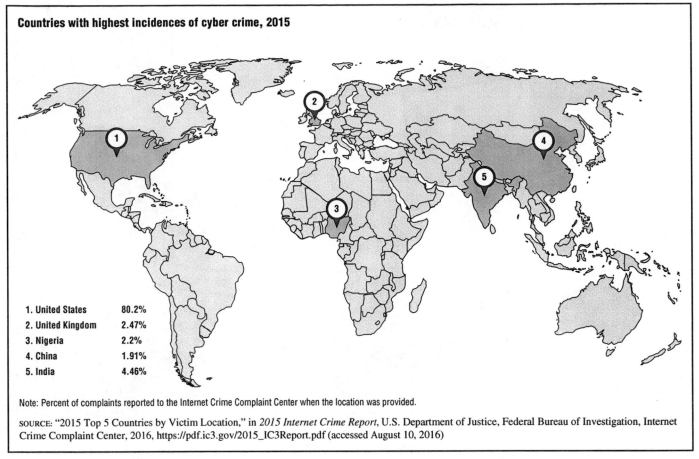

**Countries with highest incidences of cyber crime, 2015**

| | |
|---|---|
| 1. United States | 80.2% |
| 2. United Kingdom | 2.47% |
| 3. Nigeria | 2.2% |
| 4. China | 1.91% |
| 5. India | 4.46% |

Note: Percent of complaints reported to the Internet Crime Complaint Center when the location was provided.

SOURCE: "2015 Top 5 Countries by Victim Location," in *2015 Internet Crime Report*, U.S. Department of Justice, Federal Bureau of Investigation, Internet Crime Complaint Center, 2016, https://pdf.ic3.gov/2015_IC3Report.pdf (accessed August 10, 2016)

In other cases hackers have conspired to perpetrate cybercrimes on a global scale. One notable plot was uncovered in July 2013, when four Russians and a Ukrainian were indicted for breaking into the computer records of several retailers, payment processing firms, and banks, stealing more than 160 million credit card numbers and selling the information on the black market. Targets of the scheme included the convenience store chain 7-Eleven, the banking giant Citigroup, and the French retailer Carrefour. David Voreacos reports in "5 Hackers Charged in Latest Data-Breach Scheme in the U.S." (Bloomberg.com, July 26, 2013) that it was the largest data breach in U.S. history. Between November and December 2013 the retail giant Target was affected by a massive data breach that compromised the credit card records of 40 million customers, as well as the contact information of another 70 million customers.

Another technique thieves use to acquire personal information is known as phishing. Thieves will often send out bogus e-mail messages to scores of people. Typically, these e-mails will look like authentic e-mails from a prominent Internet service provider or bank. The e-mail will inform the receivers that there is something wrong with their account and that the problem can be fixed by clicking on a hyperlink. When victims click on the link, they are then taken to an official-looking site, where they are asked to provide passwords, Social Security information, and even credit card information. The moment the victims type in their personal information, the thieves have them. Once crooks have a credit card in another person's name, the Internet makes it easy to purchase items. No longer do criminals have to risk being caught using someone else's account in a shopping mall or grocery store.

By 2016 hackers were also selling stolen personal data over the Dark Web, an area of the Internet that is accessible only through the use of special software or other computer programs. Because activities that occur on the Dark Web are difficult to trace, individuals can use it to commit online crimes without fear of detection. In "It's Cheaper Than Ever to Buy Someone's Stolen Identity off the Internet" (BGR.com, April 7, 2016), Chris Smith explains that an individual's complete financial information can be acquired for as little as $15 on the Dark Web. Known as a "Fullz" package, the information sold includes an individual's Social Security number, credit card numbers, and other sensitive data.

### Efforts to Combat Identity Theft

In response to these threats, federal law enforcement agencies have established unique task forces and initiatives aimed at countering identity theft. As part of its counteroffensive, the government has also placed a high priority on keeping citizens informed about potential risks. The FBI provides information about cybercrime on its Identity Theft

**FIGURE 4.4**

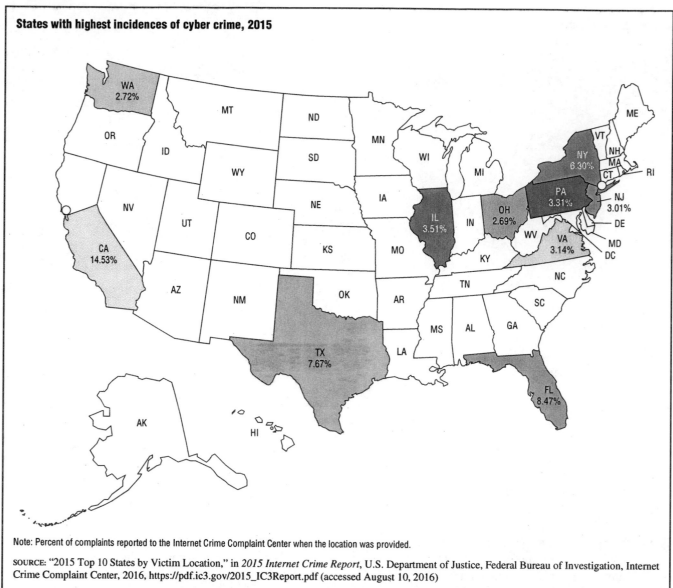

**States with highest incidences of cyber crime, 2015**

Note: Percent of complaints reported to the Internet Crime Complaint Center when the location was provided.

SOURCE: "2015 Top 10 States by Victim Location," in *2015 Internet Crime Report*, U.S. Department of Justice, Federal Bureau of Investigation, Internet Crime Complaint Center, 2016, https://pdf.ic3.gov/2015_IC3Report.pdf (accessed August 10, 2016)

page (2016, https://www.fbi.gov/scams-and-safety/common-fraud-schemes/identity-theft), which contains an overview of law enforcement initiatives that target Internet fraud, as well as valuable advice on how consumers can identify and avoid online threats. Along these lines, IC3 has created a comprehensive list of "Internet Crime Schemes" (2016, https://www.ic3.gov/crimeschemes.aspx), which contains detailed descriptions of some of the most common online scams. The federal government also maintains an Internet Fraud site (2016, https://www.usa.gov/online-safety), which provides a list of resources aimed at helping citizens understand potential Internet threats, while offering information on how to report incidences of identity theft and other online crimes. In addition, the U.S. Department of Homeland Security oversees the Cyber Crimes Center (2016, http://www.ice.gov/cyber-crimes), which is dedicated to fighting identity theft and other cybercrimes both nationally and internationally. The center consists of three

units: the Cyber Crimes Unit, which investigates various forms of Internet fraud, as well as the use of technology in activities such as drug trafficking and money laundering; the Child Exploitation Investigations Unit, which monitors the online operations of sexual predators and child pornographers; and the Computer Forensics Unit, which provides support in decoding and analyzing encrypted data.

U.S. government agencies have also become increasingly active in combating cybercrime by cooperating with law enforcement allies overseas. One major investigation came to a close in December 2012, when the Australian police arrested the fugitive hacker Tobechi Onwuhara. The FBI reports in "Scam on the Run: Fugitive Identity Thief Led Global Criminal Enterprise" (January 22, 2014, http://www.fbi.gov/news/stories/2014/january/fugitive-identity-thief-led-global-criminal-enterprise/fugitive-identity-thief-led-global-criminal-enterprise) that Onwuhara and his

## TABLE 4.8

**Complaints filed with the Internet Crime Complaint Center, by state, 2015**

[Count by victim state*]

| Rank | State | Count | Percent | Rank | State | Count | Percent |
|------|-------|-------|---------|------|-------|-------|---------|
| 1 | California | 34,842 | 14.53% | 27 | Louisiana | 2,639 | 1.10% |
| 2 | Florida | 20,306 | 8.47% | 28 | Connecticut | 2,533 | 1.06% |
| 3 | Texas | 18,392 | 7.67% | 29 | Kentucky | 2,529 | 1.05% |
| 4 | New York | 15,116 | 6.30% | 30 | Oklahoma | 2,402 | 1.00% |
| 5 | Illinois | 8,413 | 3.51% | 31 | Utah | 1,947 | 0.81% |
| 6 | Pennsylvania | 7,927 | 3.31% | 32 | Arkansas | 1,915 | 0.80% |
| 7 | Virginia | 7,534 | 3.14% | 33 | Kansas | 1,799 | 0.75% |
| 8 | New Jersey | 7,215 | 3.01% | 34 | Iowa | 1,593 | 0.66% |
| 9 | Washington | 6,518 | 2.72% | 35 | New Mexico | 1,443 | 0.60% |
| 10 | Ohio | 6,458 | 2.69% | 36 | Alaska | 1,379 | 0.58% |
| 11 | Georgia | 6,374 | 2.66% | 37 | Mississippi | 1,353 | 0.56% |
| 12 | Michigan | 6,265 | 2.61% | 38 | West Virginia | 1,083 | 0.45% |
| 13 | North Carolina | 6,112 | 2.55% | 39 | Nebraska | 1,079 | 0.45% |
| 14 | Maryland | 5,944 | 2.48% | 40 | Hawaii | 1,074 | 0.45% |
| 15 | Arizona | 5,770 | 2.41% | 41 | Idaho | 1,068 | 0.45% |
| 16 | Indiana | 5,716 | 2.38% | 42 | New Hampshire | 945 | 0.39% |
| 17 | Colorado | 5,270 | 2.20% | 43 | District of Columbia | 890 | 0.37% |
| 18 | Tennessee | 4,571 | 1.91% | 44 | Maine | 782 | 0.33% |
| 19 | Massachusetts | 4,372 | 1.82% | 45 | Delaware | 761 | 0.32% |
| 20 | Missouri | 4,210 | 1.76% | 46 | Montana | 733 | 0.31% |
| 21 | Nevada | 3,660 | 1.53% | 47 | Rhode Island | 638 | 0.27% |
| 22 | Alabama | 3,507 | 1.46% | 48 | Wyoming | 475 | 0.20% |
| 23 | Wisconsin | 3,427 | 1.43% | 49 | South Dakota | 386 | 0.16% |
| 24 | Minnesota | 3,303 | 1.38% | 50 | Vermont | 382 | 0.16% |
| 25 | Oregon | 3,294 | 1.37% | 51 | North Dakota | 368 | 0.15% |
| 26 | South Carolina | 3,099 | 1.29% | | | | |

*This information is based on the total number of complaints from each state and the District of Columbia when the complainant provided state information.

SOURCE: Adapted from "2015 Overall State Statistics," in *2015 Internet Crime Report*, U.S. Department of Justice, Federal Bureau of Investigation, Internet Crime Complaint Center, 2016, https://pdf.ic3.gov/2015_IC3Report.pdf (accessed August 10, 2016)

## TABLE 4.9

**Financial losses reported to the Internet Crime Complaint Center, by state, 2015**

[Loss by victim state*]

| Rank | State | Loss | Percent | Rank | State | Loss | Percent |
|------|-------|------|---------|------|-------|------|---------|
| 1 | California | $195,490,403 | 21.75% | 27 | Oregon | $9,630,730 | 1.07% |
| 2 | Florida | $94,526,977 | 10.52% | 28 | Minnesota | $9,310,006 | 1.04% |
| 3 | Texas | $62,976,459 | 7.01% | 29 | Louisiana | $8,255,605 | 0.92% |
| 4 | New York | $58,083,855 | 6.46% | 30 | Oklahoma | $8,027,851 | 0.89% |
| 5 | Illinois | $33,259,081 | 3.70% | 31 | Utah | $6,500,856 | 0.72% |
| 6 | Washington | $27,642,344 | 3.08% | 32 | Alaska | $6,217,134 | 0.69% |
| 7 | Pennsylvania | $26,204,814 | 2.92% | 33 | Kentucky | $6,127,717 | 0.68% |
| 8 | West Virginia | $23,346,881 | 2.60% | 34 | Arkansas | $4,817,249 | 0.54% |
| 9 | New Jersey | $21,332,409 | 2.37% | 35 | Iowa | $4,239,477 | 0.47% |
| 10 | Michigan | $20,591,750 | 2.29% | 36 | Kansas | $3,879,576 | 0.43% |
| 11 | Virginia | $20,098,497 | 2.24% | 37 | Hawaii | $3,395,581 | 0.38% |
| 12 | North Carolina | $18,901,866 | 2.10% | 38 | Mississippi | $3,099,537 | 0.34% |
| 13 | Arizona | $18,087,735 | 2.01% | 39 | New Hampshire | $3,048,031 | 0.34% |
| 14 | Georgia | $17,950,722 | 2.00% | 40 | Nebraska | $2,998,359 | 0.33% |
| 15 | Massachusetts | $16,827,318 | 1.87% | 41 | New Mexico | $2,872,694 | 0.32% |
| 16 | Maryland | $16,071,212 | 1.79% | 42 | District of Columbia | $2,729,582 | 0.30% |
| 17 | Colorado | $15,411,608 | 1.71% | 43 | Idaho | $2,493,999 | 0.28% |
| 18 | Ohio | $15,280,845 | 1.70% | 44 | Rhode Island | $1,816,091 | 0.20% |
| 19 | Missouri | $14,530,794 | 1.62% | 45 | South Dakota | $1,733,244 | 0.19% |
| 20 | South Carolina | $14,176,493 | 1.58% | 46 | Montana | $1,633,263 | 0.18% |
| 21 | Nevada | $13,192,963 | 1.47% | 47 | Delaware | $1,581,291 | 0.18% |
| 22 | Indiana | $12,275,440 | 1.37% | 48 | Wyoming | $1,507,488 | 0.17% |
| 23 | Alabama | $11,996,901 | 1.33% | 49 | Maine | $1,018,078 | 0.11% |
| 24 | Tennessee | $11,208,885 | 1.25% | 50 | North Dakota | $998,022 | 0.11% |
| 25 | Connecticut | $10,499,866 | 1.17% | 51 | Vermont | $656,631 | 0.07% |
| 26 | Wisconsin | $10,101,998 | 1.12% | | | | |

*This information is based on the total number of complaints from each state and the District of Columbia when the complainant provided state information.

SOURCE: Adapted from "2015 Overall State Statistics," in *2015 Internet Crime Report*, U.S. Department of Justice, Federal Bureau of Investigation, Internet Crime Complaint Center, 2016, https://pdf.ic3.gov/2015_IC3Report.pdf (accessed August 10, 2016)

TABLE 4.10

**Identity theft complaints received by the Consumer Sentinel Network, by victims' age, 2013–15**

| Consumer age | Calendar year 2013 | | Calendar year 2014 | | Calendar year 2015 | |
|---|---|---|---|---|---|---|
| | Complaints | Percentages | Complaints | Percentages | Complaints | Percentages |
| 19 and under | 15,226 | 6% | 15,511 | 5% | 20,905 | 5% |
| 20–29 | 48,697 | 19% | 46,765 | 17% | 55,763 | 14% |
| 30–39 | 47,682 | 19% | 49,055 | 18% | 65,850 | 16% |
| 40–49 | 45,246 | 18% | 51,569 | 18% | 81,937 | 20% |
| 50–59 | 44,084 | 17% | 55,243 | 20% | 97,308 | 24% |
| 60–69 | 31,896 | 12% | 38,392 | 14% | 62,060 | 15% |
| 70 and over | 22,103 | 9% | 21,941 | 8% | 26,305 | 6% |
| **Total reporting age** | **254,934** | | **278,476** | | **410,128** | |

Note: Percentages are based on the total number of victims reporting their age in Consumer Sentinel Network (CSN) identify theft complaints for each calendar year: calendar year 2013 = 254,934; calendar year 2014 = 278,476; and calendar year 2015 = 410,128. Of the consumers who contacted the Federal Trade Commission (FTC), 84% reported their age in calendar year 2015, 84% in calendar year 2014 and 88% in calendar year 2013.

SOURCE: "Consumer Sentinel Network Identity Theft Complaints by Victims' Age, Calendar Years 2013 through 2015," in *Consumer Sentinel Network Data Book for January–December 2015*, Federal Trade Commission, February 2016, https://www.ftc.gov/system/files/documents/reports/consumer-sentinel-network-data-book-january-december-2015/160229csn-2015databook.pdf (accessed August 10, 2016)

TABLE 4.11

**Complaints received by the Internet Crime Complaint Center, by sex, age, and amount of financial loss, 2015**

[Victims]

| Age range | Male count | Male loss | Female count | Female loss | Total count | Total loss |
|---|---|---|---|---|---|---|
| Under 20 | 6,086 | $5,535,268 | 4,349 | $2,543,810 | 10,435<br>3.62% | $8,079,077 |
| 20–29 | 26,539 | $45,744,076 | 24,763 | $25,222,975 | 51,302<br>17.81% | $70,967,050 |
| 30–39 | 30,153 | $102,334,135 | 26,866 | $54,706,343 | 57,019<br>19.80% | $157,040,478 |
| 40–49 | 28,694 | $158,386,367 | 29,559 | $105,668,109 | 58,253<br>20.23% | $264,054,476 |
| 50–59 | 31,473 | $171,954,578 | 27,655 | $115,646,653 | 59,128<br>20.53% | $287,601,231 |
| 60 and over | 29,453 | $153,157,867 | 22,422 | $129,811,342 | 51,875<br>18.01% | $282,969,208 |
| **Totals** | **152,398**<br>52.91% | **$637,112,290** | **135,614**<br>47.09% | **$433,599,232** | **288,012** | **$1,070,711,522** |

SOURCE: Adapted from "2015 Complainant Demographics," in *2015 Internet Crime Report*, U.S. Department of Justice, Federal Bureau of Investigation, Internet Crime Complaint Center, 2016, https://pdf.ic3.gov/2015_IC3Report.pdf (accessed August 10, 2016)

criminal associates operated a home equity line-of-credit scam, using the financial information of hundreds of U.S. homeowners to steal approximately $13 million. His arrest was the culmination of an international manhunt that lasted nearly five years.

In another high-profile case with an international scope, in 2014 the FBI, working with the IRS's Criminal Investigations division, uncovered an identity theft operation that had stolen $10 million from 2,400 victims over a nearly 10-year span. In "5 Indicted in Massive Identity-Fraud Scheme" (Post-Gazette.com, April 23, 2014), Rich Lord explains that the stolen funds eventually found their way to criminal organizations in Nigeria. That same year U.S. Secret Service agents arrested the hacker Roman Seleznev (1984–), the son of a Russian parliament member, on charges of stealing credit card information from financial institutions and various other businesses. According to Martha Bellisle, in "U.S. Jury Gets Case of Russian Man Charged with Hacking" (PhillyVoice.com, August 25, 2016), between 2008 and 2014 Seleznev stole approximately $170 million from banks and companies worldwide. Investigators found 1.7 million credit card numbers stored on Seleznev's laptop at the time of his arrest. In August 2016 Seleznev was convicted on 38 counts of hacking in a U.S. court.

## INTERNET FRAUD

Internet fraud takes other forms than identity theft, including auction fraud, phishing schemes, and fund-transfer scams. The FTC notes in *Consumer Sentinel Network Data Book for January–December 2015* that 52% of fraud complainants reported the method used by

TABLE 4.12

**How identity theft victims' information was misused, 2013–15**

| Theft subtype | Percentages | | |
|---|---|---|---|
| | CY-2013 | CY-2014 | CY-2015 |
| **Government documents or benefits fraud** | | | |
| Tax- or wage-related fraud | 30.1% | 32.8% | 45.3% |
| Government benefits applied for\received | 2.4% | 4.1% | 2.5% |
| Other government documents issued\forged | 1.0% | 1.3% | 1.1% |
| Driver's license issued\forged | 0.6% | 0.5% | 0.3% |
| **Total** | **34.1%** | **38.7%** | **49.2%** |
| **Credit card fraud** | | | |
| New accounts | 11.2% | 12.5% | 11.6% |
| Existing accounts | 5.7% | 4.9% | 4.2% |
| **Total** | **16.9%** | **17.4%** | **15.8%** |
| **Phone or utilities fraud** | | | |
| Utilities—new accounts | 8.9% | 7.6% | 5.1% |
| Wireless—new accounts | 3.5% | 3.5% | 3.7% |
| Unauthorized charges to existing accounts | 0.6% | 0.7% | 0.6% |
| Telephone—new accounts | 0.6% | 0.7% | 0.5% |
| **Total** | **13.6%** | **12.5%** | **9.9%** |
| **Bank fraud** | | | |
| Electronic fund transfer | 3.7% | 3.3% | 2.3% |
| New accounts | 2.2% | 2.8% | 2.0% |
| Existing accounts | 1.8% | 1.5% | 1.1% |
| Other deposit accounts[a] | — | 0.6% | 0.5% |
| **Total** | **7.7%** | **8.2%** | **5.9%** |
| **Loan fraud** | | | |
| Business\personal\student loan | 2.1% | 2.6% | 2.1% |
| Auto loan\lease | 1.1% | 1.1% | 0.8% |
| Real estate loan | 0.8% | 0.7% | 0.6% |
| **Total** | **4.0%** | **4.4%** | **3.5%** |
| **Employment-related fraud** | | | |
| Employment-related fraud | 5.6% | 4.9% | 3.3% |
| **Other identity theft** | | | |
| Uncertain | 8.5% | 11.2% | 10.8% |
| Data breach | 1.3% | 2.1% | 3.0% |
| Internet\email | 1.7% | 1.5% | 1.2% |
| Miscellaneous | 8.7% | 3.3% | 1.2% |
| Medical | 1.0% | 0.1% | 0.8% |
| Evading the law | 1.0% | 0.9% | 0.6% |
| Apartment or house rented | 0.5% | 0.6% | 0.5% |
| Insurance | 0.3% | 0.4% | 0.4% |
| Prepaid debit cards[b] | — | 0.3% | 0.3% |
| Securities\other investments | 0.2% | 0.1% | 0.1% |
| Property rental fraud | 0.1% | 0.1% | 0.1% |
| Bankruptcy | 0.1% | 0.2% | 0.1% |
| Child support | 0.1% | 0.1% | 0.1% |
| Magazines | 0.1% | <0.1% | <0.1% |
| **Total** | **23.6%** | **21.9%** | **19.2%** |
| **Attempted identity theft** | | | |
| Attempted identity theft | 7.2% | 4.8% | 3.7% |

**TABLE 4.12**

**How identity theft victims' information was misused, 2013–15** [CONTINUED]

[a]Theft subtype "Other deposit accounts" was added to the database in CY-2014.
[b]Theft subtype "Prepaid debit cards" was added to the database in CY-2014.
CY = Calendar year.
Note: Percentages are based on the total number of Consumer Sentinel Network identity complaints for each calendar year (CY): CY-2013 = 290, CY-2014 = 332,647; and CY-2015 = 490,220. Note that 14% of identity theft complaints include more than one type of identity theft in CY-2015, 17% in CY = 2014 and 16% in CY-2013.

SOURCE: "Consumer Sentinel Network Identity Theft Complaints: How Victims' Information Is Misused, Calendar Years 2013 through 2015," in *Consumer Sentinel Network Data Book for January–December 2015*, Federal Trade Commission, February 2016, https://www.ftc.gov/system/files/documents/reports/consumer-sentinel-network-data-book-january-december-2015/160229csn-2015databook.pdf (accessed August 10, 2016)

of Internet auction fraud. (See Table 4.5.) Another type of scheme involves the wire transfer of funds drawn on what turns out to be a bogus check. Typically, a victim receives overpayment for a product or service that he or she has sold and is instructed to immediately deposit the money and wire a portion to a third party; however, the initial check payment turns out to be false, leaving the victim at a loss.

Although identity theft and auction fraud make up a sizable proportion of crimes on the Internet, countless other frauds have been perpetrated over the years. These range from false merchandise advertised on a phony web page to work-at-home e-mail schemes in which the victim is told to send in money as an initial investment.

One of the more famous e-mail scams is the Nigerian letter fraud scam, which has been circulating via traditional mail since the early 1980s. In its electronic form, an e-mail purportedly from a "Nigerian dignitary" informs the victim that he or she has the opportunity to receive vast sums of money currently being held in Nigeria. When the victim responds to the message, he or she is then told that the Nigerian dignitary requires money in advance, usually to bribe government officials, so that the funds can be released and deposited in the victim's account. According to the FTC, in *Consumer Sentinel Network Data Book for January–December 2015*, Nigeria was home to the fourth-highest percentage (1%, or 7,501) of Internet fraud perpetrators in 2015, behind the United States (96%, or 1.1 million), Canada (1%, or 17,124), and the United Kingdom (1%, or 7,591).

Still other, more elaborate scams were designed to manipulate the stock market. Such scams were particularly effective in the late 1990s during the stock market bubble. The best known of these is the pump-and-dump scam. The criminals invest in a stock that is lightly traded and then trick online investors into buying it. Typically, this involves posting fake documents and press releases on financial websites or sending fake e-mail announcements,

companies to contact them: 75% were contacted by phone, 8% were solicited through e-mail, and 6% had initial contact via a website. (See Table 4.13.) In comparison, 4% were contacted by mail.

In a typical Internet auction scheme, a con artist advertises merchandise on an auction site until a buyer is found. The buyer then sends a payment but receives no merchandise. In 2015 the FTC received 2,430 complaints

**TABLE 4.13**

**Complaints received by the Consumer Sentinel Network, by perpetrator's method of contacting victim, 2013–15**

| Contact method | Calendar year 2013 | | Calendar year 2014 | | Calendar year 2015 | |
|---|---|---|---|---|---|---|
| | Complaints | Percentages | Complaints | Percentages | Complaints | Percentages |
| Phone | 230,462 | 41% | 386,807 | 54% | 485,481 | 75% |
| E-mail | 184,469 | 32% | 166,545 | 23% | 54,089 | 8% |
| Internet-web site\others | 82,757 | 15% | 79,900 | 11% | 39,728 | 6% |
| Mail | 29,089 | 5% | 29,113 | 4% | 28,127 | 4% |
| Other | 41,878 | 7% | 48,143 | 7% | 43,392 | 7% |
| **Total reporting contact method** | **568,655** | | **710,508** | | **650,817** | |

Note: Percentages are based on the total number of Consumer Sentinel Network (CSN) fraud complaints for each calendar year where consumers reported the company's method of initial contact; calendar year 2013 = 568,655; calendar year 2014 = 710,508; and calendar year 2015 = 650,817. Of the total, 52% reported this information during calendar year 2015, 45% in calendar year 2014 and 47% for calendar year 2013.

SOURCE: "Consumer Sentinel Network Fraud Complaints by Company's Method of Contacting Consumers, Calendar Years 2013 through 2015," in *Consumer Sentinel Network Data Book for January–December 2015*, Federal Trade Commission, February 2016, https://www.ftc.gov/system/files/documents/reports/consumer-sentinel-network-data-book-january-december-2015/160229csn-2015databook.pdf (accessed August 12, 2016)

telling investors that the company is either about to be bought out or has developed a new, moneymaking product. In other instances scam artists bribe lesser-known stock pundits to tout the lifeless stock. After the stock takes off, the criminals simply sell their holdings, leaving other investors holding the bag as the stock goes back down to sustainable levels.

In *2013 Internet Crime Report* (2014, https://pdf.ic3.gov/2013_IC3Report.pdf), the IC3 reports that beginning in July 2007 it began receiving complaints about an international scam targeting law firms and involving third-party debt collection. In this type of fraud, criminals approach U.S. law firms via e-mail seeking legal assistance with the wire transfer of a large sum of money. The perpetrators then send the law firms counterfeit checks, requesting that the firms subsequently wire the money in question (minus legal fees) to a third party; in some instances, fake checks were issued for amounts exceeding $100,000. In one high-profile case of this type, a Nigerian man named Emmanuel Ekhator operated a third-party debt collection scam that ultimately defrauded U.S. law firms out of more than $29 million. In August 2011 a Nigerian court ruled to allow Ekhator's extradition to the United States, where he was to stand trial on fraud charges in a U.S. district court in Pennsylvania. In 2013 Ekhator was sentenced to 100 months in prison and ordered to pay restitution of nearly $11.1 million.

## VIRUSES

The term *computer virus* is often used to refer to all malware (*mal*icious soft*ware*)—that is, programs such as viruses, worms, and Trojan horses that infect and destroy computer files. Technically speaking, viruses are self-replicating programs that insert themselves into other computer files. The virus is spread when the file is transferred to another computer via the Internet or portable media such as a CD-ROM. The first computer virus was created in 1982, when 15-year-old Rich Skrenta (1967–) wrote Elk Cloner, a virus that attached itself to an Apple DOS 3.3 operating system and spread to other computers by floppy disk.

People have all sorts of reasons for creating and sending viruses. Some viruses are written as pranks. Others are written by political activists or terrorists. Still other viruses are intended to injure specific corporations. Regardless of the virus creators' intentions, the number of viruses infecting the world's computers continues to grow. The first computer worm to attract attention appeared in 1988 and was written by Robert T. Morris (1965–), a graduate student at Cornell University. Worms are self-contained, self-replicating computer programs that spread through the Internet from computer to computer. Unlike viruses, they spread via the Internet under their own power and do not rely on people's actions or files to move from one machine to another. Like viruses, worms can destroy files and take advantage of vulnerabilities in computer programs or operating systems.

A Trojan horse does not self-replicate and is typically disguised as something more innocent, such as an e-mail attachment. When the user opens the attachment, malicious code is unleashed on the computer. As malware has become more advanced, the distinctions between types of malware have become less obvious. For example, Trojan horses often contain viruses that replicate through computer files. For this reason the term *virus* is used in this chapter to designate any type of malware, unless otherwise specified.

Viruses behave in a number of different ways. For example, the Netsky virus is typically hidden in an e-mail attachment and is launched when the user opens the attachment. Once active, Netsky sets up its own e-mail protocol, looks for e-mail accounts on the hard drive, and mass-mails itself to these accounts. Another virus named

MSBlaster appeared in August 2003 and quickly wormed its way through the Internet, infecting hundreds of thousands of computers in a day through vulnerability in the Windows operating system. Once on a personal computer, the virus instructed the computer to take part in a distributed denial-of-service (DDoS) attack on the Windowsupdate.com website. (A DDoS attack occurs when thousands of computers are used to access a single website, thus making it inaccessible.) Other viruses known as "bombs" lie dormant in a computer until a specific date is registered on the computer's clock. Still other viruses disable any virus removal program on the computer, making the virus difficult to remove. The largest DDoS attack in history occurred in October 2016, when a widespread malware attack disrupted Internet access to a number of major websites, including the NYTimes.com and Reddit.com. Lily Hay Newman reports in "What We Know about Friday's Massive East Coast Internet Outage" (Wired.com, October 21, 2016) that the target of the attack was Dyn, a domain name system services firm that connects consumers to thousands of Internet Protocol addresses worldwide. As of November 2016, the perpetrators had not yet been identified.

Meanwhile, advances in information technology have coincided with a rapid evolution in viruses. Harriet Taylor reports in "Biggest Cybersecurity Threats in 2016" (CNBC.com, December 28, 2015) that the proliferation of smartphones, connected devices, and cloud computing is creating new opportunities for hackers to create security threats. One type of virus, known as a headless worm, specifically targets smart devices such as phones, watches, and electronic medical instruments. Another virus, two-faced malware, infiltrates computers and devices by disguising itself as a harmless software program, only later transforming itself into malicious code. At the same time, Taylor notes, hackers are also developing innovative techniques for eluding detection. One notable antidetection virus is called ghostware, a type of malware that deletes all traces of its activity after it finishes infecting a system.

## Computer Emergency Response Team

Two weeks after the Morris worm was let loose on the Internet in November 1988, the Defense Advanced Research Projects Agency formed the Computer Emergency Response Team (CERT) with headquarters at Carnegie Mellon University in Pittsburgh, Pennsylvania. The purpose of the organization is to identify threats to the Internet as a whole. CERT coordinates the actions of the private and public sectors when major Internet incidents occur. Although CERT issues alerts on individual viruses that affect home users, it is more concerned with the big picture. The organization provides emergency incident response for network access ports, root dedicated name servers, and other components that make up the Internet's infrastructure. It analyzes virus code to develop solutions that thwart viruses. CERT also coordinates responses to large automated attacks against the Internet, and monitors threats to U.S. government computers in coordination with the U.S. Computer Emergency Readiness Team, which was formed in 2003 by the Department of Homeland Security.

In 2008 the Internet security researcher Dan Kaminsky discovered a vulnerability in the design of the domain name system (DNS). The security breach allowed criminals to attack the system and reroute Internet traffic to imposter websites, with users completely unaware that they had been directed to fraudulent sites. How it worked was fairly simple. Each time an address such as http://www.google.com is entered into the address bar of an Internet browser, the browser contacts one of many domain name servers distributed on the Internet. Once the browser makes the request from the DNS, the name server sends back the corresponding address number, which for Google is 209.85.225.147. The Internet browser then uses this numeric address to access the site (Google in this case). Each domain name server has a cache that stores widely used sites' names and numeric addresses for a limited time. The vulnerability, known as "cache poisoning," worked by substituting a vandal-controlled Internet address for the one normally linked with a well-known domain name. For a name not stored in its cache, a name server forwards the request to other name servers on the network until it finds the address or one very similar. The attack allowed criminals to flood the DNS with requests that would ensure that their site addresses were stored and distributed rather than the legitimate ones.

In March 2008 Internet security experts met secretly at the Microsoft Corporation's headquarters in Redmond, Washington, to discuss the problem and determine a plan of action. They did not reveal the vulnerability to the public until patches were available to fix the situation in July 2008. As reported by Stuart Corner in "Major DNS Flaw: Details Likely to Be Revealed at Black Hat" (iTWire.com, August 5, 2008), Kaminsky explained the effectiveness of the patch in his blog at DoxPara Research:

> After the attack: A bad guy has a one in 65,000 chance of stealing your Internet connection, and he can try a couple thousand times a second.

> After the patch: A bad guy has a one in a couple hundred million, or even a couple billion chance of stealing your Internet connection. He can still try to do so a couple thousand times a second, but it's going to make *a lot* of noise.

In spite of the proven success of the DNS patch, computer security breaches remain a constant threat in the second decade of the 21st century. The Internet Security firm Sophos reports in "Our Cybersecurity Predictions for 2016" (November 12, 2015, https://blogs.sophos.com/2015/12/11/our-cybersecurity-predictions-for-2016/) that the growth of mobile data, social networking platforms, and cloud computing have provided hackers and other criminals with new ways to exploit the online vulnerabilities of both businesses and individuals. Indeed, 2015 saw a sharp rise in the volume of malware attacks on Android phone platforms, and the proliferation of personal data stored on mobile devices and social networking accounts provided potential hackers with a host of new ways to access and exploit sensitive information. At the same time, corporations who used cloud computing services to manage financial data were increasingly at risk of attack.

At times, threats to Internet security originated not from criminals or hackers but from routine programming errors. The potential for system flaws to generate massive security breaches became evident in April 2014, when reports emerged that OpenSSL, an open-source encryption software used to transmit data over the Internet, contained a coding defect that enabled servers to expose sensitive user information online. In "How the Heartbleed Bug Slipped under the Radar More Than Two Years Ago" (Business Insider.com, April 10, 2014), Lisa Eadicicco explains that the security flaw, known as the Heartbleed bug, was inadvertently introduced by the German programmer Robin Seggelman in 2011 and went undetected for more than two years. Further controversy arose when it was discovered that the National Security Agency had actually discovered the bug shortly after it first emerged but had declined to reveal the fact to the public. Michael Riley notes in "NSA Said to Exploit Heartbleed Bug for Intelligence for Years" (Bloomberg.com, April 12, 2014) that the agency used the vulnerability to gather information with the potential to pose security threats to the United States. Although programmers quickly devised patches for Heartbleed, it was estimated that the bug had compromised up to two-thirds of all Internet sites in the period before its exposure.

## E-CRIME AND ORGANIZATIONS

Except for computer viruses, e-crimes that affect individuals, such as auction fraud or identity theft, are usually different from the e-crimes that affect businesses. Most large organizations are concerned about hackers breaking into their servers or dissatisfied employees sabotaging their computer network. In *US Cybersecurity: Progress Stalled—Key Findings from the 2015 US State of Cybercrime Survey* (July 2015, http://www.pwc.com/us/en/increasing-it-effectiveness/publications/assets/2015-us-cybercrime-survey.pdf), the professional services firm PricewaterhouseCoopers reports on the biggest cyberthreats confronting businesses in 2015. According to the firm, a quarter (25%) of companies surveyed said hackers posed the gravest threat to their organization in 2015; 12% reported that current employees represented the most significant risk to their cybersecurity. Another 8% of companies believed that foreign countries posed the biggest

threat, whereas 6% were most concerned about activists or other politically motivated groups or individuals.

PricewaterhouseCoopers reveals in *Global Economic Crime Survey 2016* (February 2016, http://www.pwc.com/gx/en/economic-crime-survey/pdf/GlobalEconomicCrimeSurvey2016.pdf) that in 2016 nearly one-third (32%) of organizations surveyed reported that they had been victimized by a cyberattack, while more than half (53%) believed that the risk of cybercrime had increased over the previous year. Despite this increased concern, more than one-third (37%) of these organizations had implemented a comprehensive response plan to address potential cyberthreats. Meanwhile, during this period the nature of cyberattacks on businesses and financial organizations continued to evolve. According to Kaja Whitehouse, in "Hackers Steal Directly from Banks in 'New Era' of Cyber Crime" (USAToday.com, February 16, 2015), a report issued by Kaspersky Labs, a leading antivirus software firm, revealed that a global hacking organization was using malware to seize control over the computer systems of more than 100 banks in 30 nations worldwide. Dubbed "Carbanak" by Kaspersky, the malware had enabled the hackers to steal more than $1 billion between 2013 and 2015. As of November 2016, the perpetrators had not yet been identified.

By 2016 hackers had also begun using extortion as a means of compromising large organizations. In November 2014 a group of hackers calling themselves the Guardians of Peace infiltrated the computer network of Sony Pictures, publishing unreleased films, personal information relating to Sony employees, and e-mail documents on the Internet. In "What Caused Sony Hack: What We Know Now" (CNN.com, December 29, 2014), Jose Pagliery notes that before the incident the hackers had written to several Sony executives threatening to hack into the company's network unless they received monetary compensation. Although the U.S. government initially suspected that the North Korean government was behind the attack, no conclusive evidence of its involvement ever emerged. The following year, in July 2015, an organization known as The Impact Team hacked into Ashley Madison, an online extramarital affair dating site, and gained access to the names and addresses of the site's 33 million customers. According to the article "Ashley Madison Hack Victims Receive Blackmail Letters" (BBC.com, December 15, 2015), the hackers subsequently blackmailed a number of Ashley Madison members, threatening to divulge their involvement with the site unless they received monetary compensation.

## CYBERSECURITY AND GOVERNMENT

As malware becomes increasingly sophisticated, even government information networks have proven vulnerable to hackers. Despite having access to some of the most advanced security measures in the world, the U.S.

government has fallen victim to several cyberattacks since the early 21st century. For example, Evan Perez and Shimon Prokupecz report in "U.S. Data Hack May Be 4 Times Larger Than the Government Originally Said" (CNN.com, June 24, 2015) that in June 2015 the Office of Personnel Management (OPM) revealed that its electronic records system had been infiltrated by hackers. Although the OPM maintained that the attack had compromised the personal information of roughly 4.2 million employees and job applicants, the FBI head James Comey (1960–) estimated that the total number of victims exceeded 18 million. Perez and Prokupecz note that investigators determined that the data breaches originated in China and that the Chinese government likely played a role in the attack. In "Why the OPM Hack Is Far Worse Than You Imagine" (Lawfareblog.com, March 11, 2016), Michael Adams suggests the breach represented the largest single cyberattack in U.S. history.

During the 2016 presidential election campaign foreign hackers launched a series of damaging cyberattacks in the United States, targeting political organizations, government agencies, and even individual politicians. According to Alicia Parlapiano, in "What We Know about the Cyberattack on Democratic Politicians" (NYTimes.com, August 16, 2016), between 2015 and 2016 Russian hackers gained access to the computer records of both the Democratic National Committee (DNC) and the Democratic Congressional Campaign Committee. The international activist group Wikileaks eventually obtained a large portion of the stolen data. In July 2016, on the eve of the Democratic National Convention, Wikileaks released more than 20,000 DNC e-mails online. A number of the e-mails seemed to provide evidence that DNC officials favored the presidential candidate Hillary Rodham Clinton (1947—) over Senator Bernie Sanders (1941–; I-VT) during the primary campaign, despite the fact the committee is obligated to remain neutral. In the aftermath of the e-mail leak, Representative Debbie Wasserman Schultz (1966–; D-FL) resigned from her position as DNC chair. A month after the DNC e-mails became public, a hacker named Guccifer 2.0 published the personal phone numbers and e-mail addresses of approximately 200 Democratic lawmakers, which had been obtained through stolen Democratic Congressional Campaign Committee documents. According to Parlapiano, U.S. investigators believed the hackers were employed by Russian intelligence officials. Meanwhile, in August 2016 hackers breached the voter registration systems in Illinois and Arizona, raising concerns that Russia was actively trying to tamper with the 2016 presidential election.

These data breaches came at a time when the American public's confidence in the ability of institutions to safeguard their personal information had diminished considerably. Distrust of the government's ability to protect

**TABLE 4.14**

**Confidence among Millennials and other generations that institutions will safeguard their personal data, by institution, 2016**

[% "A lot of trust"]

| | Millennials | Other generations |
|---|---|---|
| | % | % |
| Primary bank | 67 | 56 |
| Health insurance companies | 34 | 23 |
| Credit card companies | 27 | 22 |
| Cellphone platform | 25 | 16 |
| Email provider | 23 | 17 |
| Brick-and-mortar retailers | 23 | 14 |
| Cellphone carrier | 17 | 13 |
| Federal government | 19 | 12 |
| State government | 18 | 11 |
| Online retailers | 11 | 10 |
| Social networking websites or applications | 4 | 2 |

SOURCE: John Fleming and Amy Adkins, "Millennials Have the Most Trust in Institutions to Safeguard Their Personal Data," in *Data Security: Not a Big Concern for Millennials*, The Gallup Organization, June 9, 2016, http://www.gallup.com/businessjournal/192401/data-security-not-big-concern-millennials.aspx?g_source=smartphones&g_medium=search&g_campaign=tiles (accessed August 15, 2016). Copyright © 2016 Gallup, Inc. All rights reserved. The content is used with permission; however, Gallup retains all rights of republication.

sensitive data was particularly high in 2016. This trend was especially true among older generations; members of the Millennial generation, a demographic that includes people born between the early 1980s and the turn of the century, expressed somewhat more trust in the federal government's ability to safeguard personal data. As Table 4.14 shows, 19% of Millennials reported that they trusted the federal government to protect their personal information in 2016, compared with only 12% of Americans from other generations.

## INTELLECTUAL PROPERTY THEFT

Intellectual property, which includes copyrighted material such as games, software, and movies, is a huge part of the U.S. economy. These industries are important to the economy and to the people employed in them, and financial profit is critical for those who create music, video games, books, or software. As such, the issue of intellectual property theft is of vital importance to the federal government.

Intellectual property theft has posed perhaps the greatest single threat to the copyright industries since the 1990s. The Internet, along with powerful computers and the conversion of nearly every type of media into digital form, has made copying and distributing intellectual property easy even within the United States. Once a thief finds a way around the copyright protection that exists on the digitized copyrighted material, the computer provides an easy way to store the material. Because digital media do not degrade when copied, the thief can produce perfect duplicates. Distribution of the media to any country in the world is easily accomplished over the Internet using peer-to-peer networks or file transfer protocol sites, which employ standard file copying protocols to upload and download files on a server.

## Creative Industries Fight Copyright Violators

Indeed, one of the biggest threats to the music industry's profitability has been peer-to-peer networks. During the late 1990s peer-to-peer networks were created to connect music lovers around the world. Napster was the largest of these, with tens of millions of users at its peak. Like all peer-to-peer networks, Napster did not contain any music on its own website. Instead, Napster tracked the songs and albums its members had on their individual computers. By logging into the central server of the network owned by Napster, members could first locate what music files were available on the network and then proceed to download the music from another member's computer. From the music industry's point of view, the problem with peer-to-peer networks was that once an album made it on to the network, millions of people suddenly had access to it for free.

In December 1999, less than a year after the Napster website opened, the Recording Industry Association of America (RIAA) filed a case against the network in U.S. federal district court. The RIAA represented most major recording labels and claimed that Napster infringed on the companies' copyrights. The court sided with the RIAA. Napster appealed the ruling, but in September 2001 it settled with the RIAA by paying $26 million for copyright infringement. Before the case was settled, the Napster creator Shawn Fanning (1980–) sold Napster to Bertelsmann, a huge German media conglomerate. Bertelsmann dismantled the file-sharing network and constructed a database of songs that could be downloaded for a fee, part of which goes to pay the record company royalties.

The court's ruling against the practice of open music file sharing meant that the RIAA and other organizations could continue to sue peer-to-peer networks that allowed the sharing of copyrighted material for free. However, while the RIAA was suing Napster, a new problem arose. Networks began popping up that did not have a clearly defined center of operations. For example, the Kazaa and Gnutella networks had no central server to let members know who on the network had which songs. Instead, each member of the network installed a program that allowed him or her to see the individual music libraries of others on the network. Michael Desmond estimates in "Sneaky Sharing" (PCWorld.com, September 2, 2004) that despite the music industry's attempts to curb illegal file sharing, users were developing new techniques for acquiring music as sales dropped from an all-time high of $14.6 billion in 2000 to $11.9 billion in 2003, which was well after the original Napster was shut down.

In late 2003 the RIAA began going after individual file swappers. Lee Rainie et al. of the Pew Research Center report in *Data Memo: The Impact of Recording Industry Suits against Music File Swappers* (January 2004, http://www.pewinternet.org/~/media/Files/Reports/2004/PIP_File_Swapping_Memo_0104.pdf.pdf) that the RIAA filed 382 lawsuits in 2003 against individual illegal music file swappers, most of whom quickly settled their cases for between $2,500 and $10,000.

In January 2005 the RIAA announced 717 new lawsuits against individual file swappers. Six months later the U.S. Supreme Court made a landmark decision in favor of the movie and music industries. In *Metro-Goldwyn-Mayer Studios v. Grokster* (545 U.S. 913 [2005]), the court unanimously ruled that businesses that encourage others to steal intellectual property are liable for their customers' illegal actions. Because companies such as Grokster developed their technology almost solely for the purpose of swapping music and video files illegally, they likely were in violation of the ruling.

Inspired by the music industry's success, the Motion Picture Association of America (MPAA) also took steps to prevent piracy. Usually, the most damaging instances of piracy in the motion picture business occur when bootleggers digitally record movies in theaters as they watch the films. The bootleggers then transfer the recorded movies via the Internet to buyers, who then offer the movies on the Internet or make copies on a digital video disc (DVD) and sell them in foreign countries. In "It's Curtains for Video Pirates" (NewScientist.com, August 14, 2004), Barry Fox explains that the Warner cinema chain began handing out night-vision goggles to some employees in California to look for these bootleggers during premieres. In 2004 the MPAA began working with the high-tech engineering firm Cinea to develop imaging techniques that would prevent digital camcorders from recording movies in theaters. One technique involved altering the frame rate in movies so that the film would move out of synchronization with most digital camcorders' refresh rate, resulting in a copy of the movie that shudders when played. Finally, in November 2004 the MPAA announced that it, too, would be prosecuting individuals who used peer-to-peer networks to view movies. The organization filed 250 lawsuits in 2005 against individuals who downloaded movies. The MPAA also prosecuted websites such as isoHunt.com and Torrentspy.com that directed visitors to places on the web where movies could be downloaded free of charge. As a result of these lawsuits, by 2016 both isoHunt.com and Torrentspy.com had been permanently shut down.

However, even with the success of these measures online piracy remained a persistent problem for the entertainment industry. In response, the MPAA urged members of Congress to pass a new law, the Stop Online Piracy Act (SOPA), as a means of cracking down on copyright infringement. Introduced in Congress in October 2011 by Representative Lamar Smith (1947–; R-TX), SOPA was referred to the U.S. House of Representatives' Subcommittee on Intellectual Property, Competition, and the Internet in December 2011. No further action had been taken as of November 2016.

## The DOJ Begins to Crack Down

Most litigation over copyright law is conducted in civil courts where individual citizens and organizations sue one another. If the defendant is found guilty, such as in the *RIAA v. Napster* case, then the defendant typically has to pay money to the plaintiff. In a criminal case the defendant serves jail or probationary time if found guilty. The DOJ is in charge of prosecuting criminal cases against people and organizations that violate national copyright laws. The DOJ also has specialized units based in cities where high-tech theft is common. These units are known as the Computer Hacking and Intellectual Property (CHIP) units, and they identify and help prosecute intellectual-property suspects. Most of these investigations involve international copyright crime organizations or individuals who make tens of thousands of dollars stealing intellectual property.

Responding to the increased threats to intellectual property brought on by new media, the U.S. attorney general John D. Ashcroft (1942–) created the DOJ's Task Force on Intellectual Property in March 2004. The task force was assigned to examine the entire range of intellectual property theft from counterfeit automotive parts to the theft of trade secrets to copyright infractions in the entertainment industry. In October 2004 the task force published *Report of the Department of Justice's Task Force on Intellectual Property* (http://www.justice.gov/olp/ip_task_force_report.pdf), which included its recommendations on how to address the rise in intellectual property theft. The task force suggested that Congress pass an act making it illegal for people to post copyrighted material they do not own on the Internet.

In 2005 President George W. Bush (1946–) signed the Family Entertainment Copyright Act into law. Under this act any attempt to record a movie in a theater can result in federal prosecution, fines, and up to three years in prison. A similar sentence can be given to anyone who distributes a creative work that is intended for commercial distribution but has not been released, such as a video game or movie that is still in production. Since the passing of the act, a number of people have been prosecuted by the DOJ for violating the law (although most litigation still takes place in civil courts). Manuel Sandoval, a 70-year-old retired painter from Los Angeles, was the first person to be convicted under the new act in April 2006. He was caught recording the matinee showing of *The Legend of Zorro* in Los Angeles in October 2005.

Meanwhile, the prosecution of intellectual property crimes reached global proportions, requiring the collaboration of law enforcement agencies from throughout the world. One high-profile case emerged in January 2012, when authorities in New Zealand, working with the DOJ, arrested Kim Schmitz (1974–; alias Kim Dotcom), founder of the popular file-sharing site Megaupload, on charges of copyright infringement. In "Feds Shutter Megaupload, Arrest Executives" (Wired.com, January 19, 2012), David Kravets reports that at the time Megaupload accounted for 4% of all traffic on the Internet, receiving roughly 50 million visits per day. In December 2012 authorities in Cambodia arrested Gottfrid Svartholm Warg (1984–), cofounder of Pirate Bay, the largest file-swapping site on the Internet. Warg had fled Sweden earlier that year to avoid serving prison time for his role in a copyright infringement case dating to 2009. Another Pirate Bay cofounder, Peter Sunde (1978–), was arrested in Sweden in May 2014, while the cofounder Fredrik Neij (1978–) was arrested in Thailand in November 2014.

Still, some experts questioned whether lawsuits or prosecutions were having any real impact on deterring intellectual property theft. Nolan Feeney reports in "Pirate Bay Co-founder Arrested in Sweden" (Time.com, June 1, 2014) that Pirate Bay continued to operate even after its owners were detained by authorities. In "The Pirate Bay Sails Back to Its .org Domain" (CNET.com, May 25, 2016), Aloysius Low reports that the site resumed operating in May 2016 under its original url address (ThePirateBay.org) after a Swedish court ruled that the site's existing url addresses, ThePirateBay.se and PirateBay.se, be shut down. Low notes that Neij, who had been released from prison in June 2015, vowed to appeal the decision.

## CHILD PORNOGRAPHY AND OTHER INTERNET-RELATED CRIMES

Unlike any other technology in human history, the Internet has enabled individuals to communicate with unprecedented speed and frequency. One of the downsides of the Internet's ability to help people share information more easily, however, is that it also provides criminals and other predators with a powerful weapon to use against potential victims. One area of major concern to law enforcement officials is the proliferation of child pornography on the Internet. The National Center for Missing and Exploited Children (NCMEC) monitors reports of child pornography and other forms of sexual exploitation through its CyberTipline (http://www.missingkids.com/CyberTipline), an online reporting system. Between 1998 and June 2016 the CyberTipline received more than 12.7 million reports of child exploitation. The NCMEC reports in "Key Facts" (2016, http://www.missingkids.com/KeyFacts) that it received 4.3 million calls related to missing or exploited children between 1984 and 2016. During this span, the NCMEC assisted in the recovery of 232,000 missing children.

Technological innovations have also created avenues for new forms of online criminal behavior. One disturbing new trend that emerged with the increasingly widespread popularity of wireless handheld devices was called sexting. Sexting is defined as the practice through which individuals share sexually suggestive images of each other via text message. In *Teens, Technology and Romantic Relationships* (October 1, 2015, http://www.pewinternet.org/files/2015/10/PI_2015-10-01_teens-technology-romance_FINAL.pdf), Amanda Lenhart, Aaron Smith, and Monica Anderson note that among teens aged 13 to 17 years with dating experience in 2015, nearly a quarter (23%) had sent "sexy or flirty" photographs or videos of themselves as a way of expressing romantic interest in someone.

Online classifieds sites can also make it easier for sexual predators to attract victims. In one notable case, the Boston University Medical School student Philip Markoff (1986–2010) was arrested in April 2009 for the murder of Julissa Brisman (1983–2009), a masseuse whom Markoff had contacted through the adult services section on Craigslist. Dubbed the "Craigslist Killer," Markoff killed himself in his jail cell in August 2010 before standing trial for the murder. In the wake of these and other incidents, law enforcement officials urged Craigslist to shut down its adult services listings altogether. Evan Hansen reports in "Censored! Craigslist Adult Services Banned in U.S." (Wired.com, September 4, 2010) that the website's adult services listings often served as a cover for prostitution and other forms of illegal sex-trafficking. As Hansen reports, the adult services section accounted for roughly 30% of the company's total revenues in 2010. Still, negative publicity and increased pressure from state attorneys continued to plague the online classifieds site, and in September 2010 Craigslist abruptly discontinued its adult services listings, replacing it with a black bar that read "Censored." In spite of these measures other sites, notably Backpage.com, soon replaced Craigslist as popular sources of adult services listings.

## THE DEEP WEB AND THE DARK WEB

One area of growing concern to law enforcement in 2016 was the potential for criminals to conduct illegal activity on the Deep Web. Generally speaking, the Deep Web refers to anonymous Internet activity that is inaccessible on conventional web browsers, making it undetectable by search engines. Although a significant portion of the Deep Web is composed of databases, academic journals, and other web pages that do not come up in searches, a substantial amount of Deep Web activity occurs on secret websites that are hosted by anonymous networks. The portion of the Deep Web where sites are deliberately encrypted for the purpose of concealment is known as the Dark Web.

One of the most prominent secret networks on the Dark Web is Tor. The idea of Tor was first proposed in 1996 by a small team of scientists at the U.S. Naval Research Laboratory. Originally known as the Onion Router, Tor encrypted Internet traffic to the point of making it thoroughly untraceable. The first Tor network was launched in 2003. In its conception, Tor was designed to enable government agencies to engage in a range of secret activities, from conducting criminal investigations anonymously to exchanging classified documents. However, Tor soon attracted a range of other users, who were drawn to the possibility of using the Internet with complete anonymity.

The prospect of using the Internet in total secrecy had obvious appeal to criminals, and an area of the Deep Web commonly known as the DarkNet emerged. Tor quickly became a haven for illegal activity on the DarkNet, ranging from terrorist communications to the exchange of malware programs among computer hackers; it also gave rise to an illicit economy, where Internet users could acquire controlled substances, weapons, and child pornography outside the scrutiny of law enforcement. For some politically minded individuals, Tor represented an opportunity to exist outside of the control of government. These libertarian tendencies were at the heart of Silk Road, an online marketplace where users could buy and sell illegal drugs. In "The Secret Web: Where Drugs, Porn and Murder Live Online" (Time.com, November 11, 2013), Lev Grossman and Jay Newton-Small indicate that the site was first launched in January 2011 by Ross Ulbricht (1985–; alias Dread Pirate Roberts), who quickly became an "antiestablishment hero" in the eyes of many Silk Road users. Although most visitors used the site to acquire drugs, Silk Road also provided access to books, erotica, and a range of digital goods. As Grossman and Newton-Small note, Silk Road was considered especially secure because all of its transactions were conducted with Bitcoin, a virtual currency that cannot be traced to its users.

In spite of this extraordinary level of secrecy, law enforcement eventually discovered clues linking Dread Pirate Roberts to Ulbricht, and he was arrested in October 2013 while accessing Silk Road at a public library in San Francisco. Among the charges leveled against Ulbricht were drug trafficking, money laundering, and conspiracy to commit murder. In two and a half years, roughly 1 million customers spent $1.2 billion on Silk Road transactions, while Ulbricht collected an estimated $80 million in transaction fees. Following Silk Road's closure, the FBI posted a notification on the site announcing that it had been seized. Despite the site's closure, new DarkNet pages appeared to take its place. One site, Silk Road 2.0, became the leading online marketplace for illegal drugs until November 2014, when the FBI arrested the site's founder, Blake Benthall (1988?–). As of November 2016, other successors to Silk Road, notably Silk Road 3.0 and Silk Road Reloaded, remained in operation.

## HIGH-TECH LAW ENFORCEMENT

Criminals have not been the only ones taking advantage of high tech. Since the 1980s new technologies have provided law enforcement with myriad resources to combat crime and protect citizens. Video cameras have helped tremendously in identifying thieves who rob automated teller machines, banks, and convenience stores. Wiretaps and surveillance equipment have allowed law enforcement officials to catch criminals without putting themselves in harm's way. However, the biggest boon to law enforcement by far has been the increased access law enforcement officers have had to information. During the 1970s, for example, if a law enforcement officer in New York wanted the records of a criminal in California, he or she would have to call a police station in California and have the information read over the phone. Computer databases and communications technologies have connected law enforcement offices and provided them easy access to criminal records across the country. In 1995 the FBI launched Law Enforcement Online (LEO), an online communication and data system that enables law enforcement agencies from around the world to exchange information about criminal investigations. In December 2012 LEO was modernized and relaunched as the Law Enforcement Online Enterprise Portal, which subsequently became the Law Enforcement Enterprise Portal (https://www.cjis.gov/CJISEAI/EAIController). In 2014 the FBI launched Malware Investigator (https://www.malwareinvestigator.gov/), a site that is dedicated to identifying and preventing cyberattacks. At the same time, phone networks and portable computers have also given the police the ability to access criminal records and information on vehicle registrations and license holders from within the patrol car. Electronic credit and debit card networks, bank machines, and rental car records have all provided law enforcement with easily accessible, real-time information on where criminals have been and where they are going.

Communications technologies have also allowed law enforcement agencies to inform communities of terrorism, kidnapping, or other criminal activity to bring the perpetrators to justice. America's Missing: Broadcast Emergency Response (AMBER) Plan is named after nine-year-old Amber Hagerman (1986–1996), who was kidnapped and murdered in Arlington, Texas, in 1996. After her murder Texas instituted the first statewide AMBER Plan in 1999. Since that time the program has been introduced by the DOJ into the 49 other states. When an AMBER Alert is issued, the regional Emergency Alert System is used to tell the public about the missing child. Programs on television and radio stations are interrupted and followed by pertinent information about the abduction. All law enforcement officers are put on alert, and digital emergency signs above highways tell drivers where to receive more information about the abduction. According to the DOJ (2016, https://www.amberalert.gov/statistics.htm), as of December 2015, 800 children had been recovered as a result of the plan. In *National Center for Missing and Exploited Children 2014 AMBER Alert Report* (2015, http://www.amberalert.gov/pdfs/2014AMBERAlertReport.pdf), the NCMEC analyzes the effectiveness of AMBER Alert broadcasts. In more than half (56%) of cases in which children were safely recovered in 2014, either a law enforcement official or another individual recognized the vehicle described in an AMBER Alert (35%), or else an individual or law enforcement official recognized either the child or the abductor after hearing an AMBER Alert broadcast (21%). In 13% of cases the abductor released the victim after hearing the Amber Alert.

# CHAPTER 5
# ELECTRONICS, THE INTERNET, AND ENTERTAINMENT MEDIA

For many Americans, new technologies mean new toys. Figure 5.1 shows changes in electronic device ownership among adults between 2000 and 2015. In 2000 just over 50% of adults owned cell phones; by 2015 this figure exceeded 90%. Whereas only 20% of adults had MP3 players in 2006, by 2010 nearly half (47%) of adults owned MP3 players; this number subsequently dipped between 2010 and 2015, in large part due to the increasing popularity of smartphones and music streaming services. As Figure 5.1 shows, the technologies that saw the most substantial increases in popularity between 2010 and 2015 included electronic readers (e-readers or eBook readers), tablet computers, and smartphones. Overall, 45% of American adults owned a tablet in 2015. (See Figure 5.2.) A strong correlation exists between educational attainment and tablet ownership. For example, 62% of adults with college degrees owned a tablet in 2015; by comparison, only 19% of adults who never completed high school owned tablets that year. (See Table 5.1.)

Young adults are typically the most avid consumers of new technologies. Table 5.2 offers a detailed breakdown of changes in device ownership among young adults between 2010 and 2015. Whereas smartphone ownership was negligible in 2010, by 2015 it had been adopted by 86% of American adults aged 18 to 29 years. Adults in this age group were also most likely to use their smartphones to engage with various forms of media. For example, three-quarters (75%) of adults aged 18 to 29 years watched videos on their smartphones in 2015, and nearly two-thirds (64%) used their devices to listen to music or podcasts. (See Figure 5.3.) Other technologies that saw dramatic rises in use between 2010 and 2015 among adults aged 18 to 29 years included tablet computers, which rose from 5% to 50% during this period, and e-readers, which rose from 5% to 18%. By contrast, ownership of MP3 players among this age group dropped considerably during this span, from 75% in 2010 to only 51% in 2015. (See Table 5.2.)

## ELECTRONIC GAMING

Video and computer games represent a major form of entertainment in the United States. Video games, also known as console and arcade games, are played using a computer that is specifically designed to play games. By contrast, computer games are just one type of program that can be run on standard personal computers. The difference between the two types of games is in how they are accessed, not necessarily in their content. Many games can be played using either a video game system or a computer. Thus, the terms *video game* and *computer game* are sometimes used interchangeably. Maeve Duggan of the Pew Research Center reports in *Gaming and Gamers* (December 15, 2015, http://www.pewinternet.org/files/2015/12/PI_2015-12-15_gaming-and-gamers_FINAL.pdf) that 49% of American adults played video games in 2015. Men (50%) were only slightly more likely than women (48%) to play video games that year. (See Figure 5.4.) As Table 5.3 shows, two in five (40%) American adults owned video game consoles in 2015. Hispanics (45%) were more likely than African Americans (43%) and whites (39%) to own video game consoles that year. Despite the popularity of video games, attitudes toward them were decidedly mixed. As Figure 5.5 indicates, in 2015 just over one-quarter (26%) of all American adults viewed most video games as a waste of time; another one-third (33%) thought that only some games were a waste of time. On the other hand, 80% of adults who played video games in 2015 believed that at least some video games helped develop problem solving skills, while about two-thirds (63%) felt that at least some video games promoted communication and teamwork, with 15% saying that most games promote teamwork and 48% saying that some games do. (See Figure 5.6.)

### Rise of Video and Computer Games

Computer and video games are almost as old as computers. Many credit Alexander Shafto Douglas (1921–2010)

## FIGURE 5.1

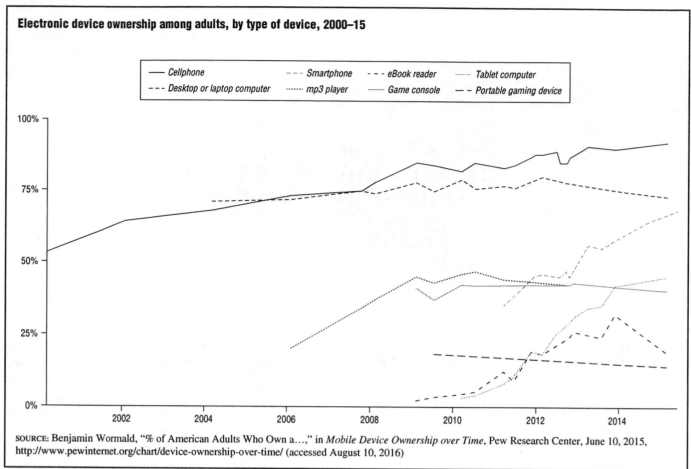

**Electronic device ownership among adults, by type of device, 2000–15**

Legend:
— Cellphone
- - - Desktop or laptop computer
- – - Smartphone
······ mp3 player
- - - eBook reader
—— Game console
········ Tablet computer
— – Portable gaming device

SOURCE: Benjamin Wormald, "% of American Adults Who Own a…," in *Mobile Device Ownership over Time*, Pew Research Center, June 10, 2015, http://www.pewinternet.org/chart/device-ownership-over-time/ (accessed August 10, 2016)

## FIGURE 5.2

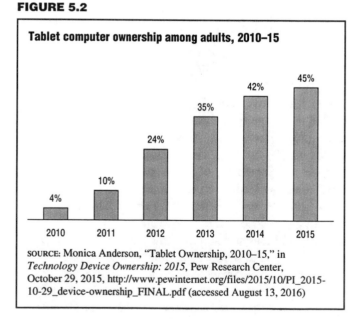

**Tablet computer ownership among adults, 2010–15**

2010: 4%
2011: 10%
2012: 24%
2013: 35%
2014: 42%
2015: 45%

SOURCE: Monica Anderson, "Tablet Ownership, 2010–15," in *Technology Device Ownership: 2015*, Pew Research Center, October 29, 2015, http://www.pewinternet.org/files/2015/10/PI_2015-10-29_device-ownership_FINAL.pdf (accessed August 13, 2016)

with creating the first graphics-based computer game at Cambridge University in England in 1952. Part of his doctoral research on human-computer interaction, the game was played on an enormous Electronic Delay Storage Automatic Calculator (EDSAC) computer, which was one of the first computers in existence and was made primarily from rows and rows of vacuum tubes. The EDSAC display screen was a 35 x 16 array of monochromatic dots. The name of Douglas's game was *OXO*, or *Noughts and Crosses*, a human-versus-machine version of tic-tac-toe in which the human player chose the first square. Ten years later, computer games were developed on mainframe computers and eventually on ARPANET, the nationwide network of military defense computers that preceded the Internet.

One of the more popular games that spread to computer mainframes across the United States during the 1960s was *Spacewar!* The game was created in 1961 by Steve Russell (1937–), Martin Graetz (1935–), and Wayne Wiitanen (1935–) at the Massachusetts Institute of Technology to test the capabilities of the $120,000 Digital Equipment Corporation PDP-1 computer. The game consisted of two low-resolution ships, one shaped like a needle and the other like a wedge, flying around a dot that represented a sun in the middle of the screen. The object was to destroy the other player's ship while maneuvering through the sun's gravitational pull.

In 1971 Nutting Associates released *Computer Space*, the first video game for the general public. *Computer Space*, a direct imitator of *Spacewar!*, was set in a futuristic arcade-style cabinet. Most people considered the game too complicated at the time, so Nutting made only 1,500 units and then stopped production. The next year, however, Atari released *Pong*. In this monochromatic game, a small cube was bounced back and forth between two slightly larger rods controlled by the player(s). The video game was a smash hit, and Atari sold more than 800,000 arcade cabinets. A month earlier, Magnavox released the Odyssey, which was the first home-console video game system that ran on a television set. The Odyssey, which sold for $100 (about $595 in 2016 dollars), had several different games installed on it, all of which involved hitting a pixilated square (or squares) on the screen with rectangles. According to the Atari Museum (2016, http://www.atarimuseum.com/videogames/dedicated/homepong.html), the Atari home version of *Pong* was released in 1975 and sold over 150,000 units during the holiday season alone.

## Golden Age of Video Games

Within a year after these initial offerings, video games quickly gained a foothold in the United States. A steady stream of unremarkable cabinet games was released throughout the 1970s. For most of the decade, video games were novelties that sat next to pinball machines in bowling alleys, bars, and roller-skating rinks. With the arrival of *Asteroids* and *Space Invaders* in 1978, arcade video games came into their own. *Space Invaders*, a game in which the player shot row after row of advancing aliens, triggered a nationwide coin shortage in Japan so severe the Japanese government had to more than double yen production. Namco introduced the first color game in 1979 with the arrival of *Galaxian*, and then in 1980 the company released *Pac-Man*. The original name of the game was *Puckman*, derived from the Japanese *pakupaku*, which means "flapping open and closed" (e.g., the character's mouth). Despite the game's simple concept of guiding a yellow, dot-eating ball around a maze, more than 100,000 arcade units were sold in the United States. The game inspired an entire line of merchandise from lunch boxes to stuffed toys. Between 1980 and 1983 many colorful, engaging video games were released, including *Centipede*, *Defender*, *Donkey Kong*, *Frogger*, and *Ms. Pac-Man*, which still holds the record for the most arcade games sold at 115,000, according to William Hunter in "Player 2 Stage 4: Two Superstars" (2016, http://www.emuunlim.com/doteaters/play2sta4.htm). Video arcades sprang up in every mall and town in the United States. On January 18, 1982, the cover of *Time* magazine read: GRONK! FLASH! ZAP! VIDEO GAMES ARE BLITZING THE WORLD. In the cover story, "Games That Play People," John Skow reported that in 1981 nearly $5 billion

**TABLE 5.1**

**Tablet computer ownership, by gender, race and ethnicity, and other demographic characteristics, 2010–15**

[In percent]

| | |
|---|---|
| **U.S. adults** | 45 |
| **Sex** | |
| Men | 43 |
| Women | 47 |
| **Race/ethnicity** | |
| White | 47 |
| Black | 38 |
| Hispanic | 35 |
| **Age group** | |
| 18–29 | 50 |
| 30–49 | 57 |
| 50–64 | 37 |
| 65+ | 32 |
| **Household income** | |
| <$30K | 28 |
| $30K–$49,999 | 44 |
| $50K–$74,999 | 51 |
| $75K+ | 67 |
| **Educational attainment** | |
| Less than high school | 19 |
| High school | 35 |
| Some college | 49 |
| College+ | 62 |
| **Community type** | |
| Urban | 42 |
| Suburban | 50 |
| Rural | 37 |

SOURCE: Monica Anderson, "Tablet Owners More Likely to be Younger, More Affluent and Highly Educated," in *Technology Device Ownership: 2015*, Pew Research Center, October 29, 2015, http://www.pewinternet.org/files/2015/10/PI_2015-10-29_device-ownership_FINAL.pdf (accessed August 13, 2016)

**TABLE 5.2**

**Device ownership among adults aged 18–29, by type of device, 2010–15**

| | 2010 | 2011 | 2012 | 2013 | 2014 | 2015 |
|---|---|---|---|---|---|---|
| Cellphone | 96 | 95 | 93 | 97 | 98 | 98 |
| Computer | 88 | 88 | 89 | — | — | 78 |
| MP3 player | 75 | 71 | — | 62 | — | 51 |
| Game console | 62 | — | — | 71 | — | 56 |
| Smartphone | — | 52 | 65 | 79 | 85 | 86 |
| Tablet computer | 5 | 13 | 32 | 36 | 48 | 50 |
| E-book reader | 5 | 8 | 27 | 24 | 28 | 18 |

SOURCE: Monica Anderson, "MP3, Computer Ownership Has Dropped among Younger Adults since 2010," in *Technology Device Ownership: 2015*, Pew Research Center, October 29, 2015, http://www.pewinternet.org/files/2015/10/PI_2015-10-29_device-ownership_FINAL.pdf (accessed August 10, 2016)

## FIGURE 5.3

**Percentage of smartphone owners who use their devices to engage with various media, by age group, 2014**

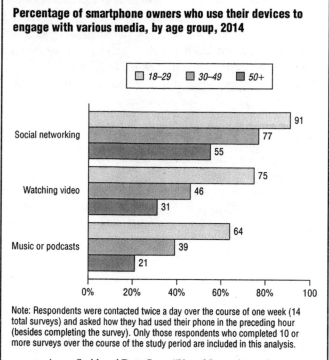

Legend: ☐ 18–29 ☐ 30–49 ■ 50+

Social networking: 91 / 77 / 55
Watching video: 75 / 46 / 31
Music or podcasts: 64 / 39 / 21

(x-axis: 0% 20% 40% 60% 80% 100)

Note: Respondents were contacted twice a day over the course of one week (14 total surveys) and asked how they had used their phone in the preceding hour (besides completing the survey). Only those respondents who completed 10 or more surveys over the course of the study period are included in this analysis.

SOURCE: Aaron Smith and Dana Page, "Use of Smartphones for Social Media, Video Watching, and Music/Podcasts Is Especially Common among Young Users," in *U.S. Smartphone Use in 2015*, Pew Research Center, April 1, 2015, http://www.pewinternet.org/files/2015/03/PI_Smartphones_0401151.pdf (accessed August 10, 2016)

## FIGURE 5.4

**Percentage of adults who play video games or who identify as "gamers," by gender and age group, 2015**

[% of all adults who...]

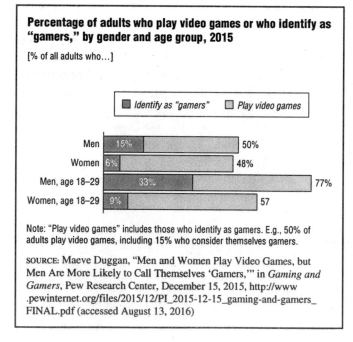

Legend: ■ Identify as "gamers" ☐ Play video games

Men: 15% / 50%
Women: 6% / 48%
Men, age 18–29: 33% / 77%
Women, age 18–29: 9% / 57

Note: "Play video games" includes those who identify as gamers. E.g., 50% of adults play video games, including 15% who consider themselves gamers.

SOURCE: Maeve Duggan, "Men and Women Play Video Games, but Men Are More Likely to Call Themselves 'Gamers,'" in *Gaming and Gamers*, Pew Research Center, December 15, 2015, http://www.pewinternet.org/files/2015/12/PI_2015-12-15_gaming-and-gamers_FINAL.pdf (accessed August 13, 2016)

## TABLE 5.3

**Game console ownership among adults, by gender, race and ethnicity, and other demographic characteristics, 2015**

[In percent]

| | |
|---|---|
| **U.S. adults** | 40 |
| **Sex** | |
| Men | 37 |
| Women | 42 |
| **Race/ethnicity** | |
| White | 39 |
| Black | 43 |
| Hispanic | 45 |
| **Age group** | |
| 18–29 | 56 |
| 30–49 | 55 |
| 50–64 | 30 |
| 65+ | 8 |
| **Household income** | |
| <$30K | 33 |
| $30K–$49,999 | 43 |
| $50K–$74,999 | 50 |
| $75K+ | 54 |
| **Educational attainment** | |
| Less than high school | 21 |
| High school | 35 |
| Some college | 54 |
| College+ | 37 |
| **Community type** | |
| Urban | 41 |
| Suburban | 41 |
| Rural | 34 |

SOURCE: Monica Anderson, "Four-in-Ten American Adults Have a Game Console; Ownership Varies by Age, Household Income and Education," in *Technology Device Ownership: 2015*, Pew Research Center, October 29, 2015, http://www.pewinternet.org/files/2015/10/PI_2015-10-29_device-ownership_FINAL.pdf (accessed August 13, 2016)

At the same time, game consoles were gaining popularity in living rooms across the United States. In 1977 Atari launched the Atari VCS (later named the Atari 2600) for $250 (about $995 in 2016 dollars). By Christmas 1979 sales were brisk as people realized that the system could support more than just *Pong*. With the release of *Space Invaders* on the system the following year, units flew off the shelves at $150 apiece (roughly $440 in 2016 dollars). Tekla E. Perry and Paul Wallich explain in "Design Case History: The Atari Video Computer System" (*IEEE Spectrum*, March 1983) that Atari sold more than 12 million consoles between 1977 and 1983. More than 200 games were made for the system. Other video systems such as Intellivision and Colecovision gained huge followings as well. Skow noted that 600,000 Intellivision units were sold in 1981. Overall, 1981 sales for home video games exceeded $1 billion (approximately $2.7 billion in 2016 dollars).

### Video Game Industry Stumbles

By 1984 the Commodore 64 home computer had debuted at $1,000 (about $2,315 in 2016 dollars), and the Apple IIc was introduced at the comparatively affordable

in quarters (about $13 billion in 2016 dollars) was spent playing arcade games. By comparison, the U.S. film industry took in $2.8 billion that year (about $7.4 billion in 2016 dollars).

**FIGURE 5.5**

## Attitudes among adults toward video games, 2015

[% of all adults who think the following qualities are…]

| | ■ … true for most games | ■ … true for some games, but not others | ■ … not true for most games | □ Unsure |
|---|---|---|---|---|

| | | | | |
|---|---|---|---|---|
| Are a waste of time | 26% | 33% | 24% | 16% |
| Help develop good problem solving skills | 17% | 47% | 16% | 20% |
| Promote teamwork and communication | 10% | 37% | 23% | 28% |
| Are a better form of entertainment than TV | 11% | 34% | 30% | 24% |

SOURCE: Maeve Duggan, "Mixed Feelings, Uncertainty among General Public toward Video Games," in *Gaming and Gamers*, Pew Research Center, December 15, 2015, http://www.pewinternet.org/files/2015/12/PI_2015-12-15_gaming-and-gamers_FINAL.pdf (accessed August 13, 2016)

**FIGURE 5.6**

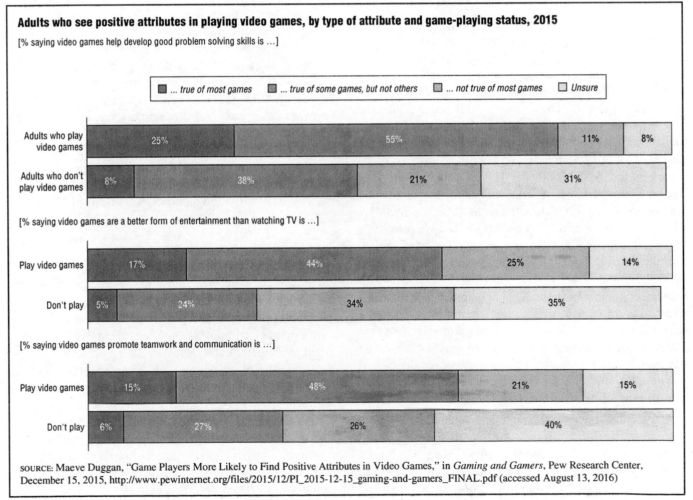

## Adults who see positive attributes in playing video games, by type of attribute and game-playing status, 2015

[% saying video games help develop good problem solving skills is …]

| | ■ … true of most games | ■ … true of some games, but not others | ■ … not true of most games | □ Unsure |
|---|---|---|---|---|

| | | | | |
|---|---|---|---|---|
| Adults who play video games | 25% | 55% | 11% | 8% |
| Adults who don't play video games | 8% | 38% | 21% | 31% |

[% saying video games are a better form of entertainment than watching TV is …]

| | | | | |
|---|---|---|---|---|
| Play video games | 17% | 44% | 25% | 14% |
| Don't play | 5% | 24% | 34% | 35% |

[% saying video games promote teamwork and communication is …]

| | | | | |
|---|---|---|---|---|
| Play video games | 15% | 48% | 21% | 15% |
| Don't play | 6% | 27% | 26% | 40% |

SOURCE: Maeve Duggan, "Game Players More Likely to Find Positive Attributes in Video Games," in *Gaming and Gamers*, Pew Research Center, December 15, 2015, http://www.pewinternet.org/files/2015/12/PI_2015-12-15_gaming-and-gamers_FINAL.pdf (accessed August 13, 2016)

price of $1,300 ($3,010 in 2016 dollars). Such computers not only offered better graphics than the contemporary video game consoles, but also they were useful for practical applications such as spreadsheets and word processors. Consequently, people began losing interest in video game systems and bought home computers instead. In 1983, faced with a collapsing video game market, losses of hundreds of millions of dollars, and far too much inventory, Atari loaded 14 tractor-trailer trucks with thousands of unsold cartridges and pieces of hardware. It drove the surplus out to a landfill site in Alamogordo, New Mexico, and buried the inventory in a concrete bunker under the desert. The following year Warner Communications, the owner of Atari, sold the game and computer divisions of Atari to Jack Tramiel (1928–2012), the founder of Commodore. Mattel, the maker of Intellivision, also shed its electronics division, and hundreds of arcades closed as well.

For several years gaming was relegated to the computer. Before 1983 computer games were low on graphics and heavy on text, but by 1984 a number of colorful and entertaining games became available for home computers, including the *Ultima* and *King's Quest* series. However, toy and electronics manufacturers in the United States were wary of investing in video game consoles after the Atari disaster.

Japanese companies were not nearly as pessimistic and continued to invest money into video console development. Nintendo, a company that originally manufactured Japanese playing cards, surprised the entire gaming market in 1986 when it released the Nintendo Entertainment System (NES). The games looked better than most arcade games from the early 1980s and took as long to play through as computer games. After two years on the market, the NES found its way into almost as many homes as the Atari 2600. Pat Davies reported in "The Hottest Game in Town" (*Globe and Mail*, May 19, 1989) that the sales of NES video games in 1988 reached $1.7 billion ($3.5 billion in 2016 dollars) in the United States alone. Arcades at the time also enjoyed a brief revival with the advent of complex fighting games such as *Mortal Kombat* and *Street Fighter II. Mortal Kombat*, which eventually made it onto the NES, inspired a congressional investigation into violence in video games and led to the establishment in 1994 of the Entertainment Software Rating Board, an industry self-regulatory organization that monitors the content of video games for depictions of violence, nudity, profanity, and other material that parents might find objectionable for young children.

## Current and Future Gaming

Since the late 1980s the U.S. electronic gaming market has continued its rise, with the majority of the gaming industry's revenues coming from console systems and games. After the NES ran its course with estimated sales of 60 million units worldwide, the Sega Genesis video game system enjoyed a period of popularity. The electronics giant Sony entered the fray in 1995 when it released PlayStation in the United States. Nintendo answered Sony's challenge with Nintendo 64 in 1996, which sold 1.7 million units in the United States in the first three months, according to Michael Miller in "A History of Home Video Game Consoles" (InformIT.com, April 1, 2005). In 2000 Sony PlayStation launched the PlayStation2. Taking note of the profits brought in by successful gaming systems, Microsoft, the largest software firm in the United States, launched the Xbox in 2001. Both Sony and Microsoft funded enormous advertising campaigns to promote their systems, and Microsoft sold its system at a loss to introduce it into more homes. Peter Lewis stated in "Should You Wait for the PS3?" (CNN.com, November 22, 2005) that over 96 million PlayStation 2 consoles and 25 million Xbox systems had sold worldwide by the end of 2005. With the release of the Xbox 360 in 2005 and the PlayStation 3 and Nintendo Wii in 2006, the video game market enjoyed double-digit year-over-year growth.

By decade's end, however, overall sales began to slip. The marketing research firm NPD Group reports in the press release "2009 U.S. Video Game Industry and PC Game Software Retail Sales Reach $20.2 Billion" (January 14, 2010, http://www.npd.com/press/releases/press_100114.html) that retail video games produced roughly $19.7 billion in sales in 2009, an 8% drop from 2008 revenues of $21.4 billion. Sales of console hardware saw the biggest decline (13%), whereas console and portable software also saw sales decrease by approximately 10%. Sales declined further after 2010. Rachel Weber writes in "NPD: 2015 Video Game Sales Flat Compared to 2014" (January 14, 2016, http://www.gamesindustry.biz/articles/2016-01-14-npd) that by 2015 annual revenues in the retail video game market fell to $13.1 billion, a 39% decline since 2008.

Overall, the computer game market grew at a slower pace than the video game market. During the 1990s with the advent of Microsoft's Windows operating system, the computer game market split in two. Solitaire and countless other card and puzzle games found their way onto personal computers, laptops, and tablets and provided a brief escape from work or schoolwork. At the same time, computers also became the platform for cutting-edge strategy and shooting games, which are generally played by a relatively small, devoted computer-gaming audience. Graphics-intensive games such as *Quake* and *Half Life 2* led to increased sales in computer components as gamers bought extra memory and bigger hard drives to boost computer performance to handle advanced graphic engines.

In the mid-1990s computer games began to go online. Hardcore fans of card games and battle and quest adventures found competitors on the Internet. The next generation of console systems also enabled gamers to go online and play against one another. In "The Future of Online Gaming" (PCMag.com, March 27, 2003), Cade Metz noted that by 2002 online gaming traffic made up nearly 9% of the overall traffic along the Internet backbone in the United States. The fastest-growing segment of online gaming appeared to be in the console game market. Xbox Live, an online service for the Xbox, gained 350,000 subscriptions at the beginning of 2003. In 2005 Microsoft launched a more advanced version of the console, the Xbox 360, and in 2013 it launched yet another version, the Xbox One. According to ZhugeEx, in the blog post "U.S. Console Market in 2015—Year in Review" (January 21, 2016, https://zhugeex.com/2016/01/us-console-market-in-2015-year-in-review/), an estimated 5 million Xbox One consoles were sold in 2015, second only to the Sony PlayStation 4, which sold 5.7 million units. ZhugeEx also reports that the biggest-selling video games of 2015 (in order of popularity) were *Call of Duty: Black Ops III*, *Madden NFL 16*, and *Fallout 4*. Meanwhile, other highly anticipated video games were expected to hit the market at mid-decade. Shaun Prescott reports in "Star Wars Battlefront 2 Will Release in 2017" (PCGamer.com, May 10, 2016) that in May 2016 video game maker Electronic Arts (EA) announced plans to release a follow-up to its popular *Star Wars Battlefront* game in 2017, while also unveiling additional titles each year through the end of the decade.

Meanwhile, new technological advances continued to shape the evolution of the video game industry. Adi Robinson reports in "How Virtual Reality Gaming Is Blowing Its Big Chance in 2016" (Verge.com, June 21, 2016) that the 2016 Electronic Entertainment Expo (E3) in Los Angeles witnessed several new developments in the evolution of virtual reality (VR) gaming systems. At the event, Sony announced that it would be unveiling a new virtual reality gaming headset, the PlayStation VR, in October 2016. The new product was designed to be compatible with the PlayStation 4 video game console, and would compete with existing VR headsets such as the Oculus Rift and the HTC Hive. At the same time, the increasing popularity of mobile devices was changing the way that consumers engaged with video games. According to the video game market research firm Newzoo, in "The Global Games Market Reaches $99.6 Billion in 2016, Mobile Generating 37%" (Newzoo.com, April 21, 2016), games for smartphones and tablets accounted for one-third (33%) of the video game market in 2015.

## Gaming Violence and Addiction

Over the years games have grown exceedingly more complex and engaging. The *Sims* series by EA has provided gamers with a "real-life" fantasy world where they can simulate alternate lives. Game series such as *Doom* and *Grand Theft Auto* allow people to take out their aggressions on virtual demons or rival gang members. Massively multiplayer online role-playing games (MMORPGs; in which a large number of players interact with each other in a virtual world that continues even when a player is offline), such as *World of Warcraft*, open up entire fantasy worlds where players are free to roam and embark on quests with other gamers.

As the complexity of games has grown, so, too, has the temptation for many to play video games in excess to escape their problems. Although still a relatively unstudied phenomenon, gaming addiction appears to be more and more commonplace. In "Video Games: Are They Really a Source of Addiction?" (June 2013, http://psychcentral.com/blog/archives/2013/07/21/video-games-are-they-really-a-source-of-addiction/), Kristi A. DeName cites an American Medical Association (AMA) report claiming that, of the 90% of children and young adults who played video games in 2013, 15% showed signs of video game addiction. Among these signs are forgoing sleeping or eating to continue playing, having reduced social contacts, losing a sense of time while playing the game, and allowing school, work, or other responsibilities to lapse.

Furthermore, video game addiction appears to be a greater risk for children suffering from developmental disorders. Serena Gordon writes in "Video Game 'Addiction' More Likely with Autism, ADHD" (Health.USNews.com, July 29, 2013) that children who struggle in social situations, in particular those with autism or attention deficit disorders, are more likely to view video games as a form of escape.

Many psychologists believe games provide a means of escape for people with stressful lives or mental problems in much the same way as drugs and alcohol. A number of symptoms that accompany gaming addiction are similar to those of other impulse control disorders, including alcoholism and drug abuse. These include preoccupation with gaming life over real-life events, failed attempts to stem gaming behavior, having a sense of well-being while playing games, craving more game time as well as feeling irritable when not playing, neglecting family and friends, lying about the amount of time spent gaming, and denying the adverse effects of too much gaming. In June 2007 the Council on Science and Public Health urged the AMA to classify excessive gaming an addiction. In response to mounting concerns about gaming and other forms of online addiction, in 2012 the American Psychiatric Association decided to list "Internet use disorder" as a subject "recommended for further study" in the fifth edition of the *Diagnostic and Statistical Manual for Mental Disorders*, published in May 2013.

Another problem people have with video games is violence. Many parents and teachers have expressed concern that violent games may lead to violent aggressive behavior. Such fears were fueled in 1999 by the shootings at Columbine High School in Littleton, Colorado, where two teenage students killed 15 people. In their suicide note, the murderers said they drew inspiration from the video game *Doom*. In *Grand Theft of Innocence? Teens and Video Games* (September 16, 2003, http://www.gallup.com/poll/9253/Grand-Theft-Innocence-Teens-Video-Games.aspx), Steve Crabtree of the Gallup Organization indicates that many parents and educators are concerned about the violence in video games such as *Grand Theft Auto*. Nevertheless, nearly three-quarters (74%) of teens played video games at least one hour per week in 2003, and 60% of teens had at some point played a game in the *Grand Theft Auto* series. Not only do such violent games give teens a false impression of adult life, but also studies show that the games may hinder social development in some teens. According to Crabtree, a 2001 study at Tokyo University indicated that violent games stunt the development of the brain's frontal lobe, which is the part of the brain that controls antisocial behavior. However, other studies have found that there is no proven connection between violent video game content and aggression. In "Aggression from Video Games 'Linked to Incompetence'" (BBC.com, April 7, 2014), Dave Lee cites a study conducted by researchers at Oxford University and the University of Rochester, which indicated that feelings of aggression were related to a player's inability to succeed at video games, rather than the game's violent content.

The ease with which young teens were able to obtain violent video games was also a cause for concern. To confront this trend, some state governments began to craft legislation aimed at keeping violent video games out of the hands of children. In 2005 the state of California passed a law making it illegal to sell violent video games to minors. The Entertainment Software Association challenged the legislation in federal court, and in 2009 the U.S. Ninth Court of Appeals declared the law unconstitutional. Bill Mears reports in "California Ban on Sale of 'Violent' Video Games to Children Rejected" (CNN.com, June 27, 2011) that in June 2011 the Supreme Court of the United States ruled the California law unconstitutional by a 7 to 2 vote.

In spite of the negative consequences sometimes associated with video games, several studies examining the positive effects of gaming have emerged over the years. In *Video Games and Your Family* (2016, http://mediasmarts.ca/sites/default/files/pdfs/tipsheet/VideoGameTipSheet_Final_EN.pdf), the Media Awareness Network outlined numerous benefits that video games offered children. According to the report, video games had the potential to teach reading and other learning skills, promote socialization with other game players, and help young people feel more comfortable with technology. At the same time, the report cautions that the violent images found in some video games can have a negative impact on a young child's development, and that parents should play a role in steering their children away from potentially traumatizing games. Other researchers have questioned the link between violent video games and aggressive behavior altogether. In "The Hitman Study: Violent Video Game Exposure Effects on Aggressive Behavior, Hostile Feelings, and Depression" (*European Psychologist*, 2010), Christopher J. Ferguson and Stephanie M. Rueda of Texas A&M International University find that there is no proven connection between violent games and aggression, while suggesting that in some cases violent games can actually help individuals suffering from depression or other mood disorders. In "Video Games May Provide Learning, Health, Social Benefits, Review Finds" (November 25, 2013, http://www.apa.org/news/press/releases/2013/11/video-games.aspx), the American Psychological Association asserts that video games have the potential to improve a child's memory, to teach them problem-solving techniques, and to foster values such as teamwork and cooperation, notably in collaborative game environments.

## Online Gambling

There is no doubt inside or outside the scientific community that gambling can be addictive. One troubling development at the turn of the 21st century was the continued rise in online gambling. According to a congressional statement by the U.S. deputy assistant attorney general John G. Malcolm (March 18, 2003, http://banking.senate.gov/03_03hrg/031803/malcolm.htm), 700 Internet gambling sites existed in 1999. By 2003 the U.S. Department of Justice estimated that 1,800 gambling sites were in place, bringing in roughly $4.2 billion. The article "Global Online Gambling Market Growing at 11 Percent Clip" (CardPlayer.com, February 26, 2016) indicates that by 2015 online gambling generated roughly $37 billion in revenues worldwide.

Many of these sites allow gamblers to transfer money from their checking accounts into a gambling account run by the casino. When the player wishes to gamble, he or she simply goes online and begins a session. Because most of these big online gambling operations are based in foreign nations in the Caribbean or South America, the U.S. government cannot regulate them. Malcolm pointed to instances in which the online houses manipulated the software so that the odds of games such as blackjack are skewed heavily in the house's favor. Other fly-by-night gambling operations had simply run off with people's money. Even when these gambling houses are honest, they are still perceived as a threat to society by many lawmakers. People addicted to gambling, for example, might log in and gamble unfettered for hours at a time from work or home. They might lose hundreds or thousands of dollars with a few clicks of the mouse.

Malcolm also addressed the issue of money laundering through online casinos. Criminals who make their money from illegal activities such as drugs are known to use online casino accounts to stash their profits. Once the money is in the casino, the crooks use the games themselves to transfer money to their associates. Some criminals set up private tables at online casino sites and then intentionally lose their money to business associates at the table. In other instances, the casino is part of the crime organization. All the criminal has to do in these cases is to lose money to the casino.

In October 2006 Congress approved the Unlawful Internet Gambling Enforcement Act (Title VIII of the Security and Accountability for Every Port Act of 2006), which made it illegal for banks and credit card companies in the United States to make payments to Internet gambling sites, effectively ending online gambling nationwide. The prohibition was rooted in the Federal Wire Act of 1961, which outlawed the use of wire communication to transmit bets or wagers. Michael McCarthy and Jon Swartz report in "New Legislation May Pull the Plug on Online Gambling" (USAToday.com, October 3, 2006) that PartyGaming, the world's largest online gambling company, generated 80% of its $1 billion revenues in 2005 from 920,000 active customers in the United States. At the time of the ban, the U.S. market accounted for an estimated 50% to 60% of online gambling worldwide. After the passage of the act, several bills came under consideration to review and revise the regulation of online gaming. Among the items introduced were the Skill Game Protection Act, a bill sponsored by Representative Robert Wexler (1961–; D-FL) in 2007, which set out to exempt such games as poker, backgammon, and other games requiring skill from regulation under the Unlawful Internet Gambling Enforcement Act; the Internet Gambling Regulation, Consumer Protection, and Enforcement Act, sponsored by Representative Barney Frank (1940–; D-MA) in 2009, which proposed legalizing online gambling under a new system of federal oversight and regulation; and the Internet Gambling Regulation and Tax Enforcement Act, a bill sponsored by Representative Jim McDermott (1936–; D-WA) in 2010, which proposed licensing operators of Internet gambling sites and imposing taxes and fees on both gamers and site operators. A turning point in the legal struggle over online gambling came in December 2011, when the Department of Justice declared that the 1961 Wire Act applied solely to sports-related gambling. Nathan Vardi reports in "Department of Justice Flip-Flops on Internet Gambling" (Forbes.com, December 23, 2011) that the decision enabled states to begin selling lottery tickets online, while also creating a legal opening for Internet poker and other forms of casino gambling sites.

As of November 2016, three states (Nevada, New Jersey, and Delaware) had legalized Internet gambling.

In "U.S. Should Go All In with Online Gambling" (BloombergView.com, November 25, 2013), Bloomberg-View projected that tax revenues on Internet gambling had the potential to generate up to $41 billion between 2013 and 2023. Nevertheless, as Brad Tuttle notes in "So Far, Online Gambling Revenues Have Been Pathetic" (Time.com, April 3, 2014), online gambling in New Jersey generated only $4.2 million in tax revenues between November 2013 and February 2014, far below the $160 million in annual tax revenues originally projected by proponents of legalization. However, as Chris Grove notes in "No Summer Slump for NJ Online Casinos as New Revenue Records Abound" (OnlinePokerReport.com, August 14, 2016), monthly revenues from online gambling operations in New Jersey grew considerably during the next two years and topped $17.3 million by July 2016.

## RECORDED MUSIC

The conversion from analog recordings to digital music during the 1980s changed the way Americans listened to music. Humans talk and listen in analog. When people speak, they create vibrations in their throats that then travel through the air around them like ripples in a pond. A membrane in the ear, known as an eardrum, picks up these vibrations, allowing people to hear. Patterns in these vibrations enable people to differentiate sounds from one another. Before compact discs (CDs) and MP3 files, all music was recorded in analog form. On a record player, the vibrations that create music are impressed into grooves on a vinyl disc. A needle passing over this impression vibrates in the same way, turning those vibrations into electrical waveforms that travel along a wire to an amplifier and into a speaker. With tape players, the analog waveforms are recorded in electronic form nearly verbatim on a magnetic tape.

The biggest problem with analog recordings is that each time the music is recorded or copied, the waveform degrades in quality, much like a photocopy of an image. Digitizing the music resolves this problem of fidelity. To record and play music digitally, an analog-to-digital converter (ADC) and a digital-to-analog converter (DAC) are needed. In the recording process, the analog music is fed through the ADC, which samples the analog waveforms and then breaks them down into a series of binary numbers represented by zeros and ones. The numbers are then stored on a disc or a memory chip like any other type of digital information. To play the music back, these numbers are fed through a DAC. The DAC reads the numbers and reproduces the original analog waveform that then travels to the headphones or speakers. Because the numbers always reproduce a high-quality version of the original recording, no quality (fidelity) is lost, regardless of how many times the song is transferred or recorded.

## Compact Discs

Digital music was first introduced into the U.S. mainstream in 1983 in the form of CDs. Klaas Compaan, a Dutch physicist, originally came up with the idea for the CD in 1969 and developed a glass prototype a year later at Philips Corporation. Over the next nine years both Philips and Sony worked on various prototypes of a CD player. In 1979 the two companies came together to create a final version and set the standards for the CD. The first CD players were sold in Japan and Europe in 1982 and then in the United States in 1983.

With a standard CD, music is recorded digitally on the surface of a polycarbonate plastic disc in a long spiral track 0.00002 inches (0.00005 cm) wide that winds from the center of the disk to the outer edges. A space 0.00006 inches (0.00015 cm) wide separates each ring of the spiral track from the one next to it. Tiny divots, or pits, a minimum of 0.00003 inches (0.00008 cm) long, are engraved into the surface of the track. The polycarbonate disc is then covered by a layer of aluminum, followed by a layer of clear acrylic. As the disc spins in the disc drive, a laser follows this tiny track counterclockwise, and a light sensor, sitting next to the laser, tracks the changes in the laser light as it reflects off the CD. The laser strikes a nondivoted section of track, which causes the laser light to bounce off the aluminum and then back to the light sensor uninterrupted. However, each time the laser hits one of the divots along the CD track, the light is scattered. These flashes of light represent the binary code that makes up the music. Electronics in the disc player read this code. The ones and zeros are then fed into a digital signal processor, which acts as a DAC, and the analog waveform for the music moves to the headphones or speakers.

When CD players were first released in the United States by both Sony and Philips in 1983, they were priced close to $900 apiece ($2,175 in 2016 dollars). The CDs themselves, which occupied a small section of the music store at the time, went for close to $20 apiece ($48 in 2016 dollars). Despite the high costs, the U.S. Census Bureau indicates in *Statistical Abstract of the United States: 2003* (2004, http://www.census.gov/prod/2004pubs/03statab/inforcomm.pdf) that 22.6 million CDs were sold in 1985. By 1990, 286.5 million CDs were sold. As reported in the *Proquest Statistical Abstract of the United States: 2014*, by 2000 this number peaked at 942.5 million, before plummeting to 210.9 million by 2012 because of competition from MP3 players and other digital and online music formats. Over the years CD players have become much more compact and have been equipped with many more features, often designed to increase sound quality. By 2016 personal CD players and portable CD stereo units were widely available for less than $50.

## Rise of the MP3 Format

In 1985 the first CD read-only memory (CD-ROM) players were released for computers, again by Sony and Philips. CD-ROM players can read computer data from CD-ROMs as well as music from CDs. Although people with early CD-ROMs were able to listen to CD music, downloading it onto a computer was difficult. A three-minute song on a CD consisted roughly of 32 megabytes. (Each byte consists of a string of eight ones and zeros that can be used to represent binary numbers from 0 to 255. In binary, which is a base-two number system, 1 is 00000001, 2 is 00000010, 3 is 00000011, and so on up to 255, which is represented as 11111111.) During the late 1980s and early 1990s most computer hard drives were only big enough to hold a few songs straight from an audio CD. In 1987 researchers at the Fraunhofer Institute for Integrated Circuits in Germany began to look into ways to compress digital video and sound data into smaller sizes for broadcasting purposes. Out of this work, the MP2 (MPEG-1 Audio Layer II) and then the MP3 (MPEG-1 Audio Layer III) audio file formats emerged. Other compression formats, such as Windows Media Audio and Advanced Audio Coding, have come onto the market since then but are not nearly as well known.

Using such compression formats and encoding software, digital songs can be compressed from 32 megabytes per song to as little as 3 megabytes per song. CD recordings pick up any and every sound in a studio or concert. Compression systems, such as MP3, work by cutting out sounds in CD recordings that people do not pay attention to or do not hear. This may include sounds drowned out by louder instruments. In classical music, an MP3 encoder might cut out a nearly indiscernible note from a flutist or the sound of a faint cough in the audience. It then condenses the recording to one-tenth its previous size. When played back, the encoder reconstructs the song. The compressed files sound nearly as good as CD tracks and much better than audiotapes.

At first, these compression formats and encoding software existed only on home computers. In February 1999 Diamond Multimedia released the first hard drive–based music player. Because early players played mainly MP3 formats, all hard drive–based music players, such as the Apple iPod, became known as MP3 players. All MP3 players consist of a hard drive (many were available in the 20-gigabyte to 60-gigabyte range in 2016) and all the electronic circuitry necessary to transform MP3 and other compressed music files into analog music. Using a cable, these players can be hooked up directly to a home computer. Once the device is connected, the user can download thousands of songs onto the hard drive of the MP3 device. When the user selects a song, a microprocessor in the player pulls the song from the hard drive. A built-in signal processor decompresses the MP3 file (or other type of compressed music file) into a digital CD format, converts the digital signal to an analog signal, and then sends the analog waveform to the headphones. Although compressed music files do not sound quite as good as CD tracks, people can place their entire music collection on a player smaller than the palm of their hand. Since 1999 significant advances in technology have led to major improvements in iPods and other MP3 players. In 2016 most new players had color screens and the ability to play video files, which typically were compressed using an MPEG-4 video compression format.

### MP3 and Peer-to-Peer File Sharing

The widespread use of MP3 files and the increased size of hard drives in the late 1990s caused a transformation in the music industry almost as big as the advent of digital music. People suddenly had the ability to store entire music libraries on their computers and swap music for free using peer-to-peer file-sharing networks. According to Michael Gowan, in "Requiem for Napster" (PCWorld.com, May 17, 2002), the Napster file-sharing service had approximately 80 million subscribers at its peak. However, the availability of free music cut deeply into the recording industry's sales, and the Recording Industry Association of America (RIAA) sued Napster and the users of other peer-to-peer networks who shared music files (see Chapter 4). Some high-profile bands at the time, such as Metallica and Creed, joined the RIAA in its attempt to close down Napster. Other musicians, however, did not seem fazed by Internet file sharing. Radiohead released its 2000 album *Kid A* on the Internet three weeks before it was released in stores. The buzz generated by the Internet prerelease catapulted the album to number one in the United States after it hit record stores. Before *Kid A*, Radiohead had never had a number-one album in the United States.

The lawsuits brought on by the RIAA succeeded in putting an end to much of the free file-swapping on the Internet. The free Napster website shut down in July 2001 and reopened later as a pay music service where users could buy songs. After the RIAA began going after private citizens, traffic on many of the remaining peer-to-peer sites diminished greatly. The number of people using noncentralized peer-to-peer networks such as Kazaa dropped precipitously after the RIAA became litigious with file swappers in 2003. Lee Rainie et al. reported in the Pew data memo "The Impact of Music Industry Suits against Music File Swappers" (January 2004, http://www.pewinternet.org/~/media//Files/Reports/2004/PIP_File_Swapping_Memo_0104.pdf.pdf) that only 14% of American adults downloaded music from the Internet in the last two months of 2003, compared with 29% only six months earlier. However, even after the demise of Napster, revenues in the recording industry decreased. Tim Ingham reports in "Global Record Industry Income Drops below $15bn for First Time in Decades" (MusicBusinessWorldwide.com, April 14, 2015) that global revenues from recorded music fell from $22.4 billion in 2004 to just under $15 billion in 2014.

**FIGURE 5.7**

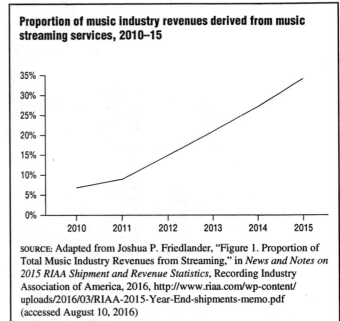

**Proportion of music industry revenues derived from music streaming services, 2010–15**

SOURCE: Adapted from Joshua P. Friedlander, "Figure 1. Proportion of Total Music Industry Revenues from Streaming," in *News and Notes on 2015 RIAA Shipment and Revenue Statistics*, Recording Industry Association of America, 2016, http://www.riaa.com/wp-content/uploads/2016/03/RIAA-2015-Year-End-shipments-memo.pdf (accessed August 10, 2016)

After the RIAA took legal steps to combat free music-sharing sites, sales of digital music downloads increased. According to Apple (2016, http://www.apple.com/pr/products/ipodhistory), after launching its iTunes service in April 2003, the company sold 25 million songs by year's end. By February 2010 the total number of songs sold on iTunes had climbed to 10 billion. During this time, more Americans were also turning to online music streaming services, such as Pandora and Spotify, to gain personalized access to extensive digital music libraries. As Figure 5.7 shows, streaming services accounted for 7% of all recorded music revenues in 2010; by 2015 this figure had risen to 34%. Overall, streaming services and digital downloads accounted for about two-thirds (68%) of all recorded music sales in 2015. (See Figure 5.8.)

## TELEVISION

Although inventors had been trying to create a television as early as 1877, many people consider Philo Farnsworth (1906–1971) to be the father of the first modern, electronic television. He demonstrated his device for the first time in San Francisco in 1927, when he transmitted an image of a dollar sign. Using Farnsworth's design, Radio Corporation of America (RCA; then the owner of the National Broadcasting Company [NBC] network) began work on the first commercial television system during the late 1930s. In 1939 the first commercial televisions were introduced. Early televisions had tiny screens and were as big as small dressers. The pictures were in black and white, and at first the major networks broadcast only in the largest cities. Full-scale broadcasting began nationwide in 1947.

**FIGURE 5.8**

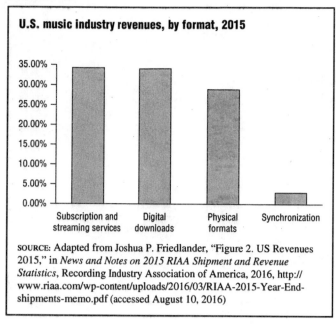

**U.S. music industry revenues, by format, 2015**

SOURCE: Adapted from Joshua P. Friedlander, "Figure 2. US Revenues 2015," in *News and Notes on 2015 RIAA Shipment and Revenue Statistics*, Recording Industry Association of America, 2016, http://www.riaa.com/wp-content/uploads/2016/03/RIAA-2015-Year-End-shipments-memo.pdf (accessed August 10, 2016)

Since the early 1960s television has been the most popular medium of entertainment for Americans. In *There's No Place Like Home to Spend an Evening, Say Most Americans* (January 10, 2002, http://www.gallup.com/poll/5164/theres-place-like-home-spend-evening-say-most-americans.aspx), Lydia Saad of the Gallup Organization reports that 27% of Americans in a December 1960 poll said their favorite way of spending their evening was in front of a television. Resting, reading, and entertaining and visiting friends were ranked second, third, and fourth, respectively. Television appeared to hit its peak between the mid-1960s and early 1970s. A full 46% of people polled in February 1974 rated watching television as their favorite evening activity, followed by reading (14%), dining out (12%), and "staying at home with the family" (10%).

By the second decade of the 21st century, however, television viewership had begun to decline. Victor Luckerson reports in "Fewer People Than Ever Are Watching TV" (Time.com, December 3, 2014) that the average amount of time an individual spent watching TV each month fell from 147 hours in 2011 to 141 hours in 2014, due largely to the increasing popularity of the Internet and video streaming services. This decline in TV viewership was particularly evident among young people. According to the marketing analysis site MarketingCharts, in "Traditional TV Viewing: What a Difference 5 Years Makes" (July 5, 2016, http://www.marketingcharts.com/television/are-young-people-watching-less-tv-24817/), between 2011 and 2016, television viewing fell among almost all age demographics, with the notable exception of people aged 65 years and older. The decline was most notable among adults aged 18 to 24 years, where TV viewing fell 39.1% over a five-year span, followed by teens aged 12 to 17 years

(36.4%); TV viewership also saw a significant drop among adults aged 25 to 34 years (21.9%) and 35 to 49 (11.7%). By contrast, TV viewership among seniors aged 65 years and older increased by 4.6% between 2011 and 2016.

**Developments in Television Technology**

In terms of television accessories, the big development during the late 1990s was the digital video disc (also known as "digital versatile disc" or DVD). DVDs work almost exactly in the same way as music CDs, but the standard DVD can hold up to seven times more information per disc, which allows the DVD to carry the data needed for much larger video files. After its release in 1997, the DVD quickly rose to become the preferred format for watching recorded movies, supplanting the videocassette recorder (VCR) that had dominated the market since the early 1980s. A higher-quality DVD format known as Blu-ray was introduced in Japan in 2003 and marketed globally in 2006. Capable of storing between 25 gigabytes and 50 gigabytes of data, Blu-ray discs produced a picture definition that was far sharper than that offered by conventional DVDs. Chris Morris writes in "Blu-ray Struggles in the Streaming Age" (Fortune.com, January 8, 2016) that by 2015 roughly 43.5 million U.S. households owned Blu-ray players.

The design and quality of TV sets also experienced a radical evolution beginning in the 1990s. Among the most significant innovations was the development of flat-screen (or flat-panel) televisions. Flat-screen televisions offered numerous advantages over traditional television sets. For one, flat screens were more streamlined and energy-efficient than traditional televisions, which used bulky cathode-ray tubes to generate images. At the same time, flat screens offered the potential for a higher-resolution picture quality. The two principal technologies behind the emergence of flat screens were liquid crystal display (LCD) and plasma. Widely used in calculators and laptop computers, LCD screens are composed of two polarized panels containing millions of liquid crystals, each of which controls a particular aspect of the light being projected through the screen. Plasma screens, on the other hand, contain tubes of gases that emit light when charged with electricity. By manipulating light in this way, LCD and plasma technologies are able to project images onto a television screen. The first flat-screen plasma televisions became widely available to consumers in 1997, and cost more than $7,000 ($10,495 in 2016 dollars). While LCD technology developed more gradually, by the early part of the new century LCD TVs began to compete with plasma models. Many higher-quality LCD televisions also began to use light-emitting diode (LED) backlighting technology, which produced a sharper picture quality while requiring less energy.

**Cable Television**

Cable television began in 1948 in Mahanoy City, Pennsylvania. John Walson (1915–1993), the owner of an electronics shop, began selling televisions in 1947. However, few customers in the local area wanted to buy a television because of the bad reception caused by the surrounding mountains. To increase sales potential, Walson erected an antenna on a nearby mountaintop, ran a cable from the antenna to his store, and connected it to his television. He then agreed to attach cables from his antenna to the houses of those who bought televisions from him. From then until the early 1970s, cable networks were generally used only in rural or mountainous areas. At most, early cable television programming included local broadcasts and a broadcast or two from a nearby region.

As early as 1965 the U.S. government and various contractors began putting up a communications satellite network. A satellite network remedied the biggest obstacle faced by broadcasters during the 1960s, which was the curvature of the earth. If the earth were flat, televisions could receive broadcast signals from thousands of miles away. However, because of the curvature of the earth, these broadcast signals escape into space after traveling about 100 miles (161 km). With a satellite system in place, a transmitter on the East Coast can beam a signal to a satellite above Kansas. The satellite then relays the signal to the West Coast without interruption.

Home Box Office (HBO) became the first pay cable station in 1972 and was the first television broadcaster to take advantage of a satellite communications network. HBO began in Wilkes-Barre, Pennsylvania, and broadcast its movies and shows to a limited number of cable networks in and around the state. In 1975, to expand the subscription television market, HBO leased the right to use one of the uplinks on RCA's *Satcom I* communications satellite. Once HBO was on the satellite network, any cable network provider in the United States could buy a 9.8-foot (3-m) satellite dish and provide HBO for any house on the network. By 1978 HBO had 1 million customers. Ted Turner (1938–), who put his Atlanta-based station, WTBS, on the satellite network in 1976, created the Cable News Network (CNN) in 1980. The Music Television Network (MTV) and a number of other stations followed in 1981 and launched an era of exponential growth for the cable industry.

Since the 1980s advances in cable, satellite, and digital technology have steadily changed the way Americans watch television. According to *Proquest Statistical Abstract of the United States: 2014*, the number of people who subscribed to cable and satellite television providers (also known as multichannel video programming distributors, or MVPDs) peaked in 2001, when 66.7 million adults subscribed to cable TV. As the 21st century progressed, however, cable television began to be eclipsed by other technologies. Myles Udland reports in "This Is the Scariest Chart in the History of Cable TV"

(BusinessInsider.com, August 18, 2015) that the percentage of U.S. households that subscribed to some form of MVPD fell from just over 88% in 2010 to 80% in 2015. Much of this decline was driven by the increasing popularity of "cord-cutting," a trend that saw many former MVPD customers cancel their subscriptions to take advantage of video content available over broadband Internet. Luckerson reports that between 2013 and 2014 the proportion of U.S. households that relied exclusively on broadband for viewing videos and other streaming content more than doubled, rising from 1.1% to 2.8%. Meanwhile, Udland notes that the nation's eight leading cable and satellite television companies, a group that includes Comcast, Cox Communications, Charter-Time Warner, DISH Network, and DirectTV, saw their total number of subscribers fall by 463,000 during the second quarter of 2015.

## Advances in Broadcasting Technology

In 1994 a new way of broadcasting movies and television shows became available when RCA released its Direct Satellite System (DSS). The DSS was the first affordable satellite receiver available to the American public. By installing an 18-inch (46-cm) satellite dish on their houses, Americans could receive nearly 200 channels in their living rooms. To squeeze so many channels into a stream of data small enough to travel through space and back, the direct broadcasting satellite provider had to use a form of digital compression known as MPEG-1. The MPEG-1 compression format works much like an MP3 format. (The MP3 format was developed from the audio portion of the MPEG-1 format.) To employ the MPEG-1 format, all television shows recorded in analog must first be transformed by ADCs into a digital format. MPEG-1 encoders, owned by the direct broadcasting satellite provider, then compress the digital data largely by removing redundant scenery between frames. For example, if a character's face movement is the only discernible change between two frames in a movie, then the background from the first frame is applied to both frames, cutting out the redundant information in the second frame. The compressed signal is then beamed to the satellite network. On receiving the signal, the satellite network broadcasts the signal to homes all across the country. A DSS box in the home decompresses the signal and delivers it to the viewer.

DIGITAL CABLE. Several years after the first direct broadcast satellites were released, cable companies introduced digital cable. Digital cable works in much the same way as direct broadcast satellites but uses a slightly more advanced MPEG-2 format for compression. By digitally compressing their programming, cable providers found they could transmit 10 times more television stations than before along their cables. Many cable providers added music stations, pay-per-view movies, and multiple movie channels to their services. The only drawback with both the digital cable and satellite systems is that the decoder can work only on one television at a time, and it is usually bulky.

## Digital Television

Many confuse the concept of digital cable with digital television. Digital cable simply uses digital technology to compress the size of broadcasts so the customer has more channels. The digital signal also does not degrade as it travels across miles of coaxial cable. Most of the programming fed through the digital cable systems is not digitally recorded. Digital television, however, is digital from start to finish. Digital cameras are used to record the broadcast; cables, satellite systems, and broadcast towers send a digital signal; and digital televisions play the broadcast. The result is a television picture that more closely resembles an image on a computer monitor than an image on a television set.

The Federal Communications Commission (FCC) established a number of standards for digital television, which became mandatory for full-power stations on June 12, 2009. Standard-definition television (SDTV) has the resolution of an analog television, which is roughly 480 x 440 dots per inch (dpi) or 210,000 pixels in total. The next step up in visual quality is enhanced-definition television (EDTV), which generally has the same overall resolution as SDTV but features a wider screen. High-definition television (HDTV) offers resolutions up to 1,920 dpi horizontally and 1,080 dpi vertically. Overall, HDTV has more than 2 million pixels to display each image, which provides the viewer with 10 times the detail of SDTV. Ultra-high-definition (UHD, also known as 4K) has 4,096 x 2,160 resolution, or 8.3 million pixels.

CONVERSION TO DIGITAL TELEVISION. The FCC standards for digital television were adopted after Congress passed the 1996 Telecommunications Act. The act called for a full conversion to digital television across the United States within 10 years. By 2006 every television station serving every market in the United States would be required to air digital programming. In addition, broadcasters would no longer have to air analog content. Americans with an analog television set would be required to buy either a digital television or a $50 to $100 ADC device to watch television. In 2005, however, only a small percentage of Americans had HDTV or even EDTV. Consequently, in 2005 Congress pushed the deadline for the digitization of television to February 17, 2009. This deadline, too, was later extended to June 2009.

On January 1, 2008, the National Telecommunications and Information Administration of the U.S. Department of Commerce began issuing $40 coupons that defrayed the cost of converter boxes, allowing consumers to continue using older, analog television sets after the conversion to digital broadcasting. Households were eligible to receive two coupons and were required to redeem them toward the purchase of converter boxes within 90 days. In December 2009 the TV Converter Box Coupon Program (December 9, 2009, http://www.ntia.doc.gov/legacy/dtvcoupon/reports/NTIA_DTVWeekly_120909.pdf) released the final number of coupon requests that had been received, processed, and redeemed. As of December 9, 2009, the program had received 64.1 million requests, and had approved coupons for 34.8 million households.

## 3-D and 4K Television

By 2010 a number of television manufacturers had introduced three-dimensional (3-D) television sets. Most of the new models projected 3-D images to viewers wearing special glasses, but in late 2010 Toshiba debuted the Regza GL1, a flat-panel 3-D television that required no glasses. Instead, Dan Reisinger reports in "Digital Home" (CNET.com, October 4, 2010) that the Regza presented multiple images of each two-dimensional frame that viewers' brains "superimposed...to create a three-dimensional impression of the image." At the time of the product release, the sets were available only in 12-inch and 20-inch (30.5- cm and 50.8-cm) models, and the 3-D effect was viewable within only a limited area two to three feet (0.61 m to 0.91 m) from the screen.

By 2016 interest in 3-D television technology had somewhat waned as the higher-resolution 4K gained popularity, and televisions with high dynamic range (HDR) were introduced. HDR improved the performance of pixels to provide brighter, clearer, more colorful images onscreen. However, as of 2016 limited programming was available in 4K, primarily through such streaming services as Netflix and Amazon Prime. According to "Watch the 2016 Rio Olympic Games in 4K Ultra HD" (July 28, 2016, http://www.nbcolympics.com/4khdr), NBC Universal used 4K technology to cover a number of events from the 2016 Summer Olympics in Rio de Janeiro, releasing the 4K programming available to the public one day after the original live broadcast.

## Television and the Internet

As higher connection speeds and faster computers became more widespread, the Internet became a popular source of video entertainment. Several video-sharing websites enabled Internet users from around the world to post videos and other recorded content online. Of these sites, YouTube quickly emerged as one of the most popular. Created in February 2005, YouTube allowed visitors to view and upload videos free of charge, while also enabling users to create their own accounts and video libraries. In "Video Websites Pop Up, Invite Postings" (USAToday.com, November 22, 2005), Jefferson Graham reports that the site had more than 200,000 registered users by late 2005. Traditional media outlets quickly recognized the marketing potential of YouTube, and soon clips from television programs, movie trailers, news features, and other mainstream content became available on the video site. YouTube's rapidly increasing popularity soon attracted the attention of major media and technology corporations, who regarded the site as a means of reaching new audiences of younger consumers. Indeed, the site's growth was staggering; as Andrew Ross Sorkin reports (NYTimes.com, October 10, 2006), by October 2006 YouTube visitors were watching more than 100 million videos per day, a 4,900% increase in less than a year. A month later, Google acquired YouTube for $1.7 billion.

The success of YouTube inspired a range of other online outlets for video content. Prominent among these was Hulu, a streaming video site that airs shows and movies produced by major studios and TV networks, and Netflix, which began offering streaming services to its subscribers in 2007. The spread of streaming video channels was accompanied by a rise in the popularity of the Roku player, a device that enabled users to stream Internet content directly into their TV sets. As of 2016, premium cable channels such as HBO and Showtime also made content available to consumers through online streaming services. Amanda Walgrove writes in "The Explosive Growth of Online Video, in 5 Charts" (Contently.com, July 6, 2015) that in 2011 the average American adult watched 39 minutes of digital video each day; by 2015 this figure had climbed to one hour and 55 minutes per day.

# CHAPTER 6
# HIGH TECHNOLOGY AND EDUCATION

Computer literacy and Internet access have become central to modern education. Not having access to information technology restricts a person's ability to search for a job, communicate with others, and efficiently perform a range of everyday activities from viewing movie or real estate listings to buying tickets for a sporting event. Aware of this, high schools and colleges in the late 1990s increased efforts to expose students to computers and the Internet before graduation. Most elementary and secondary schools installed computers with Internet access in classrooms and libraries. Many schools set up programs wherein their students could borrow laptops and handheld computers for extended periods. College administrations provided widespread broadband access to students on campus, and many professors required the use of the Internet and computer programs in college courses.

Providing students with access to high technology, however, has not been without problems. The Internet, computers, and cell phones have introduced a great deal of distraction into the life of many young people. They allow teenagers, and even younger children, access to illicit material, such as pornography, that they normally could not obtain so easily. In addition, these technologies open up avenues for cheating and plagiarism. Largely because of the Internet, academic cheating and plagiarism skyrocketed around the start of the 21st century. Some students appeared to have no qualms about copying text from the Internet and pasting it verbatim into reports and papers.

In spite of these potential drawbacks, by 2016 technology was deeply interwoven into the educational experience of most U.S. students. According to Pearson Education, in "Pearson Student Mobile Device Survey 2015" (June 2015, http://www.pearsoned.com/wp-content/uploads/2015-Pearson-Student-Mobile-Device-Survey-Grades-4-12.pdf), more than eight out of 10 (83%) of all students in grades four through 12 used a laptop to do schoolwork in 2015. More than half of students surveyed (58%) used either a tablet or smartphone for school-related purposes that year. Elementary school students (78%) were more likely than middle school students (69%) or high school students (49%) to use tablets to perform school work in 2015. Conversely, 82% of high school students used smartphones to complete school work that year, compared with 66% of middle school students and 53% of elementary school students.

## TECHNOLOGY AT SCHOOL

In February 1996 President Bill Clinton (1946–) signed the Telecommunications Act into law. This legislation ushered in the E-Rate Program, which provided elementary and secondary public schools with discounts of between 20% and 90% when purchasing computers for classrooms and libraries. The program had a tremendous impact on computer and Internet accessibility in public schools, and in 2014 program funding was increased from $2.4 billion to $3.9 billion in an effort to expand high-speed broadband access to the Internet in U.S. schools and libraries. According to Pearson Education, in the "Pearson Student Mobile Device Survey 2015," by 2015 about two-thirds (68%) of all public school students had wireless Internet access available at their schools. (In the same survey, 96% of students reported having wireless Internet access at home.)

### Technology and Instruction

As Figure 6.1 shows, in 2015 public school district administrators and principals held similar views concerning the value of using technology to facilitate student learning. In general, school district administrators were more likely to support the notion that online tools, mobile apps, learning management systems, and online classes were useful in promoting personalized learning for their students; the one exception was in the category of online textbooks, which principals were more likely than administrators to find useful as educational tools. High school

FIGURE 6.1

**Attitudes among school principals, district administrators, high school students, and parents concerning the use of various technologies for personalized learning, by type of technology, 2015**

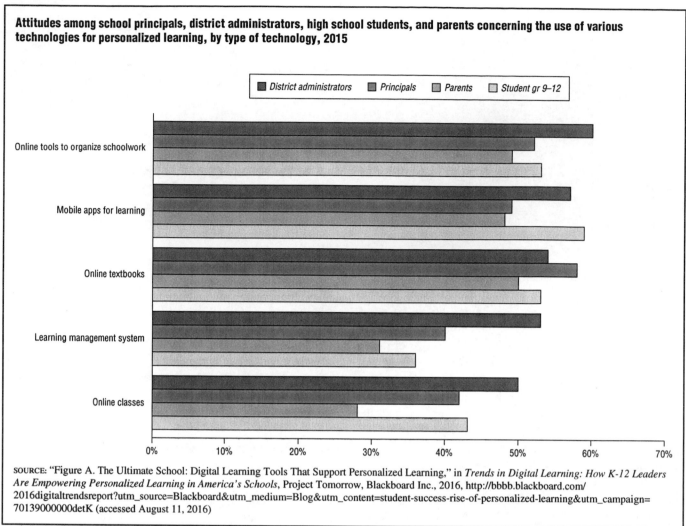

SOURCE: "Figure A. The Ultimate School: Digital Learning Tools That Support Personalized Learning," in *Trends in Digital Learning: How K-12 Leaders Are Empowering Personalized Learning in America's Schools*, Project Tomorrow, Blackboard Inc., 2016, http://bbbb.blackboard.com/ 2016digitaltrendsreport?utm_source=Blackboard&utm_medium=Blog&utm_content=student-success-rise-of-personalized-learning&utm_campaign= 70139000000detK (accessed August 11, 2016)

students were more likely than teachers, principals, or their parents to see the value of mobile apps in their educational experience. By comparison, parents expressed more support for the use of online textbooks in personalized learning than for any other technology.

Overall, a majority of public school principals thought that the use of digital content in the classroom provided multiple benefits to both students and teachers. More than three-quarters (77%) of public school principals in 2015 believed that digital content helped students become more engaged in the learning process, and nearly three-quarters (72%) of high school principals thought that digital educational content played a role in extending the learning experience beyond the classroom. (See Table 6.1.) Under two-thirds (63%) of principals reported that digital content helped improve the quality of the school curriculum, while also making it more relevant. As Table 6.1 shows, 70% of principals in urban schools reported that digital content helped personalize the learning experience for individual students in 2015, compared with 59% of principals in suburban schools, and

51% of principals in rural schools. Overall, only two in five (41%) public school principals in 2015 believed that digital content helped make teachers more productive.

Public school teachers also identified a range of benefits associated with using digital learning tools in the classroom. In "Teachers Still Struggling to Use Tech to Transform Instruction, Survey Finds" (EdWeek.org, June 6, 2016), Anthony Rebora evaluates attitudes toward digital technology among public school teachers. In 2016, 86% of teachers surveyed reported that they had employed digital technology at some point during the school year to oversee learning drills, review content, or conduct practice exercises during class time; nearly two-thirds (64%) of public school teachers reported using digital technology in this manner at least a few times a week, month, or year, and more than one in five (22%) teachers did so on a daily basis. (See Figure 6.2.) In addition, 88% of teachers in 2016 reported that their students had used digital technology to complete individual school projects, and 86% stated that their students had used digital learning tools to conduct research.

**TABLE 6.1**

Attitudes among school principals toward benefits of using digital content in education process, by type of school district, 2015

| Benefits of digital content usage | All principals | School principals that have implemented competency-based learning | | |
| --- | --- | --- | --- | --- |
| | | Principals in rural schools | Principals in suburban schools | Principals in urban schools |
| Students are more engaged in learning | 77% | 79% | 74% | 82% |
| Learning is extended beyond the school day | 72% | 71% | 72% | 75% |
| Curriculum is more relevant and higher quality | 63% | 65% | 68% | 69% |
| Learning is more personalized for each student | 58% | 51% | 59% | 70% |
| Differentiates school as innovative in the use of technology | 56% | 55% | 54% | 61% |
| Improves teachers skills with technology | 54% | 55% | 47% | 66% |
| Improves teacher productivity | 41% | 40% | 37% | 45% |

SOURCE: "Table 2. What Are the Benefits of Using Digital Content within Instruction?" in *Trends in Digital Learning: How K-12 Leaders Are Empowering Personalized Learning in America's Schools*, Project Tomorrow, Blackboard Inc., 2016, http://bbbb.blackboard.com/2016digitaltrendsreport?utm_source=Blackboard&utm_medium=Blog&utm_content=student-success-rise-of-personalized-learning&utm_campaign=70139000000detK (accessed August 11, 2016)

**FIGURE 6.2**

Use of digital technologies in the classroom by educators, by technology type and frequency, 2016

THIS SCHOOL YEAR, HOW OFTEN HAVE YOUR STUDENTS USED DIGITAL DEVICES/TECHNOLOGY FOR THE FOLLOWING PURPOSES IN YOUR CLASSROOM?

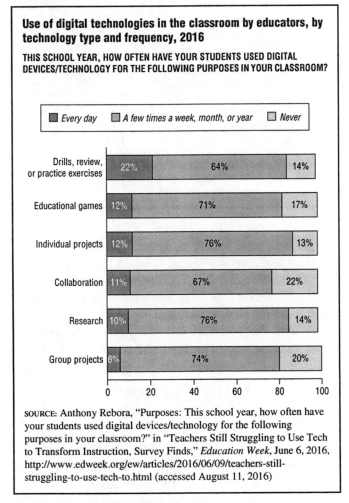

SOURCE: Anthony Rebora, "Purposes: This school year, how often have your students used digital devices/technology for the following purposes in your classroom?" in "Teachers Still Struggling to Use Tech to Transform Instruction, Survey Finds," *Education Week*, June 6, 2016, http://www.edweek.org/ew/articles/2016/06/09/teachers-still-struggling-to-use-tech-to.html (accessed August 11, 2016)

**FIGURE 6.3**

Individuals or groups who influence educators to use digital technologies in the classroom, 2016

IN YOUR VIEW, HOW INFLUENTIAL ARE THE FOLLOWING INDIVIDUALS OR GROUPS IN DECIDING WHAT DIGITAL TECHNOLOGIES AND TOOLS WILL BE USED IN YOUR CLASSROOM?

[Percent "very influential"]

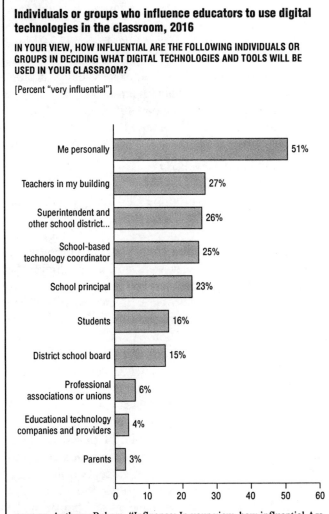

SOURCE: Anthony Rebora, "Influence: In your view, how influential Are the following individuals or groups in deciding what digital technologies and tools will be used in your classroom?" in "Teachers Still Struggling to Use Tech to Transform Instruction, Survey Finds," *Education Week*, June 6, 2016, http://www.edweek.org/ew/articles/2016/06/09/teachers-still-struggling-to-use-tech-to.html (accessed August 11, 2016)

Rebora notes that in 2016 just over half (51%) of public school teachers reported that their own judgment was "very influential" in helping them decide which digital learning tools to use in the classroom. (See Figure 6.3.) Twenty-seven percent stated that the opinions of their fellow teachers played an important role in guiding their use of technology during class time; 26% cited their district superintendent and administrators as exerting an influence on their use of learning technology, and 25% acknowledged their school's technology coordinator as a primary factor. Other individuals or groups that teachers cited as having a strong influence on their use of in-class digital technologies in 2016 included their school's principal (23%), their students (16%), and their local school board (15%). Only 3% of public school teachers surveyed reported that parents exerted an influence on their use of digital learning tools for teaching purposes.

At the same time, Rebora reports on the various challenges that digital learning technologies posed to public school teachers in 2016. As Figure 6.4 indicates, 42% of teachers surveyed reported that an inadequate supply of digital learning devices represented a "very significant" challenge to their ability to use technology in the classroom effectively. Furthermore, one-third (33%) of public school teachers thought that a lack of training presented a significant obstacle to the implementation of digital learning tools for instructional purposes, and 30% cited their district's curriculum requirements as presenting a challenge to the effective use of educational technology during class time. Others in the survey cited a range of technological problems, such as slow or unreliable Internet service (28%), a lack of adequate technical support from staff (21%), and problems with software (19%). (See Figure 6.4.)

## PREVENTING ACCESS TO INAPPROPRIATE MATERIAL

In 2000 Congress passed the Children's Internet Protection Act (CIPA). Under CIPA, public schools and libraries that could not prove they use filtering or blocking technology to keep children from viewing pornographic or sexually explicit websites were no longer eligible for the E-Rate Program. Signed into law in April 2001, CIPA promptly became the target of a legal challenge launched by the American Library Association (ALA) and the American Civil Liberties Union (ACLU). In the lawsuit, the ALA and the ACLU argued that CIPA violated free speech rights guaranteed in the First Amendment. In June 2003 the U.S. Supreme Court upheld the legality of CIPA in *United States v. American Library Association* (539 U.S. 194). By 2005, 100% of U.S. public schools were in compliance with the law. In spite of this widespread acceptance of CIPA, some educators have raised questions about the law's potential to prevent students from engaging in legitimate research. Paul T. Jaeger and Zheng Yan suggest in "One Law with Two Outcomes: Comparing the Implementation of CIPA in Public Libraries and Schools" (*Information Technology & Libraries*, vol. 28, no. 1, March 2009) that although opposition to CIPA in schools has been "very small," there are still some concerns that "filters in schools may create two classes of students— ones with only filtered access at school and ones who also

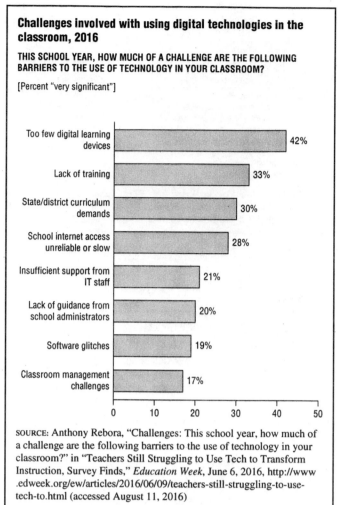

**FIGURE 6.4**

**Challenges involved with using digital technologies in the classroom, 2016**

THIS SCHOOL YEAR, HOW MUCH OF A CHALLENGE ARE THE FOLLOWING BARRIERS TO THE USE OF TECHNOLOGY IN YOUR CLASSROOM?

[Percent "very significant"]

| Challenge | Percent |
|---|---|
| Too few digital learning devices | 42% |
| Lack of training | 33% |
| State/district curriculum demands | 30% |
| School internet access unreliable or slow | 28% |
| Insufficient support from IT staff | 21% |
| Lack of guidance from school administrators | 20% |
| Software glitches | 19% |
| Classroom management challenges | 17% |

SOURCE: Anthony Rebora, "Challenges: This school year, how much of a challenge are the following barriers to the use of technology in your classroom?" in "Teachers Still Struggling to Use Tech to Transform Instruction, Survey Finds," *Education Week*, June 6, 2016, http://www.edweek.org/ew/articles/2016/06/09/teachers-still-struggling-to-use-tech-to.html (accessed August 11, 2016)

can get unfiltered access at home." In "Minors' First Amendment Rights: CIPA and School Libraries" (*Knowledge Quest*, vol. 31, no. 1, September–October 2010), Theresa Chmara raises questions concerning the impact of CIPA on the first amendment rights of children, suggesting that the scope of the law has the potential to restrict students' access to legitimate educational material.

## COLLEGES AND UNIVERSITIES

College students are among the most tech-savvy Americans and are typically the first to embrace new technologies. The marketing research firm Student Monitor (August 2016, http://www.studentmonitor.com/computing.php) reports that in 2016, 86% of full-time undergraduate college students owned their own computers before starting college, and 17% planned to buy a new computer within the next year. The firm also reports that 88% of college students accessed the Internet at least once per day. With a weekly average of 19 hours, students spent twice as much time online in 2016 as those interviewed in 2000. Student Monitor also notes that nearly nine out of ten (88%) full-time undergraduate students had a cell phone.

College students in 2016 typically lived a connected life, accessing the Internet for everything from academic research and class assignments to entertainment, transportation, social networking, shopping, and ordering food. Scott A. Peterson, Tun Aye, and Padao Yang Wheeler observe in "Internet Use and Romantic Relationships among College Students" (*North American Journal of Psychology*, vol. 16, no. 1, March 2014) that the average college student spent a little over 19.5 hours per week online in 2014. Peterson, Aye, and Wheeler note that most of this time was dedicated to activities unrelated to academic work. According to the study, nearly one-third (6.3 hours per week) of all time spent online by college students in 2014 was devoted to social networking; this figure was more than double the 2.9 hours per week devoted to school work.

For male college students, relationship status appeared to have an influence on their Internet activities, according to Peterson, Aye, and Wheeler. Male students involved in a romantic relationship spent a little under four hours per week on social media sites; among male students who were not romantically involved, this figure rose to 7.2 hours a week. By comparison, female students involved in romantic relationships (6.5 hours per week) devoted roughly the same amount of time as female students who were not romantically involved (6.7 hours per week) to social networking on the Internet.

## Technology and College Academics

The Internet has transformed college life from beginning to end, from the selection process undertaken by high school students considering different institutions to the employment and career services offered online to recent college graduates. High school students research prospective colleges and universities online, take virtual campus and dormitory tours, and download recruitment materials and application forms. College students enroll in classes, pay fees, order books and course materials, and take some classes and tests online. For some professors, electronic textbooks (e-textbooks) have supplanted traditional textbooks as a means of assigning reading to their students. In many instances, the Internet is the primary mode of communication between students and faculty. In the *2015 Higher Education Survey of Faculty Attitudes toward Technology* (InsideHigherEd.com, October 14, 2015), Carl Straumsheim, Scott Jaschik, and Doug Lederman report that more than three-quarters (77%) of college faculty members "always" used online learning platforms such as Moodle, Blackboard, and OpenClass to provide their students with information concerning a course syllabus. In addition, Straumsheim, Jaschik, and Lederman note that more than two-thirds (67%) of faculty members either "always" (44%) or "usually" (23%) used such platforms to communicate with their students.

The Internet has also radically transformed the ways that university libraries allocate their financial resources. The Publishers Communication Group reports in *Library Budget Predictions for 2016* (2016, http://www.pcgplus.com/wp-content/uploads/2016/05/Library-Budget-Prediction-2016-Final.pdf) that in 2005 North American university and research libraries devoted just under one-third (31.4%) of their annual budgets to electronic resources. By 2015 this figure was nearly 72%. At the same time, in 2015 more than three-quarters (76%) of all journal subscriptions in North American university and research libraries were available only in electronic formats; by contrast, during that same year 13% of all journal subscriptions at North American university and research libraries were available in print-only editions. Another 11% of journals at North American university and research libraries in 2015 were available in both print and electronic versions.

## The Internet and College Social Life

Since the 1990s technology has had a profound impact on everyday campus life. The Internet and mobile phones have transformed the way that college students communicate with each other, whether they are discussing academic coursework or simply making plans for the weekend. In particular, social networking sites such as Facebook have played an important role in shaping the social relationships of college students in the 21st century. Many students view social networking sites as a way to maintain contact with old friends and meet new people. Reynol Junco of Lock Haven University finds in "In-Class Multitasking and Academic Performance" (*Computers in Human Behavior*, vol. 28, no. 6, November 2012) that in 2012 between 87% and 92% of college undergraduates used Facebook every day, compared with 73% who sent or received text messages daily. On average, students who used Facebook spent more than an hour and 40 minutes on the site each day. Junco notes that 34% of college students reported texting during class at least sometimes, and 13% reported using Facebook 50% or more of the time they were in class.

At times, social media can also provide college advisers with crucial insights into potential problems confronted by their student residents. Lauren E. Kacvinsky and Megan A. Moreno report in "Facebook Use between College Resident Advisors and Their Residents: A Mixed Method Approach" (*College Student Journal*, vol. 8, no. 1, Spring 2014) that 40% of college freshmen surveyed had become friends with their resident advisers (RAs) on Facebook. According to Kacvinsky and Moreno, these students were nearly 50% more likely than their RAs to have initiated the friend request. Among the RAs interviewed by Kacvinsky and Moreno, many believed that the images and status updates posted by their residents offered important indications of potential struggles students might be facing, particularly with alcohol abuse. At the same time, RAs generally agreed that following up on potential issues in person was vital to building trusting relationships with their students.

Still, for most college students social media is primarily a means of making connections with their peers. The Institute of Politics (IOP) at Harvard University's Kennedy School of Government reports in "Use of Social Networking Technology" (2016, http://iop.harvard.edu/use-social-networking-technology) that Facebook remained the dominant social networking platform on college campuses in 2016, with 87% of all undergraduates reporting they had a Facebook account that year. Other popular social media sites among college students in 2016 included Twitter, which was used by nearly half (47%) of all undergraduates, followed by Instagram (45%), Pinterest (37%), Snapchat (34%), and Tumblr (19%).

Another mobile social networking platform that had gained popularity among college students in 2016 was Yik Yak (https://www.yikyak.com/home). Launched by Brooks Buffington and Tyler Droll in 2013, Yik Yak serves as an electronic bulletin board, allowing users within a 1.5-mile (2.4-km) radius of each other to post and read anonymous comments. Soon after its initial launch, the Yik Yak app quickly gained popularity among college students. Alyson Shontell reports in "How 2 Georgia Fraternity Brothers Created Yik Yak, a Controversial App That Became a $400 Million Business in 365 Days" (BusinessInsider.com, March 12, 2015) that by 2015 Yik Yak had users on 1,600 college campuses nationwide. As it grew in popularity, however, Yik Yak also found itself mired in controversy, as some individuals began using the app as a forum for hate speech and other offensive messages. Rebecca Schuman writes in "It's Not about Yik Yak" (Slate.com, October 27, 2015) that by 2015 individual Yik Yak users had also become targets of cyberbullying and harassment. In some cases, female students were singled out with threats of sexual violence. These attacks prompted outrage among feminists and other activists, and in October 2015 more than 70 women's groups and civil rights organizations sent a letter to the U.S. Department of Education, insisting that college administrators should take measures to curb abusive behavior on the site.

## DISTANCE LEARNING

Besides providing students with a host of valuable new research tools, the Internet has also made education more widely available to a greater portion of the population. In the past, people who lived in remote areas of the country, had limited access to transportation, suffered from illness or other disabilities, or were constrained by work or other obligations struggled to pursue educational opportunities. With the emergence of distance learning programs, however, students were able to take classes online from their own home.

Thomas D. Snyder, Cristobal de Brey, and Sally A. Dillow report in *Digest of Education Statistics 2014* (April 2016, http://nces.ed.gov/pubs2016/2016006.pdf) that in 2002–03 a total of 317,070 students in kindergarten to 12th grade were enrolled in distance learning courses in the United States; by 2009–10 this number had risen to 1.8 million, an increase of 473%. High school students (1.3 million) accounted for the majority of distance learning enrollments in 2009–10, followed by middle school students (154,970), and elementary school students (78,040). By region, the highest proportion of school districts offering distance learning in 2009–10 was in the Southeast, where 78% of all schools offered distance education courses; by comparison, 39% of school districts in the Northeast, 51% of school districts in the West, and 62% of school districts in the Central region offered distance learning opportunities to their students.

Distance learning programs also became widespread at colleges and universities in the early 21st century. Indeed, for some students taking online courses was a more attractive option than attending classes in person. There are many reasons students prefer distance learning to traditional college course offerings. For some, geographical distance or scheduling conflicts make it difficult to attend traditional classes, and online courses offer far greater flexibility and convenience. Figure 6.5 provides a breakdown of college students enrolled exclusively in distance learning courses in fall 2014. As Figure 6.5 shows, 60% of all students enrolled in private, four-year, for-profit institutions took only online classes in the fall of 2014. By comparison, 13% of students enrolled in private, four-year, nonprofit institutions and 11% of students enrolled in two-year public institutions were enrolled exclusively in distance learning classes that term. Only 3% of students enrolled in two-year, private, nonprofit colleges were enrolled exclusively in distance learning courses in fall 2014.

Figure 6.6 offers an overview of distance learning participation among postbaccalaureate students in fall 2014. Postbaccalaureate students are those who continue taking courses at the undergraduate level even after completing their college degrees. As Figure 6.6 shows, 67% of all postbaccalaureate students enrolled at degree-granting postsecondary institutions took no online classes in the fall of 2014. These percentages were highest for students enrolled at public (74%) and private nonprofit (72%) institutions. Among postbaccalaureate students enrolled at private, for-profit institutions, on the other hand, 15% took no distance learning classes in the fall of 2014. Among postbaccalaureate students enrolled exclusively in distance-learning classes that term, the highest proportion were enrolled at private, for-profit postsecondary institutions, where 81% of all postbaccalaureate students were taking online courses exclusively.

**FIGURE 6.5**

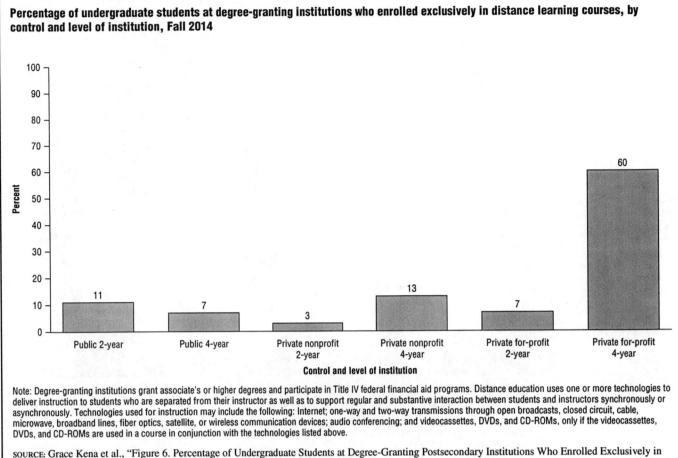

Percentage of undergraduate students at degree-granting institutions who enrolled exclusively in distance learning courses, by control and level of institution, Fall 2014

Note: Degree-granting institutions grant associate's or higher degrees and participate in Title IV federal financial aid programs. Distance education uses one or more technologies to deliver instruction to students who are separated from their instructor as well as to support regular and substantive interaction between students and instructors synchronously or asynchronously. Technologies used for instruction may include the following: Internet; one-way and two-way transmissions through open broadcasts, closed circuit, cable, microwave, broadband lines, fiber optics, satellite, or wireless communication devices; audio conferencing; and videocassettes, DVDs, and CD-ROMs, only if the videocassettes, DVDs, and CD-ROMs are used in a course in conjunction with the technologies listed above.

SOURCE: Grace Kena et al., "Figure 6. Percentage of Undergraduate Students at Degree-Granting Postsecondary Institutions Who Enrolled Exclusively in Distance Education Courses, by Control and Level of Institution: Fall 2014," in *The Condition of Education 2016*, U.S. Department of Education, National Center for Education Statistics, May 2016, http://nces.ed.gov/pubs2016/2016144.pdf (accessed August 11, 2016)

Table 6.2 provides a breakdown of distance learning in the United States in 2013. Of the 4,716 degree-granting postsecondary institutions in the United States that year, 61, or 1.3%, were primarily dedicated to offering online courses to their students. Overall, nearly 2.7 million students enrolled in degree-granting postsecondary institutions in 2013 took distance learning courses exclusively. (See Table 6.3.) Of these, nearly 1.4 million took online classes offered by institutions in the state where they lived, whereas just over 1.1 million participated in distance-learning classes offered by colleges or universities located in another state. In addition, 35,767 students who were enrolled exclusively in online classes in 2013 lived outside the United States.

I. Elaine Allen and Jeff Seaman of the Babson Survey Research Group report in *Online Report Card: Tracking Online Education in the United States* (February 2016, http://onlinelearningsurvey.com/reports/onlinereportcard.pdf) that online learning has become increasingly central to the long-term goals of degree-granting postsecondary institutions in the United States. In 2002, just under 50% of colleges and universities reported that distance learning was an integral aspect of their long-term strategic vision. This figure topped 70% in 2014, before dropping to just over 63% in 2015. (See Figure 6.7.) At the same time, academic officers at degree-granting postsecondary institutions reported that a majority of faculty members at their schools rejected the notion that distance learning was beneficial to students. As Figure 6.8 shows, in 2002 fewer than 30% of faculty members at degree-granting postsecondary institutions acknowledged that online classes added value to the educational process. By 2007 this proportion rose to just under 35%, before gradually falling below 30% again by 2015. Overall, the proportion of academic officers who believed that distance learning was as beneficial as or superior to traditional learning rose substantially between 2003 and 2015. In 2003 about 57% of academic officers thought that online courses provided educational benefits that either equaled, were somewhat superior, or were superior to traditional classes, whereas about 43% believed online courses were somewhat inferior or inferior to traditional learning; by 2012 those holding the opinion that online learning was equal to or superior to traditional learning reached 77%, before falling back to 71% in 2015. (See Figure 6.9.)

**FIGURE 6.6**

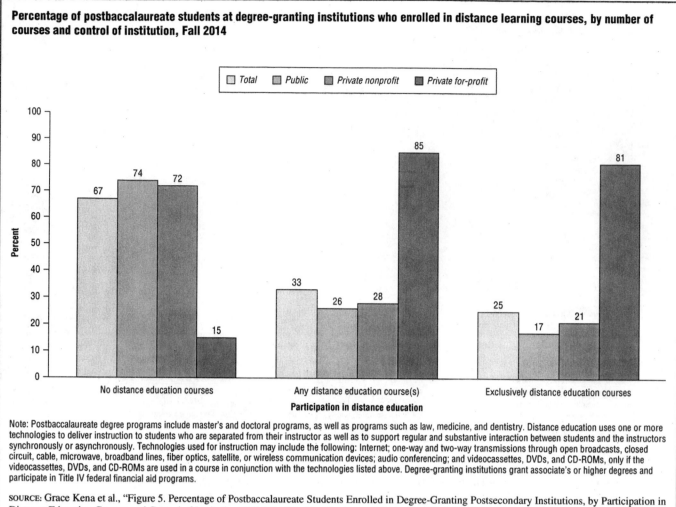

Percentage of postbaccalaureate students at degree-granting institutions who enrolled in distance learning courses, by number of courses and control of institution, Fall 2014

Note: Postbaccalaureate degree programs include master's and doctoral programs, as well as programs such as law, medicine, and dentistry. Distance education uses one or more technologies to deliver instruction to students who are separated from their instructor as well as to support regular and substantive interaction between students and the instructors synchronously or asynchronously. Technologies used for instruction may include the following: Internet; one-way and two-way transmissions through open broadcasts, closed circuit, cable, microwave, broadband lines, fiber optics, satellite, or wireless communication devices; audio conferencing; and videocassettes, DVDs, and CD-ROMs, only if the videocassettes, DVDs, and CD-ROMs are used in a course in conjunction with the technologies listed above. Degree-granting institutions grant associate's or higher degrees and participate in Title IV federal financial aid programs.

SOURCE: Grace Kena et al., "Figure 5. Percentage of Postbaccalaureate Students Enrolled in Degree-Granting Postsecondary Institutions, by Participation in Distance Education Courses and Control of Institution: Fall 2014," in *The Condition of Education 2016*, U.S. Department of Education, National Center for Education Statistics, May 2016, http://nces.ed.gov/pubs2016/2016144.pdf (accessed August 11, 2016)

Among the general public, support for online postsecondary education rose steadily between 2011 and 2015. The Gallup Organization reports in *Americans Value Postsecondary Education: The 2015 Gallup-Lumina Foundation Study of the American Public's Opinion on Higher Education* (April 12, 2016, http://www.gallup.com/file/services/190583/Lumina_Report_2015%20Survey_of_Americans_Attitudes_Toward_Postsecondary_Education_FINAL.pdf) that in 2011, 30% of Americans either agreed or strongly agreed that online colleges and universities offered students a quality education; by 2015 this proportion had risen to 46%. (See Figure 6.10.) According to the Gallup Organization, 39% of Americans in 2015 either strongly agreed (16%) or agreed (23%) that online colleges and universities provided an educational experience that was equal to that offered by traditional postsecondary institutions.

## LIFELONG LEARNING

Digital technology has also made it easier for adults to continue to pursue learning opportunities long after they have completed their formal education. John Horrigan of

the Pew Research Center reports in *Lifelong Learning and Technology* (March 22, 2016, http://www.pewinternet.org/files/2016/03/PI_2016.03.22_Educational-Ecosystems_FINAL.pdf) that adults who use broadband Internet and smartphones at home are considerably more likely to engage in personal learning activities than adults without access to those technologies. For example, in 2015 roughly one-quarter (24%) of adults who had both smartphones and a home broadband connection had taken an online course; by contrast, among adults without access to either technology at home, only 3% participated in distance learning opportunities that year. In addition, 60% of adults with both home broadband and smartphones pursued personal learning opportunities over the Internet in 2015, compared with only 19% of adults who had access to neither technology at home. Horrigan notes that race and ethnicity appear to play a role in determining whether or not American adults pursue educational opportunities online. As Figure 6.11 shows, a majority (53%) of white adults used the Internet to engage in personal learning in 2015, compared with 46% of Hispanic adults and 45% of African American adults.

TABLE 6.2

**Degree-granting postsecondary institutions primarily offering online programs, by select characteristics and control of institution, 2013**

| Selected characteristic | All institutions | Primarily online institutions[a] | | | | | Other institutions[a] | | | |
|---|---|---|---|---|---|---|---|---|---|---|
| | | Total | Percent of all institutions | Public | Nonprofit | For-profit | Total | Public | Nonprofit | For-profit |
| 1 | 2 | 3 | 4 | 5 | 6 | 7 | 8 | 9 | 10 | 11 |
| Number of institutions, fall 2013 | 4,716 | 61 | 1.3 | 4 | 14 | 43 | 4,655 | 1,621 | 1,661 | 1,373 |
| **Fall 2013 enrollment** | | | | | | | | | | |
| Total enrollment | 20,375,789 | 778,619 | 3.8 | 39,490 | 100,424 | 638,705 | 19,597,170 | 14,706,068 | 3,873,580 | 1,017,522 |
| Full-time | 12,597,112 | 480,269 | 3.8 | 5,075 | 52,929 | 422,265 | 12,116,843 | 8,459,734 | 2,933,124 | 723,985 |
| Males | 5,682,166 | 155,592 | 2.7 | 2,235 | 20,755 | 132,602 | 5,526,574 | 3,946,970 | 1,292,282 | 287,322 |
| Females | 6,914,946 | 324,677 | 4.7 | 2,840 | 32,174 | 289,663 | 6,590,269 | 4,512,764 | 1,640,842 | 436,663 |
| Part-time | 7,778,677 | 298,350 | 3.8 | 34,415 | 47,495 | 216,440 | 7,480,327 | 6,246,334 | 940,456 | 293,537 |
| Males | 3,178,620 | 118,952 | 3.7 | 17,612 | 20,109 | 81,231 | 3,059,668 | 2,602,022 | 359,757 | 97,889 |
| Females | 4,600,057 | 179,398 | 3.9 | 16,803 | 27,386 | 135,209 | 4,420,659 | 3,644,312 | 580,699 | 195,648 |
| Undergraduate | 17,474,835 | 573,888 | 3.3 | 32,143 | 82,694 | 459,051 | 16,900,947 | 13,314,859 | 2,674,753 | 911,335 |
| Full-time | 10,938,494 | 353,921 | 3.2 | 4,314 | 40,252 | 309,355 | 10,584,573 | 7,681,355 | 2,221,471 | 681,747 |
| Part-time | 6,536,341 | 219,967 | 3.4 | 27,829 | 42,442 | 149,696 | 6,316,374 | 5,633,504 | 453,282 | 229,588 |
| Postbaccalaureate | 2,900,954 | 204,731 | 7.1 | 7,347 | 17,730 | 179,654 | 2,696,223 | 1,391,209 | 1,198,827 | 106,187 |
| Full-time | 1,658,618 | 126,348 | 7.6 | 761 | 12,677 | 112,910 | 1,532,270 | 778,379 | 711,653 | 42,238 |
| Part-time | 1,242,336 | 78,383 | 6.3 | 6,586 | 5,053 | 66,744 | 1,163,953 | 612,830 | 487,174 | 63,949 |
| White | 11,590,717 | 422,826 | 3.6 | 27,549 | 68,776 | 326,501 | 11,167,891 | 8,336,597 | 2,406,397 | 424,897 |
| Black | 2,872,126 | 229,118 | 8.0 | 4,960 | 16,197 | 207,961 | 2,643,008 | 1,881,831 | 472,550 | 288,627 |
| Hispanic | 3,091,112 | 70,839 | 2.3 | 3,666 | 7,832 | 59,341 | 3,020,273 | 2,473,823 | 346,554 | 199,896 |
| Asian | 1,198,545 | 16,916 | 1.4 | 1,486 | 3,305 | 12,125 | 1,181,629 | 904,096 | 236,244 | 41,289 |
| Pacific Islander | 61,053 | 5,271 | 8.6 | 207 | 539 | 4,525 | 55,782 | 38,964 | 9,414 | 7,404 |
| American Indian/Alaska Native | 162,563 | 7,292 | 4.5 | 239 | 711 | 6,342 | 155,271 | 124,376 | 21,015 | 9,880 |
| Two or more races | 559,362 | 19,257 | 3.4 | 750 | 2,649 | 15,858 | 540,105 | 412,604 | 98,635 | 28,866 |
| Nonresident alien | 840,311 | 7,100 | 0.8 | 633 | 415 | 6,052 | 833,211 | 533,777 | 282,771 | 16,663 |
| 4-year institutions | 13,407,050 | 777,916 | 5.8 | 39,490 | 100,424 | 638,002 | 12,629,134 | 8,080,927 | 3,841,382 | 706,825 |
| Full-time | 9,764,196 | 479,868 | 4.9 | 5,075 | 52,929 | 421,864 | 9,284,328 | 5,929,777 | 2,909,069 | 445,482 |
| Part-time | 3,642,854 | 298,048 | 8.2 | 34,415 | 47,495 | 216,138 | 3,344,806 | 2,151,150 | 932,313 | 261,343 |
| 2-year institutions | 6,968,739 | 703 | ª | 0 | 0 | 703 | 6,968,036 | 6,625,141 | 32,198 | 310,697 |
| Full-time | 2,832,916 | 401 | ª | 0 | 0 | 401 | 2,832,515 | 2,529,957 | 24,055 | 278,503 |
| Part-time | 4,135,823 | 302 | ª | 0 | 0 | 302 | 4,135,521 | 4,095,184 | 8,143 | 32,194 |
| **Earned degrees conferred, 2012–13** | | | | | | | | | | |
| Associate's | 1,006,961 | 47,040 | 4.7 | 901 | 2,391 | 43,748 | 959,921 | 771,687 | 53,226 | 135,008 |
| Males | 388,846 | 15,223 | 3.9 | 588 | 969 | 13,666 | 373,623 | 302,349 | 19,162 | 52,112 |
| Females | 618,115 | 31,817 | 5.1 | 313 | 1,422 | 30,082 | 586,298 | 469,338 | 34,064 | 82,896 |
| Bachelor's | 1,840,164 | 83,981 | 4.6 | 4,213 | 8,965 | 70,803 | 1,756,183 | 1,159,407 | 526,771 | 70,005 |
| Males | 787,231 | 31,539 | 4.0 | 2,002 | 3,781 | 25,756 | 755,692 | 508,329 | 217,056 | 30,307 |
| Females | 1,052,933 | 52,442 | 5.0 | 2,211 | 5,184 | 45,047 | 1,000,491 | 651,078 | 309,715 | 39,698 |
| Master's | 751,751 | 52,735 | 7.0 | 1,217 | 4,517 | 47,001 | 699,016 | 345,596 | 322,467 | 30,953 |
| Males | 301,575 | 18,010 | 6.0 | 603 | 1,598 | 15,809 | 283,565 | 141,102 | 130,973 | 11,490 |
| Females | 450,176 | 34,725 | 7.7 | 614 | 2,919 | 31,192 | 415,451 | 204,494 | 191,494 | 19,463 |
| Doctor's[b] | 175,038 | 3,064 | 1.8 | 0 | 71 | 2,993 | 171,974 | 86,427 | 81,468 | 4,079 |
| Males | 85,104 | 1,112 | 1.3 | 0 | 18 | 1,094 | 83,992 | 42,581 | 39,680 | 1,731 |
| Females | 89,934 | 1,952 | 2.2 | 0 | 53 | 1,899 | 87,982 | 43,846 | 41,788 | 2,348 |
| **First-time students' rates of graduation from and retention at first institution attended** | | | | | | | | | | |
| **Among full-time bachelor's degree-seekers starting at 4-year institutions in 2007, percent earning bachelor's degree** | | | | | | | | | | |
| Within 4 years after start | 39.4 | 8.0 | † | ‡ | 29.0 | 7.3 | 39.5 | 33.5 | 52.8 | 23.8 |
| Within 5 years after start | 55.1 | 12.8 | † | ‡ | 31.8 | 12.1 | 55.2 | 52.3 | 63.2 | 29.0 |
| Within 6 years after start | 59.4 | 14.8 | † | ‡ | 33.6 | 14.1 | 59.5 | 57.7 | 65.3 | 33.3 |
| **Among full-time degree/certificate-seekers starting at 2-year institutions in 2010, percent completing credential within 150 percent of normal time** | 29.4 | 14.7 | † | ‡ | ‡ | 14.7 | 29.4 | 19.5 | 53.6 | 62.8 |
| **Among degree-seekers starting in 2012, percent returning in 2013** | | | | | | | | | | |
| Full-time entrants | 72.9 | 38.4 | † | ‡ | 69.9 | 38.0 | 73.0 | 71.4 | 80.3 | 64.4 |
| Part-time entrants | 43.1 | 43.2 | † | 56.5 | 26.2 | 43.3 | 43.1 | 43.3 | 40.4 | 39.7 |

For adults without smartphones or home broadband, public libraries often provide access to a range of digital technologies that allow users to engage in personal learning.

Unfortunately, many adults remain unaware of the technological resources available at their local libraries. Although nearly two-thirds (62%) of adults knew that

**TABLE 6.2**

**Degree-granting postsecondary institutions primarily offering online programs, by select characteristics and control of institution, 2013** [CONTINUED]

†Not applicable.
#Rounds to zero.
‡Reporting standards not met (too few cases for a reliable estimate).
aPrimarily online institutions have more than 90 percent of their students attending classes exclusively online. Other institutions may have some online offerings, but they are not primarily online.
bIncludes Ph.D., Ed.D., and comparable degrees at the doctoral level. Includes most degrees formerly classified as first-professional, such as M.D., D.D.S., and law degrees.
Note: Degree-granting institutions grant associate's or higher degrees and participate in Title IV federal financial aid programs.

SOURCE: Thomas D. Snyder, Cristobal de Brey, and Sally A. Dillow, "Table 311.33. Selected Statistics for Degree-Granting Postsecondary Institutions That Primarily Offer Online Programs, by Control of Institution and Selected Characteristics: 2013," in *Digest of Educational Statistics 2014*, U.S. Department of Education, Institute of Education Statistics, National Center for Education Statistics, April 2016, http://nces.ed.gov/pubs2016/2016006.pdf (accessed August 11, 2016)

their local libraries offered e-books and digital audio books in 2015, only 41% realized that libraries provide access to online career and job resources, and only 26% knew that libraries enabled patrons to take online General Educational Development (GED) or high school equivalency courses. (See Figure 6.12.) Furthermore, people who use public libraries tend to be more technologically savvy than those who do not use their local libraries. As Figure 6.13 shows, in 2015 adults who had visited a library during the previous year were more likely than nonlibrary users to use the Internet (93% vs. 83%), to have a smartphone (76% vs. 64%), to have broadband access at home (74% vs. 62%), and to use social media (74% vs. 58%). (See Figure 6.13.)

## CHEATING AND HIGH TECHNOLOGY

Cheating is one of the biggest problems facing academia and includes any instance in which a student breaks the rules for an assignment or test to gain an advantage over fellow classmates. A specific type of cheating known as plagiarism occurs when a student submits someone else's work as his or her own. Plagiarism itself has several forms, including purchasing a previously written paper, copying sentences or ideas from an original source document without proper attribution, or paying someone else to complete the work. In June 2005 Donald L. McCabe of Rutgers University, the founder of the International Center for Academic Integrity (http://www.academicintegrity.org), published the results of a three-year survey of 50,000 college students at 60 campuses across the country. Of those who admitted cheating in 2005, a quarter said they had cheated seriously on a test, and half said they had cheated seriously on a written assignment. As of 2015, McCabe and the International Center for Academic Integrity had surveyed more than 71,300 undergraduate students on the topic of academic cheating. More than two-thirds (68%) admitted cheating on written assignments or tests, including 39% who had cheated on tests and 62% who had plagiarized a written assignment. Among high school students, cheating was even more prevalent. The International Center for Academic Integrity reports that as

of 2015 it had surveyed more than 70,000 high school students, of whom 95% admitted to some form of cheating, including 64% who admitted to cheating on a test, and 58% who admitted to plagiarizing a written assignment.

In another assessment of academic integrity, the Josephson Institute of Ethics states in *2012 Report Card on the Ethics of American Youth, Installment 1: Honesty and Integrity* (November 20, 2012, https://charactercounts.org/wp-content/uploads/2014/02/ReportCard-2012-Data-Tables.pdf) that nearly one-third (32%) of high school students had copied a document from the Internet for a class assignment in 2012. The institute reports that male students (37%) were more likely than female students (27%) to have plagiarized from the Internet. Of those surveyed, 52% admitted to having cheated on a test at least once.

The Internet and other types of information technology have only served to fuel the cheating epidemic in the United States. Phones with text messaging allow students the opportunity to communicate with outsiders or others in class during a test. Companies that specialize in writing papers for students, commonly known as "paper mills," can deliver papers discreetly to students via e-mail. In general, the Internet provides an endless source of documents and papers from which students might copy material. Catching plagiarism on the Internet, however, involves combing through countless articles and websites. The issue of plagiarism from web sources is further complicated by the fact that the Internet has obscured the distinction between what information requires attribution and what is public knowledge.

To catch plagiarizers, some schools use high-technology services such as Turnitin.com. This online service receives papers from students and teachers and scans them into a database. The papers are then checked against more than 9 billion web pages, previously submitted student papers, and a number of books and encyclopedias. Turnitin.com (2016, http://turnitin.com/en_us/about-us/our-company) indicates that it had built a database of 500 million student submissions by 2014.

As of 2016, Princeton University and many other leading schools were still not using antiplagiarism

# TABLE 6.3

## Students attending degree-granting postsecondary institutions, by participation in distance education and control and level of institution, Fall 2012 and Fall 2013

Columns under **Number of students** (2–11) and **Percent of students** (12–21). Columns 6–11 and 16–21 fall under "Taking any distance education course(s) / Exclusively distance education courses by location of student."

| Year, level of enrollment, and control and level of institution (1) | Total (2) | No distance education courses (3) | Total, any distance education course(s) (4) | At least one, but not all, of student's courses (5) | Total (6) | Same state (7) | Different state (8) | State not known (9) | Outside of the United States (10) | Location unknown (11) | Total (12) | No distance education courses (13) | Total, any distance education course(s) (14) | At least one, but not all, of student's courses (15) | Total (16) | Same state (17) | Different state (18) | State not known (19) | Outside of the United States (20) | Location unknown (21) |
|---|---|---|---|---|---|---|---|---|---|---|---|---|---|---|---|---|---|---|---|---|
| **Fall 2012** | | | | | | | | | | | | | | | | | | | | |
| **All students, total** | 20,642,819 | 15,198,118 | 5,444,701 | 2,806,048 | 2,638,653 | 1,336,873 | 1,176,009 | 36,779 | 33,561 | 55,431 | 100.0 | 73.6 | 26.4 | 13.6 | 12.8 | 6.5 | 5.7 | 0.2 | 0.2 | 0.3 |
| Public | 14,880,343 | 11,227,331 | 3,653,012 | 2,405,021 | 1,247,991 | 1,031,658 | 145,655 | 23,173 | 13,277 | 34,228 | 100.0 | 75.5 | 24.5 | 16.2 | 8.4 | 6.9 | 1.0 | 0.2 | 0.1 | 0.2 |
| Private | | | | | | | | | | | | | | | | | | | | |
| Nonprofit | 3,953,578 | 3,226,385 | 727,193 | 259,696 | 467,497 | 183,450 | 253,173 | 9,050 | 7,378 | 14,446 | 100.0 | 81.6 | 18.4 | 6.6 | 11.8 | 4.6 | 6.4 | 0.2 | 0.2 | 0.4 |
| For-profit | 1,808,898 | 744,402 | 1,064,496 | 141,331 | 923,165 | 121,765 | 777,181 | 4,556 | 12,906 | 6,757 | 100.0 | 41.2 | 58.8 | 7.8 | 51.0 | 6.7 | 43.0 | 0.3 | 0.7 | 0.4 |
| 4-year | 8,120,417 | 6,244,659 | 1,875,758 | 1,255,372 | 620,386 | 462,008 | 128,232 | 7,062 | 8,834 | 14,250 | 100.0 | 76.9 | 23.1 | 15.5 | 7.6 | 5.7 | 1.6 | 0.1 | 0.1 | 0.2 |
| 2-year | 6,625,141 | 4,756,657 | 1,868,484 | 1,206,990 | 661,494 | 603,206 | 31,405 | 17,339 | 3,884 | 5,660 | 100.0 | 71.8 | 28.2 | 18.2 | 10.0 | 9.1 | 0.5 | 0.3 | 0.1 | 0.1 |
| **Fall 2013** | | | | | | | | | | | | | | | | | | | | |
| **All students, total** | 20,375,789 | 14,853,595 | 5,522,194 | 2,862,991 | 2,659,203 | 1,388,195 | 1,119,577 | 30,244 | 35,767 | 85,420 | 100.0 | 72.9 | 27.1 | 14.1 | 13.1 | 6.8 | 5.5 | 0.1 | 0.2 | 0.4 |
| 4-year | 13,407,050 | 9,790,774 | 3,616,276 | 1,638,507 | 1,977,769 | 778,853 | 1,074,387 | 12,905 | 31,867 | 79,757 | 100.0 | 73.0 | 27.0 | 12.2 | 14.8 | 5.8 | 8.0 | 0.1 | 0.2 | 0.6 |
| 2-year | 6,968,739 | 5,062,821 | 1,905,918 | 1,224,484 | 681,434 | 609,342 | 45,190 | 17,339 | 3,900 | 5,663 | 100.0 | 72.7 | 27.3 | 17.6 | 9.8 | 8.7 | 0.6 | 0.2 | 0.1 | 0.1 |
| Public | 14,745,558 | 11,001,316 | 3,744,242 | 2,462,362 | 1,281,880 | 1,065,214 | 159,637 | 24,401 | 12,718 | 19,910 | 100.0 | 74.6 | 25.4 | 16.7 | 8.7 | 7.2 | 1.1 | 0.2 | 0.1 | 0.1 |
| 4-year | 8,120,417 | 6,244,659 | 1,875,758 | 1,255,372 | 620,386 | 462,008 | 128,232 | 7,062 | 8,834 | 14,250 | 100.0 | 76.9 | 23.1 | 15.5 | 7.6 | 5.7 | 1.6 | 0.1 | 0.1 | 0.2 |
| 2-year | 6,625,141 | 4,756,657 | 1,868,484 | 1,206,990 | 661,494 | 603,206 | 31,405 | 17,339 | 3,884 | 5,660 | 100.0 | 71.8 | 28.2 | 18.2 | 10.0 | 9.1 | 0.5 | 0.3 | 0.1 | 0.1 |
| Private | | | | | | | | | | | | | | | | | | | | |
| Nonprofit | 3,974,004 | 3,178,594 | 795,410 | 275,020 | 520,390 | 205,897 | 289,967 | 2,349 | 9,435 | 12,742 | 100.0 | 80.0 | 20.0 | 6.9 | 13.1 | 5.2 | 7.3 | 0.1 | 0.2 | 0.3 |
| 4-year | 3,941,806 | 3,148,416 | 793,390 | 273,802 | 519,588 | 205,493 | 289,569 | 2,349 | 9,435 | 12,742 | 100.0 | 79.9 | 20.1 | 6.9 | 13.2 | 5.2 | 7.3 | 0.1 | 0.2 | 0.3 |
| 2-year | 32,198 | 30,178 | 2,020 | 1,218 | 802 | 404 | 398 | | | 0 | 100.0 | 93.7 | 6.3 | 3.8 | 2.5 | 1.3 | 1.2 | 0.0 | 0.0 | 0.0 |
| For-profit | 1,656,227 | 673,685 | 982,542 | 125,609 | 856,933 | 117,084 | 669,973 | 3,494 | 13,614 | 52,768 | 100.0 | 40.7 | 59.3 | 7.6 | 51.7 | 7.1 | 40.5 | 0.2 | 0.8 | 3.2 |
| 4-year | 1,344,827 | 397,699 | 947,128 | 109,333 | 837,795 | 111,352 | 656,586 | 3,494 | 13,598 | 52,765 | 100.0 | 29.6 | 70.4 | 8.1 | 62.3 | 8.3 | 48.8 | 0.3 | 1.0 | 3.9 |
| 2-year | 311,400 | 275,986 | 35,414 | 16,276 | 19,138 | 5,732 | 13,387 | | 16 | 3 | 100.0 | 88.6 | 11.4 | 5.2 | 6.1 | 1.8 | 4.3 | 0.0 | * | * |
| **Undergraduate** | | | | | | | | | | | | | | | | | | | | |
| **Total** | 17,474,835 | 12,847,210 | 4,627,625 | 2,645,183 | 1,982,442 | 1,114,983 | 757,448 | 26,211 | 21,105 | 62,695 | 100.0 | 73.5 | 26.5 | 15.1 | 11.3 | 6.4 | 4.3 | 0.1 | 0.1 | 0.4 |
| 4-year | 10,506,096 | 7,784,389 | 2,721,707 | 1,420,699 | 1,301,008 | 505,641 | 712,258 | 8,872 | 17,205 | 57,032 | 100.0 | 74.1 | 25.9 | 13.5 | 12.4 | 4.8 | 6.8 | 0.1 | 0.2 | 0.5 |
| 2-year | 6,968,739 | 5,062,821 | 1,905,918 | 1,224,484 | 681,434 | 609,342 | 45,190 | 17,339 | 3,900 | 5,663 | 100.0 | 72.7 | 27.3 | 17.6 | 9.8 | 8.7 | 0.6 | 0.2 | 0.1 | 0.1 |
| Public | 13,347,002 | 9,949,253 | 3,397,749 | 2,337,560 | 1,060,189 | 916,864 | 96,899 | 22,988 | 8,958 | 14,480 | 100.0 | 74.5 | 25.5 | 17.5 | 7.9 | 6.9 | 0.7 | 0.2 | 0.1 | 0.1 |
| 4-year | 6,721,861 | 5,192,596 | 1,529,265 | 1,130,570 | 398,695 | 313,658 | 65,494 | 5,649 | 5,074 | 8,820 | 100.0 | 77.2 | 22.8 | 16.8 | 5.9 | 4.7 | 1.0 | 0.1 | 0.1 | 0.1 |
| 2-year | 6,625,141 | 4,756,657 | 1,868,484 | 1,206,990 | 661,494 | 603,206 | 31,405 | 17,339 | 3,884 | 5,660 | 100.0 | 71.8 | 28.2 | 18.2 | 10.0 | 9.1 | 0.5 | 0.3 | 0.1 | 0.1 |
| Private | | | | | | | | | | | | | | | | | | | | |
| Nonprofit | 2,757,447 | 2,271,597 | 485,850 | 194,886 | 290,964 | 108,191 | 169,663 | 758 | 4,655 | 7,697 | 100.0 | 82.4 | 17.6 | 7.1 | 10.6 | 3.9 | 6.2 | 0.3 | 0.2 | 0.3 |
| 4-year | 2,725,249 | 2,241,419 | 483,830 | 193,668 | 290,162 | 107,787 | 169,265 | 758 | 4,655 | 7,697 | 100.0 | 82.2 | 17.8 | 7.1 | 10.6 | 4.0 | 6.2 | * | 0.0 | 0.0 |
| 2-year | 32,198 | 30,178 | 2,020 | 1,218 | 802 | 404 | 398 | | | 0 | 100.0 | 93.7 | 6.3 | 3.8 | 2.5 | 1.3 | 1.2 | 0.0 | 0.0 | 0.0 |
| For-profit | 1,370,386 | 626,360 | 744,026 | 112,737 | 631,289 | 89,928 | 490,886 | 2,465 | 7,492 | 40,518 | 100.0 | 45.7 | 54.3 | 8.2 | 46.1 | 6.6 | 35.8 | 0.2 | 0.5 | 3.0 |
| 4-year | 1,058,986 | 350,374 | 708,612 | 96,461 | 612,151 | 84,196 | 477,499 | 2,465 | 7,476 | 40,515 | 100.0 | 33.1 | 66.9 | 9.1 | 57.8 | 8.0 | 45.1 | 0.2 | 0.7 | 3.8 |
| 2-year | 311,400 | 275,986 | 35,414 | 16,276 | 19,138 | 5,732 | 13,387 | | 16 | 3 | 100.0 | 88.6 | 11.4 | 5.2 | 6.1 | 1.8 | 4.3 | 0.0 | * | * |
| **Postbaccalaureate** | | | | | | | | | | | | | | | | | | | | |
| **Total** | 2,900,954 | 2,006,385 | 894,569 | 217,808 | 676,761 | 273,212 | 362,129 | 4,033 | 14,662 | 22,725 | 100.0 | 69.2 | 30.8 | 7.5 | 23.3 | 9.4 | 12.5 | 0.1 | 0.5 | 0.8 |
| Public | 1,398,556 | 1,052,063 | 346,493 | 124,802 | 221,691 | 148,350 | 62,738 | 1,413 | 3,760 | 5,430 | 100.0 | 75.2 | 24.8 | 8.9 | 15.9 | 10.6 | 4.5 | 0.1 | 0.3 | 0.4 |
| Private | | | | | | | | | | | | | | | | | | | | |
| Nonprofit | 1,216,557 | 906,997 | 309,560 | 80,134 | 229,426 | 97,706 | 120,304 | 1,591 | 4,780 | 5,045 | 100.0 | 74.6 | 25.4 | 6.6 | 18.9 | 8.0 | 9.9 | 0.1 | 0.4 | 0.4 |
| For-profit | 285,841 | 47,325 | 238,516 | 12,872 | 225,644 | 27,156 | 179,087 | 1,029 | 6,122 | 12,250 | 100.0 | 16.6 | 83.4 | 4.5 | 78.9 | 9.5 | 62.7 | 0.4 | 2.1 | 4.3 |

**TABLE 6.3**

**Students attending degree-granting postsecondary institutions, by participation in distance education and control and level of institution, Fall 2012 and Fall 2013** [CONTINUED]

ᵃRounds to zero.

Note: Degree-granting institutions grant associate's or higher degrees and participate in Title IV federal financial aid programs.

SOURCE: Thomas D. Snyder, Cristobal de Brey, and Sally A. Dillow, "Table 311.15. Number and Percentage of Students Enrolled in Degree-Granting Postsecondary Institutions, by Distance Education Participation, Location of Student, Level of Enrollment, and Control and Level of Institution: Fall 2012 and Fall 2013," in *Digest of Educational Statistics 2014*, U.S. Department of Education, Institute of Education Statistics, National Center for Education Statistics, April 2016, http://nces.ed.gov/pubs2016/2016006.pdf (accessed August 11, 2016)

**FIGURE 6.7**

**Percentage of degree-granting postsecondary institutions that believe that online learning is a critical aspect of their long-term strategic vision, 2002–15**

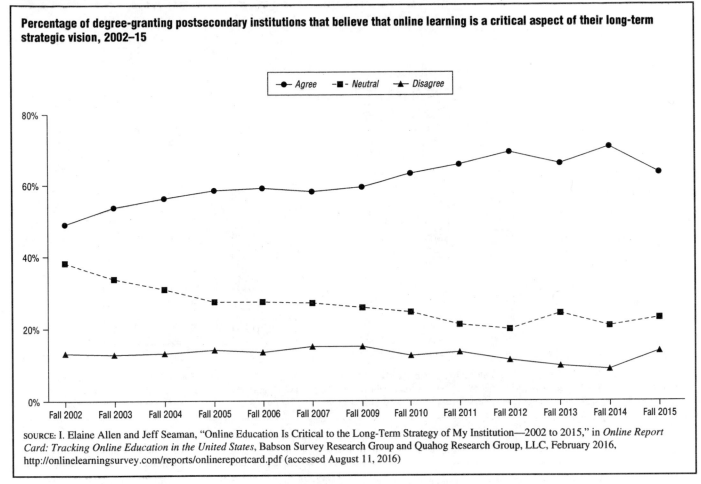

SOURCE: I. Elaine Allen and Jeff Seaman, "Online Education Is Critical to the Long-Term Strategy of My Institution—2002 to 2015," in *Online Report Card: Tracking Online Education in the United States*, Babson Survey Research Group and Quahog Research Group, LLC, February 2016, http://onlinelearningsurvey.com/reports/onlinereportcard.pdf (accessed August 11, 2016)

services, holding to the belief that their campuses did not foster a culture in which cheating is acceptable. Paul Craft writes in "Some Schools Resist Anti-cheating Software" (*Washington Monthly College Guide*, July 13, 2010) that Emily Aronson, a spokesperson for Princeton, asserted that although the university had considered implementing Turnitin software, it ultimately decided that "adopting this kind of software sends a message to our students that is not one that we want to send. We don't want to presume that they aren't approaching their work honestly. We want to presume that they're behaving with integrity." Regardless, cheating remains a serious problem even at the nation's most elite institutions.

This adherence to principles suffered a serious challenge in 2012, after details emerged concerning a major plagiarism scandal at Harvard University. According to Hana N. Rouse and Justin C. Worland, in "Faust Addresses Cheating Scandal" (*Harvard Crimson*, October 4, 2012), 125 students enrolled in a government course were accused of plagiarizing or illegally collaborating on a take-home exam. Citing the university president Drew Faust's response to the incident, Rouse and Worland report that the scandal "sparked an important discussion about cheating in higher education" during the fall of 2012, both

at Harvard and other Ivy League institutions. Richard Pérez-Peña reports in "Students Disciplined in Harvard Scandal" (NYTimes.com, February 1, 2013) that in early 2013 Harvard forced 70 students involved in the scandal to withdraw from school. Pérez-Peña notes that in an average year 17 Harvard students are dismissed from the university for academic dishonesty.

Technology was misused in a different way in a case at Dartmouth College in 2014 that resulted in disciplinary action against 64 students who used electronic "clickers" to misrepresent lecture attendance. Some students were disciplined for answering questions using clickers that had been assigned to students who were absent, whereas other students were disciplined for giving their clickers to someone else to impersonate them in class. As reported by Matt Rocheleau in "64 Dartmouth College Students Face Discipline over Cheating" (BostonGlobe.com, January 8, 2015), "Administrators were alerted to the possible cheating after the professor, Randall Balmer, chairman of the religion department, noticed that the electronic system was receiving a significantly higher number of responses than the number of students he could see sitting in front of him in the lecture hall." Calling the matter "very sad and regrettable on many

**FIGURE 6.8**

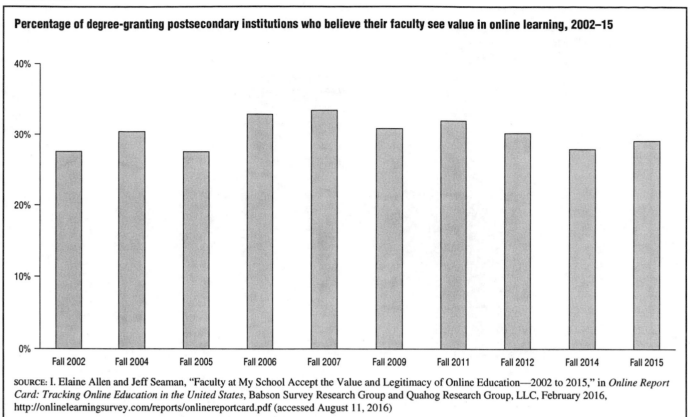

Percentage of degree-granting postsecondary institutions who believe their faculty see value in online learning, 2002–15

SOURCE: I. Elaine Allen and Jeff Seaman, "Faculty at My School Accept the Value and Legitimacy of Online Education—2002 to 2015," in *Online Report Card: Tracking Online Education in the United States*, Babson Survey Research Group and Quahog Research Group, LLC, February 2016, http://onlinelearningsurvey.com/reports/onlinereportcard.pdf (accessed August 11, 2016)

**FIGURE 6.9**

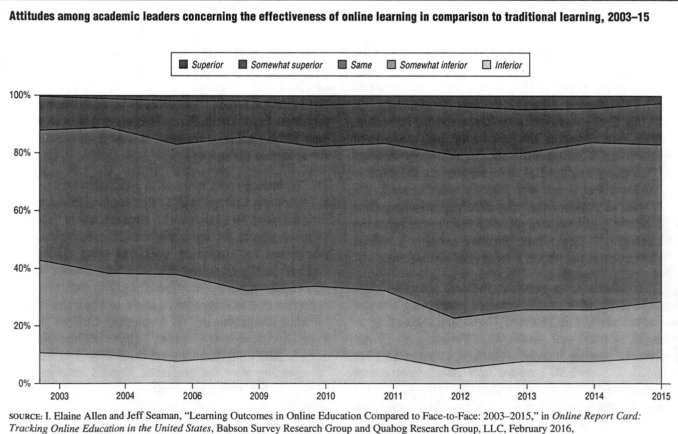

Attitudes among academic leaders concerning the effectiveness of online learning in comparison to traditional learning, 2003–15

SOURCE: I. Elaine Allen and Jeff Seaman, "Learning Outcomes in Online Education Compared to Face-to-Face: 2003–2015," in *Online Report Card: Tracking Online Education in the United States*, Babson Survey Research Group and Quahog Research Group, LLC, February 2016, http://onlinelearningsurvey.com/reports/onlinereportcard.pdf (accessed August 11, 2016)

## FIGURE 6.10

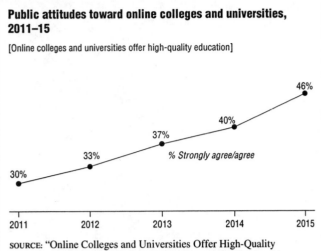

**Public attitudes toward online colleges and universities, 2011–15**

[Online colleges and universities offer high-quality education]

46%
40%
37%
33%
30%
% Strongly agree/agree

2011  2012  2013  2014  2015

SOURCE: "Online Colleges and Universities Offer High-Quality Education," in *The 2015 Gallup-Lumina Foundation Study of the American Public's Opinion on Higher Education*, The Gallup Organization, April 12, 2016, http://www.gallup.com/file/services/190583/Lumina_Report_2015%20Survey_of_Americans_Attitudes_Toward_Postsecondary_Education_FINAL.pdf (accessed August 11, 2016). Copyright © 2016 Gallup, Inc. All rights reserved. The content is used with permission; however, Gallup retains all rights of republication.

## FIGURE 6.11

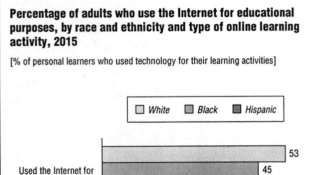

**Percentage of adults who use the Internet for educational purposes, by race and ethnicity and type of online learning activity, 2015**

[% of personal learners who used technology for their learning activities]

☐ White  ◼ Black  ■ Hispanic

Used the Internet for personal learning: 53, 45, 46

Most/all learning took place online: 31, 27, 26

Taken an online course: 17, 12, 12

0  20  40  60

Note: Based on the 74% of adults who are classified in this survey as personal learners.

SOURCE: John B. Horrigan, "Whites Are More Likely to Have Used the Internet for Personal Learning," in *Lifelong Learning and Technology*, Pew Research Center, March 22, 2016, http://www.pewinternet.org/files/2016/03/PI_2016.03.22_Educational-Ecosystems_FINAL.pdf (accessed August 11, 2016)

## FIGURE 6.12

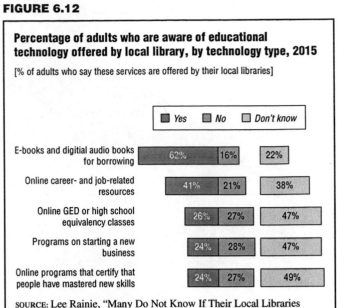

**Percentage of adults who are aware of educational technology offered by local library, by technology type, 2015**

[% of adults who say these services are offered by their local libraries]

◼ Yes  ◼ No  ☐ Don't know

E-books and digitial audio books for borrowing: 62% | 16% | 22%

Online career- and job-related resources: 41% | 21% | 38%

Online GED or high school equivalency classes: 26% | 27% | 47%

Programs on starting a new business: 24% | 28% | 47%

Online programs that certify that people have mastered new skills: 24% | 27% | 49%

SOURCE: Lee Rainie, "Many Do Not Know If Their Local Libraries Offer Key Learning and Education Resources," in *Libraries and Learning*, Pew Research Center, April 7, 2016, http://www.pewinternet.org/files/2016/04/PI_2016.04.07_Libraries-and-Learning_FINAL.pdf (accessed August 11, 2016)

## FIGURE 6.13

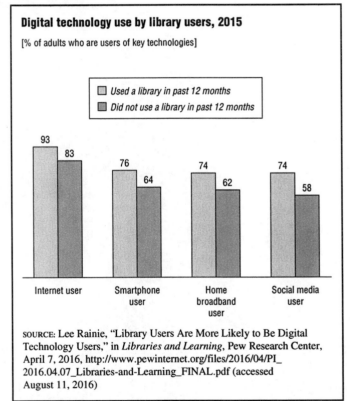

**Digital technology use by library users, 2015**

[% of adults who are users of key technologies]

☐ Used a library in past 12 months
◼ Did not use a library in past 12 months

Internet user: 93, 83
Smartphone user: 76, 64
Home broadband user: 74, 62
Social media user: 74, 58

SOURCE: Lee Rainie, "Library Users Are More Likely to Be Digital Technology Users," in *Libraries and Learning*, Pew Research Center, April 7, 2016, http://www.pewinternet.org/files/2016/04/PI_2016.04.07_Libraries-and-Learning_FINAL.pdf (accessed August 11, 2016)

levels," Ballmer told Rocheleau at the time, "I think honor no longer is something that has a lot of resonance in society, and I suppose in some ways it's not surprising that students would want to trade the nebulous notion of honor with what they perceive as some sort of advantage in professional advancement."

# CHAPTER 7
# INFORMATION TECHNOLOGY AND GOVERNMENT

Since the 1990s government bodies in the United States at the local, state, and federal levels have made a concerted effort to use the Internet and other types of information technology (IT) to streamline their operations and dealings with the public. Much of this effort has been focused on making information available via the Internet. Local and municipal governments post meeting minutes and agendas online. States have erected websites that allow citizens to renew registrations, obtain licenses, and track legislation online. The federal government has brought myriad services and information to the Internet, allowing Americans to do everything from applying for a patent online to reviewing the holdings of the Smithsonian Institution. The American public has taken advantage of these services in large numbers. John B. Horrigan, Lee Rainie, and Dana Page of the Pew Research Center report in *Americans' Views on Open Government Data* (April 21, 2015, http://www.pewinternet.org/files/2014/10/PI_OpenData_072815.pdf) that in December 2014, nearly two-thirds (65%) of American adults went online to find information about the government at some point during the previous 12 months. Overall, 37% of adults used the Internet to learn about the federal government, 34% went online to find information about state government, and 32% went online to learn about local government in 2014. (See Figure 7.1.)

Various government entities have employed other forms of IT to streamline services outside of cyberspace. After the hotly contested 2000 presidential race between Governor George W. Bush (1946–; R-TX) and Vice President Al Gore Jr. (1948–; D-TN), state election commissions replaced many of the aging mechanical voting systems with electronic touch screen and optical scanning systems. These systems made the voting booth accessible for many disabled people and presumably led to more accurate ballot totals in elections. Advances in communications and detection systems have also given rise to networks along U.S. highways that monitor traffic and

weather conditions on a real-time basis. For example, in 1999 the federal government designated 511 as the universal phone number by which people can access these systems to obtain details on traffic and weather in their area. In addition, technology has enabled the federal government to undertake ambitious and far-reaching improvements to the nation's infrastructure. For example, the Energy Independence and Security Act of 2007 included a provision calling for the creation of a smart grid, with the aim of streamlining the transmission and distribution of electricity throughout the United States.

Although U.S. citizens are constantly interacting with their government online, their attitudes toward the effectiveness with which government makes data accessible are mixed. As Figure 7.2 shows, in 2014 fewer than half (44%) of American adults thought that the federal government was either very effective (5%) or somewhat effective (39%) at sharing government data with the public. By contrast, 54% of adults reported that the federal government was either not very effective (39%) or not effective at all (15%) at making data accessible that year. On the other hand, a slight majority (52%) of adults in 2014 believed that their local government was either very effective (7%) or somewhat effective (45%) at sharing information with the public.

In general, Americans believe that making government data more accessible could have some potential benefits. As Figure 7.3 shows, 56% of adults in 2014 believed that making government data more accessible would enable journalists to write about government affairs more thoroughly, and 53% thought that an open government would make government officials more accountable to the public. These attitudes varied widely according to an individual's overall level of trust in the federal government. For example, more than three-quarters (76%) of adults who expressed a basic trust in the federal government in 2014 thought that greater access to government data would make officials more accountable to the public. By contrast, fewer than half (47%) of Americans who did not trust the federal government believed that more accessible data would lead to greater accountability. (See Figure 7.4.) As Figure 7.5 shows, Democrats were more likely than Republicans to believe that open government data could provide a range of benefits to the public in 2014. For instance, 54% of Democrats thought that making government data more accessible would improve the quality of government services in 2014, compared with 45% of Republicans who expressed the same opinion. At the same time, a correlation exists between adults' educational attainment and their faith in the ability of open government data to bring positive change to society. In 2014 more than two-thirds (68%) of college graduates thought that making government data more accessible would enable journalists to provide better coverage of government activities; by comparison only 52% of noncollege graduates thought that open government data would lead to better reporting on government affairs. (See Figure 7.6.)

## FEDERAL GOVERNMENT AND INTERNET TECHNOLOGIES

Since the early 1990s hundreds of federal government websites have been established on the Internet. In the beginning each agency or division developed its website in a unique way, offering varying levels of accessibility to the user. Some were useful and informative. For example, in 1994 the U.S. Census Bureau launched the first U.S. government World Wide Web portal. From the start, hundreds of U.S. census records from decades past could be easily viewed on the website.

The Internal Revenue Service (IRS) also maintained a useful site. In 1997 the IRS began allowing people to download tax forms and file their taxes electronically. Nearly a million tax returns were filed from home computers that first year. Filing taxes online quickly became one of the most popular forms of Internet contact with the federal government. The IRS (May 19, 2016, https://www.irs.gov/uac/newsroom/filing-season-statistics-for-week-ending-may-13-2016) reports that during the 2015 filing

**FIGURE 7.1**

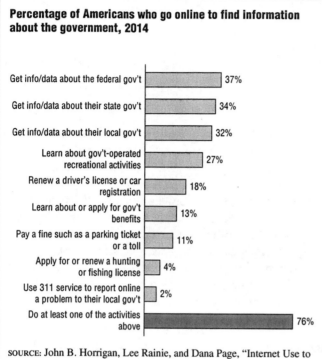

Percentage of Americans who go online to find information about the government, 2014

SOURCE: John B. Horrigan, Lee Rainie, and Dana Page, "Internet Use to Find Data or Information Pertaining to the Government," in *Americans' Views on Open Government Data* Pew Research Center, April 21, 2015, http://www.pewinternet.org/files/2014/10/PI_OpenData_072815.pdf (accessed August 13, 2016)

**FIGURE 7.2**

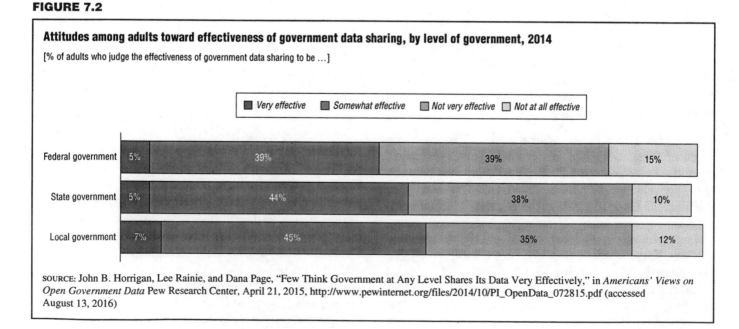

Attitudes among adults toward effectiveness of government data sharing, by level of government, 2014

[% of adults who judge the effectiveness of government data sharing to be ...]

SOURCE: John B. Horrigan, Lee Rainie, and Dana Page, "Few Think Government at Any Level Shares Its Data Very Effectively," in *Americans' Views on Open Government Data* Pew Research Center, April 21, 2015, http://www.pewinternet.org/files/2014/10/PI_OpenData_072815.pdf (accessed August 13, 2016)

## FIGURE 7.3

### Attitudes among adults toward potential advantages of government data sharing, by type of advantage, 2014

[% of adults who say these things about the possible impact of government data sharing]

Government data ...

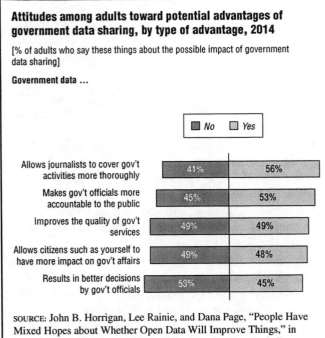

| | No | Yes |
|---|---|---|
| Allows journalists to cover gov't activities more thoroughly | 41% | 56% |
| Makes gov't officials more accountable to the public | 45% | 53% |
| Improves the quality of gov't services | 49% | 49% |
| Allows citizens such as yourself to have more impact on gov't affairs | 49% | 48% |
| Results in better decisions by gov't officials | 53% | 45% |

SOURCE: John B. Horrigan, Lee Rainie, and Dana Page, "People Have Mixed Hopes about Whether Open Data Will Improve Things," in *Americans' Views on Open Government Data* Pew Research Center, April 21, 2015, http://www.pewinternet.org/files/2014/10/PI_OpenData_072815.pdf (accessed August 13, 2016)

## FIGURE 7.4

### Attitudes among adults toward potential advantages of government data sharing, by type of advantage and level of trust in government, 2014

[% of adults who believe there are benefits to government sharing data]

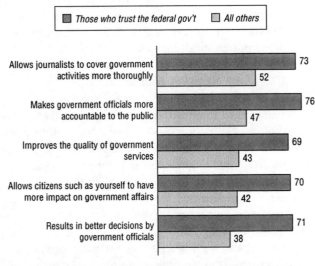

| | Those who trust the federal gov't | All others |
|---|---|---|
| Allows journalists to cover government activities more thoroughly | 73 | 52 |
| Makes government officials more accountable to the public | 76 | 47 |
| Improves the quality of government services | 69 | 43 |
| Allows citizens such as yourself to have more impact on government affairs | 70 | 42 |
| Results in better decisions by government officials | 71 | 38 |

Note: "Those who trust the federal gov't" refers to those who trust the federal government "just about always" or "most of the time."

SOURCE: John B. Horrigan, Lee Rainie, and Dana Page, "Those Who Trust Government Are More Likely to Think There Are Benefits to Opening Government Data," in *Americans' Views on Open Government Data* Pew Research Center, April 21, 2015, http://www.pewinternet.org/files/2014/10/PI_OpenData_072815.pdf (accessed August 13, 2016)

## FIGURE 7.5

### Attitudes among adults toward potential advantages of government data sharing, by type of advantage and political party affiliation, 2014

[% of adults in each group who believe open government data helps each outcome]

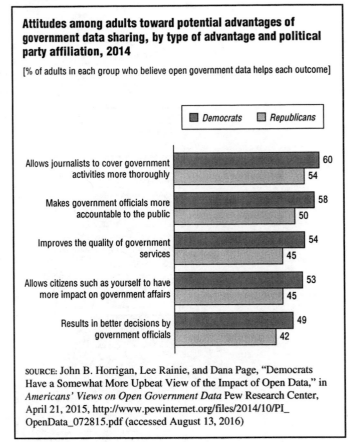

| | Democrats | Republicans |
|---|---|---|
| Allows journalists to cover government activities more thoroughly | 60 | 54 |
| Makes government officials more accountable to the public | 58 | 50 |
| Improves the quality of government services | 54 | 45 |
| Allows citizens such as yourself to have more impact on government affairs | 53 | 45 |
| Results in better decisions by government officials | 49 | 42 |

SOURCE: John B. Horrigan, Lee Rainie, and Dana Page, "Democrats Have a Somewhat More Upbeat View of the Impact of Open Data," in *Americans' Views on Open Government Data* Pew Research Center, April 21, 2015, http://www.pewinternet.org/files/2014/10/PI_OpenData_072815.pdf (accessed August 13, 2016)

year, as of May 13, 2016, it had received 123.7 million individual tax returns online. This was a 2.6% increase over the number of e-filings during the same period in the previous year (120.6 million) and represented 88% of the total number of individual returns received in 2016.

### Government Paperwork Elimination Act

When they were first developed many federal government websites, such as the National Oceanic and Atmospheric Administration (NOAA) website, offered citizens little in the way of practical information or accessibility. By 2016 the NOAA site (http://www.noaa.gov/) had been dramatically improved with tools and resources pertaining to weather forecasting, climate data, satellite imagery, wildlife restoration projects, and more, but during the 1990s profit-driven commercial websites far surpassed most government websites in both appearance and functionality. Seeing the untapped potential of many government websites, Congress and the White House put through a series of initiatives and laws to make federal government websites and services more accessible to the American people.

One of the first major congressional acts designed to improve the functionality of government websites was the Government Paperwork Elimination Act (GPEA) of 1998. The GPEA required that by October 2003 each

FIGURE 7.6

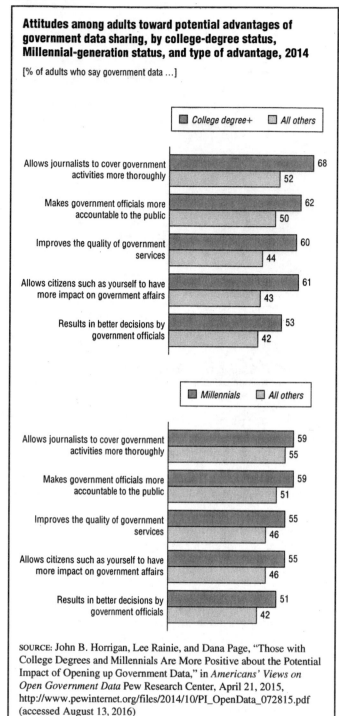

**Attitudes among adults toward potential advantages of government data sharing, by college-degree status, Millennial-generation status, and type of advantage, 2014**

[% of adults who say government data ...]

**College degree+** / **All others**

| | College degree+ | All others |
|---|---|---|
| Allows journalists to cover government activities more thoroughly | 68 | 52 |
| Makes government officials more accountable to the public | 62 | 50 |
| Improves the quality of government services | 60 | 44 |
| Allows citizens such as yourself to have more impact on government affairs | 61 | 43 |
| Results in better decisions by government officials | 53 | 42 |

**Millennials** / **All others**

| | Millennials | All others |
|---|---|---|
| Allows journalists to cover government activities more thoroughly | 59 | 55 |
| Makes government officials more accountable to the public | 59 | 51 |
| Improves the quality of government services | 55 | 46 |
| Allows citizens such as yourself to have more impact on government affairs | 55 | 46 |
| Results in better decisions by government officials | 51 | 42 |

SOURCE: John B. Horrigan, Lee Rainie, and Dana Page, "Those with College Degrees and Millennials Are More Positive about the Potential Impact of Opening up Government Data," in *Americans' Views on Open Government Data* Pew Research Center, April 21, 2015, http://www.pewinternet.org/files/2014/10/PI_OpenData_072815.pdf (accessed August 13, 2016)

use paper. Similarly, individuals were to have the option to apply for a patent online or to fill out a U.S. Census survey on the Internet. By 2016 thousands of forms for more than 170 agencies were available online.

### E-Government Act

In 2001 President Bush introduced the President's Management Agenda, which contained a number of initiatives that were intended to expand the role of the Internet in the federal government beyond the scope of the GPEA. Many of these initiatives were made law in 2002, when Congress passed the E-Government Act. The E-Government Act was a broad-reaching piece of legislation that was designed to streamline government websites and provide a wide range of services to the American people via the Internet. The act established the E-Government Fund to provide money for agencies that could not afford IT and website development. In *FY 2015 Annual Report to Congress: E-Government Act Implementation* (June 17, 2016, https://www.whitehouse.gov/sites/default/files/omb/assets/egov_docs/egov_implementation_report_6_17_16.pdf), the Office of Management and Budget (OMB) notes that in 2015, just under $6 million of the fund was dedicated to promoting greater transparency, in large part through the implementation of the Federal Funding Accountability and Transparency Act of 2006. In addition, more than $6.8 million of the fund was devoted to improving cloud computing and security protections within the federal IT system, and $1.25 million was dedicated to enhancing Performance.gov, a site dedicated to promoting federal initiatives that are aimed at improving government accountability and efficiency.

Many of these goals established standards for government websites that were already in operation. Existing government websites were required to provide links to organization policy and hierarchy on the front page and to present their information in a way that was easily searchable. Many agencies with multiple websites, such as NASA or the U.S. Environmental Protection Agency (EPA), were asked to consolidate their sites so that all the information for the public could be reached within a few clicks of the agency's main page. The E-Government Act also supported new websites that were designed to provide basic services for American citizens. The site FirstGov.gov was deemed the official portal for all federal government websites. FirstGov.gov, which began operating in February 2000, provided links to more than 22,000 federal and state websites as well as a hierarchical index of all government organizations. In January 2007 FirstGov.gov was renamed USA.gov; three years later the administration of President Barack Obama (1961–) launched an updated version of USA.gov that featured a new design and a wider range of applications, including the U.S. Government Services and Information portal (https://www.usa.gov/topics) offering services for both citizens and federal employees.

government agency should provide people, wherever possible, with the option of submitting information or transacting business electronically. The act mandated that forms and documents involved in government transactions be placed online and that electronic signature systems be put in place to replace paper signatures. For example, companies that made electronic components for the National Aeronautics and Space Administration (NASA) were required to have the option to bid for contracts, complete all paperwork with regard to sale of the merchandise, and receive payment without having to

Another website that the E-Government Act officially authorized was Regulations.gov, which was launched in January 2003. Regulations.gov lists pending regulations that are proposed by government agencies and allows citizens and nongovernmental agencies to comment on the regulations. The government agencies are then required to review the comments on Regulations.gov before putting a regulation into effect. This process provides the American people with the ability to influence government regulation, a privilege that was previously available primarily to organized lobbyists.

As a result of these White House initiatives and congressional acts supporting e-government, federal agencies have come to offer many valuable online services to Americans. For example, the EPA oversees the web portal My Environment (http://www.epa.gov/myenvironment), which enables citizens to search for information about environmental issues such as air quality and water conditions, report violations, and find ways to communicate and collaborate with other environmental activists in their area. In December 2008 the Social Security Administration launched an online application system for retirees aimed at streamlining the benefits process for the nation's seniors.

In January 2011 President Obama signed the GPRA Modernization Act. The law effectively updated the 1993 Government Performance and Results Act, which attempted to make the management of government programs more efficient. Overseen by the director of the OMB, the GPRA Modernization Act requires government agencies to make information about programs, strategic objectives, and other aspects of their work more accessible to Congress and the public, both by improving their websites and by publishing all plans and reports in "searchable, machine-readable" formats.

In April 2011, in recognition of the increasing importance of the Internet as a means for U.S. citizens to interact with the federal government, President Obama issued Executive Order 13571, Streamlining Service Delivery and Improving Customer Service (April 27, 2011, http://www.whitehouse.gov/the-press-office/2011/04/27/executive-order-streamlining-service-delivery-and-improving-customer-ser), in which he called on government agencies to focus on developing "lower-cost, self-service options accessed by the Internet or mobile phone and improved processes that deliver services faster and more responsively." In order to create greater overall transparency and access in the sharing of government information, on May 9, 2013, President Obama issued an executive order, Making Open and Machine Readable the New Default for Government Information (May 9, 2013, http://www.whitehouse.gov/sites/default/files/omb/memoranda/2013/m-13-13.pdf). Also known as the Open Government Initiative, the order intended to "institutionalize the principles of effective information management at each stage of the information's life cycle to promote interoperability and openness."

**SATISFACTION WITH GOVERNMENT WEBSITES.** Although some dissatisfaction exists with federal government websites, users seem to be happy with the improvements in e-government. Since 2003 the U.S. government has tracked websites in its annual ForeSee E-Government Satisfaction Index. This index measures how satisfied the American people are with various aspects of the federal government. Table 7.1 shows that, out of all government websites during the first quarter of 2016, users were happiest with two Social Security Administration sites: the Extra Help with Medicare Prescription Drug Plan Costs site (https://secure.ssa.gov/i1020/start), which helps retirees choose a prescription drug plan, and the Retirement Estimator (http://www.ssa.gov/estimator), a site that is designed to help retirees calculate their potential benefits. These two sites were also the top-ranked on the list of government websites that facilitated transactions or e-commerce. (See Table 7.2.) The lowest score in the overall survey (51 out of a possible 100 points) was received by va.gov, the home page of the U.S. Department of Veterans Affairs. (See Table 7.1.)

Among departmental portals or main sites, the NASA website (https://www.nasa.gov) and the U.S. Citizenship and Immigration Services Resource Center Español (https://www.uscis.gov/es) scored highest, each with satisfaction ratings of 85 out of a possible 100 points. (See Table 7.3.) Among government employment portals, the Central Intelligence Agency recruitment page (https://www.cia.gov/careers) scored highest, with a score of 83 points out of 100. (See Table 7.4.) The most highly rated government news and information website during the first quarter of 2016 was the U.S. Department of Health and Human Services MedlinePlus en Español site (https://medlineplus.gov/spanish/), which scored a rating of 88 out of 100. (See Table 7.5.)

The ForeSee E-Government Satisfaction Index also measures customer satisfaction with government mobile sites and apps. As Table 7.6 shows, overall satisfaction with the federal government's apps and mobile sites rose from 76 out of 100 during the second quarter of 2015 to 81 out of 100 during the fourth quarter of 2015, before dipping to 79 out of 100 during the first quarter of 2016. Overall, the government collected customer satisfaction data for 16 mobile sites and apps in the first quarter of 2016, with overall satisfaction scores ranging from 60 to 89. (See Table 7.7.)

One notable government IT failure occurred in October 2013, when the Obama administration unveiled HealthCare.gov, the enrollment portal for Americans seeking health insurance through the Patient Protection and Affordable Care Act of 2010 (often informally referred to as "Obamacare"). Andrew Couts writes in "We Paid over $500 Million for the Obamacare Sites and All We Got Was This Lousy 404" (DigitalTrends.com, October 8,

**TABLE 7.1**

**ForeSee E-Government Satisfaction Index scores for e-government websites, first quarter 2016**

| Department | Website | Satisfaction |
|---|---|---|
| SSA | Extra Help with Medicare Prescription Drug Plan Costs—socialsecurity.gov/i1020 | 91 |
| SSA | SSA Retirement Estimator—ssa.gov/estimator | 91 |
| SSA | SSA iClaim—socialsecurity.gov/applyonline | 90 |
| Treasury | Electronic Federal Tax Payment System—eftps.com | 88 |
| HHS | MedlinePlus en español—medlineplus.gov/esp | 88 |
| SSA | SSA - my Social Security | 88 |
| DHS | U.S. Citizenship and Immigration Services Resource Center—uscis.gov/portal/site/uscis/citizenship | 86 |
| HHS | MedlinePlus—medlineplus.gov | 86 |
| HHS | National Women's Health Information Center (NWHIC) main website—womenshealth.gov | 86 |
| NASA | NASA main website—nasa.gov | 85 |
| SSA | Social Security Business Services Online—ssa.gov/bso/bsowelcome.htm | 85 |
| DHS | U.S. Citizenship and Immigration Services Español—uscis.gov/portal/site/uscis-es | 85 |
| NIH | National Institute on Aging - Go4Life—go4life.nia.nih.gov | 84 |
| HHS | National Cancer Institute Site en Español—cancer.gov/espanol | 84 |
| HHS | NIAMS public website—niams.nih.gov | 84 |
| HHS | NIDDK—www2.niddk.nih.gov | 84 |
| PBGC | U.S. PBGC My Plan Administration Account—egov.pbgc.gov/mypaa/ | 84 |
| HHS | CDC main website—cdc.gov | 83 |
| CIA | Recruitment website—cia.gov/careers | 83 |
| DOD | DoD Navy—navy.mil | 83 |
| HHS | AIDSinfo—aidsinfo.nih.gov | 82 |
| SEC | U.S. Securities and Exchange Commission—investor.gov | 82 |
| SSA | SSA.gov iClaim – Disability—ssa.gov/applyfordisability | 82 |
| DOD | arlingtoncemetery.mil | 81 |
| Treasury | IRS Direct Pay—irs.gov/payments/direct-pay | 81 |
| DOC | National Geodetic Survey, National Oceanic and Atmospheric Administration website—ngs.noaa.gov | 81 |
| HHS | National Institute of Dental and Craniofacial Research—nidcr.nih.gov | 81 |
| HHS | National Library of Medicine Genetics Home Reference website—ghr.nlm.nih.gov | 81 |
| HHS | SAMHSA Store—store.samhsa.gov | 81 |
| DOD | DoD Marines—marines.mil | 80 |
| FTC | FTC Complaint Assistant website—ftccomplaintassistant.gov | 80 |
| HHS | National Cancer Institute main website—cancer.gov | 80 |
| SSA | SSA iAppeals - Disability Appeal—ssa.gov/disabilityssi/appeal.html | 80 |
| DOC | NOAA NWS—weather.gov | 80 |
| DOS | Recruitment website—careers.state.gov | 79 |
| DHS | U.S. Citizenship and Immigration Services—uscis.gov/e-verify | 79 |
| HHS | infosida.nih.gov | 79 |
| OPM | Recruitment website—applicationmanager.gov | 78 |
| DOJ | FBI main website—fbi.gov | 78 |
| GAO | GAO main public website—gao.gov | 78 |
| DOJ | National Institute of Justice—nij.gov | 78 |
| SBA | SBA main website—sba.gov | 78 |
| NRC | U.S. Nuclear Regulatory Commission website—nrc.gov | 78 |
| Treasury | U.S. Mint Online Catalog and main website—usmint.gov | 78 |
| HHS | Agency for Healthcare Research and Quality—ahrq.gov | 77 |
| DOD | DoD Air Force—af.mil | 77 |
| HHS | National Library of Medicine main website—nlm.nih.gov | 77 |
| VA | MyHealtheVet- https://www.myhealth.va.gov | 77 |
| DOS | Department of State - Bureau of Educational and Cultural Affairs—alumni.state.gov/ | 76 |
| VA | MyCareer@VA- http://mycareeratva.va.gov/ | 76 |
| PBGC | MyPBA—https://egov.pbgc.gov/mypba | 76 |
| NIST | National Institute of Standards and Technology main website—nist.gov | 76 |
| DOL | Bureau of Labor Statistics—bls.gov | 75 |
| FDIC | FDIC Applications—www2.fdic.gov | 75 |
| HHS | ClinicalTrials.gov—clinicaltrials.gov | 75 |
| DOS | Bureau of Consular Affairs—travel.state.gov | 75 |
| OPM | Recruitment website—usajobs.gov | 75 |
| DHS | U.S. Citizenship and Immigration Services—uscis.gov/portal/site/uscis | 75 |
| DOI | U.S. Geological Survey—usgs.gov | 75 |
| Boards, commissions, and committees | American Battle Monuments Commission—abmc.gov | 74 |
| DOD | Department of Defense portal—defense.gov | 74 |
| DOC | NOAA Tides and Currents | 74 |
| DOI | National Park Service main website—nps.gov | 74 |
| ITC | U.S. International Trade Commission main website—usitc.gov | 74 |
| FDIC | FDIC main website—fdic.gov | 73 |
| DOC | NOAA Fisheries—nmfs.noaa.gov | 73 |
| DOT | U.S. Department of Transportation—fhwa.dot.gov | 72 |
| FTC | FTC main website—ftc.gov | 72 |
| PBGC | U.S. PBGC main website—pbgc.gov | 72 |
| SEC | U.S. Securities and Exchange Commission—sec.gov | 72 |
| SSA | Social Security Online main website—socialsecurity.gov | 72 |

**TABLE 7.1**

**ForeSee E-Government Satisfaction Index scores for e-government websites, first quarter 2016** [CONTINUED]

| Department | Website | Satisfaction |
|---|---|---|
| DOT | Federal Aviation Administration—faa.gov | 71 |
| DOT | Federal Railroad Administration main website—fra.dot.gov | 71 |
| USDA | Recreation One-Stop—recreation.gov | 71 |
| HHS | SAMHSA website—samhsa.gov | 71 |
| DOC | BEA main website—bea.gov | 70 |
| USDA | ERS main website—ers.usda.gov | 70 |
| HHS | U.S. Food and Drug Administration main website—fda.gov | 70 |
| DOS | Department of State blog website—blogs.state.gov | 69 |
| USDA | FSIS main website—fsis.usda.gov | 69 |
| HHS | Health Resources and Services Administration main website—hrsa.gov | 69 |
| USDA | NRCS website—nrcs.usda.gov | 69 |
| GSA | GSA Auctions—gsaauctions.gov | 68 |
| DOJ | Bureau of Justice Statistics—bjs.gov | 66 |
| DOS | Department of State main website—state.gov | 66 |
| DOT | DOT Research and Innovative Technology Administration website—rita.dot.gov | 66 |
| EPA | U.S. Environmental Protection Agency—epa.gov | 66 |
| Treasury | IRS main website—irs.gov | 66 |
| Treasury | Treasury main website—treasury.gov | 66 |
| DOC | U.S. Patent and Trademark Office—uspto.gov | 66 |
| NARA | NARA main public website—archives.gov | 65 |
| DOC | U.S. Census Bureau main website—census.gov | 65 |
| Treasury | U.S. Alcohol and Tobacco Tax and Trade Bureau—ttb.gov | 65 |
| GSA | GSA main website—gsa.gov | 64 |
| USDA | Forest Service main website—fs.usda.gov | 63 |
| DOD | TRICARE—tricare.mil | 62 |
| HHS | HHS—grants.gov | 61 |
| DOE | U.S. Department of Education—ed.gov | 61 |
| DOC | NOAA Satellite and Information Service—nesdis.noaa.gov | 60 |
| DOL | Disability—Disability.gov | 58 |
| VA | VA main website—va.gov | 51 |

SOURCE: Dave Lewan, "Figure 2. Q1 2016 E-Government Satisfaction Index," in *ForeSee E-Government Satisfaction Index, Q1 2016*, copyright ForeSee, 2016, http://www.foresee.com/assets/eGov-Q1-2016.pdf (accessed August 11, 2016).

**TABLE 7.2**

**ForeSee E-Government Satisfaction Index scores for government e-commerce and transactional sites, first quarter 2016**

| Department | Website | Satisfaction |
|---|---|---|
| Aggregate satisfaction for federal e-commerce and transactional websites | | 82 |
| SSA | Extra Help with Medicare Prescription Drug Plan Costs—socialsecurity.gov/i1020 | 91 |
| SSA | SSA Retirement Estimator—ssa.gov/estimator | 91 |
| SSA | SSA iClaim—socialsecurity.gov/applyonline | 90 |
| Treasury | Electronic Federal Tax Payment System—eftps.com | 88 |
| SSA | SSA - my Social Security | 88 |
| SSA | Social Security Business Services Online—ssa.gov/bso/bsowelcome.htm | 85 |
| PBGC | U.S. PBGC My Plan Administration Account—egov.pbgc.gov/mypaa/ | 84 |
| SSA | SSA.gov iClaim - Disability—ssa.gov/applyfordisability | 82 |
| Treasury | IRS Direct Pay—irs.gov/payments/direct-pay | 81 |
| HHS | SAMHSA Store—store.samhsa.gov | 81 |
| FTC | FTC Complaint Assistant website—ftccomplaintassistant.gov | 80 |
| SSA | SSA iAppeals - Disability Appeal—ssa.gov/disabilityssi/appeal.html | 80 |
| Treasury | U.S. Mint Online Catalog and main website—usmint.gov | 78 |
| PBGC | MyPBA—https://egov.pbgc.gov/mypba | 76 |
| USDA | Recreation One-Stop—recreation.gov | 71 |
| GSA | GSA Auctions—gsaauctions.gov | 68 |

SSA = Social Security Administration.
PBGC = Pension Benefit Guaranty Corp.
HHS = Health & Human Services.
FTC = Federal Trade Commission.
USDA = United States Department of Agriculture.
GSA = General Services Administration.

SOURCE: Dave Lewan, "Figure 4. Federal E-Commerce and Transactional Websites," in *ForeSee E-Government Satisfaction Index, Q1 2016*, copyright ForeSee, 2016, http://www.foresee.com/assets/eGov-Q1-2016.pdf (accessed August 12, 2016).

2013) that the government devoted roughly $363 million over a three-year period to make the website operational by its official launch date of October 1, 2013. In spite of this considerable investment, the portal's launch was

# TABLE 7.3

**ForeSee E-Government Satisfaction Index scores for e-government portals and main websites, first quarter 2016**

| Department | Website | Satisfaction |
|---|---|---|
| Aggregate satisfaction for federal portals and department main websites | | 72 |
| NASA | NASA main website—nasa.gov | 85 |
| DHS | U.S. Citizenship and Immigration Services Español—uscis.gov/portal/site/uscis-es | 85 |
| HHS | NIAMS public website—niams.nih.gov | 84 |
| HHS | CDC main website—cdc.gov | 83 |
| HHS | National Institute of Dental and Craniofacial Research—nidcr.nih.gov | 81 |
| HHS | National Cancer Institute main website—cancer.gov | 80 |
| DOJ | FBI main website—fbi.gov | 78 |
| GAO | GAO main public website—gao.gov | 78 |
| SBA | SBA main website—sba.gov | 78 |
| HHS | National Library of Medicine main website—nlm.nih.gov | 77 |
| VA | MyHealtheVet- https://www.myhealth.va.gov | 77 |
| NIST | National Institute of Standards and Technology main website—nist.gov | 76 |
| DHS | U.S. Citizenship and Immigration Services—uscis.gov/portal/site/uscis | 75 |
| DOD | Department of Defense portal—defense.gov | 74 |
| DOC | NOAA Tides and Currents | 74 |
| DOI | National Park Service main website—nps.gov | 74 |
| ITC | U.S. International Trade Commission main website—usitc.gov | 74 |
| FDIC | FDIC main website—fdic.gov | 73 |
| FTC | FTC main website—ftc.gov | 72 |
| PBGC | U.S. PBGC main website—pbgc.gov | 72 |
| SSA | Social Security Online main website—socialsecurity.gov | 72 |
| DOT | Federal Railroad Administration main website—fra.dot.gov | 71 |
| HHS | SAMHSA website—samhsa.gov | 71 |
| HHS | U.S. Food and Drug Administration main website—fda.gov | 70 |
| DOS | Department of State main website—state.gov | 66 |
| EPA | U.S. Environmental Protection Agency—epa.gov | 66 |
| Treasury | IRS main website—irs.gov | 66 |
| Treasury | Treasury main website—treasury.gov | 66 |
| DOC | U.S. Patent and Trademark Office—uspto.gov | 66 |
| NARA | NARA main public website—archives.gov | 65 |
| GSA | GSA main website—gsa.gov | 64 |
| DOE | U.S. Department of Education—ed.gov | 61 |
| DOL | Disability—Disability.gov | 58 |
| VA | VA main website—va.gov | 51 |

SOURCE: Dave Lewan, "Figure 6. Federal Portals and Department Main Websites," in *ForeSee E-Government Satisfaction Index, Q1 2016*, copyright ForeSee, 2016, http://www.foresee.com/assets/eGov-Q1-2016.pdf (accessed August 11, 2016)

# TABLE 7.4

**ForeSee E-Government Satisfaction Index scores for e-government career and recruitment sites, first quarter 2016**

| Department | Website | Satisfaction |
|---|---|---|
| Aggregate satisfaction for federal career and recruitment sites | | 78 |
| CIA | Recruitment website—cia.gov/careers | 83 |
| DOS | Recruitment website—careers.state.gov | 79 |
| OPM | Recruitment website—applicationmanager.gov | 78 |
| VA | MyCareer@VA—http://mycareeratva.va.gov/ | 76 |
| OPM | Recruitment website—usajobs.gov | 75 |

CIA = Central Intelligence Agency.
DOS = Department of State.
OPM = Office of Personnel Management.
VA = Veterans Affairs.

SOURCE: Dave Lewan, "Figure 7. Federal Career and Recruitment Websites," in *ForeSee E-Government Satisfaction Index, Q1 2016*, copyright ForeSee, 2016, http://www.foresee.com/assets/eGov-Q1-2016.pdf (accessed August 11, 2016)

marred by numerous technical problems experienced by users, including repeated system shutdowns. According to Couts, the website's problems were primarily related to "poorly written code," which left the site unprepared to process the massive volume of applications filed following its launch. At the same time, as Tom Cohen notes in "Contractors Blame Government for Obamacare Website Woes" (CNN.com, October 25, 2013), contractors hired to build the portal cited a lack of adequate testing in the weeks leading up to the launch for the website's failure. Despite the problems surrounding the site's initial launch, the HealthCare.gov portal was soon fully operational.

## Government Regulation

The federal government has passed few laws that are designed to control Internet commerce or content compared with other broadcasting media. The Federal Communications Commission (FCC), which regulates all television and radio content, treats the Internet more like print media than like broadcast media. Unless a major law is being violated, people can publish all manner of pornography, illicit writing, and misleading information on the Internet without fear of repercussion. Activities that are illegal in many states or the United States as a whole, such as purchasing an item under a trade embargo,

TABLE 7.5

**ForeSee E-Government Satisfaction Index scores for e-government news and information sites, first quarter 2016**

| Department | Website | Satisfaction |
|---|---|---|
| Aggregate satisfaction for federal news and information websites | | 75 |
| HHS | MedlinePlus en español—medlineplus.gov/esp | 88 |
| DHS | U.S. Citizenship and Immigration Services Resource Center—uscis.gov/portal/site/uscis/citizenship | 86 |
| HHS | MedlinePlus—medlineplus.gov | 86 |
| HHS | National Women's Health Information Center (NWHIC) main website—womenshealth.gov | 86 |
| NIH | National Institute on Aging - Go4Life—go4life.nia.nih.gov | 84 |
| HHS | National Cancer Institute Site en Español—cancer.gov/espanol | 84 |
| HHS | NIDDK—www2.niddk.nih.gov | 84 |
| DOD | DoD Navy—navy.mil | 83 |
| HHS | AIDSinfo—aidsinfo.nih.gov | 82 |
| SEC | U.S. Securities and Exchange Commission—investor.gov | 82 |
| DOD | arlingtoncemetery.mil | 81 |
| DOC | National Geodetic Survey, National Oceanic and Atmospheric Administration website—ngs.noaa.gov | 81 |
| HHS | National Library of Medicine Genetics Home Reference website—ghr.nlm.nih.gov | 81 |
| DOD | DoD Marines—marines.mil | 80 |
| DOC | NOAA NWS—weather.gov | 80 |
| DHS | U.S. Citizenship and Immigration Services—uscis.gov/e-verify | 79 |
| HHS | infosida.nih.gov | 79 |
| DOJ | National Institute of Justice—nij.gov | 78 |
| NRC | U.S. Nuclear Regulatory Commission website—nrc.gov | 78 |
| HHS | Agency for Healthcare Research and Quality—ahrq.gov | 77 |
| DOD | DoD Air Force—af.mil | 77 |
| DOS | Department of State - Bureau of Educational and Cultural Affairs—alumni.state.gov/ | 76 |
| DOL | Bureau of Labor Statistics—bls.gov | 75 |
| FDIC | FDIC Applications—www2.fdic.gov | 75 |
| HHS | ClinicalTrials.gov—clinicaltrials.gov | 75 |
| DOS | Bureau of Consular Affairs—travel.state.gov | 75 |
| DOI | U.S. Geological Survey—usgs.gov | 75 |
| Boards, Commissions, and Committees | American Battle Monuments Commission—abmc.gov | 74 |
| DOC | NOAA Fisheries—nmfs.noaa.gov | 73 |
| DOT | U.S. Department of Transportation—fhwa.dot.gov | 72 |
| SEC | U.S. Securities and Exchange Commission—sec.gov | 72 |
| DOT | Federal Aviation Administration—faa.gov | 71 |
| DOC | BEA main website—bea.gov | 70 |
| USDA | ERS main website—ers.usda.gov | 70 |
| DOS | Department of State blog website—blogs.state.gov | 69 |
| USDA | FSIS main website—fsis.usda.gov | 69 |
| HHS | Health Resources and Services Administration main website—hrsa.gov | 69 |
| USDA | NRCS website—nrcs.usda.gov | 69 |
| DOJ | Bureau of Justice Statistics—bjs.gov | 66 |
| DOT | DOT Research and Innovative Technology Administration website—rita.dot.gov | 66 |
| DOC | U.S. Census Bureau main website—census.gov | 65 |
| Treasury | U.S. Alcohol and Tobacco Tax and Trade Bureau—ttb.gov | 65 |
| USDA | Forest Service main website—fs.usda.gov | 63 |
| DOD | TRICARE—tricare.mil | 62 |
| HHS | HHS—grants.gov | 61 |
| DOC | NOAA Satellite and Information Service—nesdis.noaa.gov | 60 |

HHS = United States Department of Health & Human Services.
DHS = Department of Homeland Security.
NIH = National Institutes of Health.
DOD = United States Department of Defense.
SEC = Securities and Exchange Commission.
DOC = Department of Commerce.
DOJ = United States Department of Justice.
NRC = Nuclear Regulatory Commission.
DOS = Department of State.
DOL = United States Department of Labor.
FDIC = Federal Deposit Insurance Corporation.
DOI = Department of the Interior.
DOT = Department of Transportation.
USDA = United States Department of Agriculture.

SOURCE: Dave Lewan, "Figure 5. Federal News and Information Websites," in *ForeSee E-Government Satisfaction Index, Q1 2016*, copyright ForeSee, 2016, http://www.foresee.com/assets/eGov-Q1-2016.pdf (accessed August 12, 2016)

can be done online with little fear of prosecution. In addition, most purchases made on the Internet were not subject to local sales tax as of 2016, and states and municipalities were forbidden by the Internet Tax Freedom Act of 1998 to tax Internet use.

For the most part, Congress has been reluctant to place restrictions or taxes on the Internet. In 2005 a bill to make spyware illegal was rejected in the U.S. Senate, and in November 2007 Congress extended the tax ban on both interstate Internet commerce and Internet service to

**TABLE 7.6**

ForeSee E-Government Satisfaction Index aggregate scores for
e-government mobile sites and apps, first quarter 2016

| | First quarter 2016 | Fourth quarter 2015 | Third quarter 2015 | Second quarter 2015 |
|---|---|---|---|---|
| Aggregate satisfaction score (100 point scale) | 79 | 81 | 76 | 76 |

SOURCE: Dave Lewan, "Figure 8. Mobile Sites and Apps," in *ForeSee E-Government Satisfaction Index, Q1 2016*, copyright ForeSee, 2016, http://www.foresee.com/assets/eGov-Q1-2016.pdf (accessed August 12, 2016)

**TABLE 7.7**

ForeSee E-Government Satisfaction Index scores and usage data
for e-government mobile sites and apps, first quarter 2016

| | |
|---|---|
| Number of sites measured | 16 |
| Number of responses collected | 68,011 |
| Average e-government satisfaction score (out of 100) | 78.7 |
| Highest satisfaction score | 89 |
| Lowest satisfaction score | 60 |
| Number of e-government sites achieving excellent rating (80 or higher) | 10 |
| Number of e-government sites rated lowest satisfaction (70 or lower) | 2 |

SOURCE: Dave Lewan, "Figure 9. Mobile Details for Q1 2016," in *ForeSee E-Government Satisfaction Index, Q1 2016*, copyright ForeSee, 2016, http://www.foresee.com/assets/eGov-Q1-2016.pdf (accessed August 12, 2016)

2014; the tax ban was subsequently made permanent in February 2016. As for content, Congress is wary of potential public backlash that it would encounter if it regulates activities such as Internet pornography. Furthermore, enforcing strict regulations would be difficult. Unlike radio or television, publishing content on the web is exceedingly easy. Anyone, provided he or she has willing participants, can set up a web server, take pornographic pictures, and post them on the Internet. If the U.S. government did make Internet pornography illegal altogether, such sites could easily be moved offshore, where U.S. laws would not apply. Another option the government has is to place restrictions and controls on all computers and web browsers in the United States. Such a plan may have been feasible back in the early 1990s, when Internet backbones and browsers were still in the development phase. Placing such controls, however, on the tens of millions of current computers and web browsers now in use would be neither well received nor easily implemented.

**NETWORK NEUTRALITY.** During the first decade of the 21st century the issue of network neutrality became the subject of fierce debate among policymakers, private corporations, and consumer advocates. Network neutrality, or net neutrality, is a legal principle aimed at guaranteeing open and unlimited access to all legal content, applications, and other products and services on the Internet, without regulation or other forms of interference from Internet service providers (ISPs) or the government.

The concept of net neutrality first became widespread in 2003, with the publication of Tim Wu's "Network Neutrality, Broadband Discrimination" (*Journal of Telecommunications and High Technology Law*, vol. 2, 2003). In this influential paper, Wu, a law professor at the University of Virginia, argues that legislation guaranteeing net neutrality is the best way to ensure that all online content and applications remain equally available to Internet users. Wu's position arose partly in response to an emerging tendency among some telecommunications companies to privilege some online content or applications over others. Specifically, some cable providers had begun blocking certain applications or content or transmitting some data faster than other data, typically by establishing unique contracts with individual companies. In doing so, cable providers granted companies that were willing to pay additional charges a clear advantage over their competitors, while simultaneously denying consumers equal access to rival information or products.

Two years after Wu's paper was published, the FCC released its "Broadband Policy Statement" (September 23, 2005, http://www.publicknowledge.org/pdf/FCC-05-151A1.pdf), in which it outlined four basic principles that were intended to guarantee the right to unlimited Internet access for all U.S. citizens: "*To encourage broadband deployment and preserve and promote the open and interconnected nature of the public Internet*, consumers are entitled to access the lawful Internet content of their choice.... [To] run applications and use services of their choice, subject to the needs of law enforcement.... [To] connect their choice of legal devices that do not harm the network.... [To] competition among network providers, application and service providers, and content providers." Also known as the "Internet Policy Statement," the FCC's position was largely aimed at preventing telecommunications companies from unfairly controlling the flow of information online.

Proponents of net neutrality generally believe that free, unregulated access to online information and services is vital to guaranteeing the rights of all citizens to view the Internet content of their choice. Furthermore, supporters of net neutrality have argued that maintaining an open Internet is the best way to ensure continued technological innovation in the digital age. A number of major corporations, notably Microsoft and Google, have been outspoken in their support of net neutrality. Opponents of net neutrality, such as cable providers and network hardware manufacturers, have insisted that the right to offer tiered services (in other words, different levels of service based on different fees) is guaranteed by law. Opponents have also asserted that tiered service plans ultimately promote free market competition on the

Internet. The question of net neutrality has also sparked a wide range of opinions among lawmakers. Some members of Congress have attempted to grant the federal government additional powers to oversee and regulate telecommunications companies, with the specific aim of safeguarding net neutrality. Notable among these was the Internet Freedom Preservation Act of 2009, introduced by Representative Edward Markey (1946–: D-MA). That same year the FCC introduced two additional principles to its original "Broadband Policy Statement" that were aimed at preventing ISPs from discriminating against certain Internet content, while also granting consumers the right to total access to all ISP policies.

The battle between the federal government and the telecommunications companies became more intense in 2008. That year the FCC ruled that the telecommunications firm Comcast had illegally blocked its subscribers from using certain Internet software applications. In March 2010 a federal court overturned the FCC's judgment against Comcast, throwing the agency's power to ensure net neutrality into doubt. In response to the ruling, the FCC began exploring other means of guaranteeing the right to neutral broadband use. Joe Nocera reports in "The Struggle for What We Already Have" (NYTimes.com, September 3, 2010) that the commission hoped to use a broader interpretation of the Telecommunications Act of 1996 to impose tighter controls over ISPs.

The FCC attempted to reach a compromise in December 2010, when it voted 3–2 to prohibit telecommunications companies from controlling Internet traffic in ways that favored certain subscribers over others; however, the new restriction did not apply to smartphones or tablets. According to David Lieberman, in "Net Neutrality Vote Irks Many" (USAToday.com, December 21, 2010), the FCC ruling provoked harsh criticism from supporters on both sides of the issue. Net neutrality advocates complained that the regulation contained loopholes that would enable telecommunications companies to continue manipulating certain forms of web traffic. On the contrary, John Boehner (1949–; R-OH), the Speaker of the U.S. House of Representatives, asserted that the ruling represented a "power grab" on the part of the federal government and promised to fight it in Congress. Indeed, the FCC decision remained the subject of intense debate over the next two years. In "No Neutrality on Net" (*Daily Variety*, October 13, 2012), Ted Johnson reports that opposition to the government's net neutrality rules prompted a legal challenge from the telecommunications giant Verizon, while also forming a key component of the Republican Party's presidential election platform in 2012.

Opponents of net neutrality appeared to achieve a victory in January 2014, when the U.S. Court of Appeals for the District of Columbia Circuit ruled that the FCC did not have the authority to force telecommunications companies to treat all of their customers equally. Nevertheless, the FCC retained the authority to impose regulations on Internet access. In the press release "FCC Launches Broad Rulemaking on How Best to Protect and Promote the Open Internet" (May 15, 2014, http://transition.fcc.gov/Daily_Releases/Daily_Business/2014/db0515/DOC-327104A1.pdf), the FCC announced that it would seek public opinion on how best to ensure fair and equal use of the Internet. Leticia Miranda writes in "The FCC's Net Neutrality Proposal Explained" (Nation.com, May 21, 2014) that many advocates of net neutrality wanted the FCC to reclassify broadband as a public utility, thus empowering the agency to impose tighter restrictions on the telecommunications industry. The deadline for members of the public to submit their proposals was September 10, 2014.

Rebecca R. Ruiz reports in "F.C.C. Sets Net Neutrality Rules" (NYTimes.com, March 12, 2015) that in February 2015 the FCC unveiled a comprehensive set of rules aimed at protecting consumer access to legal Internet content, while preventing broadband providers from interfering with the flow of online information in any way. According to the FCC, in "Open Internet" (https://www.fcc.gov/general/open-internet), the Open Internet rules were designed to "protect free expression and innovation on the Internet and promote investment in the nation's broadband networks." At the same time, the order gave the FCC broad authority to impose future regulations aimed at protecting net neutrality. The Open Internet Order prompted strong criticism from the telecommunications industry, and in July 2015 the U.S. Telecom Association filed a lawsuit claiming the FCC had overstepped its authority. Cecilia Kang writes in "Court Backs Rule Treating Internet as Utility, Not Luxury" (NYTimes.com, June 14, 2016) that in June 2016 the U.S. Court of Appeals for the District of Columbia voted 2–1 in support of the new Open Internet rules. Kang notes that the telecommunications industry intended to appeal the ruling to the Supreme Court. As of November 2016, the status of the appeal was still unresolved.

**CONTROLLING THE ASSAULT OF NON-SOLICITED PORNOGRAPHY AND MARKETING ACT.** What little Internet regulation the federal government has enacted has been met with mixed results. On January 1, 2004, the Controlling the Assault of Non-Solicited Pornography and Marketing (CAN-SPAM) Act went into effect. The act required that all unsolicited commercial e-mail contain a legitimate return address as well as instructions on how to opt out of receiving additional solicitations from the sender. Spam must also state in the subject line if the e-mail is pornographic in nature. Violators of these rules were to be subject to heavy fines. As of 2016, the largest fine ever imposed under the CAN-SPAM Act was an $873 million judgment awarded to the social networking site Facebook in 2008. Jessica Guynn reports in "Facebook Wins $873-Million Judgment against Spammer" (LATimes.com, November 24, 2008) that the Canadian citizen Adam Guerbuez (1976?–) was found guilty of sending more than 4 million spam messages to Facebook users over a two-month period. The judgment was nearly four times greater than the $230 million won by the rival social networking site MySpace in a similar case the previous May.

CHILDREN'S INTERNET PROTECTION ACT. A more successful regulation is the Children's Internet Protection Act (CIPA) of 2000. Under the act, public schools and libraries were required to keep minors from viewing explicitly sexual content on public school and library computers. If these organizations did not comply, they would no longer receive government assistance in buying IT equipment. Public school systems throughout the country were quick to adapt to the new law, and by 2005, 100% of U.S. public schools had complied with CIPA. Regulations involving children's welfare have always been warmly received by the public, so this fact may account for CIPA's success.

ADAM WALSH CHILD PROTECTION AND SAFETY ACT. Another effort using IT and the Internet in an attempt to protect the innocence and safety of children is the Adam Walsh Child Protection and Safety Act of 2006. It established a tiered system of sexual offenses and required that convicted sexual offenders register and update their whereabouts with local law enforcement agencies for designated periods based on the seriousness of their offenses. Named after Adam John Walsh (1974–1981), a Florida boy who was abducted from a shopping mall and murdered, the act established the National Sex Offender Public Registry Website (renamed the Dru Sjodin National Sex Offender Public Website in 2006; https://www.nsopw.gov), a national database of registered sex offenders that is searchable by name, state, county, town, or zip code. Table 7.8 shows the information that convicted offenders are required to provide to law enforcement agencies under the Adam Walsh Child Protection and Safety Act, Title I, which is known as the Sex Offender Registration and Notification Act. Nonetheless, the public website discloses only the personal data that are presented in Table 7.9. In "Department of Justice Releases First National Strategy for Child Exploitation Prevention and Interdiction" (August 2, 2010, http://www.justice.gov/opa/pr/2010/August/10-opa-887 .html), the U.S. Department of Justice announced that it was launching a nationwide law enforcement operation aimed at apprehending the 500 most dangerous sex offenders who were not in compliance with registry requirements. As reported in a press release by the U.S. Marshals Service (May 7, 2013, https://www .usmarshals.gov/news/chron/2013/050713c.htm), the

**TABLE 7.8**

**Required registration information under the Sex Offender Registration and Notification Act**

- Criminal history
- Date of birth
- DNA sample
- Driver's license or identification card
- Employer address
- Fingerprints
- Internet identifiers
- Name
- Palm prints
- Passport and immigration documents
- Phone numbers
- Photograph
- Physical description
- Professional licensing information
- Resident address
- School address
- Social Security number(s)
- Temporary lodging information
- Text of registration offense
- Vehicle license plate number and description

SOURCE: Laura L. Rogers, "VI. Required Registration Information: SORNA, §114," in *The Adam Walsh Act: A National Endeavor to Protect Children and Families*, U.S. Department of Justice, Office of Justice Programs, SMART Office, July 2008, http://www.search.org/files/ppt/SMARTOffice Update0708.ppt (accessed August 11, 2016)

**TABLE 7.9**

**Public website information required under the Sex Offender Registration and Notification Act**

- Name
- Photograph
- Physical description
- Current offense & prior sex offenses
- Employer address
- Resident address
- School address
- Vehicle(s) license plate number and description

SOURCE: Laura L. Rogers, "VII. Disclosure and Sharing of Information: Public Website Required Information," in *The Adam Walsh Act: A National Endeavor to Protect Children and Families*, U.S. Department of Justice, Office of Justice Programs, SMART Office, July 2008, http://www.search .org/files/ppt/SMARTOfficeUpdate0708.ppt (accessed August 11, 2016)

operation concluded in May 2013, with the arrest of 345 individuals who had failed to register with state authorities as required by law. Overall, the investigators located 427 noncompliant offenders, including 82 individuals found outside the United States. According to the National Center for Missing and Exploited Children (June 17, 2016, http://www.missingkids.com/en_US/ documents/Sex_Offenders_Map.pdf), by 2016 there were 851,870 registered sex offenders in the United States.

## TECHNOLOGY AND NATIONAL SECURITY

The use of IT has become central to issues of national security in the 21st century. The speed at which information in the modern age can be retrieved has played a key role in the War on Terror that began in the aftermath of the attacks on the United States on September 11, 2001 (9/11). Identifying the terrorists who were responsible for the attacks would have been an arduous if not impossible task were it not for electronic records of the terrorists' credit card and rental car use. The Federal Bureau of Investigation (FBI) was able to post a full list of the suspected terrorists within three days of the attacks, giving the White House the necessary information it needed to plan retaliatory measures.

In the aftermath of 9/11, many new technologies have been designed to catch terrorists before they strike. Data mining is by far the most controversial and perhaps the most powerful of the new technologies that are being developed. Since 2002 the U.S. Department of Homeland Security has spent a tremendous amount of time and money trying to create a database and database-searching techniques that enable authorities to view records of millions of citizens within seconds and determine if they have a link to terrorism. According to John Borland, in "A Global Assault on Anonymity" (CNET.com, October 20, 2004), one attempt at such a system was called the Multistate Anti-Terrorism Information Exchange (MATRIX). The system contained the data from five state law enforcement centers as well as nationwide financial and commercial data of millions of Americans. Before its termination, the system was reportedly able to match criminal records with financial records to assess whether or not a person was a terrorist threat. The database held much more information than a typical criminal database and could be used, for instance, to do a background check on someone applying for a license to drive hazardous materials across the country. The project was canceled in April 2005 after many complaints from concerned citizens and civil rights organizations such as the American Civil Liberties Union (ACLU).

Many believed that other data mining systems were still being developed by the federal government following the cancellation of MATRIX. In "Pentagon Sets Its Sights on Social Networking Websites" (*New Scientist*, June 9, 2006), Paul Marks explains that the National Security Agency (NSA) was funding a program called the Disruptive Technology Office in 2006. The reported role of the program was to combine data on people from many different sources, including phone records and online social networks such as MySpace. The existence of the program was not beyond the realm of reason. Leslie Cauley reports in "NSA Has Massive Database of Americans' Phone Calls" (USAToday.com, May 11, 2006) that in 2006 the NSA was already secretly analyzing billions of phone records in an effort to find potential terrorists in the United States. The NSA did not obtain a court's approval before searching the phone records, which many considered to be an illegal act. In August 2006 Judge Anna Diggs Taylor (1932–) of the U.S. District Court declared the program unconstitutional and ordered it to stop. However, the

program continued while the case was appealed and Congress worked to develop a modified system of surveillance.

In July 2008 President Bush signed into law the FISA Amendments Act of 2008 (also called the Foreign Intelligence Surveillance Act of 1978 Amendments Act of 2008). Besides broadening the ability of the federal government to conduct high-tech investigations that are aimed at identifying foreign terrorist activity, the act shields U.S. telecommunications firms from lawsuits that stem from their cooperation in government wiretap investigations of their customers. On the day the new law was passed, the ACLU filed a lawsuit in federal court contending that the law violated the U.S. Constitution on numerous grounds, including the right to privacy. Although the case was dismissed by a district court judge in August 2009, a federal appeals court reversed the district judge's decision in March 2011, reinstating the ACLU's lawsuit against the government. In May 2012 the U.S. Supreme Court agreed to hear the case, and oral arguments were heard that October. In February 2013 the Supreme Court voted 5–4 to dismiss the case.

Even as IT serves as a vital tool in the War on Terror, it can also pose a serious challenge to the government's control of classified information. The extent to which government secrets were vulnerable in the information age was exposed in April 2010, when WikiLeaks, an activist media website, released a classified video that showed a U.S. Apache helicopter killing 11 unarmed civilians in Iraq in 2007. The following month Private First Class Bradley Manning (1987–; later Chelsea Manning), a U.S. Army intelligence analyst, was arrested on charges of illegally copying the video, along with more than 250,000 classified diplomatic cables, and sending them to the website. David Dishneau and Ben Nuckols report in "Prosecutors to Question Manning in WikiLeaks Case" (Yahoo.com, November 30, 2012) that Manning's actions represented "the biggest leak of classified material in U.S. history." Although many politicians and U.S. officials saw Manning as a traitor, a number of free-speech advocates and political activists considered him to be a hero. Eventually, his supporters established the website BradleyManning.org (later ChelseaManning.org) to help promote Manning's legal defense.

In "WikiLeaks' Julian Assange Suffering from Chronic Lung Condition" (Time.com, November 29, 2012), Sorcha Pollak indicates that Julian Assange (1971–), the Australian founder of WikiLeaks, also faced the possibility of extradition to the United States for his role in making the classified documents public. However, no legal action had proceeded against him in the United States as of November 2016.

One of the most damaging leaks of classified materials in American history occurred in June 2013, when it emerged that the Foreign Intelligence Surveillance Court (FISC) had ordered the telecommunications firm Verizon to turn over the private phone data of millions of U.S. citizens to the NSA and the FBI. In "NSA Collecting Phone Records of Millions of Verizon Customers Daily" (Guardian.com, June 5, 2013), Glenn Greenwald reports that the court's secret order, dated April 25, 2013, granted the government unlimited access to the "metadata" of Verizon customers, information that included contact and location data, call durations, and other details relating to individual telephone records. In the ensuing days, other classified information, including the revelation that the NSA had been monitoring the online activities of U.S. citizens through a program called Prism, became public.

Days after the initial story became public, an NSA contractor named Edward Snowden (1983–) disclosed that he had leaked thousands of classified NSA documents to Greenwald. Noam Schreiber reports in "Why'd He Do It?" (NewRepublic.com, June 10, 2013) that Snowden revealed his motivations in an interview conducted in Hong Kong, where he had fled after leaking the

documents. "I don't want to live in a world where there's no privacy and therefore no room for intellectual exploration and creativity," Schreiber quotes Snowden as saying. In the face of extradition efforts on the part of the U.S. government, Snowden left Hong Kong for Russia, where he was granted temporary asylum. He remained in exile in Russia as of November 2016.

In *Americans' Attitudes about Privacy, Security and Surveillance* (May 20, 2015, http://www.pewinternet.org/files/2015/05/Privacy-and-Security-Attitudes-5.19.15_FINAL.pdf), Mary Madden and Lee Rainie of the Pew Research Center examine American attitudes toward the question of privacy in the digital age. As Figure 7.7 reveals, in 2014 U.S. adults were generally wary of allowing corporations, the government, or other entities to retain records of their online activities indefinitely. That year, less than a quarter (22%) of adults thought that government agencies should never save information concerning the online activities of U.S. citizens; 16% thought that the government should retain such information for only a few weeks (8%) or

**FIGURE 7.7**

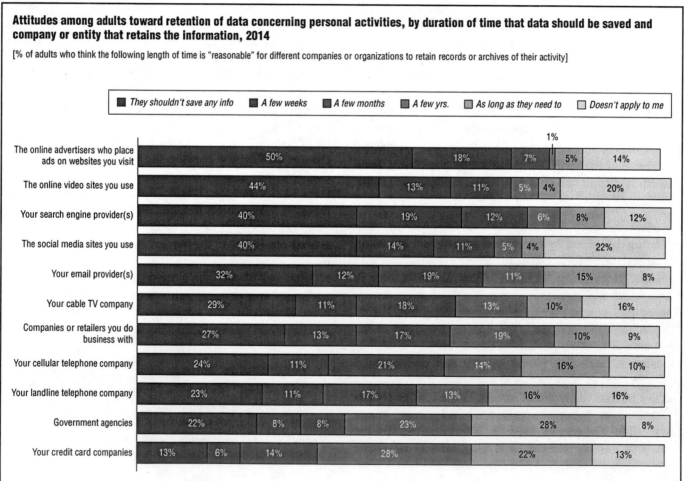

Attitudes among adults toward retention of data concerning personal activities, by duration of time that data should be saved and company or entity that retains the information, 2014

[% of adults who think the following length of time is "reasonable" for different companies or organizations to retain records or archives of their activity]

Notes: Population = 498. Refused responses not shown.

SOURCE: Mary Madden and Lee Rainie, "Most Expect Limits on How Long the Records of Their Activity Are Stored," in *Americans' Attitudes about Privacy, Security and Surveillance*, Pew Research Center, May 20, 2015, http://www.pewinternet.org/files/2015/05/Privacy-and-Security-Attitudes-5.19.15_FINAL.pdf (accessed August 13, 2016)

few months (8%), and 23% believed the government should be allowed to keep records of individual online activities for no more than a few years. (See Figure 7.7.)

Attitudes toward online privacy in 2014 appeared to be stronger among people who had heard "a lot" about government surveillance. As Figure 7.8 shows, majorities of adults who had heard a lot about government surveillance programs thought that search engines (54%) or social media sites (55%) should never save records of their online activities. Among adults who had heard only "a little" about government surveillance, by contrast, 38% thought that search engines should not keep any records of Internet activity, and 35% thought that social networking sites should not keep such information. (See Figure 7.8.) Overall, adults who had heard a lot about government surveillance also expressed less trust that their privacy was being protected online. For example, 59% of adults who had heard a lot about government surveillance in 2014 reported they were "not at all confident" that their social media sites were keeping their online activities private, compared with 45% of adults who had heard a little about government surveillance that year. (See Figure 7.9.)

IT also has the capacity to inflict damage that goes beyond the exchange of classified data. With the emergence in government agencies and private industry of increasingly complex computer systems, terrorists, hackers,

and governments soon developed the power to disrupt, and even destroy, real physical targets. The extent of this threat first achieved widespread attention in 2010, when cybersecurity experts became aware of a new form of malware that had the capacity to infiltrate massive industrial control systems and seize control of the systems' functions. Dubbed Stuxnet, this highly sophisticated cyberworm had the potential to trigger a catastrophic chain of events at a high-security site, such as a nuclear power plant. Indeed, Mark Clayton reports in "Stuxnet Malware Is 'Weapon' out to Destroy ... Iran's Bushehr Nuclear Plant?" (CSMonitor.com, September 21, 2010) that in 2010 many cybersecurity experts believed Stuxnet had infected the Bushehr nuclear power plant in Iran, which is one of the most sensitive, high-risk nuclear sites in the world. According to Ellen Nakashima and Joby Warrick, in "Stuxnet Was Work of U.S. and Israeli Experts, Officials Say" (WashingtonPost.com, June 1, 2012), the operation against the Iranian nuclear program was later discovered to have been launched as a joint mission between the United States and Israel and authorized by President Obama. In the end, the Stuxnet attack destroyed roughly one-sixth of Iran's uranium centrifuges.

By 2012 the potential for other sophisticated forms of cyberwarfare had emerged as a new type of threat to U.S. national security. In *Occupying the Information High Ground: Chinese Capabilities for Computer Network Operations and Cyber Espionage* (March 7, 2012, http://origin .www.uscc.gov/sites/default/files/Research/USCC_Report _Chinese_Capabilities_for_Computer_Network_Operations _and_Cyber_%20Espionage.pdf), a report prepared for the U.S.-China Economic and Security Review Commission by Northrop Grumman Corporation, authors Bryan Krekel, Patton Adams, and George Bakos assert that in 2012 China was in the process of developing a strategy known as "information confrontation," making "the ability to exert control over an adversary's information and information systems" one of its key defense priorities in the early 21st century. The article "How to Survive a Cyberwar" (Bloomberg.com, August 2, 2012) notes that according to General Keith Alexander (1951–), the head of the U.S. Cyber Command, electronic breaches of U.S. targets resulted in roughly $1 trillion in intellectual property losses between 2009 and 2011. In the face of these burgeoning threats, in October 2012 President Obama issued "Presidential Policy Directive 20" (http://fas .org/irp/offdocs/ppd/ppd-20.pdf), a classified order that established new guidelines for the "cyber-operations of military and federal agencies."

Sandra I. Erwin reports in "NSA Chief: Military Not Organized for Cyber Warfare" (NationalDefenseMagazine .org, June 12, 2014) that U.S. Cyber Command, a Pentagon division formed in 2009, had a $500 million annual budget dedicated to combating cyberattacks

**FIGURE 7.8**

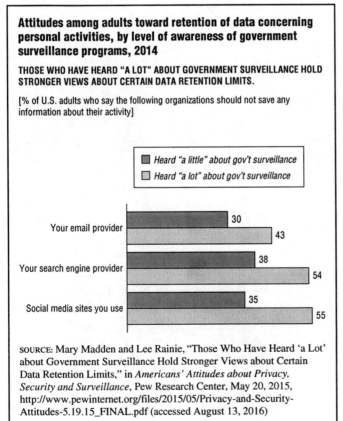

Attitudes among adults toward retention of data concerning personal activities, by level of awareness of government surveillance programs, 2014

THOSE WHO HAVE HEARD "A LOT" ABOUT GOVERNMENT SURVEILLANCE HOLD STRONGER VIEWS ABOUT CERTAIN DATA RETENTION LIMITS.

[% of U.S. adults who say the following organizations should not save any information about their activity]

■ Heard "a little" about gov't surveillance
□ Heard "a lot" about gov't surveillance

Your email provider — 30 / 43
Your search engine provider — 38 / 54
Social media sites you use — 35 / 55

SOURCE: Mary Madden and Lee Rainie, "Those Who Have Heard 'a Lot' about Government Surveillance Hold Stronger Views about Certain Data Retention Limits," in *Americans' Attitudes about Privacy, Security and Surveillance*, Pew Research Center, May 20, 2015, http://www.pewinternet.org/files/2015/05/Privacy-and-Security-Attitudes-5.19.15_FINAL.pdf (accessed August 13, 2016)

**FIGURE 7.9**

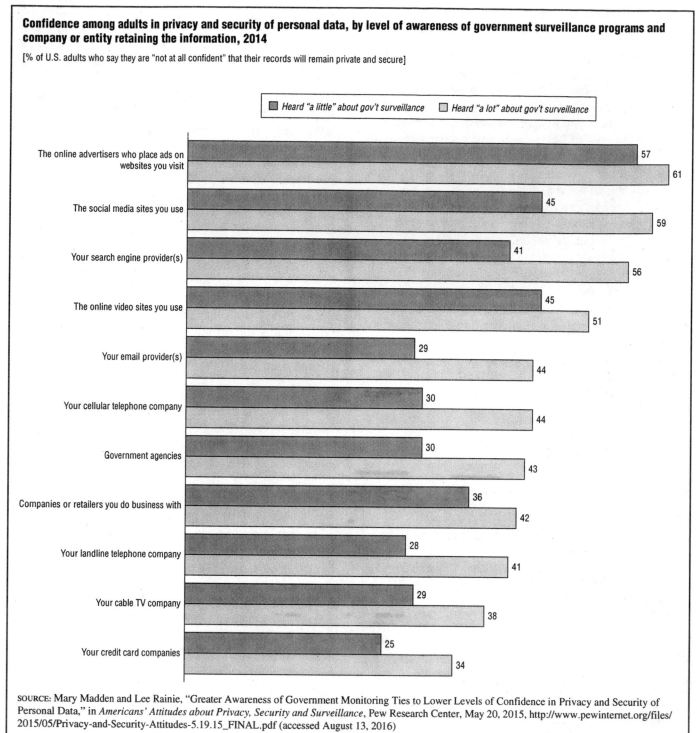

**Confidence among adults in privacy and security of personal data, by level of awareness of government surveillance programs and company or entity retaining the information, 2014**

[% of U.S. adults who say they are "not at all confident" that their records will remain private and secure]

■ Heard "a little" about gov't surveillance   □ Heard "a lot" about gov't surveillance

| Category | Heard "a little" | Heard "a lot" |
|---|---|---|
| The online advertisers who place ads on websites you visit | 57 | 61 |
| The social media sites you use | 45 | 59 |
| Your search engine provider(s) | 41 | 56 |
| The online video sites you use | 45 | 51 |
| Your email provider(s) | 29 | 44 |
| Your cellular telephone company | 30 | 44 |
| Government agencies | 30 | 43 |
| Companies or retailers you do business with | 36 | 42 |
| Your landline telephone company | 28 | 41 |
| Your cable TV company | 29 | 38 |
| Your credit card companies | 25 | 34 |

SOURCE: Mary Madden and Lee Rainie, "Greater Awareness of Government Monitoring Ties to Lower Levels of Confidence in Privacy and Security of Personal Data," in *Americans' Attitudes about Privacy, Security and Surveillance*, Pew Research Center, May 20, 2015, http://www.pewinternet.org/files/2015/05/Privacy-and-Security-Attitudes-5.19.15_FINAL.pdf (accessed August 13, 2016)

against the United States. Erwin notes, however, that in 2014 Cyber Command was still contending with the U.S. military's "hidebound culture and outdated procurement system," which hindered the division's efforts to develop an effective defense against cyberwarfare. "Our greater challenge is not technology but organization," Erwin quotes Admiral Michael S. Rogers (1959–), head of both the NSA and Cyber Command, as saying. "Military commanders must 'own' cyber." Karen Parrish reports in

"Cyber Guard 2016 Seeks to Manage Complexity in Invisible Domain" (June 18, 2016, http://www.defense.gov/News/Article/Article/803018/cyber-guard-2016-seeks-to-manage-complexity-in-invisible-domain) that in June 2016 the Joint Chiefs of Staff of the U.S. Department of Defense oversaw Cyber Guard 2016, a nine-day exercise that included more than 800 participants from 100 U.S. organizations and foreign allies designed to test the military's preparedness for a large-scale cyberattack.

## ELECTIONS AND POLITICS

The Internet has not only influenced how people interact with the government but also how people engage with politics. Aaron Smith of the Pew Research Center reports in *Cell Phones, Social Media and Campaign 2014* (November 23, 2014, http://www.pewinternet.org/files/2014/10/PI_CellPhonesSocialMediaCampaign2014_110314.pdf) that by 2014 social media had become an increasingly important source of political information for many American adults. That year, 16% of all registered voters in the United States followed a politician or political party on social media. Younger voters in particular have been quick to adopt social networking as a way of remaining politically informed. In 2014 nearly one-quarter (24%) of all registered voters between the ages of 18 and 29 years followed a politician or political party on social media, and more than one-fifth (21%) of voters aged 30 to 49 years used social media as a way to follow the activities of a political party or politician. Overall, 41% of registered voters reported that learning about political news before other people was a "major reason" they followed politicians or parties on social networking sites.

By 2014 mobile devices had become another important tool for finding political news and information. Smith notes that more than one-quarter (28%) of registered voters used their cell phones to keep informed about political or election news in 2014. Voters aged 18 to 29 years (43%) were most likely to use their mobile devices to learn about political developments that year, followed by voters aged 30 to 49 years (40%), voters aged 50 to 64 years (22%), and voters aged 65 years and older (11%). Smith also notes a correlation between party affiliation and the use of mobile devices to learn about political news. In 2014 independents (32%) were the most likely to learn about politics through their mobile devices, followed by Democrats (29%) and Republicans (25%).

### IT and the Voting Booth

To help bring IT into voting booths, in 2002 Congress passed and President Bush signed the Help America Vote Act (HAVA). The act was a direct response to the hotly contested 2000 presidential campaign in which disputes over punch-card ballots in Florida contributed to a month-long delay of nationwide presidential election results. The punch-card ballots were prone to human error in that people would sometimes punch out the wrong perforated circle or not punch the card all the way through. HAVA required states to upgrade to electronic voting systems by the 2006 national election. The bill allotted $3.9 billion to help states replace old punch-card and lever systems with new voting machines. Although HAVA did not specify precisely which voting machines states were required to use, the act did provide a list of features the machines should have. Among other things, the machines should keep an electronic and paper record of the votes, be accessible to those with disabilities, allow voters to review their ballots before they are cast, and notify voters if they misvote (e.g., vote twice for the same office).

The two types of machines that came closest to meeting HAVA's requirements were used heavily in subsequent elections. The first type is the optical scanning (Marksense) voting system. This system operates much like the paper-based standardized tests given in high schools and colleges. Using a dark lead pencil or black ink pen, voters darken ovals next to the names of candidates for whom they wish to vote. The sheet is then fed into a scanner. If the ballot is acceptable, the machine scans the ballot using lasers and the votes are registered in the machine. The problem with optical scanning systems, however, is that they are not accessible to disabled people who have trouble seeing or do not have complete control of their fine motor skills.

The second type of machine, known as a direct recording electronic (DRE) voting system, covers all the requirements laid down by HAVA. DRE systems are akin to touch-screen automated teller machines. The voter stands in front of the touch screen and a list of candidates for a given political contest is displayed on the screen. The voter simply touches the candidate's name to vote for that person, and the machine displays the next list of candidates. The machine notifies the voter if he or she has misvoted and allows for a review of votes on a final checkout screen before they are cast. The machine prints out a paper record resembling a spreadsheet at the end of the voting day. Proponents claim that the DRE system is better than the optical system because the DRE system eliminates the potential human error involved in coloring in circles and is easier for the disabled.

Although DRE systems meet HAVA's requirements, controversy still surrounds their use. Many people are concerned that hackers can somehow tap into these systems and change the votes. A second concern is that the complicated computer hardware and software in these systems can malfunction. In "Is E-Voting Safe?" (PCWorld.com, April 28, 2004), Paul Boutin discusses a study on DRE systems that was conducted by computer scientists at the California Institute of Technology and the Massachusetts Institute of Technology (MIT) in 2001. The study concluded that touch-screen machines were slightly more accurate than punch-card machines. The residual margin of error for the DRE machines, which equates to the percentage of votes that are thrown out because of error, was 2.3%. This was only marginally better than the 2.5% error rate generated by punch-card systems. By contrast, optically scanned paper ballots had an error rate of only 1.5%.

The new voting machines did appear to make some difference in the 2004 presidential election. Charles Stewart III of MIT states in "Measuring the Improvement (or Lack of Improvement) in Voting since 2000 in the U.S." (January 14, 2006, http://web.mit.edu/cstewart/www/papers/measuring_2.pdf) that the number of votes that had to be thrown out because of error between the 2000 and 2004 presidential elections dropped from 1.9% to 1.1% among those states and counties where the statistics were available. (It should be noted that the reported/detected error from election officials may have been lower than the actual error.) Although many factors could have contributed to this reduction, those counties that updated to optical scanning voting machines or DRE systems showed some of the most significant drops in voting error.

In spite of these promising signs, by 2008 a number of states, notably Florida, were compelled to replace many of the voting machines they had installed only six years earlier, amid concerns that the machines were vulnerable to error or security risks. The article "Voting Shouldn't Be a Game of Chance" (WashingtonPost.com, November 2, 2008) reports numerous problems that were related to early electronic voting in the weeks preceding the 2008 presidential election, including instances where voters were unable to select the candidates they wanted on touch-screen voting systems. Even with a record turnout of 132.6 million voters for the November 4 election, incidences of problems with electronic voting machines were relatively minor. Still, the question of the reliability of e-voting remained a subject of debate, particularly as one-third of all states did not require paper records of electronic ballots. In August 2010 a number of lawmakers, led by Representative Rush D. Holt Jr. (1948–; D-NJ), submitted a letter to the U.S. attorney general Eric Holder Jr. (1951–) recommending that the Department of Justice require all states to generate paper voting records during the November 2010 elections. As of November 2016, however, systems were still in place in 15 states that did not generate paper voting records.

VOTING AND THE INTERNET. As the normalcy of conducting many personal transactions over the Internet became more widespread during the early 21st century, some observers began anticipating online voting and suggested that the convenience of voting online would increase voter participation in elections. A turning point in the evolution of online voting came in October 2009, with the passage of the Military and Overseas Voter Empowerment Act. Under the new law, states were empowered to send electronic voter registration forms, election information, and even blank ballots to Americans living overseas, thereby saving the time and money associated with sending materials through conventional mail. Perhaps more significant, the new system made it possible for the votes of military personnel and other overseas Americans to be counted in a timely manner, eliminating the lag time that was traditionally associated

with counting absentee voting ballots. A month after the law passed, Massachusetts became the first state to adopt the new procedures. In "States Move to Allow Overseas and Military Voters to Cast Ballots by Internet" (NYTimes.com, May 8, 2010), Ian Urbina notes that by May 2010, 33 states had instituted laws allowing Americans abroad to vote via e-mail or fax. The shift to Internet voting caused a great deal of concern among Internet security experts and other voting advocates. Urbina quotes John Bonifaz of the voting rights organization Voter Action as saying that the move toward online voting "basically takes the hazards we've seen with electronic voting and puts them on steroids." Indeed, following the hacking of election systems in Illinois and Arizona in August 2016 (discussed in Chapter 4), the prospect of online voting appeared increasingly unlikely for the foreseeable future.

## GOVERNMENT IMPROVEMENTS IN DAILY LIFE

### 511 Travel Information System

Using advanced technology, the federal and state governments have begun to put into place a nationwide travel information system known as 511. The 511 system is an attempt to unify the many automated information systems that were already operated by state and local governments. Dozens of cities and states set up these systems during the 1990s, when cell phones and advanced communications became affordable. Callers and Internet users could retrieve information on traffic jams and road conditions over the phone or on the Internet. For example, the Advanced Regional Traffic Interactive Management and Information System (ARTIMIS) was set up in 1995 to monitor traffic and alert people to traffic problems on 88 miles (142 km) of freeway in the Cincinnati, Ohio, metropolitan area. ARTIMIS (now part of OHGo, which is maintained by the Ohio Department of Transportation) used cameras and hundreds of detectors to monitor the flow of traffic along these freeways. People could dial into the system at any time to retrieve the information.

Most of these systems, however, had one big flaw. To access them by phone, drivers typically had to remember an unfamiliar, seven-digit number. Consequently, these services were rarely used. Noticing this problem, the U.S. Department of Transportation (DOT) approached the FCC and asked that a three-digit number be established to connect users to local travel information anywhere in the country. The FCC chose 511. The number was short and would automatically be associated with the more widely used 411 and 911. Ultimately, the DOT wanted all driver information systems to adopt the 511 number so that any driver in the country could receive information by simply dialing 511.

With the support of the DOT, the 511 Deployment Coalition was formed in 2001 by a number of federal and state agencies to establish guidelines and procedures for implementing local 511 travel information systems. The coalition explains in *America's Travel Information Number: Implementation and Operational Guidelines for 511 Services* (September 2005, http://www.ops.fhwa.dot.gov/511/resources/publications/511guide_ver3/511guide3.htm) that 511 services should allow a driver to access automated recordings on travel conditions through a series of voice commands or touch-tone commands on the phone. At bare minimum, the system should provide conditions for major arteries in the designated region.

Many previously developed systems such as the TravInfo service in San Francisco, California, quickly adopted the number for their travel services. The DOT also awarded $100,000 grants to states or cities without traffic advisory systems to fund implementation plans. Figure 7.10 displays the states that used the 511 number and those that received funding to implement a system as of June 2016.

### National Do Not Call Registry

Another attempt by the federal government to respond to the everyday concerns of the American public is the National Do Not Call Registry (https://www.donotcall.gov/default.aspx), which is managed by the Federal Trade Commission (FTC). Launched in June 2003, the registry was established with the simple goal of reducing the number of unwanted telemarketing calls received by consumers. Under the Telemarketing Sales Rule that outlined the program, commercial telemarketers were

**FIGURE 7.10**

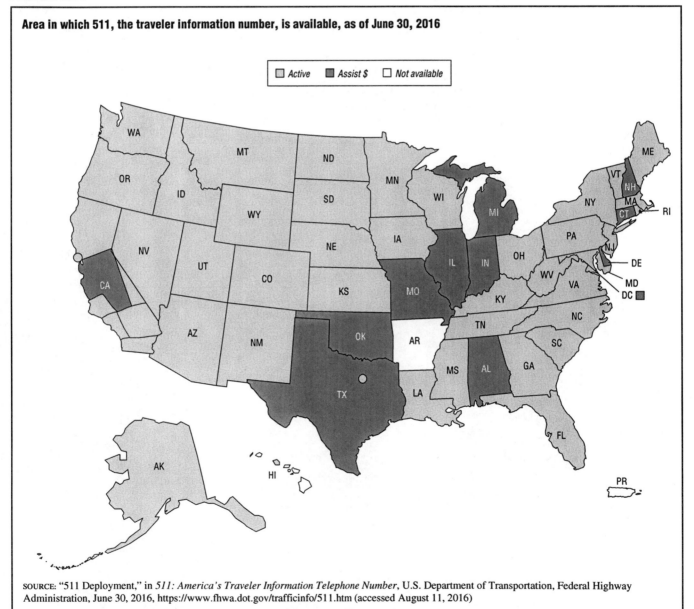

Area in which 511, the traveler information number, is available, as of June 30, 2016

Legend: Active | Assist $ | Not available

SOURCE: "511 Deployment," in *511: America's Traveler Information Telephone Number*, U.S. Department of Transportation, Federal Highway Administration, June 30, 2016, https://www.fhwa.dot.gov/trafficinfo/511.htm (accessed August 11, 2016)

allowed to access the list for a fee to continue making unsolicited calls to numbers in their area that were not registered. In addition, telemarketers could continue to call those on the list with whom they had an established business relationship within the preceding 18 months. The Do Not Call Registry contained more than 142 million phone numbers within its first four years of operation, according to the FTC in *The FTC in 2007: A Champion for Consumers and Competition* (April 2007, http://www .ftc.gov/sites/default/files/documents/reports_annual/annual-report-2007/chairmansreport2007_0.pdf). The FTC indicates in *National Do Not Call Registry Data Book FY 2015* (November 2015, https://www.ftc.gov/system/files/documents/reports/national-do-not-call-registry-data-book-fiscal-year-2015/dncdatabookfy2015.pdf) that in 2015, 222.8 million phone numbers had been submitted to the service, which covered all U.S. states and territories. (See Figure 7.11.) As Table 7.10 shows, California led the nation in both active Do Not Call registrations (25.2 million) and

complaints (543,477) in 2015. Among the states, New Hampshire had the highest proportion of active registrations in 2015, with 89,203 out of every 100,000 residents registered that year. (See Figure 7.12.)

Although the implementation of the national registry limited many unwanted telemarketing phone calls, by 2013 Internet phone services enabled unscrupulous marketers to flout the system, sending thousands of automated phone calls, dubbed "robocalls," per minute to numbers on the Do Not Call Registry. Megan Kowalski and Meghan Hoye report in "Robocallers Doing a Number on the Do Not Call List" (USAToday.com, August 26, 2013) that complaints to the FTC increased to 308,000 per month in 2012, an increase of 63% over the previous year. In "Robocalls Ring off the Hook Despite Do Not Call Registry" (CNBC.com, May 21, 2016), Erin Barry reports that "many of the scammers originate overseas and spoof or fake the number on caller ID, making it harder for law enforcement to catch the criminals."

FIGURE 7.11

**Do Not Call registrations and complaints, 2003–15**

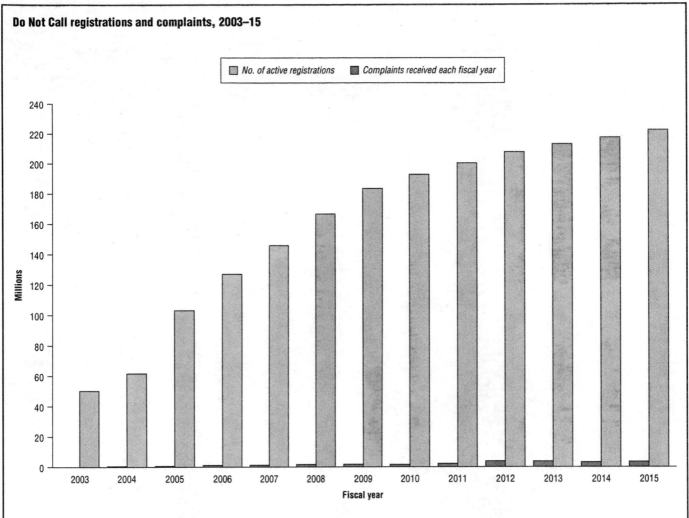

| Fiscal year | No. of active registrations | Increase in active registrations | No. of cumulative complaints | Complaints received each fiscal year |
|---|---|---|---|---|
| 2003 | 50,267,097 | 50,267,097 | 0 | 0 |
| 2004 | 61,741,124 | 11,474,027 | 579,838 | 579,838 |
| 2005 | 103,193,927 | 41,452,803 | 1,249,312 | 669,474 |
| 2006 | 126,981,844 | 23,787,917 | 2,399,130 | 1,149,818 |
| 2007 | 145,756,274 | 18,774,430 | 3,696,995 | 1,297,865 |
| 2008 | 166,582,471 | 20,826,197 | 5,464,793 | 1,767,798 |
| 2009 | 183,505,798 | 16,923,327 | 7,273,144 | 1,808,351 |
| 2010 | 192,917,741 | 9,411,943 | 8,906,957 | 1,633,813 |
| 2011 | 200,520,793 | 7,603,052 | 11,180,473 | 2,273,516 |
| 2012 | 207,938,719 | 7,417,926 | 15,021,029 | 3,840,556 |
| 2013 | 213,400,640 | 5,461,921 | 18,769,675 | 3,748,646 |
| 2014 | 217,855,659 | 4,455,019 | 22,010,761 | 3,241,086 |
| 2015 | 222,841,484 | 4,985,825 | 25,589,481 | 3,578,720 |

FTC = Federal Trade Commission.
Note: Active registration and complaint figures reflect the total number of phone numbers registered and the total number of National Do Not Call Registry complaints submitted to the FTC as of September 30, 2015.

SOURCE: "National Do Not Call Registry Active Registration and Complaint Figures," in *National Do Not Call Registry Data Book: FY 2015*, Federal Trade Commission, November 2015, https://www.ftc.gov/system/files/documents/reports/national-do-not-call-registry-data-book-fiscal-year-2015/dncdatabookfy2015.pdf (accessed August 11, 2016).

**TABLE 7.10**

## Do Not Call registrations and complaints, by state, 2015

| | Active registrations | | FY 2015 complaints | |
|---|---|---|---|---|
| Consumer state | Active registrations[a] | Active registrations per 100,000 population[b] | FY 2015 complaints[c] | FY 2015 complaints per 100,000 population[b] |
| Alabama | 3,283,842 | 67,717 | 46,264 | 954 |
| Alaska | 358,716 | 48,690 | 2,035 | 276 |
| Arizona | 4,464,376 | 66,321 | 93,787 | 1,393 |
| Arkansas | 1,957,045 | 65,974 | 29,331 | 989 |
| California | 25,201,180 | 64,947 | 543,477 | 1,401 |
| Colorado | 4,341,567 | 81,062 | 77,069 | 1,439 |
| Connecticut | 3,087,422 | 85,841 | 52,710 | 1,466 |
| Delaware | 725,325 | 77,524 | 14,426 | 1,542 |
| District of Columbia | 593,057 | 90,008 | 8,760 | 1,330 |
| Florida | 14,191,227 | 71,337 | 244,717 | 1,230 |
| Georgia | 6,869,990 | 68,038 | 99,102 | 981 |
| Hawaii | 760,824 | 53,596 | 8,417 | 593 |
| Idaho | 1,129,590 | 69,111 | 20,251 | 1,239 |
| Illinois | 9,707,760 | 75,367 | 181,890 | 1,412 |
| Indiana | 3,944,861 | 59,799 | 30,984 | 470 |
| Iowa | 2,427,757 | 78,135 | 27,546 | 887 |
| Kansas | 2,295,049 | 79,030 | 27,242 | 938 |
| Kentucky | 3,230,323 | 73,193 | 32,621 | 739 |
| Louisiana | 2,729,396 | 58,701 | 30,867 | 664 |
| Maine | 1,050,374 | 78,970 | 11,346 | 853 |
| Maryland | 4,543,895 | 76,031 | 91,679 | 1,534 |
| Massachusetts | 5,643,946 | 83,671 | 99,215 | 1,471 |
| Michigan | 7,699,127 | 77,691 | 114,024 | 1,151 |
| Minnesota | 4,208,768 | 77,124 | 50,356 | 923 |
| Mississippi | 1,574,141 | 52,575 | 19,769 | 660 |
| Missouri | 3,920,400 | 64,655 | 36,187 | 597 |
| Montana | 767,960 | 75,027 | 9,892 | 966 |
| Nebraska | 1,448,706 | 76,997 | 17,261 | 917 |
| Nevada | 1,893,287 | 66,686 | 41,601 | 1,465 |
| New Hampshire | 1,183,553 | 89,203 | 17,085 | 1,288 |
| New Jersey | 7,086,459 | 79,283 | 141,944 | 1,588 |
| New Mexico | 1,512,415 | 72,518 | 24,089 | 1,155 |
| New York | 13,622,666 | 68,989 | 247,164 | 1,252 |
| North Carolina | 6,594,478 | 66,316 | 89,467 | 900 |
| North Dakota | 506,783 | 68,532 | 3,044 | 412 |
| Ohio | 8,818,031 | 76,056 | 125,108 | 1,079 |
| Oklahoma | 2,587,322 | 66,717 | 33,127 | 854 |
| Oregon | 2,883,597 | 72,630 | 50,614 | 1,275 |
| Pennsylvania | 9,934,851 | 77,694 | 138,079 | 1,080 |
| Rhode Island | 791,228 | 74,986 | 12,250 | 1,161 |
| South Carolina | 2,955,560 | 61,160 | 40,601 | 840 |
| South Dakota | 615,857 | 72,184 | 6,559 | 769 |
| Tennessee | 4,518,402 | 68,990 | 64,524 | 985 |
| Texas | 14,951,105 | 55,463 | 225,190 | 835 |
| Utah | 1,861,025 | 63,238 | 26,700 | 907 |
| Vermont | 480,480 | 76,685 | 5,884 | 939 |
| Virginia | 5,990,170 | 71,943 | 107,944 | 1,296 |
| Washington | 5,019,456 | 71,082 | 86,986 | 1,232 |
| West Virginia | 1,198,211 | 64,757 | 14,874 | 804 |
| Wisconsin | 4,476,128 | 77,743 | 41,326 | 718 |
| Wyoming | 444,075 | 76,020 | 6,996 | 1,198 |

[a]"Active Registrations" reflect the total number of phone numbers registered on the National Do Not Call Registry as of September 30, 2015.
[b]Population estimates are based on the 2014 U.S. Census population estimates.
[c]"FY 2015 Complaints" reflect National Do Not Call Registry complaints received by the Commission during fiscal year 2015.
FY = fiscal year.

SOURCE: "Fiscal Year 2015 National Do Not Call Registry Registration and Complaint Figures by State Population," in *National Do Not Call Registry Data Book: FY 2015*, Federal Trade Commission, November 2015, https://www.ftc.gov/system/files/documents/reports/national-do-not-call-registry-data-book-fiscal-year-2015/dncdatabookfy2015.pdf (accessed August 11, 2016).

FIGURE 7.12

**State rankings for Do Not Call registrations, by proportion of population registered, 2015**

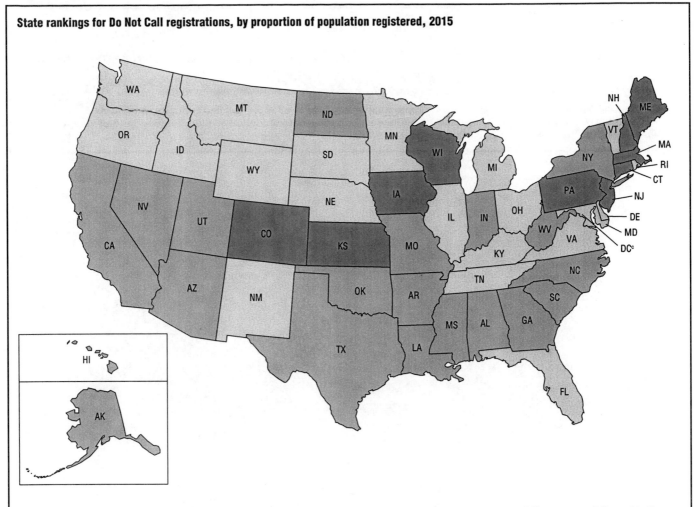

| Rank[a] | Consumer state | Active registrations | Active registrations per 100,000 population[b] | Rank[a] | Consumer state | Active registrations | Active registrations per 100,000 population[b] |
|---|---|---|---|---|---|---|---|
| 1 | New Hampshire | 1,183,553 | 89,203 | 26 | Virginia | 5,990,170 | 71,943 |
| 2 | Connecticut | 3,087,422 | 85,841 | 27 | Florida | 14,191,227 | 71,337 |
| 3 | Massachusetts | 5,643,946 | 83,671 | 28 | Washington | 5,019,456 | 71,082 |
| 4 | Colorado | 4,341,567 | 81,062 | 29 | Idaho | 1,129,590 | 69,111 |
| 5 | New Jersey | 7,086,459 | 79,283 | 30 | Tennessee | 4,518,402 | 68,990 |
| 6 | Kansas | 2,295,049 | 79,030 | 31 | New York | 13,622,666 | 68,989 |
| 7 | Maine | 1,050,374 | 78,970 | 32 | North Dakota | 506,783 | 68,532 |
| 8 | Iowa | 2,427,757 | 78,135 | 33 | Georgia | 6,869,990 | 68,038 |
| 9 | Wisconsin | 4,476,128 | 77,743 | 34 | Alabama | 3,283,842 | 67,717 |
| 10 | Pennsylvania | 9,934,851 | 77,694 | 35 | Oklahoma | 2,587,322 | 66,717 |
| 11 | Michigan | 7,699,127 | 77,691 | 36 | Nevada | 1,893,287 | 66,686 |
| 12 | Delaware | 725,325 | 77,524 | 37 | Arizona | 4,464,376 | 66,321 |
| 13 | Minnesota | 4,208,768 | 77,124 | 38 | North Carolina | 6,594,478 | 66,316 |
| 14 | Nebraska | 1,448,706 | 76,997 | 39 | Arkansas | 1,957,045 | 65,974 |
| 15 | Vermont | 480,480 | 76,685 | 40 | California | 25,201,180 | 64,947 |
| 16 | Ohio | 8,818,031 | 76,056 | 41 | West Virginia | 1,198,211 | 64,757 |
| 17 | Maryland | 4,543,895 | 76,031 | 42 | Missouri | 3,920,400 | 64,655 |
| 18 | Wyoming | 444,075 | 76,020 | 43 | Utah | 1,861,025 | 63,238 |
| 19 | Illinois | 9,707,760 | 75,367 | 44 | South Carolina | 2,955,560 | 61,160 |
| 20 | Montana | 767,960 | 75,027 | 45 | Indiana | 3,944,861 | 59,799 |
| 21 | Rhode Island | 791,228 | 74,986 | 46 | Louisiana | 2,729,396 | 58,701 |
| 22 | Kentucky | 3,230,323 | 73,193 | 47 | Texas | 14,951,105 | 55,463 |
| 23 | Oregon | 2,883,597 | 72,630 | 48 | Hawaii | 760,824 | 53,596 |
| 24 | New Mexico | 1,512,415 | 72,518 | 49 | Mississippi | 1,574,141 | 52,575 |
| 25 | South Dakota | 615,857 | 72,184 | 50 | Alaska | 358,716 | 48,690 |

**FIGURE 7.12**

**State rankings for Do Not Call registrations, by proportion of population registered, 2015 [CONTINUED]**

ªRankings are based on the "Active registrations per 100,000 population." "Active registrations" reflect the total number of phone numbers registered on the National Do Not Call Registry as of September 30, 2015.
ᵇPopulation estimates are based on the 2014 U.S. Census population estimates.
ᶜNumbers for the District of Columbia are as follows: Active registrations = 593,057; and Active registrations per 100,000 population = 90,008.

SOURCE: "State Rankings for National Do Not Call Registry Registrations by State Population," in *National Do Not Call Registry Data Book: FY 2015*, Federal Trade Commission, November 2015, https://www.ftc.gov/system/files/documents/reports/national-do-not-call-registry-data-book-fiscal-year-2015/dncdatabookfy2015.pdf (accessed August 11, 2016)

# CHAPTER 8

# HEALTH RESOURCES IN THE INFORMATION AGE

Before the Internet, finding the latest information on a health issue typically required access to a university or medical library. Most medical studies and information existed in expensive books and journals, which were generally written for those with formal training. The Internet gave rise to a plethora of accessible, informative websites that average consumers could comprehend. The rise of online pharmacies also allowed people the convenience of ordering and receiving prescription drugs and medical supplies at home. Despite some problems such as the online sale of counterfeit medications and the existence of faulty medical information on the web, a majority of Americans used the Internet to research health-related matters in 2016. Susannah Fox, Maeve Duggan, and Kristen Purcell of the Pew Research Center report in *Family Caregivers Are Wired for Health* (June 20, 2013, http://www.pewinternet.org/files/old-media//Files/Reports/2013/PewResearch_Family Caregivers.pdf) that in 2012, 84% of caregivers who used the Internet went online to research medical or health issues. Among other adult Internet users, this figure was 64%.

The Internet has also benefited those who work in the health care fields. The Internet allows medical researchers to share information as never before. Enormous databases accessible on the Internet contain references to nearly all published medical papers, sparing researchers the tedium of hunting through print indexes. The Internet also provides the perfect medium for posting health care research data, such as statistics on disease prevalence, and research organizations can post data from thousands of disease studies. The availability of research data has fostered a new era of scientific cooperation wherein medical results from laboratories halfway around the world can be brought together via a quick online search using a web browser or mobile app.

## HEALTH CARE ON THE INTERNET

In their report, Fox, Duggan, and Purcell examine the types of topics Internet users research online. Overall, 71% of all online adults not suffering from a chronic condition researched a specific health topic on the Internet in 2012. By comparison, 73% of online adults with one chronic condition researched a specific health topic on the Internet that year, and 76% of adult Internet users with two or more chronic conditions searched for health-related information online. Less than two-thirds (62%) of online adults with two or more chronic conditions researched a specific disease or health problem in 2012, whereas a little more than half (52%) of adult Internet users not suffering from a chronic condition conducted the same type of research. That year, online adults with no chronic health problems (13%) were slightly more likely than those with one chronic condition (12%) or those with two or more chronic conditions (6%) to search for information about pregnancy online.

Libraries also provide Americans with an opportunity to research health topics over the Internet. John Horrigan of the Pew Research Center reports in *Libraries at the Crossroads* (September 15, 2015, http://www.pewinternet.org/files/2015/09/2015-09-15_libraries_FINAL.pdf) that of all Americans 16 years of age and older who have used online services at a public library, 42% have done so in order to conduct research about health-related topics. According to Horrigan, this figure represents 10% of all U.S. residents in this age group.

As more adults go online for health information, many health care officials have begun to worry that Americans are using the Internet to diagnose their own ailments in the hope of avoiding time-consuming but necessary visits to the doctor's office. The biggest problem with self-diagnosis is that it is rarely objective. Using advice from online websites is especially problematic in that it is often incomplete. In "Find Good Health

Information" (2016, http://www.mlanet.org/resources/userguide.html), the Medical Library Association (MLA) provides a list of recommendations that those seeking health information on the Internet should follow. These recommendations include identifying each site's sponsor, checking the date of information on the site, and verifying that the material is rooted in fact, as opposed to opinion.

**Top Websites for Health Information**

According to the MLA, in "MLA Top Health Web Sites" (2016, http://www.mlanet.org/p/cm/ld/fid=397), the most useful medical websites in 2016 were:

- Cancer.gov, National Cancer Institute (http://www.cancer.gov)

- Centers for Disease Control and Prevention (CDC; http://www.cdc.gov)

- Familydoctor.org, American Academy of Family Physicians (http://familydoctor.org)

- Healthfinder, National Health Information Center (http://www.healthfinder.gov)

- HIV InSite, University of California, San Francisco Center for HIV Information (http://hivinsite.ucsf.edu)

- KidsHealth, Nemours Foundation (http://www.kidshealth.org)

- Mayo Clinic (http://www.mayoclinic.com)

- MedlinePlus, U.S. National Library of Medicine (http://www.medlineplus.gov)

- NetWellness, Universities of Cincinnati, Ohio State, and Case Western Reserve (http://www.netwellness.org)

- NIHSeniorHealth, National Institutes of Health (NIH) health and wellness information for older adults (http://nihseniorhealth.gov)

These websites were evaluated in part on their credibility, content, sponsorship/authorship, purpose, and design. The general medicine websites noted by the MLA (Healthfinder.gov, Familydoctor.org, MedlinePlus.gov, and MayoClinic.com) contain information on many medical diseases and conditions. The nonprofit Kidshealth.org focuses on health care for children from prenatal care through adolescence. Facts on the human immunodeficiency virus (HIV) are available at HIVInsite.com, and Cancer.gov presents information on cancer types, causes, and treatments. Cancer.gov also maintains a database of clinical trials that are being conducted all over the country for those who seek information on alternative treatments. Finally, CDC.gov contains information on communicable diseases, immunization, and disease prevention.

MedlinePlus, the most comprehensive general medicine site, made its debut on the Internet in October 1998 with 22 health topics in its library. The site received more than 682,000 page hits during its first three months. By 2015 the site held information in English on more than 975 diseases and conditions, as well as Spanish-language information on 962 diseases and conditions. (See Table 8.1.) A search on MedlinePlus for a disease typically yields definitions, fact sheets, drug information, the latest news on the disease, and links to places where further information can be found. During the first quarter of fiscal year (FY) 2014 the site recorded 263 million page views, an all-time high. (See Figure 8.1.) Traffic dropped over the next year, however, falling to 202 million views during the first quarter of FY 2015. Traffic to MedlinePlus began an upward trend again, reaching 238 million page views and a record 117.2 million unique visitors during the first quarter of 2016.

**MEDICATION ONLINE**

The Internet also contains a wealth of information about prescription and nonprescription drugs. Since the late 1990s the online pharmacy business has been growing at a steady rate. Most major online pharmacies, such as Walgreens, are legitimate. They carry the Verified Internet Pharmacy Practice Sites seal of approval issued by the National Association of Boards of Pharmacy (NABP), meaning that they comply with all state and federal laws. Much like traditional pharmacies, these online drugstores require that a prescription be sent or called in by a doctor. Such pharmacies also send the drug to the patient complete with dosage and warning information on the bottle.

**TABLE 8.1**

**Annual number of health topics covered by MedlinePlus, by language, 1998–2015**

| Year | English total | Spanish total |
|------|---------------|---------------|
| 1998 | 40 | — |
| 1999 | 317 | — |
| 2000 | 430 | — |
| 2001 | 511 | — |
| 2002 | 574 | 506 |
| 2003 | 649 | 595 |
| 2004 | 686 | 623 |
| 2005 | 712 | 665 |
| 2006 | 738 | 698 |
| 2007 | 748 | 709 |
| 2008 | 777 | 737 |
| 2009 | 809 | 774 |
| 2010 | 881 | 851 |
| 2011 | 912 | 887 |
| 2012 | 938 | 919 |
| 2013 | 956 | 942 |
| 2014 | 959 | 950 |
| 2015 | 975 | 962 |

SOURCE: "Number of Health Topics by Date," in *MedlinePlus Statistics*, U.S. Department of Health and Human Services, National Institute of Health, U.S. National Library of Medicine, January 21, 2016, https://medlineplus.gov/usestatistics.html (accessed August 12, 2016)

**FIGURE 8.1**

Use of MedlinePlus, fiscal years 1999–2016

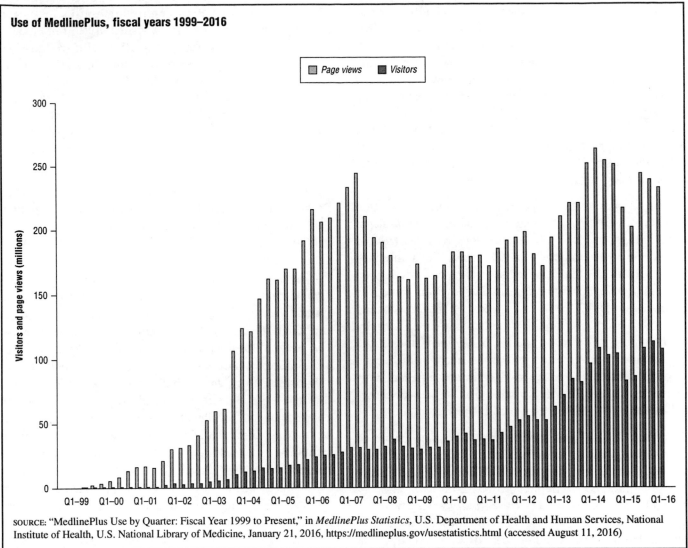

SOURCE: "MedlinePlus Use by Quarter: Fiscal Year 1999 to Present," in *MedlinePlus Statistics*, U.S. Department of Health and Human Services, National Institute of Health, U.S. National Library of Medicine, January 21, 2016, https://medlineplus.gov/usestatistics.html (accessed August 11, 2016)

Nevertheless, unlawful virtual pharmacies, which do not follow U.S. state and federal regulations, also operate on the Internet. In some cases, online pharmacies are operating illegally simply because they are based in other countries. For example, although many Canadian pharmacies follow strict standards that are comparable to those imposed on legitimate U.S. pharmacies, as of 2016 it was still illegal for individuals in the United States to buy pharmaceuticals from Canadian pharmacies. Of greater concern to health and law enforcement officials, however, is the rise of illegitimate online pharmacies. Although many online pharmacies that cater to the U.S. market claim to be located in Canada, research shows that many of them are actually located in other countries, including the United States. Many of these pharmacies will sell prescription drugs without a patient prescription, provide counterfeit or contaminated drugs, or send medications in the wrong dosages.

For many patients in the United States, the lure of online pharmacies is their convenience and low cost. In 2015, as reported by Jessica C. Barnett and Marina S. Vornovitsky of the U.S. Census Bureau in "Health Insurance Coverage in the United States: 2015" (September 2016, http://www.census.gov/content/dam/Census/library/publications/2016/demo/p60-257.pdf), 29 million Americans were without health insurance. Millions more had limited prescription drug benefits. In some cases, cheaper online pharmacies represented the difference between obtaining much-needed medications and going without them. Paul Jablow notes in "Ins, Outs of Getting Meds from Overseas" (Philly.com, January 12, 2014) that brand-name medications purchased from foreign-based online pharmacies cost 75% less than those acquired in the United States.

## Online Pharmacies, Safety, and the Law

Regardless, purchasing drugs online carries substantial risks. Illegitimate online pharmacies have generated a great deal of concern among health care professionals and government regulators in the United States. One problem is that state medical boards, which typically oversee brick-and-mortar operations, have difficulty monitoring pharmaceutical websites. Although some of these pharmacies follow many of the same standards as legitimate operations, others disregard them altogether. Besides providing drugs without a prescription, many send patients drugs without warning labels or dosage information. In an investigation of more than 11,500 online pharmacies marketing to patients in the United States, the NABP (2016, https://nabp.pharmacy/initiatives/dot-pharmacy/buying-medicine-online/) finds that only 4% adhered to standard pharmacy regulations and practices.

In response to this trend, Congress crafted legislation aimed at controlling the rapidly expanding trade in illegal online drugs. In 2008 President George W. Bush (1946–) signed the Ryan Haight Online Pharmacy Consumer Protection Act, a law that imposed several new restrictions on the sale of online pharmaceuticals. The law was named for Ryan Haight (1982–2001), a California teenager who died after overdosing on painkillers he had purchased illegally over the Internet. Among the law's key provisions is the requirement that all prescriptions be accompanied by a physical consultation between a doctor and a patient. Furthermore, the law imposed a ban on all online advertisements for illegal prescription medications.

When federal and state agencies become aware of illegitimate pharmacies in the United States, they attempt to shut them down. In a speech delivered to the Opiate Abuse Conference in September 2010, the U.S. attorney general Eric Holder Jr. (1951–; http://www.justice.gov/ag/speeches/2010/ag-speech-100910.html) asserted that, during the first nine months of 2010, the U.S. Drug Enforcement Administration (DEA) had seized "more than $62 million in proceeds and assets and . . . helped to shut down 'pill mill' pain clinics, prescription forgery rings, and illegal online pharmacies." Holder also claimed that the Ryan Haight Act had already played a major role in reducing the number of illegal online pharmacies selling prescription drugs in the United States. In "Two Indicted in Phila. in Illegal Online Drug Sales" (Philly.com, May 13, 2010), Nathan Gorenstein reports that the first prosecution under the Ryan Haight Act was initiated in May 2010, when federal prosecutors indicted two individuals, one American and one from the Bahamas, in association with an illegal online diet pill ring.

Amy Pavuk reports in "DEA Targets FedEx, UPS in Online-Pharmacy Probe" (OrlandoSentinel.com, March 26, 2013) that by 2013 the DEA had also begun investigating the role of major shipping companies in the transport of prescription drugs into the United States by illegal online pharmacies. However, government regulators can do little about controlling pharmacies that are outside of U.S. borders.

In the view of law enforcement officials, global cooperation is critical to controlling traffic in illegal online drugs. Dina Fine Maron writes in "Pill of Goods: International Counterfeit Drug Ring Hit in Massive Sting" (ScientificAmerican.com, July 3, 2013) that in July 2013 the U.S. Food and Drug Administration (FDA) closed down 1,677 illegal online pharmacies, the largest Internet-based operation of its kind. Although all of the websites claimed to be operating in Canada, Maron writes, none of the illegal prescription medications actually originated there.

In "Thousands of Illicit Online Pharmacies Shut Down in the Largest-Ever Global Operation Targeting Fake Medicines" (May 22, 2014, http://www.interpol.int/News-and-media/News/2014/N2014-089), the International Criminal Police Organization (Interpol) reports that in May 2014 approximately 200 law enforcement organizations in more than 110 countries participated in a worldwide raid aimed at disrupting global traffic in fake and illicit pharmaceuticals. Dubbed Operation Pangea VII, the raid resulted in a total of 237 arrests, as well as the confiscation of 9.4 million counterfeit and illegal prescription drugs worth an estimated $36 billion. In the course of the operation, officials deleted over 19,000 advertisements for illegal pharmaceuticals from social networking sites, while also shutting down more than 10,500 websites selling illicit medications. According to Interpol, Operation Pangea VII was the largest single enforcement action targeting counterfeit medications in history. A number of international agencies and entities participated in the operation, including the Center for Safe Internet Pharmacies, the Permanent Forum of International Pharmaceutical Crime, and the World Customs Organization. In addition, several global corporations, among them MasterCard, Microsoft, and Visa, cooperated with Interpol in the effort.

Because of the many unethical and illegal practices that are encountered by consumers making pharmaceutical purchases online, the FDA provides the guide "Buying Prescription Medicine Online: A Consumer Safety Guide" (June 12, 2015, http://www.fda.gov/Drugs/ResourcesForYou/ucm080588.htm) to reduce or eliminate many issues surrounding Internet pharmacies. The FDA recommends that patients use only sites that require a prescription, have pharmacists available to answer questions, and adequately protect the privacy of customers. It also suggests that online consumers use only state-licensed U.S. pharmacies. In 2012 the FDA launched the BeSafeRx initiative (http://www.fda.gov/drugs/resourcesforyou/consumers/buyingusingmedicinesafely/buyingmedicinesovertheinternet/besaferxknowyouronlinepharmacy/default.htm), which is aimed at providing the public with vital information concerning the dangers that are involved with purchasing drugs over the Internet.

## MEDICAL DATA REVOLUTION

Since the 1980s information technology (IT) and the Internet have transformed the field of medical research. Before launching a medical research project, a scientist must first know what has been done in the area he or she plans to study. For example, the initial step for a researcher who wants to find a cure for Alzheimer's would be to analyze previous data on the subject. Only then could the researcher formulate new theories and design experiments that advance the field. Before the Internet and the widespread use of computer databases, researchers seeking such information were required to spend days at medical libraries, sifting through thick journal indexes that cataloged thousands upon thousands of past journal articles by subject. The advent of computer databases changed all that. Huge medical indexes were put in digital form, which allowed researchers to compile a full list of research articles in minutes instead of days. MEDLINE/PubMed, which is maintained by the National Library of Medicine, is one of the most comprehensive and widely used of these databases. The National Library of Medicine (January 6, 2016, https://www.nlm.nih.gov/pubs/factsheets/dif_med_pub.html) states that in 2016 MEDLINE contained 22 million citations and abstracts summarizing papers that were published in nearly 5,600 biomedical journals in the United States and throughout the world. By simply going online to MEDLINE and typing a query, a researcher can track down every published paper on most medical topics.

The ability of computers and the Internet to store and transmit scientific data has also transformed the way medical research is conducted. The Internet allows scientists from all over the world to share data on diseases and patient attributes. Computers can then perform statistical analyses on disease data in relation to various aspects of patient histories, such as age, geographic location, and even the presence of other diseases.

The CDC's National Center for Health Statistics (NCHS; http://www.cdc.gov/nchs) database contains statistics on a variety of diseases including arthritis, heart disease, HIV, and even tooth decay. All this information is freely available for scientists to use in their research. The NCHS also provides valuable data to other government agencies. For example, in 2016 the NCHS collaborated with the Federal Interagency Forum on Child and Family Statistics, a group of government agencies that is dedicated to collecting and sharing data on children and families, to produce *America's Children in Brief: Key National Indicators of Well-Being, 2016* (July 2016, http://www.childstats.gov/pdf/ac2016/ac_16.pdf). Among the contributions provided by the NCHS to the report were data measuring premature births and low birthrates, blood-lead levels in children between the ages of one and five

years, and statistics evaluating the link between poverty and dental care in school-age children.

Computer databases and the Internet have also become invaluable resources for organ and tissue donor programs. For example, treatments for leukemia (a type of cancer) sometimes destroy the bone marrow, which produces red and white blood cells and platelets. To replace the bone marrow, a transplant from another person is needed. Finding compatible bone marrow, however, is difficult. Typically, a match may not even exist within the same family. The National Bone Marrow Donor Registry (http://bethematch.org) is a computer database of people who have agreed to donate their bone marrow to those in need. A doctor with a patient in need of a transplant can log onto the registry via the Internet and pull up all possible matches in the country. The Organ Procurement and Transplantation Network (OPTN; http://optn.transplant.hrsa.gov) maintains a similar database for internal organ transplants, including kidney, pancreas, heart, lung, and intestine. The OPTN's secure transplant information database keeps track of patients who are in need of a transplant. Table 8.2 displays the number of candidates who were waiting on the OPTN in August 2016. All necessary forms and patient histories are also included in the database. Should a donor's heart become available in a medical facility anywhere in the United States, for example, the attending physician can access the database to find patients who are waiting for a heart.

## HEALTH IT

IT is changing the way patients interact with their health care providers and the way health care providers interact with one another to ensure prompt, safe, and effective treatments. Electronic health records are expected to improve health care by keeping all information about a patient's health history, including medications, immunizations, labo-

**TABLE 8.2**

**Number of organ-transplant candidates registered with the Organ Procurement and Transplantation Network, August 2016**

| | |
|---|---|
| All | 120,045 |
| Kidney | 99,333 |
| Pancreas | 973 |
| Kidney/pancreas | 1,866 |
| Liver | 14,646 |
| Intestine | 276 |
| Heart | 4,129 |
| Lung | 1,418 |
| Heart/lung | 41 |

Note: All candidates will be less than the sum due to candidates waiting for multiple organs.

SOURCE: Adapted from "Waiting List Candidates," U.S. Department of Health and Human Services, Health Resources and Services Administration, Organ Procurement and Transplantation Network, August 2016, https://optn.transplant.hrsa.gov/data/ (accessed August 11, 2016)

FIGURE 8.2

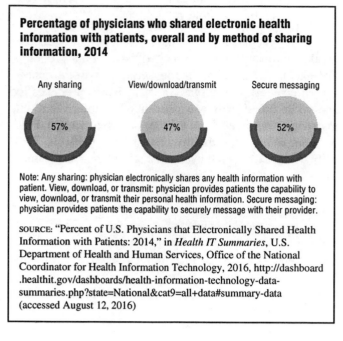

**Percentage of physicians who shared electronic health information with patients, overall and by method of sharing information, 2014**

Any sharing — 57%
View/download/transmit — 47%
Secure messaging — 52%

Note: Any sharing: physician electronically shares any health information with patient. View, download, or transmit: physician provides patients the capability to view, download, or transmit their personal health information. Secure messaging: physician provides patients the capability to securely message with their provider.

SOURCE: "Percent of U.S. Physicians that Electronically Shared Health Information with Patients: 2014," in *Health IT Summaries*, U.S. Department of Health and Human Services, Office of the National Coordinator for Health Information Technology, 2016, http://dashboard .healthit.gov/dashboards/health-information-technology-data-summaries.php?state=National&cat9=all+data#summary-data (accessed August 12, 2016)

FIGURE 8.3

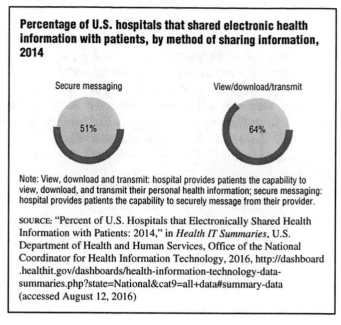

**Percentage of U.S. hospitals that shared electronic health information with patients, by method of sharing information, 2014**

Secure messaging — 51%
View/download/transmit — 64%

Note: View, download and transmit: hospital provides patients the capability to view, download, and transmit their personal health information; secure messaging: hospital provides patients the capability to securely message from their provider.

SOURCE: "Percent of U.S. Hospitals that Electronically Shared Health Information with Patients: 2014," in *Health IT Summaries*, U.S. Department of Health and Human Services, Office of the National Coordinator for Health Information Technology, 2016, http://dashboard .healthit.gov/dashboards/health-information-technology-data-summaries.php?state=National&cat9=all+data#summary-data (accessed August 12, 2016)

ratory and test results, allergies, and family history in one accessible online location. As U.S. health care systems become networked, information about a patient will be immediately available regardless of the treatment location.

To facilitate the development of a nationwide electronic health system, President Bush established in April 2004 the Office of the National Coordinator for Health Information Technology (ONC) within the U.S. Department of Health and Human Services (HHS). This office provides leadership in developing standards, policies, and the necessary infrastructure that will allow the flow of health information nationwide. *Healthcare IT News* (http://www.healthcareitnews.com), an online journal examining the role of IT in the medical profession, maintains a website that is dedicated to providing regular updates on the development of the Nationwide Health Information Network. Known as HIEWatch (http://www .hiewatch.com), the site reports on various federal, state, and local health care IT initiatives, analyzes critical surveys and studies, and provides other news relating to the Nationwide Health Information Network project.

The Health Information Technology for Economic and Clinical Health (HITECH) Act, which was part of the American Recovery and Reinvestment Act of 2009, was designed to improve and expand IT systems across the U.S. health care industry. HITECH provided the HHS with approximately $2 billion to help fund regional health care IT networks, with the aim of helping medical professionals coordinate patient care more quickly and efficiently, while reducing cases of medical errors. Supervised by the ONC, HITECH was also dedicated to maintaining online security to safeguard patient privacy.

In February 2016 the ONC presented Congress with the status report *Update on the Adoption of Health Information Technology and Related Efforts to Facilitate the Electronic Use and Exchange of Health Information* (https://www.healthit.gov/sites/default/files/Attachment_1 _-_2-26-16_RTC_Health_IT_Progress.pdf). The ONC notes that 74% of nonhospital-based primary physicians had adopted electronic health record systems by 2014. That year, more than half (57%) of all nonhospital-based physicians shared records with their patients electronically; 52% did so using a secure messaging system, whereas 47% shared electronic health records by providing their patients with the capability to download or view information online. (See Figure 8.2.) At the same time, in 2014 under two-thirds (64%) of U.S. hospitals shared electronic health records by providing patients with the capability to download or view information over the Internet, and just over half (51%) used a secure messaging system. (See Figure 8.3.)

The Agency for Healthcare Research and Quality (AHRQ), a part of HHS, maintains a website (http:// www.ahrq.gov/professionals/quality-patient-safety/index .html#online) that provides information and resources aimed at reducing incidences of medical error. The AHRQ believes that by using IT to integrate health history with medication information many deaths and injuries stemming from medical errors can be prevented. Computerized health record systems would provide attending doctors with dosage information about medications already prescribed for each patient, check for potential interactions with other medications, and alert physicians to patient allergies. Anticipated benefits of integrated health IT include electronic health records for patients that can be easily shared by health care providers; electronic transmittal of medical test results; and electronic prescription messaging, which will improve efficiency and reduce human errors in reading paper prescriptions.

Although electronic medical records provide enormous benefits to both patients and health care professionals, they also pose a number of new challenges. Alicia Gallegos indicates in "Legal Risks of Going Paperless" (AMedNews.com, March 5, 2012) that the potential for data breaches, system errors, and other problems relating to the transmission of data online leave health care professionals vulnerable to new forms of legal action. In "Benefits and Drawbacks of Electronic Health Record Systems" (*Journal of Risk Management and Healthcare Policy*, vol. 4, May 11, 2012), Nir Menachemi and Taleah H. Collum cite a number of financial disadvantages involved with implementing electronic health records, including the high costs that are related to launching and maintaining medical information online and the problems of lost productivity that are involved with the transition from paper to electronic data-keeping systems.

Despite these concerns, by 2016 adoption of health IT had become widespread across the medical profession. Between 2008 and 2015, the proportion of U.S. hospitals that transmitted or received medical test results, patient records, or drug information electronically doubled, from 41% to 82%. (See Figure 8.4.) Figure 8.5 shows the increase in electronic record sharing among nonfederal hospitals between 2014 and 2015, by domain of interoperability. In the health care industry, interoperability refers to the capacity of IT systems to exchange health and patient information with other systems. In 2015, 85% of all hospitals sent medical records electronically, up from 78% in 2014. The proportion of hospitals that received records electronically also increased during this span, from 56% to 65%, as did the percentage of hospitals that retrieved patient health records electronically, which rose from 48% to 52%. By contrast, the percentage of hospitals that integrated or otherwise used patient records from outside their own system fell slightly over this one-year period, dropping from 40% in 2014 to 38% in 2015. Overall, more than a quarter (26%) of all hospitals used medical record sharing in all four domains of interoperability in 2015, up from 23% the previous year.

Hospitals that used all four domains of medical record sharing interoperability were considerably more likely to have the capability to access patient records and other medical information from outside providers or sources. Although fewer than half (46%) of all hospitals were able to access medical information from outside providers in 2015, nearly nine out of ten (89%) hospitals that used all four domains of interoperability had the capacity to do so. (See Figure 8.6.) As Figure 8.7 indicates, 53% of U.S. hospitals reported that their providers

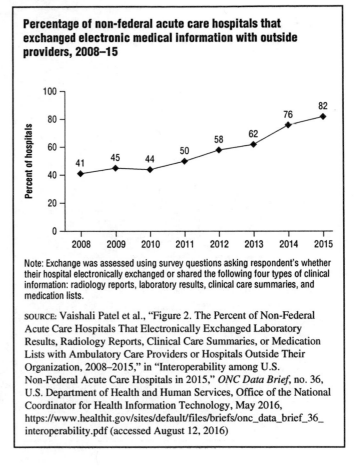

**FIGURE 8.4**

**Percentage of non-federal acute care hospitals that exchanged electronic medical information with outside providers, 2008–15**

Note: Exchange was assessed using survey questions asking respondent's whether their hospital electronically exchanged or shared the following four types of clinical information: radiology reports, laboratory results, clinical care summaries, and medication lists.

SOURCE: Vaishali Patel et al., "Figure 2. The Percent of Non-Federal Acute Care Hospitals That Electronically Exchanged Laboratory Results, Radiology Reports, Clinical Care Summaries, or Medication Lists with Ambulatory Care Providers or Hospitals Outside Their Organization, 2008–2015," in "Interoperability among U.S. Non-Federal Acute Care Hospitals in 2015," *ONC Data Brief*, no. 36, U.S. Department of Health and Human Services, Office of the National Coordinator for Health Information Technology, May 2016, https://www.healthit.gov/sites/default/files/briefs/onc_data_brief_36_interoperability.pdf (accessed August 12, 2016)

used electronic records received from outside sources either often (18%) or sometimes (35%) in 2015. Among hospitals that rarely or never used electronic records received from outside sources in 2015, more than half (53%) reported that the information was not accessible to providers in the course of their daily workflow; 45% reported difficulties related to integrating outside information into their existing electronic record systems, and 40% stated that outside information was sometimes not available when it was needed. (See Figure 8.8.)

Technological issues can also impact the way that hospitals and providers use electronic medical records. Table 8.3 provides a breakdown of some common problems confronted by hospitals when trying to exchange medical information with outside providers in 2014 and 2015. As Table 8.3 shows, 55% of hospitals cited the inability of an outside provider to receive data as a major barrier to interoperability in 2015. This figure was down slightly from the previous year, when 58% of hospitals reported that outside providers lacked the capacity to receive electronic medical data. Other technical barriers to interoperability confronted by hospitals in 2015 included the absence of any kind of electronic medical records capacity on the part of outside providers (53%), problems finding addresses of outside providers (49%), and incompatibility between electronic platforms (46%).

**FIGURE 8.5**

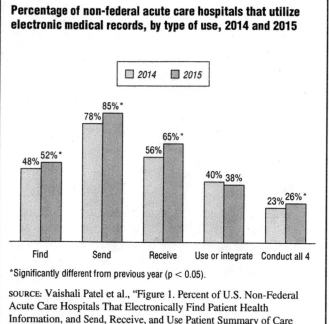

Percentage of non-federal acute care hospitals that utilize electronic medical records, by type of use, 2014 and 2015

☐ 2014  ☐ 2015

- Find: 48%, 52%*
- Send: 78%, 85%*
- Receive: 56%, 65%*
- Use or integrate: 40%, 38%
- Conduct all 4: 23%, 26%*

*Significantly different from previous year (p < 0.05).

SOURCE: Vaishali Patel et al., "Figure 1. Percent of U.S. Non-Federal Acute Care Hospitals That Electronically Find Patient Health Information, and Send, Receive, and Use Patient Summary of Care Records from Sources Outside Their Health System, 2014–2015," in "Interoperability among U.S. Non-Federal Acute Care Hospitals in 2015," *ONC Data Brief*, no. 36, U.S. Department of Health and Human Services, Office of the National Coordinator for Health Information Technology, May 2016, https://www.healthit.gov/sites/default/files/briefs/onc_data_brief_36_interoperability.pdf (accessed August 12, 2016)

**FIGURE 8.6**

Percentage of non-federal acute care hospitals that had access to electronic medical records at point of care, by adoption of electronic interoperability, 2014 and 2015

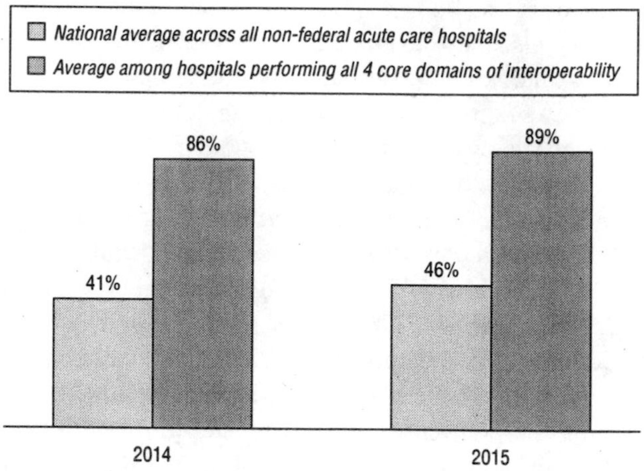

☐ National average across all non-federal acute care hospitals
☐ Average among hospitals performing all 4 core domains of interoperability

- 2014: 41%, 86%
- 2015: 46%, 89%

Notes: Four core domains of interoperability consist of find, send, receive, and integrate or use.

SOURCE: Vaishali Patel et al., "Figure 3. Percent of U.S. Non-Federal Acute Care Hospitals Whose Providers Have Electronically Available Necessary Clinical Information from Outside Providers or Sources Across All Non-Federal Acute Care Hospitals and Those That Engaged in All 4 Core Domains of Interoperability, 2014–2015," in "Interoperability among U.S. Non-Federal Acute Care Hospitals in 2015," *ONC Data Brief*, no. 36, U.S. Department of Health and Human Services, Office of the National Coordinator for Health Information Technology, May 2016, https://www.healthit.gov/sites/default/files/briefs/onc_data_brief_36_interoperability.pdf (accessed August 12, 2016)

A majority of hospitals in 2014 and 2015 used both paper and electronic methods of exchanging summary of care records with other providers. (See Figure 8.9.) In 2015, 75% of hospitals used both paper and electronic methods to receive summary of care records from outside providers, and 84% used both paper and electronic methods to send such records. That year, 7% of hospitals used electronic records sharing exclusively to receive summaries of care from other providers, whereas 9% used electronic records sharing exclusively when sending summaries of care. (See Figure 8.9.) In 2015 just over three-quarters (76%) of hospitals sent electronic medical records by way of a secure messaging system, and more than half (54%) used secure messaging systems to receive electronic medical records. (See Figure 8.10.) As Figure 8.11 indicates, more than three in five (61%) hospitals in 2015 both belonged to a state, regional, or local health information exchange organization (HIO) and employed a third-party health information exchange (HIE) vendor to exchange medical records electronically.

In 2015, 40% of U.S. hospitals received summary of care information from outside hospitals, and 37% received such records from ambulatory care providers. (See Figure 8.12.) That year, medium and large hospitals were more likely than small hospitals to use electronic methods to exchange summary of care records with other

providers. As Table 8.4 reveals, more than one-third (34%) of medium and large hospitals employed all four domains of electronic interoperability in 2015, compared with 18% of small hospitals. Of the 46% of all hospitals that had access to electronic medical records from outside providers in 2015, more than half (53%) reported using these records in providing care. (See Figure 8.13.)

Besides facilitating the electronic exchange of medical records, IT has also transformed the ways that health care professionals provide care to patients. In *Can Telemedicine Help Address Concerns with Network Adequacy? Opportunities and Challenges in Six States* (April 2016, http://www.urban.org/sites/default/files/alfresco/publication-pdfs/2000736-Can-Telemedicine-Help-Address-Concerns-with-Network-Adequacy-Opportunities-and-Challenges-in-Six-States.pdf), Sandy Ahn, Sabrina Corlette, and Kevin Lucia of the Urban Institute examine how shortages of physicians and other providers in certain communities have led to the emergence of a form of remote health care called telemedicine. According to Ahn, Corlette, and Lucia, telemedicine is a form of care that enables providers to communicate with patients electronically when an in-person visit is not possible. As Table 8.5 shows, telemedicine employs

**FIGURE 8.7**

**FIGURE 8.8**

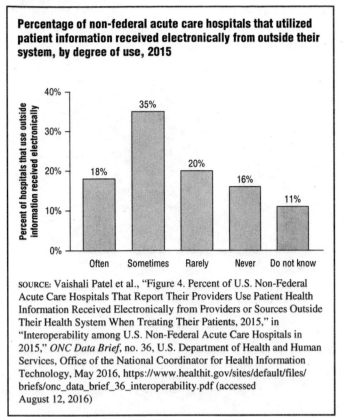

**Percentage of non-federal acute care hospitals that utilized patient information received electronically from outside their system, by degree of use, 2015**

SOURCE: Vaishali Patel et al., "Figure 4. Percent of U.S. Non-Federal Acute Care Hospitals That Report Their Providers Use Patient Health Information Received Electronically from Providers or Sources Outside Their Health System When Treating Their Patients, 2015," in "Interoperability among U.S. Non-Federal Acute Care Hospitals in 2015," *ONC Data Brief*, no. 36, U.S. Department of Health and Human Services, Office of the National Coordinator for Health Information Technology, May 2016, https://www.healthit.gov/sites/default/files/briefs/onc_data_brief_36_interoperability.pdf (accessed August 12, 2016)

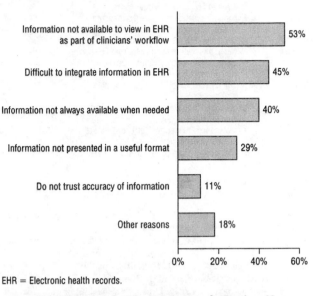

**Reasons for not utilizing electronically-received medical records among non-federal acute care hospitals that rarely or never use electronic medical records when treating patients, 2015**

[Percentage of hospitals that rarely or never use information electronically received from outside their health system]

EHR = Electronic health records.

SOURCE: Vaishali Patel et al., "Figure 5. Reasons for Rarely or Never Using Patient Health Information Received Electronically from Providers or Sources Outside Their Health System When Treating Their Patients as Reported by U.S. Non-Federal Acute Care Hospitals, 2015," in "Interoperability among U.S. Non-Federal Acute Care Hospitals in 2015," *ONC Data Brief*, no. 36, U.S. Department of Health and Human Services, Office of the National Coordinator for Health Information Technology, May 2016, https://www.healthit.gov/sites/default/files/briefs/onc_data_brief_36_interoperability.pdf (accessed August 12, 2016)

a range of technologies, including electronic record sharing, videoconferencing, and electronic monitoring devices, to help doctors maintain contact with patients throughout the treatment process.

TABLE 8.3

**Problems experienced by non-federal acute care hospitals when utilizing electronic medical records, 2014 and 2015**

| Type of barrier | Barrier | 2014 | 2015 |
|---|---|---|---|
| Technical | Exchange partners' EHR system lacks capability to receive data | 58% | 55% |
| Technical | Exchange partners' lack EHR or other system to receive data | 59% | 53% |
| Technical | Difficult to find providers' addresses | 45% | 49% |
| Technical | Experience greater challenges exchanging across different vendor platforms. | NA | 46% |
| Technical | Difficult to match or identify patients | 24% | 33% |
| Operational | Cumbersome workflow to send from EHR system | 30% | 32% |
| Operational | Many recipients of care summaries report that the information is not useful | 26% | 31% |
| Financial | Additional costs to exchange with outside providers or settings | 25% | 25% |
| Technical | Lack capability to electronically receive data from outside sources | 16% | 14% |
| Technical | Lack capability to electronically send data to outside sources | 10% | 8% |
| Operational | Don't typically share patient data with outside providers | 10% | 6% |

EHR = electronic health record.
Notes: NA or not applicable because item was not asked in 2014.

SOURCE: Vaishali Patel et al., "Table 1. Percent of U.S. Non-Federal Acute Care Hospitals That Experienced the Issues When Trying to Electronically Send, Receive, or Find Health Information to/from Other Care Settings or Organizations, 2014–2015," in "Interoperability among U.S. Non-Federal Acute Care Hospitals in 2015," *ONC Data Brief*, no. 36, U.S. Department of Health and Human Services, Office of the National Coordinator for Health Information Technology, May 2016, https://www.healthit.gov/sites/default/files/briefs/onc_data_brief_36_interoperability.pdf (accessed August 12, 2016)

**FIGURE 8.9**

**Percentage of non-federal acute care hospitals that send or receive medical information to or from outside providers, by method of sending or receiving information, 2014 and 2015**

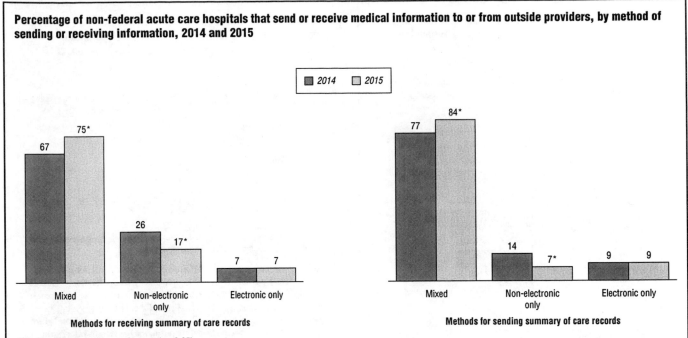

*Significantly different from prior year (p<0.05).
Notes: Non-electronic methods include mail, fax, or eFax. Electronic methods include secure messaging using an electronic health record, provider portals, or via health information exchange organizations or other third parties.

SOURCE: Vaishali Patel et al., "Figure 1. Percent of U.S. Non-Federal Acute Care Hospitals That Send or Receive Summary of Care Records to/from Outside Sources by Electronic and Non-Electronic Methods, 2014–2015," in "Variation in Interoperability among U.S. Non-Federal Acute Care Hospitals in 2015," *ONC Data Brief*, no. 37, U.S. Department of Health and Human Services, Office of the National Coordinator for Health Information Technology, July 2016, https://www.healthit.gov/sites/default/files/07.22.2016Variation_in_Interoperability_DataBrief.pdf (accessed August 12, 2016)

FIGURE 8.10

**Percentage of non-federal acute care hospitals that send or receive electronic health records, by method of sending or receiving information, 2015**

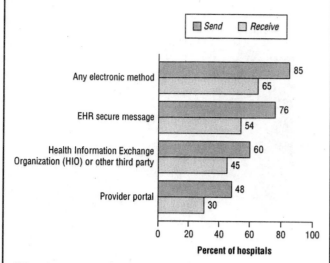

EHR = electronic health record.
Notes: Does not include "eFax." Summary of care records are in a structured format (e.g., Consolidated Clinical Document Architecture).

SOURCE: Vaishali Patel et al., "Figure 2. Percent of U.S. Non-Federal Acute Care Hospitals That Send or Receive Summary of Care Records Electronically by Method, 2015," in "Variation in Interoperability among U.S. Non-Federal Acute Care Hospitals in 2015," *ONC Data Brief*, no. 37, U.S. Department of Health and Human Services, Office of the National Coordinator for Health Information Technology, July 2016, https://www.healthit.gov/sites/default/files/07.22.2016Variation_in_Interoperability_DataBrief.pdf (accessed August 12, 2016)

FIGURE 8.11

**Percentage of non-federal acute care hospitals that shared electronic medical information via health information organizations and/or health information exchanges, 2015**

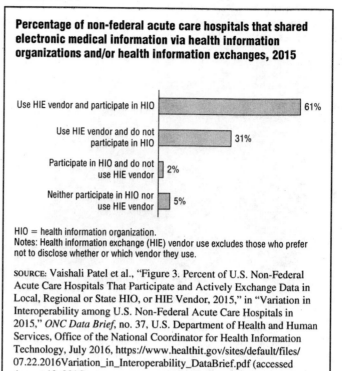

HIO = health information organization.
Notes: Health information exchange (HIE) vendor use excludes those who prefer not to disclose whether or which vendor they use.

SOURCE: Vaishali Patel et al., "Figure 3. Percent of U.S. Non-Federal Acute Care Hospitals That Participate and Actively Exchange Data in Local, Regional or State HIO, or HIE Vendor, 2015," in "Variation in Interoperability among U.S. Non-Federal Acute Care Hospitals in 2015," *ONC Data Brief*, no. 37, U.S. Department of Health and Human Services, Office of the National Coordinator for Health Information Technology, July 2016, https://www.healthit.gov/sites/default/files/07.22.2016Variation_in_Interoperability_DataBrief.pdf (accessed August 12, 2016)

**FIGURE 8.12**

Rates at which non-federal acute care hospitals sent and received electronic medical records to outside providers, by outside provider type, 2014 and 2015

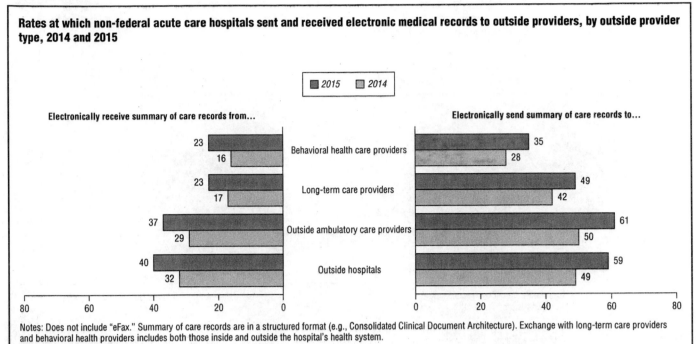

Notes: Does not include "eFax." Summary of care records are in a structured format (e.g., Consolidated Clinical Document Architecture). Exchange with long-term care providers and behavioral health providers includes both those inside and outside the hospital's health system.

SOURCE: Vaishali Patel et al., "Figure 4. Percent of U.S. Non-Federal Acute Care Hospitals That Send or Receive Summary of Care Records Electronically to/from Various Exchange Partners, 2014–2015," in "Variation in Interoperability among U.S. Non-Federal Acute Care Hospitals in 2015," *ONC Data Brief*, no. 37, U.S. Department of Health and Human Services, Office of the National Coordinator for Health Information Technology, July 2016, https://www.healthit.gov/sites/default/files/07.22.2016Variation_in_Interoperability_DataBrief.pdf (accessed August 12, 2016)

**TABLE 8.4**

Rates at which non-federal acute care hospitals utilize electronic medical records, by method of use and hospital type, 2015

|  | Send | Receive | Find | Integrate | All 4 domains |
|---|---|---|---|---|---|
| Small hospitals | 80% | 58% | 43% | 31% | 18% |
| Medium and large hospitals | 90% | 71% | 62% | 45% | 34% |
| Critical access hospitals (CAHs) | 78% | 56% | 40% | 31% | 17% |
| Non-critical access hospitals | 88% | 68% | 58% | 41% | 30% |
| Rural hospitals | 79% | 57% | 38% | 32% | 15% |
| Suburban and urban hospitals | 90% | 70% | 63% | 43% | 34% |

SOURCE: Vaishali Patel et al., "Table 1. Rates of Electronically Sending Summary of Care Records, Receiving Summary of Care Records, Querying and Integrating Summary of Care Records by Hospital Type, 2015," in "Variation in Interoperability among U.S. Non-Federal Acute Care Hospitals in 2015," *ONC Data Brief*, no. 37, U.S. Department of Health and Human Services, Office of the National Coordinator for Health Information Technology, July 2016, https://www.healthit.gov/sites/default/files/07.22.2016Variation_in_Interoperability_DataBrief.pdf (accessed August 12, 2016)

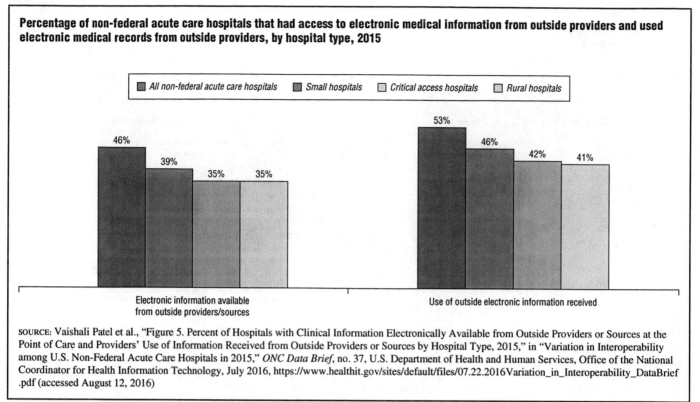

**FIGURE 8.13**

**Percentage of non-federal acute care hospitals that had access to electronic medical information from outside providers and used electronic medical records from outside providers, by hospital type, 2015**

■ All non-federal acute care hospitals  ▨ Small hospitals  ▢ Critical access hospitals  ▢ Rural hospitals

SOURCE: Vaishali Patel et al., "Figure 5. Percent of Hospitals with Clinical Information Electronically Available from Outside Providers or Sources at the Point of Care and Providers' Use of Information Received from Outside Providers or Sources by Hospital Type, 2015," in "Variation in Interoperability among U.S. Non-Federal Acute Care Hospitals in 2015," *ONC Data Brief*, no. 37, U.S. Department of Health and Human Services, Office of the National Coordinator for Health Information Technology, July 2016, https://www.healthit.gov/sites/default/files/07.22.2016Variation_in_Interoperability_DataBrief.pdf (accessed August 12, 2016)

**TABLE 8.5**

**Categories of telemedicine technology**

| Modality | Definition | Examples of Use |
|---|---|---|
| Interactive videoconferencing | Use of two-way, interactive audio-visual technology | • Postoperative consult with a surgeon while a patient is in the office of his or her primary care provider (PCP)<br>• Psychiatric consult while a patient is in a mental health clinic staffed by clinical social workers |
| Store and forward | Transmission of patient data, such as X-rays, scans, or photos, from one provider to another | • X-rays sent from a rural hospital emergency department to a radiologist at urban hospital for review<br>• Digital photos of a patient's skin condition sent from a PCP to a dermatologist for review and diagnosis |
| Remote patient monitoring | Use of digital technology to collect medical and other forms of health data from patients and to transmit it to providers in another location | • Home monitoring of blood pressure and blood sugar levels<br>• Home monitoring of postoperative patients' vital signs |

SOURCE: Sandy Ahn, Sabrina Corlette, and Kevin Lucia, "Table 1. Telemedicine Modalities," in *Can Telemedicine Help Address Concerns with Network Adequacy? Opportunities and Challenges in Six States*, The Urban Institute, April 2016, http://urbn.is/2dZVzmz (accessed August 12, 2016)

# CHAPTER 9
# HIGH TECHNOLOGY AND DAILY LIFE

Since the early 1980s high technology (high tech) has crept into every aspect of American life and has become in some instances as mundane as running water or refrigeration. Many Americans think nothing of going online to check the weather, purchase movie tickets, watch videos, or read up on their favorite hobbies. The Internet also contains an endless list of resources that most people would never have room for on their bookshelf but now take for granted nonetheless, including maps, dictionaries, phone books, and manuals on most products. The Internet has become a great way to communicate with others as well, and millions have used it to make a date, schedule appointments, or find old friends.

A sizable minority of Americans make a point of acquiring new technology products as soon as possible after they hit the market. As shown in Figure 9.1, in 2014 more than one-third (35%) of adults reported that they enjoyed using the latest smartphone, tablet, or other innovative device because they appreciated the variety of experience provided by new products, whereas 30% enjoyed the experience of sharing their experiences with new products and brands with other people. On the other hand, a slight majority (52%) of American adults in 2014 reported that they were more comfortable using technology products with which they were already familiar; 39% of adults reported that they preferred to remain loyal to certain brands of technology products, and 39% liked to wait until they had heard reviews of new products by other people before deciding to upgrade. (See Figure 9.1.)

Over time, innovations in technology have increased mobile access to the Internet, which has transformed the way that people conduct their lives. Indeed, for many Americans, mobile devices such as smartphones have become an indispensable part of their everyday experience. As Table 9.1 shows, nearly half (46%) of smartphone owners in 2015 claimed that they could not imagine life without their devices. That year, women

(51%) were more likely than men (41%) to report that their smartphones had become indispensable to their daily lives. Young adults were also more likely to report that life without their smartphones was unimaginable. For example, 51% of smartphone users between the ages of 18 and 29 years claimed that their devices had become a vital aspect of their everyday existence in 2015, compared with 40% of smartphone owners aged 65 years and older. (See Table 9.1.)

New technologies have also transformed the way that Americans interact with their mobile devices. Most smartphones in 2016 came equipped with an intelligent personal assistant (also referred to as an automated personal assistant), a voice-activated software program that enabled users to find information by asking a question to their device. Assistants such as Apple's Siri, Google Assistant, and Samsung's S Voice helped users perform tasks such as locating a restaurant or identifying the title of a song, without having to type search terms into a browser. At the same time, products such as the Amazon Echo, a type of smart speaker, acted as a form of digital hub inside a home or office, allowing individuals to initiate tasks by voice command. Amazon Echo also had the capacity to coordinate multiple smart devices at once, creating a network that enabled consumers to communicate with several smart products simultaneously.

Internet-enabled mobile devices are not the only high-tech conveniences to have become ubiquitous in everyday American life. Microchips, sensors, and display screens can be found on or in just about every appliance in the home. They allow people to do everything from control the home thermostat from a remote device to heat water with microwave radiation. Most American automobiles have dozens of complex sensors that monitor engine performance, regulate gas flow, sense obstacles, and pinpoint the vehicle's location. As of 2016, robots were increasingly making their way into U.S. homes to complete

## FIGURE 9.1

### Attitudes toward new technology among U.S. adults, 2014

[Percentage of U.S. adults who say each of the following statements describes them well when it comes to technology]

**Prefer new products**

| | |
|---|---|
| Like the variety of trying new products | 35 |
| Like being able to tell others about the new brands and products I have tried | 30 |
| Usually try new products before others | 15 |

**Prefer familiar products**

| | |
|---|---|
| Feel more comfortable using familiar brands and products | 52 |
| Prefer my tried and trusted brands | 39 |
| Wait until I hear about others' experiences before I try new products | 39 |

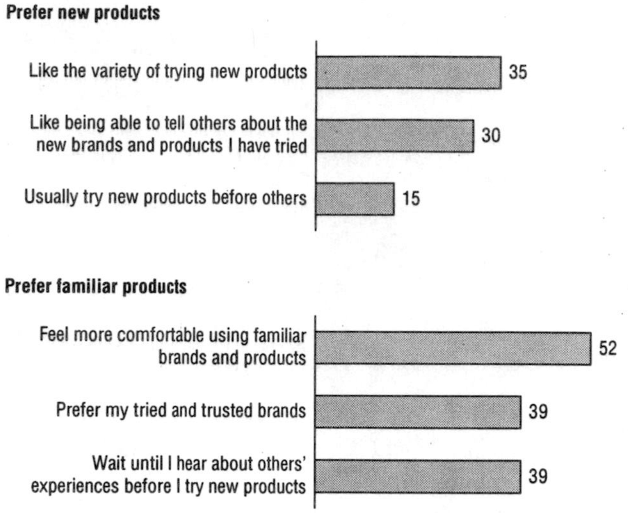

SOURCE: Brian Kennedy and Cary Funk, "When It Comes to Technology, a Minority of Americans Prefer the New over the Familiar," in *28% of Americans Are "Strong" Early Adopters of Technology*, Pew Research Center, July 12, 2016, http://www.pewresearch.org/fact-tank/2016/07/12/28-of-americans-are-strong-early-adopters-of-technology/ (accessed August 6, 2016)

## TABLE 9.1

### Percentage of smartphone users who can't imagine life without their devices, by gender, age, and type of device used, 2015

DO YOU AGREE OR DISAGREE WITH THIS STATEMENT: "I CAN'T IMAGINE MY LIFE WITHOUT MY SMARTPHONE"?

| | Agree | Disagree |
|---|---|---|
| | % | % |
| **Total** | **46** | **54** |
| Men | 41 | 59 |
| Women | 51 | 49 |
| 18 to 29 years | 51 | 49 |
| 30 to 49 years | 48 | 52 |
| 50 to 64 years | 42 | 58 |
| 65 and older | 40 | 60 |
| iPhone user | 52 | 48 |
| Android user | 43 | 57 |
| Blackberry/Windows/other user | 27 | 73 |

Gallup Panel survey by Web and mail, April 17–May 18, 2015.

SOURCE: Lydia Saad, "U.S. Smartphone Users' Bond with Their Phones," in *Nearly Half of Smartphone Users Can't Imagine Life without It*, The Gallup Organization, July 13, 2015, http://www.gallup.com/poll/184085/nearly-half-smartphone-users-imagine-life-without.aspx?g_source=devices&g_medium=search&g_campaign=tiles (accessed August 15, 2016). Copyright © 2015 Gallup, Inc. All rights reserved. The content is used with permission; however, Gallup retains all rights of republication.

## TABLE 9.2

### Frequency with which smartphone users check their devices, 2015

NEXT, WE'D LIKE YOU TO ESTIMATE HOW OFTEN YOU USE YOUR SMARTPHONE, INCLUDING TIMES YOU LOOK AT IT, CHECK IT OR USE IT FOR ANY REASON…

| | % Smartphone owners |
|---|---|
| Every few minutes | 11 |
| A few times an hour | 41 |
| About once an hour | 20 |
| A few times a day | 24 |
| About once a day | 2 |
| Less than once a day | 2 |

Gallup Panel survey via Web and mail, April 17–May 18, 2015.

SOURCE: Frank Newport, "Next, we'd like you to estimate how often you use your smartphone, including times you look at it, check it or use it for any reason…," in *Most U.S. Smartphone Owners Check Phone at Least Hourly*, The Gallup Organization, July 9, 2015, http://www.gallup.com/poll/184046/smartphone-owners-check-phone-least-hourly.aspx?g_source=devices&g_medium=search&g_campaign=tiles (accessed August 15, 2016). Copyright © 2015 Gallup, Inc. All rights reserved. The content is used with permission; however, Gallup retains all rights of republication.

time-consuming tasks such as mowing the lawn, vacuuming the living room, and mopping the kitchen floor.

## EVERYDAY ACTIVITIES AND THE INTERNET

### Mobile Connectivity

Mobile technology has played an increasingly important role in people's everyday Internet experiences. E-mail, instant messaging, social networking, and other software applications (or apps) have allowed individuals to use their mobile devices to maintain contact with family, friends, and associates. Other popular phone apps offer games, music, entertainment, health and fitness monitoring, shopping, navigation, photo sharing, video editing, and much more.

Wireless connectivity has also enabled people to work remotely, establish contact with organizations, become acquainted with others who share similar interests, or simply meet new people. Indeed, the easy portability of smartphones has enabled Americans to remain connected with other people on a constant basis, regardless of where they happened to be. For some individuals, this continual connectivity proved difficult to ignore. Table 9.2 shows the rate at which smartphone owners used their devices in 2015. Just over one out of 10 (11%) smartphone owners that year reported that they used or checked their devices every few minutes; two out of five

(41%) checked their smartphones at least a few times an hour, and one out of five (20%) checked their smartphones approximately once every hour. Only 4% of smartphone owners checked their phone once a day (2%) or less than once a day (2%) in 2015.

### Technology, Friendship, and Family

Advances in technology have radically transformed the ways that people communicate with each other, particularly

**FIGURE 9.2**

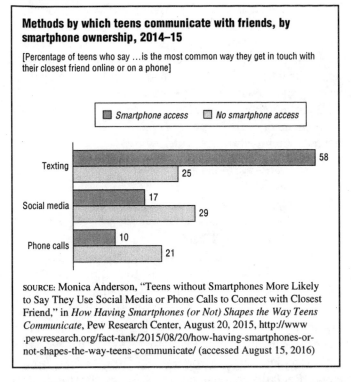

**Methods by which teens communicate with friends, by smartphone ownership, 2014–15**

[Percentage of teens who say …is the most common way they get in touch with their closest friend online or on a phone]

- Smartphone access
- No smartphone access

| | | |
|---|---|---|
| Texting | 58 | 25 |
| Social media | 17 | 29 |
| Phone calls | 10 | 21 |

SOURCE: Monica Anderson, "Teens without Smartphones More Likely to Say They Use Social Media or Phone Calls to Connect with Closest Friend," in *How Having Smartphones (or Not) Shapes the Way Teens Communicate*, Pew Research Center, August 20, 2015, http://www.pewresearch.org/fact-tank/2015/08/20/how-having-smartphones-or-not-shapes-the-way-teens-communicate/ (accessed August 15, 2016)

**FIGURE 9.3**

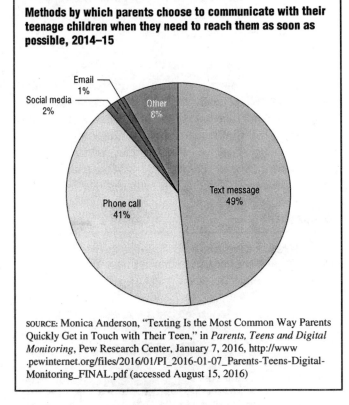

**Methods by which parents choose to communicate with their teenage children when they need to reach them as soon as possible, 2014–15**

- Email 1%
- Social media 2%
- Other 8%
- Phone call 41%
- Text message 49%

SOURCE: Monica Anderson, "Texting Is the Most Common Way Parents Quickly Get in Touch with Their Teen," in *Parents, Teens and Digital Monitoring*, Pew Research Center, January 7, 2016, http://www.pewinternet.org/files/2016/01/PI_2016-01-07_Parents-Teens-Digital-Monitoring_FINAL.pdf (accessed August 15, 2016)

among teens. Before the Internet, teenagers typically made contact with their friends by calling them on home telephones. In the 21st century, as wireless technology becomes more prevalent, young people have a wider range of options when trying to communicate with each other. In 2015 well over half (58%) of teen smartphone users reported that texting was the most common method by which they stayed in touch with their friends; among teens without access to smartphones, 29% reported that their preferred method of communicating with friends was through social media. (See Figure 9.2.) By comparison, 10% of teen smartphone users, and 21% of teens without smartphone access, cited talking on the phone as their preferred way of making contact with friends.

Technology has also exerted a profound impact on the way that parents communicate with their teenage children. In 2015 nearly half (49%) of parents reported that texting was their preferred method of making contact with their teenage children when they needed to communicate with them right away. (See Figure 9.3.) By comparison, 41% of parents claimed that calling on the phone was the most reliable way of establishing contact with their teenage children quickly. Monica Anderson of the Pew Research Center reports in *Parents, Teens and Digital Monitoring* (January 7, 2016, http://www.pewinternet.org/files/2016/01/PI_2016-01-07_Parents-Teens-Digital-Monitoring_FINAL.pdf) that this discrepancy was greater among some income groups. According to Anderson, in 2015, 57% of parents with annual household incomes of $75,000 or more reported that texting was their preferred method of communicating with their

teenage children. Among parents with incomes under $30,000 a year, fewer than one-third (31%) used texting as their preferred way of reaching their teenage children quickly.

Even as digital technology has facilitated communication between parents and their children, it has also ushered in a host of new challenges. Going online provides teenagers unprecedented access to information, but it can also pose a threat to their privacy, as well as their wellbeing. As a consequence, many parents have become vigilant about monitoring the online activities of their teenage children. As Figure 9.4 indicates, 61% of parents checked on their teenage children's Internet use in 2015, whereas a comparable proportion (60%) evaluated their children's social media profiles. At the same time, nearly half (48%) of parents reviewed their teenage children's text messages and phone records that year. Furthermore, Figure 9.5 shows that in 2015 more than half (55%) of parents of teenagers imposed limits on their children's Internet use; at the same time, nearly two-thirds (65%) of parents that year reported disciplining their teenage children by either taking away their cell phones or prohibiting them from going online. Anderson reports that Hispanic parents were considerably more active than African American or white parents in discussing appropriate online behavior with their children. For example, in 2015 more than half (56%) of Hispanic parents said they regularly discussed what content was appropriate or not appropriate for their teenage children to view online; by comparison, 43% of African American parents and 35% of white parents reported having regular conversations with their teenage children about what was appropriate for them to view online. (See Figure 9.6.)

### Social Networking

Arguably the most important development in online communication has been the rise of social networking during the early 21st century. Websites such as Facebook, Instagram, LinkedIn, and Google+ allow members to create virtual profiles on the Internet, where they can upload pictures, share personal and professional information, post messages, and forge connections with other social network users. In "Top 15 Most Popular Social Networking Sites (and 10 Apps!)" (DreamGrow.com, September 18, 2016), Liis Hainla offers a breakdown of the busiest social media sites in 2016. Facebook was the most visited social media site in September 2016, with approximately 1.7 billion monthly users. The video-sharing site YouTube was the second most popular, with 1 billion monthly visitors. Other leading social media sites in September 2016 were Instagram, with 500 million unique monthly visitors, Twitter, with 313 million monthly users, and Reddit, with 234 million monthly users.

Besides enabling Americans to form and maintain relationships over the Internet, by 2016 social networking had also become a crucial platform for political activism. Monica Anderson and Paul Hitlin of the Pew Research Center write in *Social Media Conversations about Race* (August 15, 2016, http://www.pewinternet.org/files/2016/08/PI_2016.08.15_Race-and-Social-Media_FINAL.pdf) that social media was an especially important organizing tool for the Black Lives Matter movement, a civil rights organization founded in 2013 to combat violence and systemic racism perpetrated against African Americans. Racially charged events, such as the June 2015 shooting at the Emanuel African Methodist Episcopal Church in Charleston, South Carolina, a tragedy that left nine African American parishioners dead, prompted an outpouring of race-related posts on social media. As Table 9.3 shows, the day after the Charleston shooting saw 4.3 million race-related tweets appear on Twitter; it marked the highest number of tweets about race to appear in a single day on the social media platform between January 1, 2015, and March 31, 2016.

Indeed, concern over issues of racial justice shaped much of the online content viewed by social media users in 2016. As Figure 9.7 shows, more than two-thirds (68%) of African Americans who used social networking

**FIGURE 9.4**

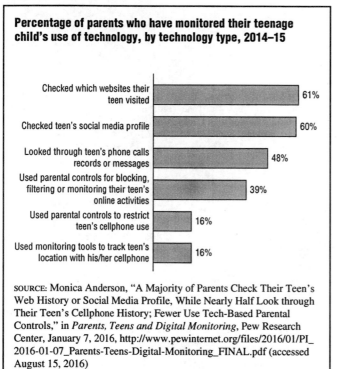

Percentage of parents who have monitored their teenage child's use of technology, by technology type, 2014–15

SOURCE: Monica Anderson, "A Majority of Parents Check Their Teen's Web History or Social Media Profile, While Nearly Half Look through Their Teen's Cellphone History; Fewer Use Tech-Based Parental Controls," in *Parents, Teens and Digital Monitoring*, Pew Research Center, January 7, 2016, http://www.pewinternet.org/files/2016/01/PI_2016-01-07_Parents-Teens-Digital-Monitoring_FINAL.pdf (accessed August 15, 2016)

**FIGURE 9.5**

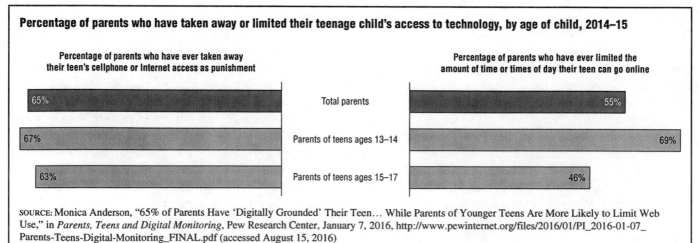

Percentage of parents who have taken away or limited their teenage child's access to technology, by age of child, 2014–15

SOURCE: Monica Anderson, "65% of Parents Have 'Digitally Grounded' Their Teen… While Parents of Younger Teens Are More Likely to Limit Web Use," in *Parents, Teens and Digital Monitoring*, Pew Research Center, January 7, 2016, http://www.pewinternet.org/files/2016/01/PI_2016-01-07_Parents-Teens-Digital-Monitoring_FINAL.pdf (accessed August 15, 2016)

FIGURE 9.6

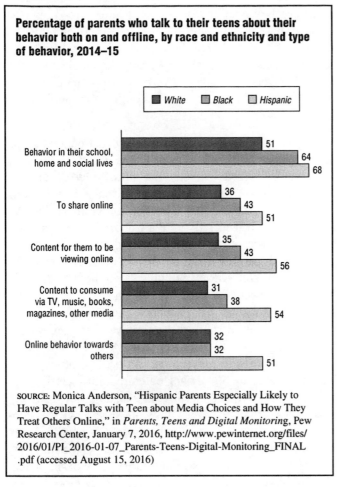

**Percentage of parents who talk to their teens about their behavior both on and offline, by race and ethnicity and type of behavior, 2014–15**

White ■ Black ■ Hispanic ▫

Behavior in their school, home and social lives: 51, 64, 68

To share online: 36, 43, 51

Content for them to be viewing online: 35, 43, 56

Content to consume via TV, music, books, magazines, other media: 31, 38, 54

Online behavior towards others: 32, 32, 51

SOURCE: Monica Anderson, "Hispanic Parents Especially Likely to Have Regular Talks with Teen about Media Choices and How They Treat Others Online," in *Parents, Teens and Digital Monitoring*, Pew Research Center, January 7, 2016, http://www.pewinternet.org/files/2016/01/PI_2016-01-07_Parents-Teens-Digital-Monitoring_FINAL.pdf (accessed August 15, 2016)

TABLE 9.3

**Ten most active days for posting tweets about race on Twitter, by date, number of tweets, and precipitating event, January 1, 2015 to March 31, 2016**

| Rank | Date | Approximate # of tweets in millions | Events |
|---|---|---|---|
| 1 | 6/18/15 | 4.3 | Day following church shooting in Charleston, S.C. |
| 2 | 4/28/15 | 3.4 | Unrest in Baltimore following death of Freddie Gray |
| 3 | 7/22/15 | 3.3 | Details are released about the death of Sandra Bland while in police custody in Texas |
| 4 | 7/29/15 | 3.0 | Protests organized by #BlackLivesMatter movement in response to death of Sandra Bland |
| 5 | 7/23/15 | 3.0 | Day after details are released about the death of Sandra Bland |
| 6 | 2/16/16 | 2.9 | Day following 2016 Grammy Awards and Kendrick Lamar's provocative performance |
| 7 | 11/11/15 | 2.9 | Missouri University of Science and Technology student is arrested after racially charged threats were posted on social media |
| 8 | 6/19/15 | 2.9 | Two days following church shooting in Charleston |
| 9 | 2/29/16 | 2.9 | Day following 2016 Oscars amid controversy over the lack of minority nominees |
| 10 | 6/29/15 | 2.9 | Day following BET Awards |

Note: Data were collected using Crimson Hexagon's machine learning algorithm and include all publically available tweets that mention race from Jan. 1, 2015 to March 31, 2016.

SOURCE: Monica Anderson and Paul Hitlin, "Ten Most Active Days on Twitter Discussing Race from Jan. 1, 2015 to March 31, 2016," in *Social Media Conversations about Race*, Pew Research Center, August 15, 2016, http://www.pewinternet.org/files/2016/08/PI_2016.08.15_Race-and-Social-Media_FINAL.pdf (accessed August 15, 2016)

that year reported that most (24%) or some (44%) of the posts they viewed on social media sites were related to issues of race; by contrast, 43% of all social networking users reported that race-related themes accounted for most (9%) or some (34%) of the posts they saw on social media. African American social media users (8%) were also more likely than white (1%) or Hispanic (4%) social media users to report that most of the content they posted or shared on social networking sites in 2016 was race related. (See Figure 9.8.) Anderson and Hitlin also report that among African American social media users who regularly talked about race relations in their day-to-day lives, nearly three-quarters (72%) reported that some or most of the posts they viewed on social networking platforms were related to issues of race; among white social media users who had regular conversations about race, this figure was 41%.

## Cyberbullying

Advances in communication have also led to new forms of negative online behavior, particularly among children and adolescents. One form of abuse that became a concern during the early part of the 21st century was cyberbullying. Cyberbullying refers to situations in which a child or teenager is harassed, humiliated, or intimidated by other children,

teens, or adults through the use of the Internet or other forms of interactive communication, such as cell phones. Cyberbullies torment their victims by sending them malicious, sometimes threatening e-mails or text messages, or by posting pernicious rumors about the victims on the Internet, typically on blogs or social networking sites. In *Teens, Kindness and Cruelty on Social Network Sites* (November 9, 2011, http://www.pewinternet.org/files/old-media//Files/Reports/2011/PIP_Teens_Kindness_Cruelty_SNS_Report_Nov_2011_FINAL_110711.pdf), Amanda Lenhart et al. of the Pew Research Center report that 8% of American teens had experienced some form of online bullying in 2011, and 9% had been bullied via text messages.

Cyberbullying is particularly damaging to the emotional health of children because of its potential to spread to wide audiences, as well as the relative ease with which it eludes the detection of parents and teachers. In addition, the physical distance separating the cyberbullies from the victims can desensitize antagonists to the harm they are inflicting, leading to behavior that is far more hateful and cruel than it would be if the perpetrators and victims were face to face. Because it uses technologies that have become omnipresent in the lives of most young people, cyberbullying also has the power to reach far beyond the schoolyard, following victims wherever they go, at any hour of the day.

## FIGURE 9.7

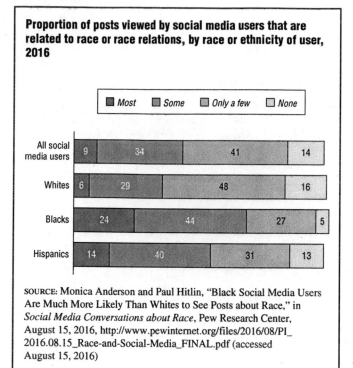

Proportion of posts viewed by social media users that are related to race or race relations, by race or ethnicity of user, 2016

Legend: ■ Most  ■ Some  □ Only a few  □ None

| | Most | Some | Only a few | None |
|---|---|---|---|---|
| All social media users | 9 | 34 | 41 | 14 |
| Whites | 6 | 29 | 48 | 16 |
| Blacks | 24 | 44 | 27 | 5 |
| Hispanics | 14 | 40 | 31 | 13 |

SOURCE: Monica Anderson and Paul Hitlin, "Black Social Media Users Are Much More Likely Than Whites to See Posts about Race," in *Social Media Conversations about Race*, Pew Research Center, August 15, 2016, http://www.pewinternet.org/files/2016/08/PI_2016.08.15_Race-and-Social-Media_FINAL.pdf (accessed August 15, 2016)

## FIGURE 9.8

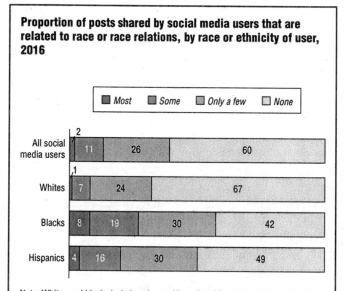

Proportion of posts shared by social media users that are related to race or race relations, by race or ethnicity of user, 2016

Legend: ■ Most  ■ Some  □ Only a few  □ None

| | Most | Some | Only a few | None |
|---|---|---|---|---|
| All social media users | 2 | 11 | 26 | 60 |
| Whites | 1 | 7 | 24 | 67 |
| Blacks | 8 | 19 | 30 | 42 |
| Hispanics | 4 | 16 | 30 | 49 |

Note: Whites and blacks include only non-Hispanics. All social media users include adult social media users of all races. "Don't know/Refused" responses are not shown.

SOURCE: Monica Anderson and Paul Hitlin, "Roughly Three-in-Ten Black Social Media Users Say Most or Some of What They Post Pertains to Race," in *Social Media Conversations about Race*, Pew Research Center, August 15, 2016, http://www.pewinternet.org/files/2016/08/PI_2016.08.15_Race-and-Social-Media_FINAL.pdf (accessed August 15, 2016)

Sometimes, cyberbullying can inflict fatal consequences. In one notorious case, Megan Meier (1992–2006), a 13-year-old girl from Missouri, committed suicide after receiving malicious communications from a teenage boy over MySpace. As it later turned out, the teenage boy was a fictitious character created by the mother of one of Megan's friends. The case prompted several states to pass anti-cyberbullying legislation the following year. In 2008 the state of Missouri passed its own statute prohibiting malicious online communications between adults and children.

Cyberbullying once again received national attention in September 2010, when Tyler Clementi (1992–2010), a freshman at Rutgers University, jumped to his death from New York's George Washington Bridge. The ensuing investigation revealed that Clementi's roommate, Dharun Ravi (1992–), had secretly used a webcam controlled from another dorm room to view Clementi engaged in sexual activity with another male; another resident of Clementi's dorm, Molly Wei, was also implicated in the incident. In a bitter irony, Clementi used his cell phone to post a brief suicide message on his Facebook page minutes before jumping off the bridge, writing simply: "Jumping off the gw bridge sorry." In February 2012 Wei entered into a plea agreement with prosecutors. As part of the deal, she was sentenced to 300 hours of community service and ordered to undergo counseling, in exchange for testifying against Ravi in court. The following May, Ravi was convicted on multiple charges relating to Clementi's death, including bias intimidation and invasion of privacy. He was sentenced to 30 days in jail, three years of probation, and 300 hours of community service; in addition, he was fined $10,000 and ordered to complete counseling related to cyberbullying. Ravi's conviction was overturned by the Appellate Division of the Superior Court of New Jersey in September 2016. A month later he pleaded guilty to one count of attempted invasion of privacy in a deal to avoid a retrial on other charges related to the case.

By 2016 legislation appeared to have some positive effect on curbing instances of cyberbullying. According to Sameer Hinduja and Justin W. Patchin of the Cyberbullying Research Center, in *State Cyberbullying Laws: A Brief Review of State Cyberbullying Laws and Policies* (January 2016, http://cyberbullying.org/Bullying-and-Cyberbullying-Laws.pdf), as of January 2016 every state in the country had passed some form of antibullying statute. Of these state laws, 48 included provisions outlawing electronic harassment; 24 states specifically prohibited cyberbullying.

## Work

Information technology has touched nearly every industry in the U.S. economy, and for many Americans communications technologies have provided the opportunity to work at home either for their primary employer or in their own home-based business. Peter J. Mateyka, Melanie A. Rapino, and Liana Christin Landivar of the U.S. Census Bureau report in *Home-Based Workers in* the *United States: 2010* (October 2012, http://www.census.gov/prod/2012pubs/p70-132.pdf), the most recent report of its kind as of November 2016, that the number of U.S. workers who did their jobs from home at least one day per week rose from 9.2 million in 1997 to 13.4 million in 2010. Over this same span, the proportion of employed Americans who worked at home one day a week increased to 9.5% from 7%. Meanwhile, the percentage of Americans who worked exclusively at home rose from 4.8% in 1997 to 6.6% in 2010. Jeffrey M. Jones of the Gallup Organization notes in *In U.S., Telecommuting for Work Climbs to 37%* (August 2015, http://www.gallup.com/poll/184649/telecommuting-work-climbs.aspx) that by 2015 more than one-third (37%) of the U.S. workforce had worked from home at some point in their lives. According to Jones, college graduates (55%) were more than twice as likely to have worked from home as noncollege graduates (26%) in 2015.

One development with the potential to revolutionize how Americans work was the rapid evolution of cloud computing technologies. Cloud computing refers to the use of software, tools, and other applications that are available on online servers, as opposed to being stored on the hard drive of a personal computer. For example, Google Docs enables users to create and save documents online, thereby allowing another user (such as a coworker) to access the information directly through his or her own Internet connection. Many popular forms of cloud computing had already gained widespread popularity by 2016, notably file-sharing sites such as Box or Dropbox, web-based e-mail services such as Hotmail and Gmail, social networking sites such as Facebook, and the status updating service Twitter. Furthermore, cloud computing has made it possible for businesses to form virtual offices, allowing workers at various remote locations to link up and collaborate with each other through a common web-based platform. For example, Microsoft SharePoint enables partners in a business enterprise to exchange documents and other files, share tools and applications, and communicate with each other all within a common Internet platform. According to Janna Quitney Anderson and Lee Rainie of the Pew Research Center, in *The Future of Cloud Computing* (June 11, 2010, http://www.pewinternet.org/~/media//Files/Reports/2010/PIP_Future_of_the_Internet_cloud_computing.pdf), a Pew survey of technology experts indicates that 71% believe the majority of Americans who use computers for their jobs will work primarily via cloud computing by 2020.

Kenneth Olmstead, Cliff Lampe, and Nicole B. Ellison of the Pew Research Center write in *Social Media and the Workplace* (June 22, 2015, http://www.pewinternet.org/files/2016/06/PI_2016.06.22_Social-Media-and-Work_FINAL.pdf) that the ability to connect with other people online, particularly through social networking, has also had a profound effect on the ways that Americans interact in the workplace. According to Olmstead, Lampe,

and Ellison, although social media provides Americans with unique opportunities to expand their professional networks, it can also pose a challenge to overall productivity during the workday. Figure 9.9 provides a breakdown of reasons Americans used social networking while at work in 2014. Just over one-third (34%) of Americans who used social media in the workplace that year reported that they did so in order to take a mental break from their day-to-day tasks. Another 27% used social media as a way of staying in contact with friends and family while at work, whereas just under one-quarter (24%) used social networking in order to maintain or build professional relationships. At the same time, Olmstead, Lampe, and Ellison note that social media has the power to shape people's opinions of their coworkers. As Figure 9.10 shows, in 2014, 29% of adults between the ages of 18 and 29 years reported that their opinion of a colleague had gone down after they had seen information about them on a social media site; conversely, nearly a quarter (23%) of people in the same age group reported that their opinion of a colleague had been raised by information discovered through social media.

## Romance

Besides hosting online dating sites such as eHarmony and Match.com, the Internet also plays a role in the way that Americans experience their romantic relationships. In "Online Dating Statistics" (July 1, 2016, http://www.statisticbrain.com/online-dating-statistics), Statistic Brain

**FIGURE 9.9**

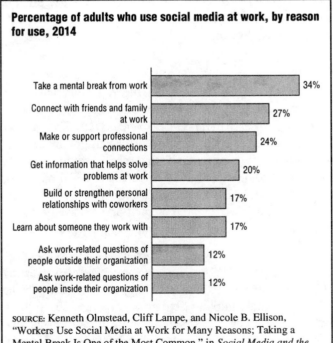

Percentage of adults who use social media at work, by reason for use, 2014

| | |
|---|---|
| Take a mental break from work | 34% |
| Connect with friends and family at work | 27% |
| Make or support professional connections | 24% |
| Get information that helps solve problems at work | 20% |
| Build or strengthen personal relationships with coworkers | 17% |
| Learn about someone they work with | 17% |
| Ask work-related questions of people outside their organization | 12% |
| Ask work-related questions of people inside their organization | 12% |

SOURCE: Kenneth Olmstead, Cliff Lampe, and Nicole B. Ellison, "Workers Use Social Media at Work for Many Reasons; Taking a Mental Break Is One of the Most Common," in *Social Media and the Workplace*, Pew Research Center, June 22, 2015, http://www.pewinternet.org/files/2016/06/PI_2016.06.22_Social-Media-and-Work_FINAL.pdf (accessed August 15, 2016)

FIGURE 9.10

**Percentage of employees who have changed their opinions of a co-worker based on information found on social media, by age group, 2014**

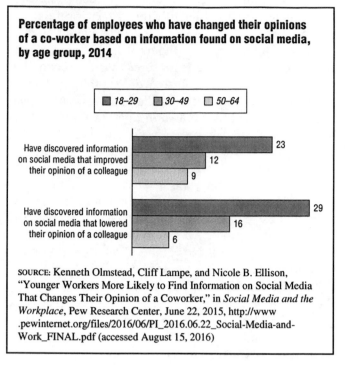

SOURCE: Kenneth Olmstead, Cliff Lampe, and Nicole B. Ellison, "Younger Workers More Likely to Find Information on Social Media That Changes Their Opinion of a Coworker," in *Social Media and the Workplace*, Pew Research Center, June 22, 2015, http://www .pewinternet.org/files/2016/06/PI_2016.06.22_Social-Media-and-Work_FINAL.pdf (accessed August 15, 2016)

FIGURE 9.11

**Percentage of adults who use online sharing or on-demand services, 2015**

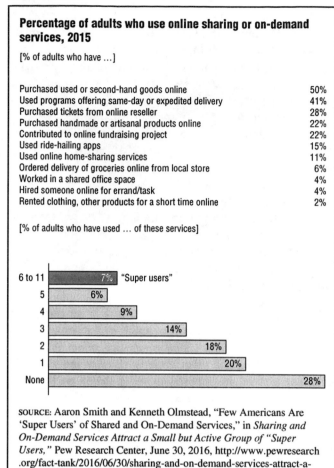

SOURCE: Aaron Smith and Kenneth Olmstead, "Few Americans Are 'Super Users' of Shared and On-Demand Services," in *Sharing and On-Demand Services Attract a Small but Active Group of "Super Users,"* Pew Research Center, June 30, 2016, http://www.pewresearch .org/fact-tank/2016/06/30/sharing-and-on-demand-services-attract-a-small-but-active-group-of-super-users/ (accessed August 6, 2016)

reports that 49.3 million American adults had tried an online dating service by 2016. That same year Match.com had nearly 23.6 million members and eHarmony had 16.5 million members. Overall, 20% of all committed relationships in 2016 originated on the Internet; likewise, 17% of marriages that had taken place in the previous year began as an online relationship. On average, married couples who met online dated for 18.5 months before marrying; by comparison, couples who did not meet online dated for an average of 42 months before marrying. By 2016 the online dating industry was generating revenues of more than $1.7 billion annually.

**Shopping**

Use of the Internet for making retail purchases has been rising steadily for several years. The Census Bureau states in *Quarterly Retail E-Commerce Sales: 2nd Quarter 2016* (August 16, 2016, http://www.census.gov/retail/mrts/www/data/pdf/ec_current.pdf) that retail e-commerce sales for the second quarter of 2016 amounted to $97.3 billion, or 8.1% of the $1.2 trillion total retail sales in the United States. The $97.3 billion figure represented an increase of 15.8% over e-commerce retail sales for the second quarter of 2015.

In "Number of Digital Shoppers in the United States from 2014 to 2019" (2016, https://www.statista.com/statistics/183755/number-of-us-internet-shoppers-since-2009/), the statistical data company Statista reports that 205 million Americans purchased something online in 2015. Madeline Farber reports in "Consumers Are Now Doing Most of Their Shopping Online" (Fortune.com, June 8, 2016) that by 2016 just over half (51%) of all Americans were doing the majority of their shopping on the Internet.

As more Americans went online to make purchases, a wider range of goods and services became available on the Internet. Aaron Smith and Kenneth Olmstead of the Pew Research Center report in *Sharing and On-Demand Services Attract a Small but Active Group of "Super Users"* (June 30, 2016, http://www.pewresearch.org/fact-tank/2016/06/30/sharing-and-on-demand-services-attract-a-small-but-active-group-of-super-users/) that by 2015 consumers were able to go online to find transportation (typically using a ride-hailing app such as Uber or Lyft), order groceries to be delivered to their home, or hire someone to run an errand, among other services. As of that year, half (50%) of all adults had bought used or secondhand goods over the Internet at some point; more than a quarter (28%) had purchased event tickets from an online reseller, and just over one out of 10 (11%) had used an Internet home-sharing program. (See Figure 9.11.)

**Alternate Realities**

As time passed, many Internet users met, developed social relationships, or spent long periods online in virtual worlds such as Second Life (http://secondlife.com), Ultima Online (http://uo.com), and other massively multiplayer online role-playing games. Even children took care of virtual pets online at such sites as Disney's Club Penguin (http://www.clubpenguin.com) or WebKinz World (http://www.webkinz.com), where among other activities players could send their pets to school; earn money by working, growing crops, or playing games; and shop for virtual groceries, vacations, and home furnishings.

Another major technological development during these years was in the field of augmented reality. Augmented reality is a form of digital technology that enables users to supplement their experience of the world with additional graphics, data, or other computer-generated content. For example, with augmented reality smartphone owners can view a shopping plaza through the lens of their mobile device and immediately learn which stores and businesses the plaza contains, what their hours of operation are, or what menu specials the restaurants are offering that day. By 2016 augmented reality had also become integrated into online games. One of the best-selling gaming apps from that year was Pokémon Go developed by Niantic, Inc. Based on the popular Japanese video game and cartoon franchise, Pokémon Go was an interactive game that allowed smartphone owners to use their mobile devices to hunt and capture Pokémon characters in the real world. Artyom Dogtiev reports in "Pokémon Go Usage and Revenue Statistics" (BusinessofApps.com, August 15, 2016) that by August 2016 Pokémon Go had been downloaded 100 million times, had 20 million daily users, and had generated $268 million in revenue.

One of the most high-profile developments in augmented reality during this time was Google Glass. Developed by Google X, the company's research and development division, Google Glass consists of a pair of eyeglasses with a small Internet-enabled computer embedded into one of the lenses, thereby allowing the user to access data about their surroundings while performing normal tasks. Amy Hubbard writes in "Sergey Brin Wears Project Glass; Google Specs Spur Fear, Punch Lines" (LATimes.com, April 6, 2012) that Google Glass made its public debut in April 2012, when Google cofounder Sergey Brin (1973–) wore a prototype of the augmented reality glasses to a charity event in San Francisco. Within a year, Claire Cain Miller notes in "New Apps Arrive on Google Glass" (NYTimes.com, May 16, 2013), Google had introduced several apps, known as Glassware, for use with Google Glass. Despite some initial enthusiasm for Google Glass, however, the product never reached the broader consumer market. BBC News reports in "Google Glass Sales Halted but Firm Says Kit Is Not Dead" (BBC.com, January 15, 2015) that early users of Google Glass soon became disappointed, complaining that the product's technological innovations were not developing in the way they originally expected. Furthermore, many restaurants and bars began prohibiting customers from wearing the glasses in their places of business, out of concern for the privacy and safety of other patrons. In January 2015 Google announced that it had discontinued production of the product. Meanwhile, Paul Lamkin reports in "The Best Smartglasses 2016: Sony, Vuzix, and More" (Wareable.com, August 30, 2016) that by 2016 a number of other companies, including Sony, had begun developing their own smartglass products.

## HOME ELECTRONICS REVOLUTION

During the 1970s and early 1980s advances in circuit manufacturing lowered the price of integrated electronic components from hundreds of dollars to less than $10 in some instances. Since then, electronic chips, displays, and sensors have worked their way into everything from washing machines to hairdryers to coffeemakers. Overall, these electronics have given people more control over the settings on their appliances, lighting, and heating and cooling systems.

### High-Tech Home Features

Many home appliances and systems have become fully programmable. For example, interactive, online thermostats come installed in many new homes. These thermostats, which can be connected to the Internet, give the homeowner the option of remotely setting and monitoring the temperature of the house from a computer or cell phone. The thermostat also alerts the user of a malfunction or a gas leak in the system. Zone lighting systems contain electronics that enable homeowners to program lighting configurations for multiple areas of the same room. With the touch of a button, one side of a room can be illuminated for reading while the other side remains dark for watching television.

Another programmable fixture that is available for the home market is the electronic keypad locking system. The advantage of the keypad over the normal lock is that it can be easily reprogrammed. If a homeowner wants to keep someone out, this can be done by simply changing the lock code. The lock can also be set to let in certain people, such as a painter, only during certain times of the day. Some keypad locks contain circuit boards that can be plugged into a broadband connection, which gives the homeowner the option of remotely changing the lock codes or keeping a record of who comes and goes. By 2016 some companies offered automated home systems that tied the lights, door locks, thermostat, and home security system into one control center that could be accessed via the Internet. These systems can be placed in different modes for when the homeowner is awake, asleep, or away. In addition, in the event a security alarm is activated, systems automatically send prerecorded messages to phone numbers that have been programmed into the system, including emergency services or the homeowner's work or cell phone.

## Smart Appliances

As technology progresses and electronics become even more affordable, makers of appliances will likely continue to add additional electronic features. By 2016 many of these advances were aimed at making appliances more energy efficient. As part of the American Recovery and Reinvestment Act of 2009, the federal government offered cash rebates to consumers who traded in older appliances for new, more eco-friendly models. The law also provided $4 billion in funding to the U.S. Department of Energy toward improvements to the nation's smart grid, a system that will allow power suppliers to "communicate" with home appliances, through a system of sensors and other digital technologies, to regulate and reduce overall electricity usage. Richard Babyak notes in "Searching for Smart Standards" (ApplianceDesign.com, January 2010) that many advances in the manufacturing of environmentally friendly appliances are being undertaken to streamline interaction with the smart grid.

## ROBOTS

Around the dawn of the 21st century the first practical, automated robots went on sale for the consumer market. Far from the convenient marvels depicted in futuristic television shows, these robots performed only simple tasks. Nevertheless, service robots began performing simple domestic chores such as sweeping, vacuuming, and mopping, and some care robots were developed to assist individuals with limited mobility to retrieve items and perform other simple household tasks. As of 2016, a number of models of robotic vacuum cleaners could be found on the market, and people were buying them. According to the iRobot Corporation (2016, http://www.irobot.com/en/us/Company/About/Our_History.aspx), the maker of Roomba robotic vacuums and Brava Jet floor cleaners, the company had sold more than 15 million home robots worldwide by 2016. Most robotic vacuum cleaners used various sensors to feel their way around the room, picking up dirt as they went. For example, the Neato Botvac (http://www.neatorobotics.com) uses a laser scan to map the cleaning area, allowing it to detect and avoid obstacles in its way as it goes back and forth across the room, sucking up dirt and recording where it has been.

Other devices available in 2016 included robotic mowers, pool cleaners, and gutter cleaners. The Robomow (http://usa.robomow.com/) automatically zigzags back and forth over a lawn, cutting the grass as it goes. Sensors are embedded in bumpers that surround the entire mower, and if it bangs into something bigger than a large piece of bark, it backs off. A low-voltage guide wire set up by the user around the perimeter of the yard lets the mower know if it is crossing the boundaries of the lawn, in which case it turns around. In addition, the mower can be programmed to leave its base station and mow the lawn at preset days and times, and then return to the base station to be recharged. In 2016 robotic lawn mower models were priced at $999 and up.

## Humanoid Robots

Several large companies and many academic laboratories have been experimenting with complex humanoid robots. The most famous of these is probably Honda's Advanced Step in Innovation Mobility (ASIMO) robot (http://world.honda.com/ASIMO). Researchers at Honda have been working on the ASIMO design since 1986. As of 2016, the robot could recognize faces programmed into its memory, walk over uneven surfaces, hop on one leg, climb stairs, and run at a speed of 5.6 miles (9 km) per hour. Honda's goal is to create a robot that can assist a handicapped person to complete basic chores around the house such as retrieving the mail, doing the dishes, or moving items from one place to another.

During the first decade of the 21st century the National Aeronautics and Space Administration (NASA) developed a humanoid robot that was designed to perform repairs and other basic operations on the outside of the *International Space Station*. A robotic torso modeled after the upper half of the human body, the Robonaut simulated the actions of an astronaut inside the space station using virtual reality technology. Whereas astronauts required several hours of preparation before entering the deadly vacuum outside the space station, the Robonaut could make the transition within a matter of minutes. By 2010 NASA, working together with engineers from General Motors (GM), had developed a faster, more dexterous version of its humanoid robot, the Robonaut 2 (R2), which employed a "touch sensitivity" technology to perform more complex tasks. The R2 successfully joined the crew of the *International Space Station* in February 2011. According to the article "Robonaut 2 Getting Its Space Legs" (RedOrbit.com, April 24, 2014), in April 2014 a NASA space capsule arrived at the *International Space Station* with a pair of legs for the R2. The legs were designed to increase the R2's mobility, enabling it to perform a greater range of tasks on its own.

Many scientists and engineers worldwide have been working on ways to make robots even more anthropomorphic (having human characteristics) than ASIMO and other humanoid robots. In late 2009 researchers at the Campus Bio-Medico in Rome successfully tested a biomechanical hand. In the experiment, the robotic hand was linked with electrodes to the arm of an amputee, who was able to make the hand move and perform basic actions with his thoughts. In October 2010 researchers working at the National Institute of Advanced Industrial Science and Technology in Japan unveiled the HRP-4C, a "female" robot that used voice and motion-capture software to simulate human singing, breathing patterns, facial expressions, and gestures. In April 2016 researchers at China's University of Science and Technology unveiled Jia Jia, a robot with lifelike female features that was capable of speech, facial expressions, and arm and eye movements. Zach Epstein reports in "Elon Musk Says His Next Mission Is to Build a Robot for Your Home" (BRG.com, June 22, 2016) that in June 2016 OpenAI, a nonprofit artificial intelligence developer cochaired by technology entrepreneur Elon Musk (1971–), announced that it had raised $1 billion in research funding to develop a humanoid robot maid. According to Epstein, the maid would be capable of performing a range of household chores, as well as engage in conversations with human beings.

## HIGH-TECH AUTOMOBILES

Technological innovations for everyday life are not just occurring in the home. Many types of advanced information technology have made it into automobiles as well. Automobile buyers in 2016 had the option to choose certain vehicle models that were equipped with rear- and night-vision cameras, lane-departure warning systems, blind-spot monitors, and proximity sensors. For example, lane-departure warning systems employ infrared sensors that scan painted road markings on each side of the vehicle and alert the driver if he or she strays out of the lane. Proximity sensors help prevent accidents by alerting the driver if something, such as a parked vehicle or a small child, is too close to the bumper. Global positioning systems (GPS) have been incorporated into many vehicles. GPS continuously picks up signals that are broadcast from a network of geostationary (nonorbiting) satellites positioned at a fixed point above the earth. By analyzing its proximity in relation to three of the satellites in the network, GPS can pinpoint its location on the earth's surface. Most systems that use GPS then combine this information with an up-to-date map of the local roads to display the vehicle's position on a street map.

Automobile makers have also developed systems that allow vehicles to communicate with one another to warn drivers of delays or of dangerous road conditions ahead. Sensor-equipped cars employing the wireless local area network (WLAN) send information via the WLAN to warn other cars in close proximity when they encounter a traffic jam or black ice. These cars then relay the information to other cars and so on until every car and driver in the area is made aware of the traffic jam or the black ice.

Among the advanced safety technologies are frontal radar and driver-state monitoring. Frontal radar is a collision-avoidance technology that works by informing drivers of obstacles in their path up to 660 feet (200 m) ahead. The technology is integrated into braking or adaptive cruise control systems to automatically slow the vehicle to keep a safe distance behind other vehicles. Driver-state monitoring incorporates infrared cameras to assess the driver's fatigue level, issuing a warning if the driver seems too tired to drive safely. Another important advancement in automobile safety has been the development of the electronic stability control (ESC) system. Using smart-braking technology, ESC helps prevent collisions and rollovers in situations where the driver is losing control of the vehicle. According to the article "Electronic Stability Control 101" (ConsumerReports.org, April 15, 2010), ESC represents the "single most important safety advance since the development of the safety belt." In "The Effect of ESC on Passenger Vehicle Rollover Fatality Trends" (*Traffic Safety Facts*, June 2014, https://crash stats.nhtsa.dot.gov/Api/Public/ViewPublication/812031), the National Highway Traffic Safety Administration indicates that ESC technology likely played a role in a 91% decline in newer passenger vehicle (vehicles five years old or newer) rollover fatalities between 2001 and 2012.

### In-Vehicle Communications Systems

By combining GPS, cell phone, and sensor technology, several companies have developed in-vehicle communications systems. GM's OnStar (2016, https://www.onstar .com/us/en/home.html) is one of the most widely used of these in-vehicle systems, with more than 6 million subscribers. The OnStar Corporation, which is a subsidiary of GM, first offered the OnStar system on GM vehicles in 1996. The system is activated when the user presses either a blue button or a red button in the vehicle or when the vehicle's air bags are deployed. Pressing the blue button instructs the OnStar cellular unit to call the main OnStar switchboard. A GPS then relays the vehicle's coordinates through the built-in mobile phone to the operator, telling him or her exactly where the vehicle is. Sensors planted on the vehicle's major systems let the operator know how it is functioning. The vehicle owner can then request roadside assistance, directions, or information on the status of the vehicle. In the event of a life-threatening emergency, the red button contacts an OnStar emergency service operator, who calls the nearest emergency service provider. The system is also triggered if the air bags are deployed. In this event, the OnStar emergency operator is called, and he or she notifies the nearest emergency service provider, telling it where the accident took place as well as the make and model of the vehicle. Furthermore, the user can call the OnStar operator from a phone outside the vehicle to open the door locks or to report a stolen vehicle. Finally, once each month owners of OnStar-equipped vehicles receive an e-mail containing a diagnostic analysis of their vehicle that covers everything from the condition of the engine and braking systems to the pressure in their tires and when they need to change their oil.

### Automated Vehicles

In October 2010 the technology company Google announced that it had developed automated vehicles that had driven more than 140,000 miles (225,000 km) without human control during testing events on U.S. roads. To navigate the streets without human control, the vehicles used a combination of video cameras, radar sensors, laser range finders, and maps. The only reported accident that occurred during road testing was when a Google automated vehicle was hit from behind by a human-operated car that failed to stop at a traffic light.

Cy Ryan reports in "Nevada Issues Google First License for Self-Driving Car" (LasVegasSun.com, May 7, 2012) that in November 2011 Nevada became the first U.S. state to allow driverless cars on public roads. In May 2012 the Nevada Department of Motor Vehicles issued the first official self-driving car license to Google, enabling the company to begin testing the vehicles on the state's streets and highways. In September 2012 Governor Jerry Brown (1938–) of California signed a similar law that allowed self-driving cars to travel on public roadways. In an interview with Miguel Helft (Fortune.com, December 11, 2012), Larry Page (1973–), the cofounder and chief executive officer of Google, described the motivation behind the company's ambitious self-driving car project. "We want to do things that will motivate the most amazing people in the world to want to work on them," Page said. "You look at self-driving cars. You know a lot of people die, and there's a lot of wasted labor. The better transportation you have, the more choice in jobs. And that's social good. That's probably an economic good. I like it when we're picking problems like that: big things where technology can have a really big impact. And we're pretty sure we can do it." As John Markoff writes in "Google's Next Phase in Driverless Cars: No Steering Wheel or Brake Pedals" (NYTimes.com, May 27, 2014), in May 2014 Google announced a plan to manufacture 100 electric driverless cars that would contain no manual control mechanisms in the vehicle. According to Markoff, the new automated car would be controlled exclusively with a smartphone app. Meanwhile, driverless car manufacturers received a significant boost in September 2016, when the government announced that the U.S. Department of Transportation would release an official Federal Automated Vehicle Policy, with the aim of encouraging further developments in self-driving automobile technology. Richard Gonzales notes in "Government Says Self-Driving Vehicles Will Save Money, Time, Lives" (NPR.org, September 19, 2016) that the new policy included safety guidelines relating to automated vehicle design, testing, and deployment, as well as recommendations for updating state and federal statutes to accommodate the registration and licensing of self-driving vehicles.

# IMPORTANT NAMES
# AND ADDRESSES

**Apple Inc.**
1 Infinite Loop
Cupertino, CA 95014
(408) 996-1010
URL: https://www.apple.com/

**Association of Public and Land-Grant
Universities**
1307 New York Ave. NW, Ste. 400
Washington, DC 20005-4722
(202) 478-6040
FAX: (202) 478-6046
E-mail: info@aplu.org
URL: http://www.aplu.org/

**Centers for Disease Control and
Prevention**
1600 Clifton Rd.
Atlanta, GA 30329-4027
1-800-232-4636
URL: http://www.cdc.gov/

**CERT Program**
4500 Fifth Ave.
Pittsburgh, PA 15213-2612
(412) 268-7090
FAX: (412) 268-6989
URL: http://www.cert.org/

**Economics and Statistics Administration
U.S. Department of Commerce**
1401 Constitution Ave. NW, Rm. 4848
Washington, DC 20230
(202) 482-6607
E-mail: ESAwebmaster@doc.gov
URL: http://www.esa.doc.gov/

**Facebook, Inc.**
1601 Willow Rd.
Menlo Park, CA 94025
(650) 543-4800
URL: http://www.facebook.com/

**Federal Bureau of Investigation**
935 Pennsylvania Ave. NW
Washington, DC 20535

(202) 324-3000
URL: http://www.fbi.gov/

**Federal Communications
Commission**
445 12th St. SW
Washington, DC 20554
1-888-225-5322
FAX: 1-866-418-0232
URL: http://www.fcc.gov/

**Federal Deposit Insurance
Corporation**
550 17th St. NW
Washington, DC 20429
1-877-275-3342
E-mail: publicinfo@fdic.gov
URL: http://www.fdic.gov/

**Federal Election Commission**
999 E St. NW
Washington, DC 20463
(202) 694-1000
1-800-424-9530
E-mail: info@fec.gov
URL: http://www.fec.gov/

**Federal Trade Commission**
600 Pennsylvania Ave. NW
Washington, DC 20580
(202) 326-2222
URL: http://www.ftc.gov/

**ForeSee**
2500 Green Rd., Ste. 400
Ann Arbor, MI 48105
1-800-621-2850
FAX: (734) 205-2601
URL: http://www.foresee.com/

**Gallup Organization**
The Gallup Building
901 F St. NW
Washington, DC 20004
(202) 715-3030
FAX: (202) 715-3045
URL: http://www.gallup.com/

**Google Inc.**
1600 Amphitheatre Pkwy.
Mountain View, CA 94043
(650) 253-0000
URL: http://www.google.com/about/
company/

**Governors Highway Safety Association**
444 N. Capitol St. NW, Ste. 722
Washington, DC 20001-1534
(202) 789-0942
FAX: (202) 789-0946
E-mail: headquarters@ghsa.org
URL: http://www.ghsa.org/

**Intelligent Transportation Society of America**
1100 New Jersey Ave. SE, Ste. 850
Washington, DC 20003
(202) 484-4847
1-800-374-8472
E-mail: info@itsa.org
URL: http://www.itsa.org/

**Intelligent Transportation Systems Joint
Program Office
Office of the Assistant Secretary for
Research and Technology
U.S. Department of Transportation**
1200 New Jersey Ave. SE
Washington, DC 20590
1-866-367-7487
E-mail: ITShelp@dot.gov
URL: http://www.its.dot.gov/

**International Center for Academic Integrity
Clemson University**
126 Hardin Hall
Clemson, SC 29634-5138
(864) 656-1293
FAX: (864) 656-2858
E-mail: CAI-L@clemson.edu
URL: http://www.academicintegrity.org/

**Internet Society**
1775 Wiehle Ave., Ste. 201
Reston, VA 20190-5108
(703) 439-2120

FAX: (703) 326-9881
E-mail: isoc@isoc.org
URL: http://www.internetsociety.org/

**Internet2**
1150 18th St. NW, Ste. 900
Washington, DC 20036
(202) 803-8995
FAX: (202) 803-8958
URL: http://www.internet2.edu/

**iRobot Corporation**
8 Crosby Dr.
Bedford, MA 01730
(781) 430-3000
FAX: (781) 430-3001
URL: http://www.irobot.com/

**Kaspersky Lab US**
500 Unicorn Park, Third Floor
Woburn, MA 01801
(781) 503-1800
1-866-328-5700
FAX: (781) 503-1818
URL: http://usa.kaspersky.com/

**Medical Library Association**
65 E. Wacker Pl., Ste. 1900
Chicago, IL 60601-7246
(312) 419-9094
FAX: (312) 419-8950
E-mail: websupport@mail.mlahq.org
URL: http://www.mlanet.org/

**Microsoft Corporation**
1 Microsoft Way
Redmond, WA 98052-6399
(425) 882-8080
1-800-642-7676
FAX: (425) 936-7329
URL: http://www.microsoft.com/

**Motion Picture Association of
America**
1600 I St. NW
Washington, DC 20006
(202) 293-1966
E-mail: contactus@mpaa.org
URL: http://www.mpaa.org/

**National Aeronautics and Space
Administration**
NASA Headquarters
300 E St. SW, Ste. 5R30
Washington, DC 20546
(202) 358-0001
FAX: (202) 358-4338
URL: http://www.nasa.gov/

**National Association of Boards of
Pharmacy**
1600 Feehanville Dr.
Mount Prospect, IL 60056
(847) 391-4406
FAX: (847) 375-1114
E-mail: help@nabp.pharmacy
URL: http://www.nabp.net/

**National Center for Education Statistics
Institute of Education Sciences**
Potomac Center Plaza
550 12th St. SW
Washington, DC 20202
(202) 403-5551
URL: http://nces.ed.gov/

**National Science Foundation**
4201 Wilson Blvd.
Arlington, VA 22230
(703) 292-5111
1-800-877-8339
E-mail: info@nsf.gov
URL: http://www.nsf.gov/

**The Nielsen Company**
85 Broad St.
New York, NY 10004
(646) 654-5000
URL: http://www.nielsen.com/

**Office of Management and Budget**
725 17th St. NW
Washington, DC 20503
(202) 395-3080
FAX: (202) 395-3888
URL: http://www.whitehouse.gov/omb/

**Pew Research Center**
1615 L St. NW, Ste. 800
Washington, DC 20036
(202) 419-4300

FAX: (202) 419-4349
URL: http://www.pewinternet.org/

**Recording Industry Association
of America**
1025 F St. NW
Washington, DC 20004
(202) 775-0101
URL: http://www.riaa.com/

**The Spamhaus Project**
18 Ave. Louis Casai
Geneva, Switzerland CH-1209
E-mail: admin-sec-ch@spamhaus.org
URL: http://www.spamhaus.org/

**United Network for Organ Sharing**
700 N. Fourth St.
Richmond, VA 23219
(804) 782-4800
URL: http://www.unos.org/

**U.S. Census Bureau**
4600 Silver Hill Rd.
Washington, DC 20233
(301) 763-4636
1-800-923-8282
URL: http://www.census.gov/

**US-CERT Security Operations Center
U.S. Department of Homeland Security**
245 Murray Ln. SW, Bldg. 410
Washington, DC 20528
1-888-282-0870
E-mail: info@us-cert.gov
URL: http://www.us-cert.gov/

**U.S. Department of Justice
Computer Crime and Intellectual
Property Section**
950 Pennsylvania Ave. NW
Washington, DC 20530-0001
(202) 514-2000
URL: http://www.justice.gov/

**U.S. Department of Labor**
Frances Perkins Building
200 Constitution Ave. NW
Washington, DC 20210
1-866-487-2365
URL: http://www.dol.gov/

# RESOURCES

Since 1999 the Pew Research Center has conducted dozens of surveys on the impact of technology on American life, including who uses the Internet and how they use it. *Americans' Internet Access: 2000–2015* (Andrew Perrin and Maeve Duggan, June 2015), *Home Broadband 2015* (John B. Horrigan and Maeve Duggan, December 2015), *Technology Device Ownership: 2015* (Monica Anderson, October 2015), and *U.S. Smartphone Use in 2015* (Aaron Smith and Dana Page, April 2015) report Pew's findings on the adoption of Internet and mobile technology in the United States. *Gaming and Gamers* (Maeve Duggan, December 15, 2015), *Parents, Teens and Digital Monitoring* (Monica Anderson, Aaron Smith, and Dana Page, January 2016), and *Social Media Conversations about Race* (Monica Anderson and Paul Hitlin, August 2016) report on specific demographic groups. *Americans' Attitudes about Privacy, Security and Surveillance* (Mary Madden and Lee Rainie, May 2015) and *Americans' Views on Open Government Data* (John B. Horrigan, Lee Rainie, and Dana Page, April 2015) illustrate how much technology shapes Americans' attitudes toward the government. *Social Media Usage: 2005–2015* (Andrew Perrin, October 2015) and *Social Media and the Workplace* (Kenneth Olmstead, Cliff Lampe, and Nicole B. Ellison, June 2015) examine social networking trends among online adults. Pew publications that examine education and the Internet include *Lifelong Learning and Technology* (John B. Horrigan, March 2016) and *Libraries and Learning* (Lee Rainie, April 2016).

Other publications by Pew that were useful in preparing this volume include *The Web at 25 in the U.S.* (Susannah Fox and Lee Rainie, February 2014), *Mobile Messaging and Social Media 2015* (Maeve Duggan, August 2015), *Teens, Social Media & Technology Overview 2015* (Amanda Lenhart and Dana Page, April 2015), *Cell Phones, Social Media and Campaign 2014* (Aaron Smith, November 2014), *Family Caregivers Are Wired for Health* (Susannah Fox, Maeve Duggan, and Kristen Purcell, June 2013), and *Libraries at the Crossroads* (John Horrigan, September 2015).

The Gallup Organization provides valuable results from polls on topics such as Internet and cell phone use, e-crime, e-commerce, and entertainment. Reports consulted for this book include *The 2015 Gallup-Lumina Foundation Study of the American Public's Opinion on Higher Education* (April 2016), *Nearly Half of Smartphone Users Can't Imagine Life without It* (Lydia Saad, July 2015), *Most U.S. Smartphone Owners Check Phone at Least Hourly* (Frank Newport, July 2015), and *Data Security: Not a Big Concern for Millennials* (John Fleming and Amy Adkins, June 2016)

A number of excellent accounts of Internet history can be found online, including Robert H. Zakon's *Hobbes' Internet Timeline 23* (January 2016, http://www.zakon.org/robert/internet/timeline/). Most of these histories are listed in the Internet Society's *Histories of the Internet* (2016, http://www.isoc.org/internet/history/). *A Brief History of the Internet* (December 2003, http://www.internetsociety.org/internet/what-internet/history-internet/brief-history-internet) was written by some of the people who gave rise to the Internet, including Vinton G. Cerf, the creator of TCP/IP. *An Atlas of Cyberspaces* (February 2007, http://personalpages.manchester.ac.uk/staff/m.dodge/cybergeography/atlas/atlas.html) by Martin Dodge and Rob Kitchin displays map after map of the Internet networks that developed in the United States after the creation of ARPANET. The Internet2 website (http://www.internet2.edu/) contains a great deal of information on the Internet2 consortium as well as on the future of the Internet.

A number of magazines and websites report on the latest developments in technology. In print, *New Scientist*, *PC World*, *Popular Science*, *Scientific American*, and *Wired* contain articles on the most recent trends in electronics and software. On the Internet, CNET.com, eWeek.com, TechWeb.com, Wired.com, and ZDNet.com post the latest news in high tech daily.

The Federal Communications Commission (FCC) is the government agency responsible for regulating which devices can use the various portions of the electromagnetic spectrum. The agency also regulates television and radio programming. The FCC website (http://www.fcc.gov/) provides information on the Children's Internet Protection Act, closed captioning, high-definition television, radio spectrum allocation, and the transition to digital television.

*Proquest Statistical Abstract of the United States* contains a number of statistics illustrating the effects of technology on American life. These include the percentage of households with computer and Internet access, the amount of time and money Americans spend on various media and media systems (e.g., television and radio), and the number of Americans with credit and debit card accounts. The U.S. Census Bureau's *E-Stats* provides financial statistics on e-commerce in the United States.

The U.S. Department of Commerce compiles reports on Internet usage and on the effects of high tech on the economy. Its landmark study *Digital Economy 2003* (December 2003) reports on how high tech transformed the U.S. economy at the dawn of the 21st century. The Department of Commerce also publishes the serial publications *Industry Economic Accounts* and *Quarterly Retail E-Commerce Sales*, which provide information on the economic impact of the Internet and information technology. In addition, the U.S. Department of Labor tracks employment statistics and trends in publications such as *Mass Layoff Statistics* (May 2013) and *Labor Productivity and Costs* (August 2016).

The Federal Trade Commission (FTC) hosts a website (https://www.consumer.ftc.gov/features/feature-0014-identity-theft) that houses a number of reports and informational brochures on identity theft and Internet fraud. The FTC publications consulted for this book include *Consumer Sentinel Network Data Book for January–December 2015* (February 2016). The U.S. Department of Justice maintains a website on cybercrime (https://www.justice.gov/criminal-ccips/) that contains reports on identity theft and Internet fraud.

The Internet Crime Complaint Center (IC3), a division of the Federal Bureau of Investigation, monitors and responds to major threats to the Internet such as large-scale hacking incidents and virus attacks. Each year, IC3,

in conjunction with the Department of Justice, the Bureau of Justice Assistance, and the National White Collar Crime Center, publishes *Internet Crime Report*, which outlines e-crime incidents reported by U.S. businesses. These crimes include anything from Internet fraud to hacking incidents to viruses. The U.S. Department of Homeland Security website (http://www.dhs.gov/) and the U.S. Computer Emergency Readiness Team website (http://www.us-cert.gov/) contain reports on how the government is using high tech to combat threats to national security.

To get more information on optical scan and digital recording electronic voting machines and about how national elections are conducted, visit the Federal Election Commission website (http://www.fec.gov/). The Intelligent Transportation Systems Joint Program Office, which is located within the U.S. Department of Transportation, contains reports on 511 deployment and operations. The American Customer Satisfaction Index scores for many of the federal government's most popular sites can be found at http://www.theacsi.org/. The Office of Management and Budget website (http://www.whitehouse.gov/omb/) provides information on President Barack Obama's e-government initiatives as well as on the E-Government Act of 2002.

The Centers for Disease Control and Prevention website (http://www.cdc.gov/) reports on how researchers are employing the Internet, global positioning systems, and other high-tech equipment to analyze the risks that are associated with major diseases. Information on the development of a nationwide health information network is presented by the U.S. Department of Health and Human Services in *Update on the Adoption of Health Information Technology and Related Efforts to Facilitate the Electronic Use and Exchange of Health Information* (February 2016).

The National Center for Education Statistics provides a number of reports that detail the use of computers and the Internet in the classroom. The reports discussed in this book are *The Condition of Education 2016* (Grace Kena et al., May 2016) and *Digest of Education Statistics 2014* (Thomas A. Snyder, Cristobal de Brey, and Sally A. Dillow, April 2016).

# INDEX

President's Management Agenda, 106
Ryan Haight Online Pharmacy
Consumer Protection Act, 130
Business, 29–35, 47, 49–50, 64
*See also* E-commerce

## C

Cable News Network (CNN), 83
Cable television, 82–84
"Cache poisoning," 63
California, 53, 54, 78, 152
Campus Bio-Medico, 150
Canadian online pharmacies, 129
Canadian Pharmacy (spam gang), 15
Cancer.gov, 128
CAN-SPAM Act, 15, 113–114
Cappel, Carl Joseph, 53
"Carbanak" malware, 64
CDC (Centers for Disease Control and
Prevention), 128, 131
CDMA (code division multiple access),
21–22, 23(f2.10)
CDs (compact discs), 80, 82
Cell phones
distracted driving, 25, 26t–27t
health risks, 25
history and development, 20
networks, 21–22
ownership, by demographic
characteristics, 23t
radio frequencies, 22f, 23(f2.10)
technology, 9–10, 21
*See also* Smartphones
Centers for Disease Control and Prevention
(CDC), 128, 131
Central Intelligence Agency (CIA), 107
Cerf, Vinton G., 5
CERN (Conseil Européen pour la
Recherche Nucléaire), 6
CERT (Computer Emergency Response
Team), 63
Charleston, SC, shooting, 144
Chaudhry, Amit, 52
Check Truncation Act, 49
Chemical Bank, 48
Child pornography, 67
Children
access to inappropriate material, 90
AMBER Alert System, 69
child pornography, 67
cyberbullying, 145–146
government Internet regulations, 114
health statistics, 131
video games, 76, 77, 78
virtual pets, 148–149
Children's Internet Protection Act (CIPA),
90, 114, 156
China, 117
CIA (Central Intelligence Agency), 107

CIPA (Children's Internet Protection Act),
90, 114, 156
Cisco Systems, 31
Classified information leaks, 115
Clementi, Tyler, 146
"Clickers," 99
Clinton, Bill, 87
Clinton, Hillary Rodham, 65
Cloud computing, 64, 147
CNN (Cable News Network), 83
Code division multiple access (CDMA),
21–22, 23(f2.10)
Cold War, 3
Colecovision, 74
Colleges and universities
cheating, 96, 99, 101
Internet history, 3–5
student electronics use, 90–91
student social life and the Internet,
91–92
technology and academics, 91
*See also* Distance learning
Columbine High School shooting, 78
Comcast, 113
Comey, James, 65
Commodore 64 home computer, 74–75
Communication technology. *See*
Telecommunications
Communication with friends and family,
142–143, 143f
Compact discs (CDs), 80, 82
Computer Emergency Response Team
(CERT), 63
Computer games, 71–72, 74, 76–77
Computer Hacking and Intellectual Property
units, Department of Justice, 67
Computer ownership, 2t
Computer Science Network, 5
*Computer Space* (game), 72–73
Computerized health records. *See* Electronic
medical records
Computers
gaming, 71–72, 74, 76–77
history, 5
ownership, 2t
sales of, 9
Consumer Sentinel Network complaints, 51,
53t, 54t, 55f, 56t, 60(t4.10), 62
Cooper, Martin, 21
Copyrighted material, 65–67, 81
"Cord-cutting," 83
Council on Science and Public Health, 77
Counterterrorism, 115
Court cases
*Metro-Goldwyn-Mayer Studios v.
Grokster*, 66
*RIAA v. Napster*, 67
*United States v. American Library
Association*, 90
Craigslist, 68

Credit cards, 47–48, 51–52
Crime
child pornography, 67
Consumer Sentinel Network complaints,
53t, 54t, 55f, 56t, 60(t4.10)
countries with highest incidences, 57f
Craigslist, 67
cyberbullying, 146
government and cybersecurity, 64–65
hacking, 64–65
intellectual property theft, 65–67, 81
Internet Crime Complaint Center
complaints, 51, 52f, 52t, 55t, 59t,
60(f4.11)
Internet fraud, 60–62
malware, 62–64
money laundering through online
gambling, 79
states with highest incidences, 58f
*See also* Identity theft
Currency, 41, 44, 47–49
Cyber Crimes Center, Department of
Homeland Security, 58
Cyber Guard, 118
Cyberbullying, 145–146
Cybercrime. *See* Crime; Identity theft
Cyberwarfare, 117–118

## D

Dark Web, 57, 68
DARPA (Defense Advanced Research
Projects Agency), 63
Dartmouth College, 99, 101
Data mining, 115
Databases, medical research, 131
Debit cards, 47–48, 49, 51–52
Debt collection scams, 62
Dedicated name servers (DNS), 5
Deep Web, 68
Defense Advanced Research Projects
Agency (DARPA), 63
Dell, 31
Democratic Congressional Campaign
Committee, 65
Democratic National Committee, 65
Democrats, 104, 105(f7.5)
Desktop computers, 9
Deutche Group case, 52–53
*Diagnostic and Statistical Manual for
Mental Disorders* (American Psychiatric
Association), 77
Diamond Multimedia, 80
Digital cable television, 83–84
Digital cell phone service, 21, 22(f2.9)
Digital divide, 7–8
Digital music recordings, 79–81
Digital signal processor (DSP), 21
Digital television, 84
Digital video, 84–85

Direct recording electronic voting system, 119

Direct Satellite System, 83

Distance learning
  academic leaders' attitudes toward, 100(f6.9)
  college students' participation in, 97t–98t
  colleges and universities, 92–94
  Internet use for, 101(f6.11)
  postbaccalaureate students, 94f
  postsecondary faculty, value to, 100(f6.8)
  postsecondary institutions, importance to, 99f
  postsecondary institutions primarily offering online programs, 95t–96t
  public attitudes toward online colleges and universities, 101(f6.10)
  undergraduate students enrolled exclusively in, 93f

Distracted driving, 25, 26t–27t

Distributed denial-of-service attacks, 63

Do Not Call Registry, 121–122, 123f, 124t, 125f–126f

Document sharing sites, 147

Domain names, 5, 7, 63

Dot-com stocks, 31

Douglas, Alexander Shafto, 71–72

DoxPara Research, 63

Dread Pirate Roberts, 68

Droll, Tyler, 92

Dru Sjodin National Sex Offender Public Website, 114

DSP (digital signal processor), 21

DVDs (digital video discs), 82

# E

eBay, 41

Eco-friendly appliances, 150

E-commerce
  government sites, 107, 109(t7.2)
  increase in, 29
  Internet Tax Freedom Act, 111–112
  manufacturing, 35–36, 37t–38t, 39t–40t
  m-commerce, 47
  online auctions, 41
  online shoppers, 148
  as percentage of total value of the economy, 35(f3.3)
  productivity, by business sector, 36f
  retail, 30f, 30t, 36, 41, 42t–43t, 44
  services industries, 44, 45t–46t, 47
  virtual goods and currencies, 41, 44

Economics, 31–35

EDSAC computer, 72

EDTV (enhanced-definition television), 84

Education
  attitudes toward technologies for personalized learning, 88f

digital content and technologies, 89f, 89t, 90f

elementary and secondary public schools, 87–90

libraries, educational technology in, 101(f6.12), 101(f6.13)

lifelong learning, 94–96

*See also* Colleges and universities; Distance learning

Educational attainment
  cell phone owners, 23t
  Internet use, 7–8
  public opinion on effectiveness of government data sharing, 104, 106f
  smartphone ownership, 24t
  social networking, 16
  tablet computer use and ownership, 8, 73(t5.1)

E-Government Act, 106–107

E-Government Satisfaction Index scores, 108t–109t, 111t, 112t

Ekhator, Emmanuel, 62

Elections, 103, 119–120

Electricity distribution, 103

Electromagnetic fields, 25

Electronic Arts, 77

Electronic device ownership, 23(f2.11), 72(f5.1), 73(t5.2)

Electronic keypad locking systems, 149

Electronic medical records
  health information organizations and health information exchanges, 138(f8.11)
  hospitals' access to, by adoption of electronic interoperability, 134(f8.6)
  hospitals' exchange of with outside providers, 133f
  hospitals' reasons for not utilizing received information, 135(f8.8)
  hospitals' use of, 131–134, 132(f8.3), 134(f8.5), 135(f8.7), 139t, 140f
  method of information transmission, 137f, 138(f8.10)
  physicians' use of, 132, 132(f8.2)
  problems experienced by hospitals when using, 136t
  rate of hospitals sending to outside providers, by outside provider type, 139f

Electronic money transfer, 48–49

Electronic stability control (ESC) system, 151

E-mail
  CAN-SPAM Act, 113–114
  history, 4, 13–14
  scams, 61
  spam, 15–16
  use, 14–15

Emanuel African Methodist Episcopal Church shooting, 144

Employment and labor
  government employment, 107, 110(f7.4)
  information technology industry, 32

social networking at work, 147f

work at home, 146–147

worker productivity, 32–35, 33t–34t, 35(f3.2)

Encrypted Internet, 68

Energy efficiency, 150

Energy Independence and Security Act, 103

Enhanced-definition television (EDTV), 84

Entertainment
  gaming, 41, 71–74, 74f, 74t, 75f, 76–78
  motion pictures, 66–67
  music, 66, 79–81
  online gambling, 78–79
  television, 81–85

Entertainment Software Association, 78

Entertainment Software Rating Board, 76

Environmental Protection Agency (EPA), 106, 107

E-Rate Program, 87, 90

ESC (electronic stability control) system, 151

Ethernet, 4

European Union, 50

E-voting, 119

Executive Order 13571, 107

Extortion, 64

# F

Facebook, 16, 17, 91–92

Family Entertainment Copyright Act, 67

Fanning, Shawn, 66

Farnsworth, Philo, 81

Faust, Drew, 99

FBI (Federal Bureau of Investigation), 57–58, 60, 69

FCC (Federal Communications Commission), 20, 84, 110, 112–113, 120

FDMA (frequency division multiple access), 21

Federal Automated Vehicle Policy, 152

Federal Bureau of Investigation (FBI), 57–58, 60, 69
  *See also* Internet Crime Complaint Center

Federal Communications Commission (FCC), 20, 84, 110, 112–113, 120

Federal Funding Accountability and Transparency Act, 106

Federal Interagency Forum on Child and Family Statistics, 131

Federal Trade Commission (FTC)
  antispam efforts, 15–16
  Consumer Sentinel Network complaints, 55f, 56t, 60(t4.10), 62t
  identity theft, 1, 51, 53–55
  National Do Not Call Registry, 121–122

Federal Wire Act, 79

File-sharing sites, 147
  *See also* Peer-to-peer file sharing

Financial services industry, 44

FirstGov.gov, 106
FISA (Foreign Intelligence Surveillance Act), 115
FISC (Foreign Intelligence Surveillance Court), 115–116
511 travel information system, 120–121, 121*f*
Flat-screen televisions, 82
Florida, 120
Foreign Intelligence Surveillance Act (FISA), 115
Foreign Intelligence Surveillance Court (FISC), 115–116
ForeSee E-Government Satisfaction Index, 107
4K television, 84
Fourth-generation cell phone service, 9–10, 22
Frank, Barney, 79
Fraud, 53, 54(*t*4.5), 58, 60–62
Freedom House, 11
Frequency division multiple access (FDMA), 21
FTC. *See* Federal Trade Commission
"Fullz" package, 57

## G

Gambling, online, 78–79
Gaming
    adults, 74*f*
    alternate realities, 148–149
    attitudes toward video games, 75*f*
    game console ownership, 74*t*
    video and computer games, 71–74, 76–78
    virtual goods and currencies, 41
Gender
    college students' Internet activities, 91
    Consumer Sentinel Network complaints, 54
    educational attainment, 18(*f*2.4)
    smartphone ownership, 24*t*
    social networking, 18(*f*2.3)
    tablet computer ownership, 73(*t*5.1)
    video gaming, 71
Global positioning system (GPS), 151
GM OnStar system, 151
Gonzalez, Albert, 52
Goods, virtual, 41
Google, 50, 85, 151–152
Google Glass, 149
Gore, Al, Jr., 7, 103
Government
    cybersecurity, 64–65
    elections and politics, 103, 119–120
    Federal Automated Vehicle Policy, 152
    511 travel information system, 120–121, 121*f*
    Internet control and regulations, 11, 110–114

Internet history, 7
    National Do Not Call Registry, 121–122, 123*f*, 124*t*, 125*f*–126*f*
    national security, 114–118
    online pharmacies, regulation of, 130
    public opinion on effectiveness of government data sharing, 104(*f*7.2), 105*f*, 106*f*
    public users of online government information, 104(*f*7.1)
    websites, 104–107, 108*t*–109*t*, 109–110, 110*t*, 111*t*, 112*t*
Government Paperwork Elimination Act, 105–106
Government Performance and Results Act (GPRA), 107
GPRA (Government Performance and Results Act), 107
GPRA Modernization Act, 107
GPS (global positioning system), 151
Graetz, Martin, 72
*Grand Theft Auto* (game), 78
*Grokster, Metro-Goldwyn-Mayer Studios v.*, 66
Guardians of Peace, 64
Guccifer 2.0, 65
Guerbuez, Adam, 114

## H

Hacking, 55–57, 58, 60, 64, 65, 119
Hagerman, Amber, 69
Haight, Ryan, 130
Hardware manufacturers, 31
Harvard University, 99
HAVA (Help America Vote Act), 119
HBO, 83
HDTV (high-definition television), 84
Health and health care
    cell phone use risk, 25
    online pharmacies, 128–130
    researching health topics, 127–128, 128*t*, 129*f*
    robotic hands, 150
    *See also* Electronic medical records
Health information exchange (HIE), 134
Health information exchange organization (HIO), 134
Health Information Technology for Economic and Clinical Health (HITECH) Act, 132
Health insurance. *See* Patient Protection and Affordable Care Act
HealthCare.gov, 107, 109–110
Heartbleed bug, 64
Helft, Miguel, 152
Help America Vote Act (HAVA), 119
HIE (health information exchange), 134
HIEWatch, 132
High Performance Computing Act, 7
High-definition television (HDTV), 84

Higher education. *See* Colleges and universities; Distance learning
High-speed Internet access, 9–10
HIO (health information exchange organization), 134
Hispanic parents, 143–144
History
    cell phones, 20–21
    e-mail, 13–14
    Internet, 3–7
HITECH (Health Information Technology for Economic and Clinical Health) Act, 132
HIVInsite.com, 128
Holder, Eric, Jr., 120, 130
Holt, Rush D., Jr., 120
Home computing. *See* Personal computers
Home electronics, 149–150
Honda, 150
Hospitals. *See* Electronic medical records
HRP-4C robot, 150–151
HTML (hypertext markup language), 6, 7
HTTP (hypertext transfer protocol), 6, 7
Humanoid robots, 150–151
Hypertext markup language, 6, 7
Hypertext transfer protocol, 6, 7

## I

IBM, 50
IC3 (Internet Crime Complaint Center), 51, 52*f*, 52*t*, 55*t*, 59*t*, 60(*f*4.11)
Identity theft, 1, 47–48, 51–58, 60, 60(*t*4.10), 61*t*
Impact Team, 64
Income
    cell phone owners, 23*t*
    Internet use, 7
    smartphone ownership, 24*t*
    social networking, 16, 19(*f*2.6)
    tablet computer use and ownership, 8, 73(*t*5.1)
India, 50
Information confrontation, 117
Information technology (IT)
    business impact, 29–30, 32–35
    industry, 29, 30–32, 49–50
    national security, 114–118
    payments, 47–49
    *See also* Electronic medical records
Instagram, 17, 18
Instant messaging, 16, 23
Insurance, health. *See* Patient Protection and Affordable Care Act
Intellectual property theft, 65–67, 81
Intelligent personal assistants, 141
Intellivision, 74
Internal Revenue Service (IRS), 3, 44, 60, 104–105
International Criminal Police Organization (Interpol), 130

Medical errors, 132
Medical Library Association (MLA), 128
Medical research online, 127–128, 128t, 129f
Medicare, 107
Medline, 107, 128, 128t, 129f, 131
Megaupload, 67
Meier, Megan, 146
Merchant wholesale e-commerce, 36
Metcalfe, Robert, 4
*Metro-Goldwyn-Mayer Studios v. Grokster*, 66
Microsoft Corporation, 31, 49–50, 76, 77
Military, 54(t4.4)
Military and Overseas Voter Empowerment Act, 120
Millennials, 65, 65t, 106f
Missing children and the AMBER Alert System, 69
MLA (Medical Library Association), 128
Mobile devices
    apps, 24–25
    banking, 49
    communication with family and friends, 142–143, 143f
    gaming, 77
    instant messaging, 16
    malware, 2–3
    m-commerce, 47
    political news and information, 119
    usage, 8–9, 13
    voice over Internet protocol, 19–20
    wireless technology, 9–10
    *See also* Cell phones; Smartphones
Mobile sites, government, 107, 112t
Money laundering, 79
Monopolies, 49–50
Morris, Robert T., 62
Mosaic X web browser, 7
Motion Picture Association of America (MPAA), 66–67
Motion picture industry, 66–67
Motorola Inc., 21
Mowers, robotic, 150
MP3 players, 80–81
MPAA (Motion Picture Association of America), 66–67
MPEG-1 format, 83
MSBlaster virus, 63
MTV, 83
Multichannel video programming distributors (MVPD), 83
Multistate Anti-Terrorism Information Exchange (MATRIX), 115
Music, 66, 79–81, 81f, 82f, 83
Musk, Elon, 151
MVPDs (multichannel video programming distributors), 83

# N

NABP (National Association of Boards of Pharmacy), 128
Napster, 66, 81
*Napster, RIAA v.*, 67
NASA (National Aeronautics and Space Administration), 106, 107
NASDAQ, 31
National Aeronautics and Space Administration (NASA), 106, 107
National Air and Space Administration, 150
National Association of Boards of Pharmacy (NABP), 128
National Bone Marrow Donor Registry, 131
National Broadcasting Company (NBC), 81
National Center for Health Statistics, 131
National Coordinator for Health Information Technology, 132
National Do Not Call Registry, 121–122, 123f, 124t, 125f–126f
National Institute of Advanced Industrial Science and Technology, 150
National Oceanic and Atmospheric Administration (NOAA), 105
National Science Foundation, 5–6
National security, 114–118
National Security Agency (NSA), 115, 116
National Sex Offender Public Registry Website, 114
National Telecommunications and Information Administration, 84
Nationwide Health Information Network, 132
NBC (National Broadcasting Company), 81
Neato Botvac, 150
Neij, Fredrik, 67
Netflix, 85
Netsky virus, 62
Network neutrality, 112–113
"Network Neutrality, Broadband Discrimination" (Wu), 112
Network Solutions, 7
Networks
    computer network hierarchy, 6f
    e-mail, 14
    Internet history, 3–5
News and information sites, 107, 111t, 119
Newspaper industry, 29–30
Nigerian letter fraud scam, 61
Nintendo game system, 76
NOAA (National Oceanic and Atmospheric Administration), 105
*Noughts and Crosses* (game), 72
NSA (National Security Agency), 115, 116
NSFNet, 6
Nutting Associates, 72–73

# O

Obama, Barack, 106, 107, 117
Obamacare, 107, 109–110

Odyssey game system, 73
Office of the National Coordinator for Health Information Technology, 132
Omidyar, Pierre, 41
On-demand services, 148, 148(f9.11)
Onion Router, 68
Online auctions, 41
Online banking, 49
Online brokerages, 44
Online gambling, 78–79
OnStar system, 151
Onwuhara, Tobechi, 58, 60
Open Government Initiative, 107
Open Internet, 113
Open music file sharing, 66, 81
OpenAI, 151
OpenSSL, 64
Operation Swiper, 52
Optical scanning voting systems, 103, 119
OPTN (Organ Procurement and Transplantation Network), 131, 131t
Organ Procurement and Transplantation Network (OPTN), 131, 131t
Overseas voters, 120
*OXO* (game), 72

# P

Packetizing data, 3
Page, Larry, 152
Pain clinics, 130
Pandora, 81
"Paper mills," 96
Parents, 143–144, 143(f9.3), 144f, 145f
PartyGaming, 79
Patient privacy, 132
Patient Protection and Affordable Care Act, 107, 109–110
Payments and information technology, 47–49
PCs. *See* Personal computers
Peer-to-peer file sharing, 66, 81
Personal communications services networks, 21
Personal computers (PCs)
    gaming, 71–72, 74, 76–77
    history, 5
    ownership, 2t
    sales of, 9
Personalized learning, 88f
Pharmacies, online, 128–130
Philips Corporation, 80
Phishing, 57
Phone records, 115–116
Phones. *See* Cell phones; Smartphones; Voice over Internet protocol
Physicians, 132
"Pill mill" pain clinics, 130
Piracy, 66–67
Plagiarism, 96
Plasma televisions, 82

PlayStation game system, 76, 77
Pokémon Go, 149
Political party affiliation, 104, 105(f7.5)
Politics, 11, 119–120
*Pong* (game), 73
Pornography, child, 67
Portals, government, 106, 107, 110(t7.3)
Postbaccalaureate education, 92, 94f
Premium cable channels, 85
Prescription drugs, 128–130
Presidential elections, 65, 120
President's Management Agenda, 106
Princeton University, 96, 99
Principals, school, 88, 89t
Prism (NSA program), 116
Privacy issues, 115–117, 116f, 118f, 132
Productivity, 32–35, 35(f3.2), 36f, 147
Public opinion
    confidence in institutions' ability to
      safeguard personal data, 65, 65t
    distance learning, 101(f6.10)
    government data sharing effectiveness,
      103–104, 104(f7.2), 105f, 106f
    government information online, access
      of, 104(f7.1)
    new technologies, 141, 142f
    privacy, 116–117, 116f, 117f, 118if
    technology for personalized learning, 88f
    video games, 75f
Public schools, technology in, 87–90
Pump-and-dump scams, 61–62

## Q

Quantum Link, 14

## R

Race/ethnicity
    broadband users, 8
    cell phone owners, 23t
    Internet use, 7
    Internet use for educational purposes,
      101(f6.11)
    lifelong learning, 94
    parents' monitoring of teen online
      activity, 143–144, 145f
    smartphone ownership and use, 8, 24t
    social networking, 16, 19(f2.6)
    social networking use related to race
      issues, 144–145, 145t, 146f
    tablet computer ownership, 73(t5.1)
    video game console ownership, 71
Radio Corporation of America (RCA), 81
Radio spectrum frequencies, 20–21, 20–22,
    22f
Radiohead, 81
Ravi, Dharun, 146
Real estate services industry, 44, 47
Recording Industry Association of America
    (RIAA), 66, 67, 81

Regulations, government
    of information technology, 110–114
    online pharmacies regulation, 130
    regulations.gov website, 107
Republican Party, 113
Republicans, 104, 105(f7.5)
Retail e-commerce, 30f, 30t, 36, 41,
    42t–43t, 44
Retirement Estimator website, 107
*RIAA v. Napster*, 67
Richmond Radiotelephone Company, 20
Ring, D. H., 20
Roberts, Lawrence, 3
"Robocalls," 122
Robonaut, 150
Robots, 150–151
Roku players, 85
Roomba, 150
Russell, Steve, 72
Russian hackers, 65
Ryan Haight Online Pharmacy Consumer
    Protection Act, 130

## S

Safety technologies, 151
Sanders, Bernie, 65
Sandoval, Manuel, 67
Satellite television, 83
Schmitz, Kim, 67
Schultz, Debbie Wasserman, 64
SDTV (standard-definition television), 84
Security systems, 149
Seggelman, Robin, 64
Seleznev, Roman, 60
Self-driving cars, 151–152
Servers, 7–8
Services industries, 44, 45t–46t, 47
Sex Offender Registration and Notification
    Act, 114
Sex offenders, 114, 114t
Sharing services, 148, 148(f9.11)
Sherman Antitrust Act, 49
Shopping, 148
Silk Road, 68
Singh, Amar, 52
Skill Game Protection Act (proposed), 79
Skoll, Jeff, 41
Smart appliances, 150
Smart grid, 103
Smartglass products, 149
Smartphones
    activities, 74(f5.3)
    apps, 24–25
    communication with friends and family,
      143
    frequency of checking, 142, 142(t9.2)
    instant messaging, 16, 23
    Internet use via, 9t
    lifelong learning, 94

    m-commerce, 47
    ownership, 8, 23–24, 24t
    teens and texting, 23, 143
    use, by activities, 24, 24f
    users' attitudes toward, 141, 142(t9.1)
Smith, Lamar, 67
Snapchat, 17–18
Snowden, Edward, 116
Social networking
    college students, 91–92
    coworkers, opinion of, 147, 148(f9.10)
    demographics, 16, 17f, 18f, 19f
    leading sites, 17
    mobile device apps, 25
    politics, 119
    race and racial justice issues, 144–145,
      145t, 146f
    teens, 17–18
    at work, 147, 147f
Social Security Administration, 107
Social Security numbers, 55–56
Software
    information technology industry, 31
    spam filtering software, 15
    *See also* Malware
Sony, 76, 77, 80
Sony Pictures, 64
South Carolina Revenue Department, 56
Soviet Union, 3
*Space Invaders* (game), 73, 74
*Spacewar!* (game), 72
Spam, 15–16, 113–114
Spamhaus Project, 15
Spotify, 81
*Sputnik 1* (satellite), 3
Standard-definition television (SDTV), 84
States
    anti-cyberbullying legislation, 146
    Consumer Sentinel Network complaints,
      56t
    cybercrime, 58f
    distracted driving laws, 25, 26t–27t
    511 travel information system, 120–121,
      121f
    identity theft, 53–54
    Internet Crime Complaint Center
      complaints, 59t
    Internet gambling, 79
    Microsoft case, 50
    National Do Not Call registrations and
      complaints, 124t, 125f–126f
    voting machines, 103
Statistical information
    adult video gamers, 74(f5.4)
    broadband users, 8f, 8t
    cell phone owners, by demographic
      characteristics, 23t
    computer ownership, 2t
    confidence in institutions' ability to
      safeguard personal data, 65t

Consumer Sentinel Network complaints, 53*t*, 54*t*, 55*f*, 56*t*, 60(*t*4.10), 62*t*

digital content and technologies, 90*f*

digital educational content and technologies, 89*f*, 89*t*

distance learning, 93*f*, 95*t*–96*t*, 97*t*–98*t*, 99*f*, 100*f*, 101(*f*6.10), 101(*f*6.11)

e-commerce, 35(*f*3.3)

e-commerce productivity, by business sector, 36*f*

e-commerce retail sales, 30*f*, 30*t*, 42*t*–43*t*

E-Government Satisfaction Index scores, 108*t*–112*t*

electronic device ownership, 72(*f*5.1), 73(*t*5.2)

electronic devices, by type, 23(*f*2.11)

game console ownership, 74*t*

government information online users, 104(*f*7.1)

hospitals' access to electronic medical records, by adoption of electronic interoperability, 134(*f*8.6)

hospitals' exchange of electronic medical records with outside providers, 133*f*

hospitals sending electronic information to outside providers, by outside provider type, 139*f*

hospitals' use of electronic medical information, by method of use and hospital type, 139*t*

hospitals' use of electronic medical records, 132(*f*8.3)

hospitals' use of electronically received patient information, 135(*f*8.7)

hospitals' use of outside providers electronic medical information, by hospital type, 140*f*

Internet Crime Complaint Center complaints, 52*f*, 52*t*, 55*t*, 59*t*, 60(*t*4.11)

Internet use, 2(*f*1.1)

Internet use, by age, 2(*f*1.2)

Internet use via smartphones, 9*t*

libraries, digital technology use in, 101(*f*6.13)

manufacturing e-commerce, 37*t*–38*t*, 39*t*–40*t*

MedlinePlus health topics, 128*t*

MedlinePlus use, 129*f*

method of transmitting electronic medical information, 137*f*, 138(*f*8.10)

music industry revenues, by format, 82*f*

music industry revenues from streaming services, 81*f*

National Do Not Call registrations and complaints, 123*f*, 124*t*, 125*f*–126*f*

online sharing or on-demand services use, 148(*f*9.11)

Organ Procurement and Transplantation Network, 131*t*

parental monitoring of online activity, 144*f*, 145*f*

physicians' use of electronic medical records, 132(*f*8.2)

postbaccalaureate distance learning, 93*f*

problems experienced by hospitals when using electronic medical records, 136*t*

productivity, by industry, 33*t*–34*t*

productivity change, 35(*f*3.2)

public awareness of educational technology in libraries, 101(*f*6.12)

public opinion on effectiveness of government data sharing, 104(*f*7.2), 105*f*, 106*f*

public opinion on new technology, 142*f*

public opinion on online privacy, 116*f*, 117*f*, 118*f*

public opinion on technology for personalized learning, 88if

public opinion on video games, 75*f*

services industries e-commerce, 45*t*–46*t*

smartphone activities, 74(*f*5.3)

smartphone checking frequency, 142(*t*9.2)

smartphone ownership, by demographic characteristics, 24*t*

smartphone use, by activity performed, 24*f*

smartphone users' attitudes toward their devices, 142(*t*9.1)

social media use related to race or race relations, 146*f*

social network information and opinion of coworkers, 148(*f*9.10)

social networking at work, 147*f*

social networking users, 17*f*, 18*f*, 19*f*

tablet computer ownership, 72(*f*5.2), 73(*t*5.1)

Stock market, 31, 44, 61–62

Stop Online Piracy Act (proposed), 66–67

Streaming
music, 81, 81*f*
videos, 83, 85

Streamlining Service Delivery and Improving Customer Service, 107

Stuxnet, 117

Suicide, 146

Sunde, Peter, 67

Surveillance, government, 115–117, 117*f*, 118*f*

## T

Tablet computers, 8–9, 72(*f*5.2), 73(*t*5.1)

Task Force on Intellectual Property, Department of Justice, 67

Taxes
electronic filing, 49, 104–105
fraud, 53
Internet gambling revenues, 79
Internet Tax Freedom Act, 111–112

Taylor, Anna Diggs, 115

TCP/IP (Transmission Control Program and the Internet Protocol), 5

TDMA (time division multiple access), 21

Teachers, 88–90

Teens
cell phones, 22–23
parental monitoring of online activity, 143–144, 144*f*, 145*f*
social networking, 17–18
texting, 143
video games, 78

Telecommunications
e-mail, 13–16
government surveillance, 115–116
instant messaging, 16
National Do Not Call Registry, 121–122, 123*f*, 124*t*, 125*f*–126*f*
network neutrality, 112–113
social networking, 16–18
state distracted driving laws, 26*t*–27*t*
voice over Internet protocol, 18–20
*See also* Cell phones; Smartphones

Telecommunications Act, 87, 113

Telecommunications Industry Association, 21

Telemarketers, 121–122

Telemedicine, 134–135

Television, 81–85

Texting, 23, 25, 26*t*–27*t*, 96, 143

Thermostats, 149

Third-generation cell phone service, 9–10

Three-dimensional television, 84

Time division multiple access (TDMA), 21

Tomlinson, Raymond, 4, 14

Tor, 68

Torrentspy.com, 66

Touch-screen voting machines, 103, 119

Tramiel, Jack, 76

Transactional government websites, 107, 109(*t*7.2)

Transmission Control Program and the Internet Protocol (TCP/IP), 5

Travel industry, 29, 44

Travel information, 120–121

Turner, Ted, 83

Turnitin.com, 96

Twitter, 17, 144, 145*t*

## U

UHD (ultra-high-definition) television, 84

Ulbricht, Ross, 68

Ultra-high-definition (UHD) television, 84

*United States v. American Library Association*, 90

Universities. *See* Colleges and universities; Distance learning

University of California, Los Angeles, 3–4

University of Science and Technology, China, 151

Unlawful Internet Gambling Enforcement Act, 79

U.S. Citizenship and Immigration Services Resource Center Español, 107

U.S. Cyber Command, 117–118
U.S. Department of Defense, 3, 117–118
U.S. Department of Health and Human Services, 132
U.S. Department of Homeland Security, 58, 115
U.S. Department of Justice, 49–50, 67, 79
U.S. Department of Transportation, 120–121, 152
U.S. Drug Enforcement Administration, 130
U.S. Food and Drug Administration, 25
U.S. government, 7
U.S. Office of Personnel Management, 65
U.S. Telecom Association, 113
USA.gov, 106
Usenet, 14

## V

Vacuum cleaners, robotic, 150
Vandervoort, Laura, 53
Verizon, 113
Video games, 71–74, 74(f5.4), 74t, 75f, 76–78

Violence and video games, 76, 77, 78
Virtual goods and currencies, 41, 44
Virtual reality gaming systems, 77
Viruses. *see* Malware
Voice over Internet protocol (VoIP), 18–20
Voice-activated assistants, 141
VoIP (voice over Internet protocol), 18–20
Voting machines, 103, 119–120

## W

Walson, John, 82–83
War on Terror, 115
Warg, Gottfrid Svartholm, 67
Web browsers, 7, 49–50
Websites
    federal government, 108t–112t
    health information, 128
    sex offender registration, 114, 114t
Wei, Molly, 146
Wexler, Robert, 79

Whitman, Meg, 41
Wholesale e-commerce, 36
Wiitanen, Wayne, 72
WikiLeaks, 65, 115
Windows, 49–50
Wireless devices. *See* Cell phones; Mobile devices; Smartphones
Wireless local area networks, 151
WLANs, 151
Work at home, 146–147
Worker productivity, 32–35, 33t–34t
World IPv6 Day, 10
World Wide Web history, 6
Wu, Tim, 112

## X

Xbox game system, 76, 77

## Y

Yik Yak, 92
YouTube, 84–85